WORLD HISTORY

WORLD HISTORY

FROM THE ANCIENT WORLD TO THE INFORMATION AGE

PHILIP PARKER

DK DELHI
Senior editor Rupa Rao
Project art editor Neha Sharma
Editor Charvi Arora
Art editors Priyanka Bansal, Amit Varma
Jacket designer Suhita Dharamjit
Jackets editorial coordinator Priyanka Sharma
Senior DTP designer Vishal Bhatia
DTP designers Ashok Kumar, Nityanand Kumar
Picture researcher Aditya Katyal
Managing jackets editor Sreshtha Bhattacharya
Picture research manager Taiyaba Khatoon
Pre-production manager Balwant Singh
Production manager Pankaj Sharma
Managing editor Kingshuk Ghoshal
Managing art editor Govind Mittal

DK LONDON
Senior editor Hugo Wilkinson
Project art editor Katie Cavanagh
US Editors Lori Hand, Kayla Dugger, Megan Douglass
Jacket design development manager Sophia MTT
Producer, pre-production David Almond
Production controller Mandy Inness
Managing editor Gareth Jones
Senior managing art editor Lee Griffiths
Associate publishing director Liz Wheeler
Art director Karen Self
Publishing director Jonathan Metcalf

First American edition published in 2010 as
Eyewitness Companions World History.
This revised edition published in the United States
in 2017 by DK Publishing, 345 Hudson Street,
New York, New York, 10014

Published in Great Britain by
Dorling Kindersley Limited.

A catalog record for this book is available from the
Library of Congress.

ISBN 978-1-4654-6240-4

DK books are available at special discounts when
purchased in bulk for sales promotions, premiums,
fund-raising, or educational use. For details, contact:
DK Publishing Special Markets, 345 Hudson Street,
New York, New York 10014
SpecialSales@dk.com

Printed and bound in Malaysia

A WORLD OF IDEAS:
SEE ALL THERE IS TO KNOW

www.dk.com

Contents

Key to symbols used in this book

🏴 Country of origin   ⬛ Date of origin

Think of **tomorrow**, the **past** can't be **mended**.

Confucius, *Analects*, 6th century BCE

History is an inescapable part of our lives. Each element of present-day society has been shaped by the actions of our ancestors, and those in turn by chains of events stretching back into an almost unimaginably remote past. The goal of history is to try to bring sense and order to our view of that past.

The past is frustratingly hard to pin down. It seems that the more we examine a historical event, the more any pleasing neatness of it simply having taken place falls away, and a chaos of complex and competing causes begins to cry out for our attention. Scores of reasons, for example, have been put forward for the fall of the Roman Empire, from an excess of other-worldliness caused by the rise of Christianity, to an excess of worldliness promoted by luxury imports into the empire from the East.

More recently, historians have begun to question whether the word "fall," with its resonance of sudden, violent change, is the right one to use at all, arguing that we should think in terms of a "transition" and look for continuity between Rome and the Germanic successor states that replaced it in western Europe.

All of these theories seem to have at least some merit, yet not one of them, in truth, is the sole explanation for the collapse of Rome. There are many books on this single subject alone, and the life of just one person in the Roman world—Julius Caesar—has been the focus of dozens of works.

Telling the story

It might seem, therefore, a daunting task to attempt a "world" history. To select which of the myriad tales should be told, and which of the countless people described in the historical records should be included in the pages of a single volume might seem almost impossible. Yet by condensing the whole of history down to its essentials—the personalities and events (as well as the causes) that shaped our world—the whole scope of the human story becomes more comprehensible.

Contrasts and comparisons

In this book, the reader can trace the history of nations, such as China—from the first villages along the banks of the Yangtze to a sophisticated 21st-century society that has sent men into space—yet also find out what was occurring in Central America, for example, while the Romans were conquering Britain.

The pace of historical change has accelerated with the coming of the 21st century. Among the updates to this new edition, there are many—such as the changes wrought in the Middle East by the Arab Spring, the dangers posed by new global terrorist groups, challenges presented by ever-growing numbers of refugees, and a rising tide of populism—which seemed to emerge from nowhere. Yet, with the benefit of a long historical viewpoint, these changes can be better understood and placed in their proper perspective.

Inevitably there has been a process of selection as to what can be included, but I hope nevertheless that this book will introduce readers to the key elements of world history and give them a glimpse of a subject which, for me, contains an almost infinite (and growing) store of fascinating stories.

The battles of the past command our attention; historians investigate their causes and consequences.

» **The tombs of the Egyptian pharaohs** give us an unparalleled insight into the history and customs of one of humankind's most ancient civilizations.

What Is History?

History is not the same as the past. We can never directly experience the past—we can never know how it felt to be a gladiator fighting in the Colosseum of ancient Rome, or exactly what Napoleon had in mind when he decided to invade Russia in 1812. What actually happened in the past is gone—history is our attempt to reconstruct the past from the evidence that remains.

The word "history," while commonly taken to mean "everything that has happened up until now," has its root in the Greek word *historein*, meaning "to find out by enquiry." The same root gives us the word "story." We could say, then, that history is our enquiry into the story of the human race.

History and fact

History is something very distinct from facts. Historians ask not only what happened, but also why it happened, how it happened, and what the consequences were, and use the answers to forge the links in chains of events, creating a continuous narrative. These are the kinds of "enquiries" that historians make, and from their conclusions, the past, for most of us, becomes a much more comprehensible place.

Even today, however, there are cultures that do not concern themselves with recording history in the conventional sense—that is, as a chronological narrative that aims to represent what actually happened in the past. Many indigenous peoples,

◄ **Passing on stories** is a vital part of the oral culture of peoples such as the San of Namibia.

especially those with a strong oral tradition, instead weave together events of the distant and recent past, and both mythological and actual happenings. The result is a body of knowledge that is relevant to that culture, which is passed down through the generations via storytelling and ritual.

Whether oral or written, history is always an incomplete puzzle, made up of fragments, hints, and selections from the evidence that is available.

Historical sources

The ingredients from which historians construct history are their "sources." These may range from the types of pollen found in an ancient Near Eastern site (revealing which crops once grew there), to a charter recording a land sale in medieval France, the writings of a historian living in ancient Rome, or the oral testimony of a World War II soldier.

The **past** is a **foreign country**, they do things **differently** there.

L.P. Hartley, *The Go-Between* (1955)

Sources are themselves subdivided into those that are primary and those that are secondary. A primary source is something produced or written at the time—the writings of the Latin author Tacitus about 1st-century CE Rome, say—while a secondary source is something written after the event itself, making use of primary sources. The distinction between the two may not always be clear, of course. For example, Niccolò Machiavelli's 16th-century study of Roman history is a secondary source about Rome, but the obvious influence on his writing of his own view of the world gives us a primary source into life and attitudes in Renaissance Italy.

In some eras, particularly the very ancient past before writing existed, there are no primary sources at all in the conventional sense. Here, archaeology—the study of bones, buildings, and artifacts recovered from past societies— must help out.

Varying perspectives

History can be written from many different viewpoints. A 19th-century European writing shortly after the French Revolution is likely to have very different interests from a Chinese bureaucrat living in the 2nd century BCE. Moreover, the interpretation of facts is always open to dispute, and historians often disagree about how one fact is linked with another.

Throughout history itself, we see evidence of different ideas about the same events. The perspective of chroniclers such as the French scholar Geoffrey of Villehardouin, who traveled with the Christian forces on the Fourth Crusade, is very different from that of his contemporary on the opposing side, the Arab historian Ibn al-Athir.

Inevitably, we are all prone to adjusting history according to our own prejudices and beliefs, but for most of us, at its simplest, history answers a very human desire for order. Names for eras and ages (the Classical world, the Medieval world, and so on), and for movements and cultures, may not necessarily have been used at the time, but today they serve to break down the past and its interpretation into convenient and digestible blocks, making history accessible for all.

Monumental remnants of long-dead civilizations inspire a host of questions about the peoples that built them.

The ancient past

The era before humankind invented writing is called "prehistory," and our knowledge of this time relies largely upon the skill of archaeologists. Once early societies developed scripts, they left not only artifacts but also written evidence from which their history could be deciphered.

Fascination with the far-distant past is not a new phenomenon. In 81 BCE, the Roman general Sertorius had his men dig up a skeleton in North Africa, doubtless that of a dinosaur, but which he decided were the bones of the giant Tingi, the traditional founder of the local town. However, it was not until the 19th century, when a fierce debate erupted over whether humanity had descended from apes—fuelled by Charles Darwin's *The Descent of Man* (1871)—that the greatest advances in the study of the ancient world were made.

Inspired by Darwin's theories, the Dutch scholar Eugene Dubois set out to find an early ancestor of humankind and in 1891 unearthed the remains

⏶ **The Sumerians** made records of, for example, livestock tallies, in a wedge-shaped script we call cuneiform.

of *Pithecanthropus erectus* or "Solo Man" (later called *Homo erectus*) in Java in Indonesia. Dubois' 20th-century successors, such as Richard and Louis Leakey working in East Africa's Rift Valley, have since discovered remains that shed valuable light on humanity's physical evolution into its modern form.

The first civilizations

European scholars and archaeologists of the 19th and early 20th centuries became fascinated by the remote past, and in particular, the rise and fall of ancient empires. This was, after all, an age of empire for Europe, and the wealthy traveled abroad as part of their education. On the "Grand Tour," as it was called, they inspected the ruins of Classical cities such as Athens and Rome, but soon the older civilizations of the Near East drew attention.

Scholars began to uncover evidence that revealed previously little-known cultures, or shed dramatic new light on more familiar ones. For example, in a single decade—the 1920s—Leonard Woolley excavated the early Sumerian city at Ur; Howard Carter discovered the tomb of Tutankhamun in Egypt's Valley of the Kings; Sir John Marshall began the first consistent study of the Indus Valley civilization with his digs at Mohenjo-Daro; and Sir Arthur Evans' work at Knossos revealed the Minoan civilization.

Written clues

The first steps to decipher Sumerian cuneiform script were also taken in the 1920s. While paintings, carvings, and other early art forms all reveal something of the ancient world, the most illuminating records were left once writing had

◀ **Howard Carter's discovery** of Tutankhamun's tomb is perhaps even more famous, as a historical event, than any of the details of the boy-pharaoh's reign.

been invented, in around the mid-4th millennium BCE. The earliest pieces of written evidence—dating to before c.3000 BCE—were not narratives about life at the time, but lists and rosters on practical matters: cuneiform records of merchants' stocks from Sumeria, and royal archives from Assyria. Hieroglyphic tomb inscriptions that identify the Egyptian dead may not provide us with stories, but give us a lot of information about how ancient peoples lived.

Myth and tradition

Perhaps the most colorful insights into the ancient world are preserved in myth and tradition. Some of the earliest stories to be told by early societies relate to the origins of their race, or its legendary heroes: Aztec tales of their wanderings before settling at Tenochtitlán, for example, or the Sumerian *Epic of Gilgamesh*. Few have survived so intact as the traditions in the Old Testament of the Bible. Stories such as the exodus of the Jews from persecution in Egypt, and their subsequent conquest of Palestine, doubtless reflect the chaotic

migrations and political instability of the Near East in the late 2nd millennium BCE. But the purpose of these accounts was primarily cultural or religious, and the task of relating the stories within them to precise historical events is not easy.

▽ **The ancient** *Epic of Gilgamesh* contains an account of a great flood, a mythic legend that has many parallels with the story of Noah's ark in the Bible.

The first historians

It was in ancient Greece that historical "enquiry" first arose, perhaps inspired by the questioning spirit of the age that also produced the world's first philosophers. In the new empires of Rome and China, scholars were prompted to investigate their people's rise to greatness.

The Classical era has left us some of the finest literature and most majestic architecture ever produced—the latter embellished with statues and inscriptions that provide crucial evidence for the power and extent of empires, their social structures, and rituals of the time. But even seemingly trivial finds give us clues about the minutiae of daily life—for example, the discovery at a watchtower in southwest Germany of a shoehorn showed that the Romans wore sandals closed at the back, while previously they were believed to have been open.

However, it is not only through art and artifacts that we can understand the Classical world. From around the 5th century BCE appear the first writers whom we can call "historians."

⏷ **Greek art provides** a window on Classical life—for example, what a hoplite soldier wore into battle.

The Greeks

Known as the "Father of History," the Greek scholar Herodotus (c.485–c.430 BCE) traveled widely throughout the Aegean and Near East in search of the raw material for his Histories.

What makes Herodotus exceptional is that he was the first chronicler of the past to state openly that he intended to discover the reasons behind events, rather than simply recording the events themselves. A generation later, Thucydides (c.460–c.411 BCE), in his *History of the Peloponnesian War*, recounts the conflict between Athens and Sparta. He gives incredibly lengthy accounts of the political and military maneuvers of each side, and his attention to detail and careful narrative were to become a model for many histories in the centuries to come.

The Romans

By the early centuries BCE, Rome, the Mediterranean's new imperial power, was inspiring histories of its own. Scholars such as Livy (59 BCE–17 CE) and Tacitus (55–120 CE) analyzed the reasons for their city's power—and the start of its perceived decline.

In the view of Tacitus, the effect of imperial rule had been to undermine the moral fabric of the state. Roman historians were also not averse to purveying gossip about their emperors, such as the salacious details of imperial habits that appear in Suetonius's *Lives of the Twelve Caesars*. More akin to the military histories of today is Julius Caesar's *Gallic Wars*, an account of the conquest of Gaul in which Caesar was the commanding general—a history that also served to glorify Caesar's reputation and promote his political career. From Pliny the

△ **Sima Qian**, a scholar in the Han court of China, sought to document imperial history, largely through a series of mini-biographies of important persons.

Younger (61–c.112 CE), we have a graphic description of the eruption of Mount Vesuvius in southern Italy in 79 CE, which destroyed the city of Pompeii and killed his uncle, the naturalist Pliny the Elder.

Although Pliny's description is almost scientific in its precision, giving no role to supernatural forces, other Romans believed that such events were caused by the anger of the gods. This was not merely common superstition: as late as the 4th century CE, even educated Roman senators sacrificed at the Altar of Victory in the Senate House, believing that abandoning the old ways might cause their city's ruin.

The Chinese

Other Classical cultures also produced histories, entirely separate from the Greco-Roman tradition that began with Herodotus. From China, in particular, much has survived from this period. There are accounts as early as 753 BCE of official scribes at the court of Ch'in tasked with compiling records of significant events, and a set of such annals covering the period 722–481 BCE in the state of Lu has survived.

Perhaps the most famous Chinese historian, Sima Qian (c.135–86 BCE), composed the *Shiji* ("Records of the Historians"), the first attempt to compile a comprehensive history of China from ancient times. Falling out of favor with the emperor, he was sentenced to castration. But rather than committing suicide (the expected outcome of such a sentence), Sima Qian accepted his punishment so that he might finish his history.

> " Many **besought** the **aid of the gods**, but still more imagined there were **no gods left**. "
>
> **Pliny the Younger, on the eruption of Vesuvius, 1st century CE**

▽ **In 79 CE, the volcano Vesuvius**, in southern Italy, erupted, burying the city of Pompeii— a catastrophic event graphically documented by Pliny the Younger.

An era of scholarship

The western Roman Empire became Christian in the early 4th century CE, but collapsed around 150 years later, leaving the Christian church in possession of the most widespread network of power throughout Europe. Its scholarship was soon matched by that of a rising eastern faith—Islam.

After the fall of the western Roman empire, a series of national histories written in Europe sought to discover, rediscover, or even invent the origins of the Germanic kingdoms that had inherited formerly Roman-occupied territory. The writers were ecclesiastical figures such as bishop Gregory of Tours and the English monk Bede. Between the 8th and 10th centuries, the European record becomes rich with chronicles.

At first simply monks' scribbled notes on ecclesiastical calendars, these became more elaborate accounts of whatever interested the author, from the Creation onward—often a litany of fables, plagues, and disasters that cannot be relied upon as historical evidence. Almost all chronicles had their origins in the Christian church, which, as virtually the sole fount of literacy at the time, controlled what books were written, copied, and circulated.

Later in the Middle Ages, however, some chronicles escaped their ecclesiastical origins and religious bias to give a more rounded view of events—for example, Geoffrey of Villehardouin's account of the Fourth Crusade.

☑ **Ecclesiastical chronicles** owed much to royal patronage; here the monk Guillaume de Nangis presents his Chroniques to Philip IV of France.

◀◀ Printed sheets
brought news to a wide audience, detailing in words and pictures events such as the Gunpowder Plot of 1605 against the British king.

The rise of Islam

The Islamic world of the 6th to 10th centuries experienced an era of expansion, political strength, and cultural creativity. Islamic scholars were interested in establishing accurate biographical information from the past, prompted by the need to determine which of the traditions about the life of the prophet Muhammad and the first caliphs were accurate. It was Muslim scholars, too—chiefly in the Abbasid capital of Baghdad—that preserved the works of many ancient Greek and Roman authors lost to Europe.

The Islamic historical tradition culminated in such great writers as Ibn Khaldun (1332–1406), a North African scholar whose monumental work, the *Muqqadimah*, covered the whole of Islamic history, and included aspects of social history and economics that European historians would investigate only some centuries later.

The European Renaissance

From the 12th century, key Classical texts such as those by the philosopher Aristotle and the medical writer Galen started to return to Europe through Muslim-controlled Sicily and Spain. Soon yet more Classical works became available, some from the dwindling Greek-speaking territories of the Byzantine Empire. The pace of scholarly change in Europe quickened into a cultural flowering known as the Renaissance.

A central preoccupation of Renaissance writers, artists, and scholars was the rediscovery of the past. The Roman era in particular was perceived as a time of scientific, literary, and artistic achievement. The study of Roman history and historians became extremely popular, and writers such as Niccolò Machiavelli produced works such as *The History of Florence* in imitation of their Roman ancestors. Renaissance authors wrote not only in Latin, but also in the vernacular, or everyday language, making their works much more accessible.

New media

The spread of printing at this time dispersed new works more widely, and also resulted in a wealth of printed "primary sources" for historians.

Pamphlets, posters, and news-sheets were used to disseminate news and also to spread new ideas to a wider audience: for example, the distribution of printed material greatly assisted the success of the radical religious changes of the Reformation as it swept through Europe in the 16th and 17th centuries.

◤ Islamic manuscripts
feature scenes and accounts of events at court and diplomatic encounters.

A new age of empire

The 18th and 19th centuries were a time of expansionism and empire, and much of our information about this era displays the bias of the empire-builders. But it was also a time of revolution, with established power structures being questioned, challenged, and often overthrown.

Le Petit Journal

⚏ **Newspapers** brought eagerly awaited news and colorful images of events and practices in far-flung lands.

During the 18th century in Europe, religion gave ground to the human-centered ideology of the Enlightenment, and it is evident from the works of thinkers and writers how the scope of history and commentary widened. The Scottish economist Adam Smith (1723–1790) included in his *Wealth of Nations* a new, historical approach to the study of capitalism. The French philosopher Voltaire (1694–1778) argued not only that social and economic history was just as important as the prevailing focus on political and diplomatic matters, but also that much could be learned by studying the histories of civilizations such as China and India.

The philosophy of Romanticism found its way into history, as Johann von Herder (1744–1803) encouraged his fellow historians to "feel" their way inside historical cultures and, through empathizing, to really come to understand how they worked.

Great powers

As European empires gathered power, other writers viewed national and imperial greatness as the pinnacle of human achievement. In Germany, historians began to concentrate on tracing the history of their nation (which was unified, politically, in 1871), while the *History of England* written by

Baron Macaulay (1800–1859) detailed what he saw as the steady, virtually uninterrupted English ascendancy to greatness.

Outside Europe, views of empire were at times similarly positive. In the view of the Indian writer Ghulam Hussain Tabatabai (in his *Siyyar al-Mutakherin* of 1781), the gradual British takeover of India was valuable in filling a power vacuum created by the decline of Mughal power. In Japan, the *Nihon Gaishi* ("Unofficial History of Japan") by Rai Sanyo (1780–1832) argued that domination by powerful military clans had been Japan's undoing, and that power rightfully belonged to the emperor alone. This proposal influenced many of the leaders of the movement that restored imperial power to Japan in 1868.

New sources

The spread of literacy in this era compared to previous centuries has left historians a wider range of sources than just the views of the educated classes. There are revealing accounts, for example, made by common

Images of slavery cast a shadow over imperialism, even though support for the sale of slaves was widespread at the time.

soldiers during the Peninsular War campaign (1808–1814) of the Napoleonic Wars. Alex de Tocqueville (1805–1859) wrote his history of the French Revolution making use of first-hand accounts of events and a huge range of administrative documents, such as the *cahiers de doléances* (lists of grievances) that the French communes sent to the legislature in 1789.

In the 19th century, the vastly increased availability of primary sources was complemented by new methods of recording events as they happened. The spread of photography from the 1830s made it possible for future historians to see what the past actually looked like. By the end of the 20th century, the first moving pictures and the first voice recordings had given us the possibility of an even more thrillingly direct insight into the past. History had come alive.

The neoclassical style in architecture allied itself to the noble ideals of the past, both in imperial Europe and, in buildings such as Washington, D.C.'s Capitol, the burgeoning new nation of the US.

Past, present, and future

The revolutions and terrible wars of the 20th century profoundly affected people's views of their times and the histories that they wrote. The 21st century has continued to confront us with deeply shocking events, on which we have yet to gain a full perspective.

The Revolution of 1917 that toppled the Russian czars had at its base a brand-new ideology—Marxism. Karl Marx (1818–1883) argued that history should be seen as a process by which societies develop through a series of stages, from ancient to feudal, then bourgeois, which would in turn be superseded by a "communist" society. Marx argued that there is an uncontrollable development from one stage to another, fueled by struggles between social classes over the ownership of wealth. In Marx's view, violent social revolution was necessary to move from one phase to another. This is exactly what occurred in Russia in 1917, but it was not, as Marx predicted, repeated in the more industrialized countries of Europe, such as Germany.

Marxism may have challenged modern historians to take a different view of history, but the advent of two world wars led to other major preoccupations. World Wars I and II devastated large parts of Europe and Asia, and profoundly affected the political systems of large parts of the world.

The sheer quantity of evidence available from a conflict such as World War II—from first-hand accounts to photographs and films—appears to make the job of the historian disarmingly simple, but it has also become dauntingly complex, in that there is so much information from every side of the conflict to be sifted through and compared.

Instant access

At the beginning of the 21st century, technology has become so advanced that it gives us multiple records of major events. These are records that can all be accessed in an instant through our television sets, personal computers, and now even our cell phones. The development of the Internet since the 1990s means that we can now capture, store, and transmit information at a speed that would have seemed supernatural only 200 years ago.

» **The Russian Revolution** of 1917 promised a new world order, yet Communism itself was overthrown in 1989.

МЫ ЗЛОМУ ВРАГУ ВСЕ ОТРЕЖЕМ ПУТИ,
ИЗ ПЕТЛИ, ИЗ ЭТОЙ ЕМУ НЕ УЙТИ!

❰❰ **The use of art** as a tool to denigrate enemies has a long history. Whereas ancient Egyptian pharaohs might be depicted trampling the enemy, this Soviet propaganda poster from World War II shows Allied powers literally tying Hitler "in knots."

Future perspectives

Access to information, as well as the first-hand accounts we can hear for ourselves from people who have made history (such as the veterans of World War II), can lull us into feeling as though somehow we "know" our recent history.

However, just as the "enquiries" of the ancient Greeks were only the first step in producing a history, so our recordings and transcriptions of events in the modern world are simply contributions to an abundance of sources that we leave for the historians who will look back on the 20th and 21st centuries. Then, as ever, it will be how historians interpret their sources that makes history, not the sources themselves. Historians perpetually revisit the past, reassessing it in the light of updated social attitudes—for example, toward women or ethnic groups—as they do so.

In many cases, it is only with hindsight that we can focus fully on the causes and consequences of events. In years to come, our own ideas and biases may well be held up for scrutiny (and perhaps disapproval) by the historians of the future. And

❝ **Revolutions** are the **locomotives** of **history**.
Karl Marx (1818–1883)

when these individuals ask not only what happened but why it happened, they may arrive at answers that are very different to those we are so certain of today.

❰❰ **Television and the Internet have become** important media for propaganda, used ably by former al-Qaeda leader Osama bin Laden to disseminate his messages worldwide.

The Prehistoric World

The world to 3000 BCE

Set against the age of the Earth itself, which is some 4.5 billion years old, human history covers a comparatively short span. Human ancestors split genetically from their apelike ancestors around 5 to 6 million years ago, though anatomically modern humans—*Homo sapiens*—only appeared about 200,000 years ago.

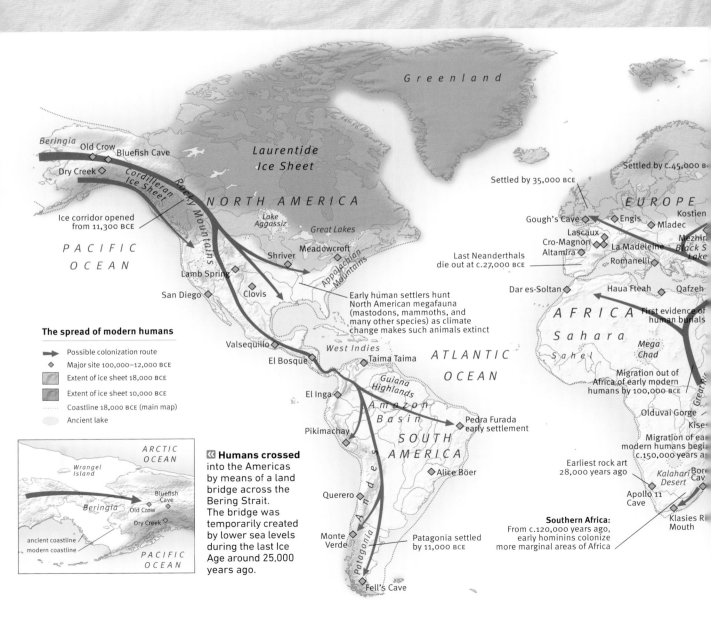

Greenland

Beringia
Old Crow
Bluefish Cave

Laurentide Ice Sheet

Settled by c.45,000 B.

Dry Creek

Cordilleran Ice Sheet

Rocky Mountains

Settled by 35,000 BCE

EUROPE

Kostien

Ice corridor opened from 11,300 BCE

NORTH AMERICA

Lake Aggassiz

Great Lakes

Gough's Cave
Engis
Mladec

Lascaux
Cro-Magnon
Altamira
La Madeleine
Romanelli

Mezhir
Black S
Lake

PACIFIC OCEAN

Meadowcroft
Shriver

Appalachian Mountains

Last Neanderthals die out at c.27,000 BCE

Lamb Spring

San Diego
Clovis

Dar es-Soltan

Haua Fteah
Qafzeh

AFRICA
First evidence of human burials

S a h a r a

The spread of modern humans

Valsequillo

West Indies

Taima Taima

ATLANTIC OCEAN

Sahel

Mega Chad

➡ Possible colonization route
◇ Major site 100,000–12,000 BCE
▢ Extent of ice sheet 18,000 BCE
▢ Extent of ice sheet 10,000 BCE
⋯ Coastline 18,000 BCE (main map)
◌ Ancient lake

El Bosque

El Inga

Guiana Highlands

Amazon Basin

Pikimachay

SOUTH AMERICA

Early human settlers hunt North American megafauna (mastodons, mammoths, and many other species) as climate change makes such animals extinct

Migration out of Africa of early modern humans by 100,000 BCE

Olduvai Gorge
Kise

Migration of ea modern humans begi c.150,000 years a

Pedra Furada early settlement

Alice Böer

Earliest rock art 28,000 years ago

Kalahari Desert

Bor
Cav

ARCTIC OCEAN

Wrangel Island

Bluefish Cave

Beringia
Old Crow

Dry Creek

ancient coastline
modern coastline

PACIFIC OCEAN

Apollo 11 Cave

Klasies R Mouth

Querero

Andes
Patagonia

Monte Verde

◀ Humans crossed into the Americas by means of a land bridge across the Bering Strait. The bridge was temporarily created by lower sea levels during the last Ice Age around 25,000 years ago.

Patagonia settled by 11,000 BCE

Southern Africa: From c.120,000 years ago, early hominins colonize more marginal areas of Africa

Fell's Cave

Humans rapidly migrated from their African homelands, and
had spread to almost the entire world by about 12,000 years ago.
Around 2,000 years later, the invention of agriculture in the Middle
East led to the emergence of settled and increasingly complex
societies—and eventually to the world's first cities.

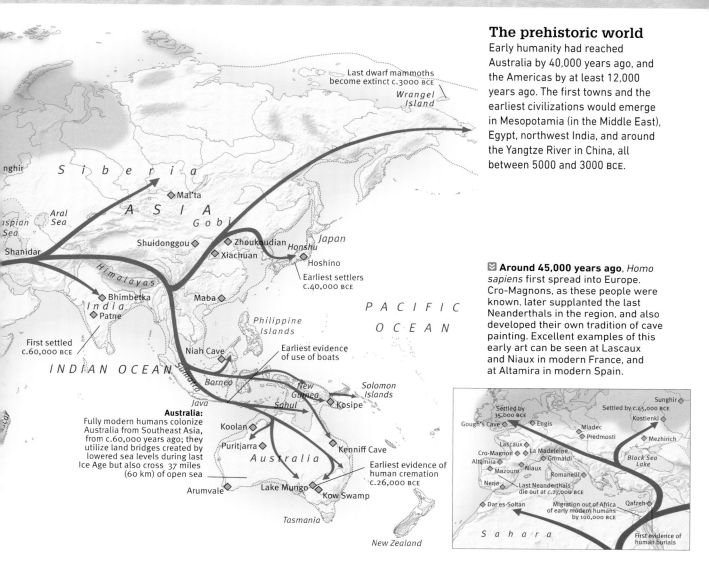

The prehistoric world

Early humanity had reached
Australia by 40,000 years ago, and
the Americas by at least 12,000
years ago. The first towns and the
earliest civilizations would emerge
in Mesopotamia (in the Middle East),
Egypt, northwest India, and around
the Yangtze River in China, all
between 5000 and 3000 BCE.

◪ **Around 45,000 years ago,** *Homo
sapiens* first spread into Europe.
Cro-Magnons, as these people were
known, later supplanted the last
Neanderthals in the region, and also
developed their own tradition of cave
painting. Excellent examples of this
early art can be seen at Lascaux
and Niaux in modern France, and
at Altamira in modern Spain.

Australia:
Fully modern humans colonize
Australia from Southeast Asia,
from c.60,000 years ago; they
utilize land bridges created by
lowered sea levels during last
Ice Age but also cross 37 miles
(60 km) of open sea

Human ancestors

The evolution of modern humans extends back millions of years, beginning with a genetic split between chimpanzees and humans 5 to 6 million years ago. The process is not easy to trace, as our evidence comes from scattered, unrelated finds. The emergence of *Homo sapiens*, modern humans, is a comparatively recent development, occurring around 200,000 years ago, and evidence of the first settled villages dates only as far back as about 10,000 BCE.

The Australopithecines

⚲ **E AFRICA** ⏳ **4.5 MILLION YEARS AGO**

Among the earliest known human ancestors are the Australopithecines ("southern ape-men"), who evolved in the East African forests. By 3 million years ago, the Australopithecines had diversified into many forms that shared a vital characteristic—they were bipedal, standing on two feet.

The Laetoli footprints and Lucy

Around 3.6 million years ago, a volcanic eruption deposited a layer of ash at Laetoli, Tanzania. This ash, made cement-like by rain, preserved the footprints of at least five Australopithecine individuals. The prints confirmed that they walked upright, with a rolling gait. The most complete Australopithecine skeleton, discovered in Ethiopia in 1975, is of a young female, dubbed "Lucy." She stood around 3 ft (1 m) tall and weighed around 60 lb (27 kg), while her pelvis shows clear signs of adaptation for an erect posture.

Walking upright enabled the Australopithecines to operate away from the forests in the open terrain of the savannah, giving them a wider food-gathering range than their competitors. By 3 million years ago, they flourished throughout much of sub-Saharan Africa.

» **The African country of Tanzania**, where archaeologists have discovered evidence of many of our earliest ancestors, has been called the "cradle of human life."

Homo habilis

E AFRICA ☒ 2.4 TO 1.4 MILLION YEARS AGO

The earliest "hominins"—human ancestors—to be placed in the same genus, Homo, as the modern human species Homo sapiens, evolved a little more than 2 million years ago. The first to be discovered, in Tanzania's Olduvai Gorge, was *Homo habilis* ("handyman"), so named for their use of stone tools.

Homo habilis resembled the Australopithecines (*see facing page*) but had a larger brain size, and teeth and hands that show a greater evolution toward those of modern humans, while still retaining a low, heavy-browed skull and long arms.

The *Homo habilis* camp site at Olduvai Gorge, where their fossil remains were first unearthed, included a scatter of simple stone tools such as shaped flints (*see p.32*) and broken animal bones, showing evidence of the deliberate breaking-up of carcasses. *Homo habilis* probably slept in trees, in relative safety from lions and other predators. There are some indications that *Homo habilis* was capable of primitive speech, permitting the development of more complicated social organization.

⊼ A skull of *Homo habilis*, one of the earliest human ancestors.

Homo erectus

E ASIA, AFRICA, EUROPE ☒ 2 MILLION TO 143,000 YEARS AGO

The very earliest examples of a new species of hominin, *Homo erectus* ("upright man"), date from around 2 million years ago in East Africa. The tools that *Homo erectus* made were of significantly improved design from those of *Homo habilis* (*see above*), and included shaped hand axes and cleaving tools, which were used for specific functions, such as butchering animals.

These early humans were skilled hunters and brilliant opportunists, quick to take advantage of different environments, which must have been a key factor in the success of the species. By 500,000 years ago, these early humans had adapted successfully to a wide variety of tropical and temperate environments, moving as far northeast as China. Numerous fragments of a species classified as *Homo erectus* were found in Zhoukoudian Cave, near Beijing—the skeletons found there were dubbed "Peking Man." They are known to have used fire, making settlement possible in cold locations, and allowing them to cook food, which in turn led to the evolution of smaller jaws and less robust teeth.

≫ *Homo erectus* was powerfully built with massive brow ridges, a large face, and a long, low skull.

Tool making and speech

Although certain species of ape, including chimpanzees, have been observed to use tools such as sticks and stones for digging, opening shellfish, or menacing enemies, it was early human ancestors who were the first to deliberately shape tools around 3 million years ago. Around the same time, our ancestors began to evolve the necessary changes in the brain and voice box to permit language.

The development of tools

The earliest stone tools were probably modified rocks found in Kenya, which date to 3.3 million years ago, although it is unclear which species made them. Later *Homo habilis* and other early human ancestors created stone artifacts, including pebbles and rock fragments, by deliberately removing flakes. They used some tools as scrapers, others as choppers, and the basic forms did not change for thousands of years. An early hominin species called *Homo heidelbergensis* may have been the first to create spears by mounting sharp stone tips on wooden shafts around 500,000 years ago in southern Africa.

Physical evolution and language

The development of articulate language was a key threshold in human evolution, because it allowed for an enhanced level of cooperation. Exactly when it emerged is difficult to define. *Homo habilis* had a slightly more human-like frontal lobe (the part of the brain that houses speech control) than the earlier Australopithecines. *Homo erectus*, around 1.8 million years ago, had a lower-positioned larynx, which would have allowed a wider variety of vocal sounds. *Homo heidelbergensis* was found to possess the hyoid bone at the root of the larynx that facilitates speech. It was only around 300,000 years ago that the base of the skull evolved to allow a full range of sounds.

Around 40,000 to 50,000 years ago, during what some anthropologists term the "Great Leap Forward," modern humans seem to have developed language of the kind we would recognize today. The first symbolic representations of the world, such as the cave art at Lascaux in France (*see p.39*), accompanied this leap. Language and art enabled our ancestors to pass on skills, traditions, and discoveries, an essential foundation for the complex societies that would emerge from around 10,000 BCE.

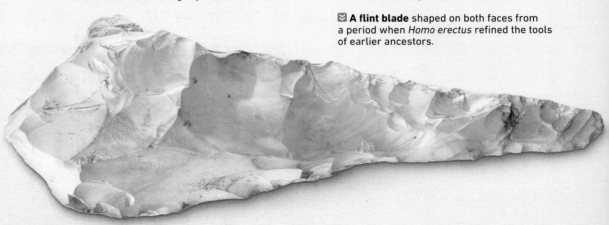

A flint blade shaped on both faces from a period when *Homo erectus* refined the tools of earlier ancestors.

The Neanderthals

AFRICA, EUROPE, W EURASIA 350,000 TO 40,000 YEARS AGO

Around 350,000 years ago, a new species, *Homo neanderthalensis*, appeared in Africa. It would be the last major human-like species before the evolution of fully modern humans. The Neanderthals spread out from Africa, by 200,000 years ago reaching as far as Uzbekistan and Iran in the east and the Iberian peninsula in the west, then moving into northern Europe. They were named for the site in Germany where one of the first specimens was discovered, in 1856. They had a short, robust build, powerful limbs, a protruding face, and heavy brow ridges, but a body shape closer to that of modern humans than preceding species.

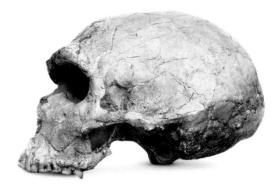

A **Neanderthal skull** shows a distinctive brow ridge. Neanderthals had large brains and more rounded heads than their predecessors.

Neanderthal lifestyle

The Neanderthals were expert hunters, who pursued animals such as bison with wooden and stone-tipped spears. They made sophisticated tools and dwelt in caves, rock shelters, and open camps. They may have been capable of speech, although their larynx is higher than in modern humans, which would have impeded the use of the broad spectrum of sounds necessary for full language. This was the first species to exhibit a sense of care for the dead. In one grave at Teshik-Tash in Uzbekistan, ibex horns had been placed in a circle around the skull, and a fire lit around the body.

DNA recovered from remains reveals that the Neanderthals were not our direct ancestors. They did, however, live alongside modern humans (*Homo sapiens*, or "wise humans"), who migrated northward from Africa into Europe around 45,000 years ago. It may be that competition with (or possibly absorption by) the newcomers caused their extinction around 40,000 years ago.

Gorham's Cave on Gibraltar is thought to have been one of the very last sites inhabited by the Neanderthals before their extinction.

The earliest humans

Modern humans, *Homo sapiens,* **evolved** around 200,000 years ago in East Africa. Physically, they were not well adapted to cold conditions, and the Ice Age that began around the time they appeared confined them to a small area of tropical Africa and southwestern Asia. Despite this, their large brain size and capacity for language left them poised to expand out of this initial heartland.

The Ice Ages

◪ **WORLDWIDE, EXCEPT TROPICAL REGIONS**   ⌛ **2 MILLION TO 11,000 YEARS AGO**

▨ **Sea levels dropped** as seawater froze during the last Ice Age. A land bridge at the Bering Strait allowed hominins to migrate from Siberia into North America.

Over millions of years, Earth has experienced a series of Ice Ages. These periods of intense cold were punctuated by intervals of milder conditions, known as interglacials. The last Ice Age began around 2.5 million years ago, and we are currently in an interglacial period that began around 11,000 years ago. During the glacial periods of the last Ice Age, the Earth's natural environments experienced major changes. Huge ice sheets formed over Scandinavia and covered most of Canada and part of the US as far south as the Great Lakes. There were ice sheets in the mountains of the Pyrenees and the Andes, and on Central Asian mountains. South of these areas, huge expanses of barren land extended from the Atlantic to Siberia. These environments suffered nine-month winters, making them uninhabitable for our ancestors, who instead moved south to more temperate and tropical regions. During interglacials, the ice sheets started to melt, sea levels rose, and humans returned north, following the animals they hunted and the plants they foraged.

Homo sapiens in Africa

AFRICA   195,000 TO 50,000 YEARS AGO

Anatomically modern humans—*Homo sapiens*—appeared almost 200,000 years ago, probably in East Africa. They were taller than their immediate predecessors, males averaging about 5½ ft (1.75 m), and heavier. Their faces were less protruding than their Neanderthal contemporaries (*see p.33*) and their brow ridge was less prominent. Brain size was larger than in most previous species, though actually somewhat smaller than the average Neanderthal brain. The larynx was lower, so they could vocalize a wide enough range of sounds to form language as we know it.

Homo sapiens were long-limbed, giving them a greater skin surface area from which heat could be lost—an adaptation suited to warmer climates. The narrow pelvic girdle necessary for a fully upright stance meant that babies had to be born at an earlier stage in their development, with smaller skulls and brains—which is why human babies are dependent on their parents for so much longer, relatively, than any other species. The shorter gestation period allowed more frequent pregnancies, enabling greater population growth.

Despite their advantages, *Homo sapiens* at this stage did not compete well with the Neanderthals in their territories in Europe and southwest Asia. The most important sites for early *Homo sapiens* lie within Africa, with a few in modern Israel. At the earliest known site,

Omo in Ethiopia, bones have been dated to around 195,000 years ago. At Klasies River Cave, South Africa, a population of *Homo sapiens* lived from about 120,000 years ago, hunting seal and antelope, and gathering roots and shellfish.

⌂ **An early *Homo sapiens* skull** discovered in South Africa shows very close affinities to the skull shapes of humans today.

Cultural advances and expansion

The development of art is taken as an important indicator of when *Homo sapiens* developed fully modern cognitive abilities, because it requires reasoning, planning, and the expression of intangible feelings. The oldest definitively dated decorative items, red ochres engraved with geometric patterns, come from Blombos Cave in South Africa and are about 77,000 years old. They mark a shift into the Upper Paleolithic period, in which *Homo sapiens*, whose population was probably only around a million, expanded both in numbers and, through a series of remarkable migrations (*see overleaf*), in their territories.

》 MITOCHONDRIAL EVE

Examination of a wide range of samples of mitochondrial DNA (matter outside the nucleus of the cell, which is passed down from every mother to her offspring) has revealed that all living humans have a common ancestor who lived in Africa around 200,000 years ago. This unknown matriarch has been dubbed "Mitochondrial Eve," and we all share at least some genetic information with her. By studying mitochondrial DNA, scientists have been able to track the movement of *Homo sapiens* across the globe.

Settling the world

⚑ **WORLDWIDE** ⌛ **50,000 TO 15,000 YEARS AGO**

The most significant of all human migrations began around 50,000 years ago during the last Ice Age (*see p.34*). This period saw the spread of *Homo sapiens* out of Africa, until they settled the whole of mainland Eurasia and crossed land bridges into the Americas. *Homo sapiens* had also mastered tropical waters with canoes or rafts, which allowed them to drift to New Guinea and Australia. Colonizing the world was not a deliberate project, but a consequence of following game migrations and searching for new animals to hunt and new food plants to gather. The adaptability of *Homo sapiens* as a species made them capable of exploiting a vast range of new environments.

The settlement of North America

The ancestors of today's Native Americans crossed into North America via a land bridge that existed at the Bering Strait up until 10,000 years ago. The earliest human sites in the Americas have long been thought to be in Alaska, at Broken Mammoth and Healy Lake; they date from around 11,000 to 12,000 years ago. However, finds at Buttermilk

⌃ **European cave paintings** date from around 32,000 years ago. This scene, from Lascaux in France, shows a bison, a common theme in prehistoric cave art.

Creek in Texas, dating to 15,000 years ago, and at Monte Verde in Chile to around 14,000 years ago, suggest much earlier settlement.

The settlers in Alaska established what is known as the Clovis culture, and this eventually extended as far south as Panama. The Clovis people may have been responsible for the

⌄ **Human footprints** found at the Willandra Lakes, New South Wales, Australia, reveal that this area was inhabited around 40,000 years ago.

widespread extinction of gigantic mammals that took place at about this time. That extinction could in turn have contributed to the end of their culture around 11,000 years ago.

Expansion into Australia

Some 50,000 years ago, Java, Sumatra, and Borneo were joined by land, but to reach Australia and New Guinea required a series of sea crossings and must have involved the use of boats. *Homo sapiens* had certainly reached the Australian mainland soon after this, as indicated by a series of rock shelters in the Northern Territory and north of Adelaide. Dating back some 40,000 years, Lake Mungo in New South Wales is the most important early site. The *Homo sapiens* remains found there were partially covered in red ocher, indicating a ritual element to the burials.

The arrival of humans in Australia coincided with the extinction of massive vertebrates that had previously inhabited the continent, although it is not clear whether the newcomers hunted them to extinction, or whether brushfires set by early humans destroyed their habitat. The early settlers, ancestors of today's Aboriginal peoples, developed an isolated and unique culture, many elements of which still survive; the earliest boomerang found—at Wyrie Swamp, Tasmania—dates from around 8000 BCE.

Expansion elsewhere

Homo sapiens gradually infiltrated almost every other habitable part of the globe, reaching southwestern Europe by around 45,000 years ago. The group of *Homo sapiens* that settled here are referred to as Cro-Magnon, and they entirely displaced the Neanderthal population in this region. By around 40,000 years ago *Homo sapiens* had migrated to eastern Europe and southwestern Siberia, colonizing Japan by around 30,000 to 35,000 years ago.

Although the Clovis people, who had colonized North America from Alaska to Panama, did not penetrate South America themselves, later groups reached the very tip of the continent by around 9000 BCE. After this, with the exception of certain Pacific islands and particularly remote regions of the globe, the long migration of *Homo sapiens* out of Africa was complete.

Clovis spear points have a bifacial, concave, and fluted shape, which was replicated throughout the entire area occupied by the culture.

Hunter-gatherers

Hunting and foraging for food was the only way of life for humans until around 12,000 years ago. It was a successful lifestyle that, in its flexibility, had significant advantages over the settled agricultural societies that would supplant it. Today, only a handful of hunter-gatherer societies survive, in the Amazon Basin and in Africa, which provide vital evidence for their prehistoric forebears' way of life.

⌃ **Spear-fishing** with barbed poles, such as this 10,000-year-old harpoon made from an antler, was widespread in later prehistoric times.

Early evidence

Hunter-gatherers have to range across a wide area for food, and so carry few possessions with them. As a result, prehistoric hunter-gatherers have left few material remains.

Rare finds of digging sticks, such as at Gwisho in Central Africa, and flint sickle blades show that people dug for tubers and harvested wild grasses. Broken animal and fish bones and plant pollens reveal details of the hunter-gatherer diet, as do deep middens (waste sites) crammed with discarded mollusk shells.

Sites such as Star Carr in northeast England, from around 9000 BCE, show that hunter-gatherers might return again and again to the same places, establishing seasonal settlements close to where game was plentiful. Small figurines and carvings of bears and mammoths discovered at Dolní Věstonice in Czechia (former Czech Republic), and remarkable fish sculptures from Lepenski Vir in Serbia, show the level of cultural sophistication that such early societies could reach.

Eventually, however, hunting-gathering was replaced by farming. Probably, as agriculturalists encroached on their territory, some hunter-gatherers adopted the new way of life, while others were forced into the margins. In marginal environments, farming always carries the risk of starvation if crops fail, and today there are still isolated groups, such as the San of the Kalahari desert in Africa, that maintain the ancient hunter-gatherer traditions.

⌃ **A hunter is depicted** in a cave painting from Faraway Bay, Western Australia, dating to around 20,000 years ago.

Art and ritual

WORLDWIDE **40,000 TO 4,000 YEARS AGO**

Around 77,000 years ago, early humans began to create the first examples of art—geometric patterns incised on ocher. By 40,000 to 50,000 years ago the repertoire had extended to images incised on animal bones, sculpted from ivory, and painted on cave walls. This artistic activity coincides with the first evidence of religious belief, and both of these developments indicate an ability to think about ideas or concepts that lie outside immediate, everyday existence.

Cave art

A tradition of cave painting arose about 40,000 years ago on the Indonesian island of Sulawesi and among the Cro-Magnon people of western Europe, where flamboyant artworks survive, sheltered from the elements. The cave paintings depict a wide range of animals, some of them, such as mammoth and woolly rhinoceros, long extinct; others, like wild horses, European bison, and reindeer, still familiar today. In a society dependent on hunting, animal paintings may have been the focus of rituals intended to ensure success and a rich supply of meat.

By contrast, human figures in cave paintings are rare, and when they do survive are highly stylized or masked. However, impressions of human hands and indecipherable signs do appear on the walls of caves, including Altamira in Spain, and Chauvet, Niaux, and Lascaux in France. One theory is that the art was created by shamans who acted as mediums with the spiritual world, communicating with ancestors and spirit totems. Other artistic creations, including carved female statuettes known as "Venus figurines," may have been

In later rock art, symbols such as this circular sign filled with dots start to feature alongside depictions of animal and human figures.

related to hunter-gatherer fertility cults, while the burial of possessions alongside bodies indicates belief in an afterlife.

From ritual to religion

As societies grew more complex, they began to devote particular areas and spaces to cult practices. At Çatalhöyük in Turkey, murals identify places used for ritual around 7000 BCE. In time, lavish temples would be built for the worship of complex pantheons of gods, who demanded elaborate rituals performed only by a priestly elite. A glimpse of hunter-gatherer beliefs can now only be seen in societies such as that of the Australian Aborigines, who continue to commemorate their ancestral spirits with spectacular rock art.

The "Venus of Willendorf," carved around 20–25,000 years ago, may have been a fertility talisman.

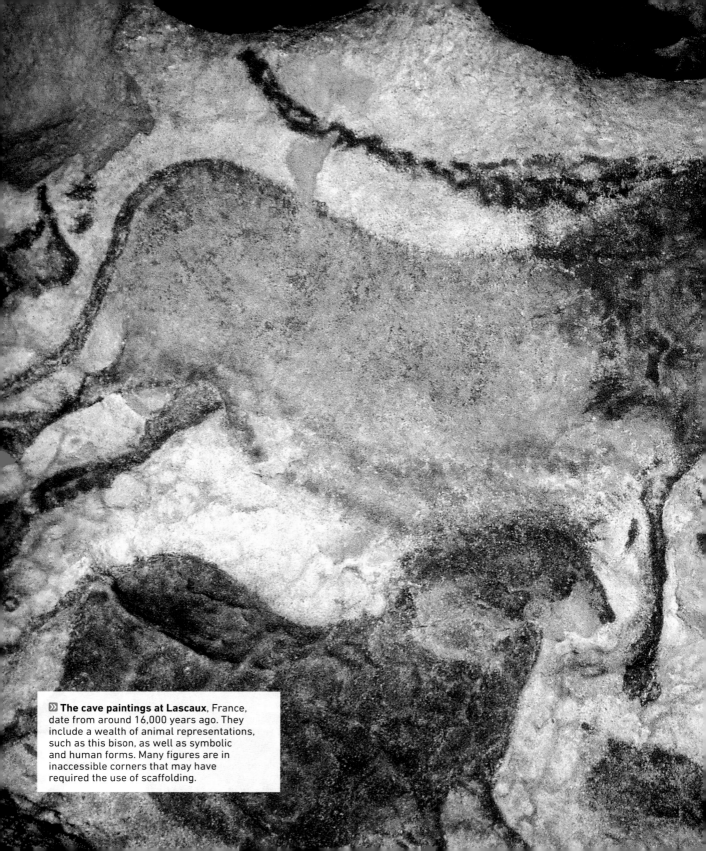

>> **The cave paintings at Lascaux**, France, date from around 16,000 years ago. They include a wealth of animal representations, such as this bison, as well as symbolic and human forms. Many figures are in inaccessible corners that may have required the use of scaffolding.

Early societies

The transition to an agricultural existence, which began around 11,000 years ago and was virtually complete by about 2000 BCE, gave rise to new ways of life, including the first settled communities. From this period of early farming, known as the Neolithic, also emerge the earliest monumental remains, including striking megalithic structures that appear across northern and western Europe.

The cradle of agriculture

TURKEY, SYRIA, IRAQ, PAKISTAN, CHINA, MESOAMERICA ⧖ **8500–6000** BCE

The end of the last Ice Age around 11,000 years ago, and the accompanying rise in temperatures, was the trigger for the switch from the hunter-gatherer lifestyle to one of agricultural and animal domestication. This first took place in around 8500 BCE, in an area known as the "Fertile Crescent" that includes Turkey, Syria, and Iraq.

The hot, dry summers and cool, wet winters, together with a wide variety of altitudes and a large number of wild cereals and legumes, provided ideal conditions for agriculture to succeed. Agriculture arose independently in other regions with favorable climatic conditions—in China's Yangtze Valley in around 7000 BCE and, a thousand years later, in Mesoamerica and possibly at Mehrgarh in Pakistan.

Early agriculture

The first plants to be adapted from their wild forms for cultivation were cereals—emmer and einkorn, barley and rye. These are found at sites such as Abu Hureyra in Syria, where a small foraging settlement became a compact farming community of mudbrick dwellings.

At around the same time, animals were domesticated—goats first, then sheep, pigs, and cattle—providing a reliable source of meat, milk, and other animal products. The settled nature of agriculture compared with hunter-gathering, and the ready availability of food, led to large increases in population—the site of Ain 'Ghazal in Jordan more than doubled in size between 7250 BCE and 6750 BCE.

⬆ **Ears of emmer**, originally a wild grass that early agriculturalists selectively bred to enhance its crop yield.

The spread of farming

WORLDWIDE ⌛ **7000–2000** BCE

Around 7000 BCE, agricultural societies of the Near East began to show signs of stress caused by growing populations. Some sites shrank in size; others were abandoned. This may have led to a dispersal of the agricultural population, and increased pastoralism (animal herding).

Farming in Europe and Asia

Farming seems to have reached the Balkans in southeast Europe by around 6500 BCE, and by around 5500 BCE had penetrated as far west as the Iberian Peninsula. Its range extended by 3500 BCE to northern Germany, Scandinavia, and the British Isles.

Agriculture moved east from the Zagros mountains of the Iran–Iraq borderlands to reach the Caucasus, Turkmenistan, and Pakistan (although farming in Pakistan may have developed independently). By 3000 BCE farming had reached India's Ganges Valley, and by 2500 BCE it extended as far as the Altai in Central Asia. In eastern Asia, an agricultural economy based on rice and millet spread from its origins in the Yangtze Valley to reach southern China by 3000 BCE and Southeast Asia by at least 2300 BCE.

Farming in Africa and the Americas

Agriculture first arrived in Egypt around 5500 BCE, and spread southwards (it may also have arisen independently in sub-Saharan Africa around 2000 BCE).

In the Americas, sunflowers were grown for food in 4000 BCE. The staple crops of native American agriculture, corn and beans, were domesticated in Central America by 3500 BCE. In the high altitudes of the Andes in South America, potatoes were cultivated as early as 5000 BCE, and llamas were domesticated around 1,000 years later.

⌂ **Agricultural living** increased the need for food storage vessels and pottery.

✉ **In Mesoamerica**, with few animals available for domestication, the llama was used as a pack animal, for meat, and for the materials woven from its hair.

The first villages

JORDAN, SYRIA, TURKEY ⌛ **9600–7000** BCE

Skara Brae, a well-preserved Neolithic settlement of stone houses on Orkney, Scotland.

Once prehistoric peoples had begun to cultivate domestic crops and keep livestock, they established permanent settlements. The earliest farming villages were compact huddles of mudbrick houses.

At Abu Hureyra, Syria, several hundred farmers lived in close proximity to their fields and to one another. By 8000 BCE, Jericho, in the Jordan Valley, had become a small, walled town, whose inhabitants lived in beehive-shaped houses with stone foundations and plastered floors (under which they were eventually buried).

Trade, society, and religion

Another highly successful settlement was Çatalhöyük in Turkey, which thrived from 7000 BCE and was inhabited for more than 1,000 years. Its population lived in rectangular houses, built very close together, which were entered through the roof. The houses were whitewashed and painted with geometric patterns. Çatalhöyük probably prospered because of its trade in obsidian, a highly prized black volcanic glass found in Turkey that was used for cutting tools. Trading networks are another sign of society's increasing sophistication. They allowed village settlements to acquire resources from elsewhere, "paying" for their goods by exchanging their agricultural surpluses.

With less time needed to find food, people had more time to specialize in other aspects of life. Some became skilled workers, such as potters and masons, while others became shamans or priests and guided the growing ancestor and fertility cults.

Göbekli Tepe, in southeastern Turkey, dates from around 9500 BCE and is thought to be the world's oldest temple building. Its monumental pillars are carved with images of animals.

Discovery of metals

EURASIA, MESOAMERICA 8000–2000 BCE

Humans had made tools out of stone, bone, and wood for thousands of years. The advent of copper-working around 7000 BCE was a significant watershed in human history and the beginning of a long association with metals.

Copper ores are relatively common around the Mediterranean, found in surface outcrops easily identifiable by their distinctive green color. The earliest copper items were hammered crude axes and beads, but it was the discovery of copper smelting—heating ore with charcoal to extract the metal—that opened the way to the development of a range of practical and decorative items. At first, smelting was done in open fires, until it was found that crucibles—heat-resistant vessels of fired clay—produced metal more efficiently.

The spread of metallurgy

This discovery of smelting seems to have occurred independently in western Asia around 6000 BCE and in East Asia before 2000 BCE. The earliest use of gold and silver dates to around 6000–5000 BCE, with both metals being used for decorative and ritual purposes, as their malleability makes them unsuitable for everyday use. Between 4000 and 2000 BCE, knowledge of metalworking reached most of Eurasia and North Africa. The demand

for metals promoted the growth of trade networks; lowland Mesopotamia, for example—the focus of the earliest civilizations—has no native metal or ore, and societies there needed to import metal from Anatolia or the Iranian plateau. In Europe, copper mines existed from around 5100 BCE at Varna in Bulgaria.

From copper to bronze

Some time after 3500 BCE, people discovered that mixing copper and tin together to create an alloy, named bronze, produced a much more durable metal, suitable for weaponry, armor, and tools. By 3300 BCE, the Mesopotamians had adopted the technique, as had the Egyptians around 3100 BCE, beginning the Bronze Age. Bronze-working was discovered in China around 2000 BCE and from there spread throughout eastern and Southeast Asia.

The discovery of copper allowed prehistoric humans to manufacture much more effective tools and weapons, such as these copper ax heads.

A grave from Varna in Bulgaria, where rich metal deposits allowed a culture to develop in which costly goods accompanied the dead.

Megaliths

As agriculture spread across Europe, new and more centralized communities—mainly in the north and west of the continent, but also as far afield as Malta—created monuments with vast pieces of stone, called megaliths. We may never know their exact purpose, but they are clearly an expression of a belief system, marking out the seasons and the cyclical movements of the sun, moon, and stars.

Barrows and henges

In the 4th millennium BCE, European farming communities created long earthen burial mounds ("barrows") and stone-chambered tombs, such as that at West Kennet in Wiltshire, southern Britain, where a passageway in a barrow leads to side chambers in which as many as 46 corpses were interred. At Newgrange in Ireland a similar chambered tomb features patterns of spirals and circles, typical of a new artistic technique that characterized the art of the megalith builders.

"Henge" monuments appeared around 3200 BCE. Henges consist of a circular or oval area enclosed by a bank, containing a circle of wooden posts or huge stones. Wooden circles have largely perished—although at Woodhenge in Wiltshire, the post-holes have survived; the deepest measure about 6 ft (2 m), indicating posts that stood some 17 ft (5.5 m) high. The stone circles, however, are the most remarkable monuments of the megalithic age. These are spread throughout northern and western Europe, with the British Isles alone containing perhaps 1,000 stone circles. The circle at Avebury, Wiltshire, 1,381 ft (420 m) in diameter, is among the largest that survive, and probably acted as the ritual focus for a large area of southwestern Britain. At Carnac in France, elaborate, long rows of standing stones form a similarly striking ensemble.

▼ **The dramatic stone circle** at Stonehenge is thought by some to have been built to mark the summer and winter solstices—critical events in farming societies.

Stonehenge

Stonehenge, in southern England, is perhaps the most famous megalithic site of all. First begun around 3100 BCE as a simple earthwork enclosure, the site was developed over the next 1,000 years in several stages. Around 2500 BCE, a central stone circle of giant sandstones (or sarsen stones) was set up, each weighing around 26 tons (23,586 kg). Each was shaped into the correct size by hammering with great stone balls or "mauls." How exactly the sarsens were erected is unknown, but the complex must have demanded a huge investment in time and labor, implying a highly centralized society. Around 2300 BCE, a circle of bluestones—transported all the way from Preseli in south Wales, a distance of some 155 miles (250 km)—was erected.

The end of the megalith age

By around 1500 BCE, the megalithic age in Europe was on the wane. Construction of stone circles ceased in Britain and northern France. The focus of religion in northern Europe turned to the ritual deposit of weaponry in lakes and bogs and the last evidence of additions at Stonehenge dates to around 1100 BCE. Some time around 1000 BCE, some of the stones were deliberately overturned. Although the monuments were not forgotten, their makers and their meaning became utterly obscure.

△ **The Mnajdra temple** complex on Malta, built around 3500 BCE, is the crowning achievement of a flourishing megalithic culture on the island.

◁ **This stone passageway** leads to a burial chamber at the 5,000-year-old megalithic passage-tomb at Newgrange, Ireland.

The first towns

⚐ NEAR EAST ⛏ 5000–3000 BCE

The world's earliest known large towns and cities developed in Mesopotamia in the 4th millennium BCE, perhaps through the need to organize the construction of irrigation channels fed by the Tigris and Euphrates rivers. At first the towns were little more than agglomerations of villages and related families, but soon they became major centers of trade with vast irrigation works that watered the countryside and produced several crops a year. The irrigated fields' increased productivity could now support larger populations; in Egypt, the Nile (*see facing page, below*) fulfilled a similar role.

Cities and hierarchies

The change was not simply a matter of size, but was accompanied by radical changes in the region's society, economy, and politics. Society became increasingly hierarchical, with rulers (often kings) at the top, who were frequently seen as living gods, and below them a small privileged class of high officials and priests. Lower down the social scale came craftsmen, lesser officials, soldiers, and the commoners. The authority of the rulers came not just from a threat of force, but from religious ideas about authority. These beliefs are commemorated by art and by writing on temple walls, and were reinforced by elaborate ceremonies. Each city clustered around temple precincts; those in Mesopotamia were built on top of mudbrick pyramids, called ziggurats.

From its original heartland in southern Mesopotamia, urbanism spread northward to sites such as Nineveh on the Tigris, Mari on the Euphrates, and Susa in western Iran. Each town or city tended to remain an independent entity (or city-state). In Egypt, however, a process of consolidation into a single state was complete as early as 3000 BCE.

⚌ Jericho, in Jordan, after 6000 BCE, developed from a permanent village into one of the first towns.

✉ Çatalhöyük in modern Turkey, founded 7500 BCE, had a population of some 8,000 at its peak, yet it did not survive into the Bronze Age to become a city.

Early Mesopotamia

⚑ IRAQ, W IRAN, SE SYRIA ⌛ 6000–3000 BCE

By around 6000 BCE, a culture known as the Halafian had become established in northern Mesopotamia. Communities lived in villages of domed houses built of clay, relied on long-distance trade, and buried their dead in distinctive shaft graves. They were replaced by the 'Ubaid culture, a pre-eminent Mesopotamian culture that was the first to use irrigation to increase crop yields. It was also at this time that the first urban centers appeared, at Eridu and Uruk.

The first cities

As with many other Mesopotamian cities, Eridu was originally a shrine. It honored the god Enki, ruler of the Abyss, who had created order from chaos. The shrine went through six or more incarnations before finally becoming an imposing step pyramid.

Uruk arose between 4800 and 3750 BCE. By 2800 BCE, it occupied around 615 acres (250 hectares) and may have housed 5,000 people. It depended on trade networks for goods in exchange for its grain, and may have had satellite colonies as far as the Zagros Mountains, several hundred miles to the north, to ensure control of key trade routes.

≫ A small statuette from 3rd millennium BCE Uruk shows a worshiper bearing offerings to the gods.

Predynastic Egypt

⚑ EGYPT ⌛ 4000–3100 BCE

In 4000 BCE, Egypt consisted of a valley of farmers living in small communities along the Nile; the river's annual flooding, or inundation, deposited rich, fertile silt on a broad strip along its banks. There were many small kingdoms, the largest of which were based in growing towns such as Abydos and Nekhen (Hierakonpolis). The first walled towns in Egypt were erected at Naqada and Hierakonpolis around 3300 BCE. Alongside them were constructed rich tombs for their rulers.

By this time there were only two main kingdoms, Upper and Lower Egypt. It was the rulers of Upper Egypt who unified the country in around 3100 BCE. Exactly which of them achieved this is unclear. Narmer, traditionally the first ruler (pharaoh) of the 1st dynasty, is often given the credit, but his successor Aha (also called Menes), who may in fact be the same person as Narmer, may have been responsible. He also seems to have strengthened the ruler's position as a divine king, and possibly founded the new royal capital at Memphis.

◀ The Palette of Narmer depicts a pharaoh, wearing a crown and bearing a mace and a flail, in a victory procession that may celebrate Egypt's unification.

The Ancient World

The world in 3000–700 BCE

By 3000 BCE, complex civilizations had arisen in the Tigris and
Euphrates valleys of Mesopotamia and along the banks of the Nile
in Egypt. China's first civilization flourished along the Yangtze River;
somewhat later, the advanced cultures of the Chavín and Olmecs
developed in Peru and Mexico respectively. Eventually, trade and

Greenland

Inuit

Inuit

Rocky Mountains

British Isles

Finno-Ugrian

Celts

Slavs **ASSYRIAN EMPIRE**

Illyrians

Thracians

Etruscans Black Sea

Rome Gordium Teushp

Great Lakes

Nomadic hunters

Great Plains

ADENA

Appalachian Mountains

Lixus Carthage Byblos
Tyre Baby

Berbers Memphis **ISRA**

EGYPT Jerusa

A T L A N T I C
O C E A N

Sahara Thebes
KUSH

Nilo-Saharan peoples Napata

OLMEC *Yucatán*
San Lorenzo La Venta *West Indies*

Niger-Congo peoples *Chadians*

Kush

Farmers

Amazon Basin

Chorrera

CHAVÍN
Chavín
de Huantar

Nomadic hunters

Andes

Khoisan peoples

P A C I F I C
O C E A N

Kalahari Desert

Patagonia

The world in 750 BCE

········· Undefined border

◉ Greek cities and territories

● Phoenician cities and territories

Small Chinese states under
the Eastern Zhou dynasty

NOTE: Settlements in italics were
not in existence in 750 BCE but were
significant during this chapter's era.

technological innovation led to increased prosperity. In the densely populated Middle East, competition between neighboring states led to warfare, and to conquest by the Egyptians, Hittites, Assyrians, and Babylonians. Europe's first sophisticated culture, the Minoans, flourished on the island of Crete around 2000 BCE.

The ancient world in 750 BCE

By 750 BCE, Egypt's New Kingdom Empire had waned, and much of the Middle East was under Assyrian control. While the Greeks had begun to colonize the Mediterranean, Rome was but a tiny village. In China, central authority had collapsed with the Zhou dynasty, while India's Indus Valley civilization had long since dissolved.

The Phoenicians of modern Lebanon had colonized much of the Mediterranean shoreline by 750 BCE, but were increasingly forced to compete with Greek colonists. In the Middle East, the dominant power was the Assyrian empire, which ruled most of the area; only Urartu remained completely independent.

The Near East

The world's first complex societies arose in the Near East within the fertile area known as Mesopotamia, between the Tigris and Euphrates rivers. By 3000 BCE, competing city-states of great wealth flourished here, with advanced irrigation plans, established trade, and grand palaces and temples. The earliest civilization, that of Sumeria, was followed by the Babylonian and Assyrian empires, which established their dominance over almost the entire region.

The Sumerians

MODERN IRAQ   c.3000–c.2340 BCE

The first civilization in Mesopotamia arose in the south, where a number of growing city-states forged trading and diplomatic ties. This Sumerian culture, as it is known, was characterized by centralized hierarchies headed by rulers who often had priestly roles but, unlike Egypt's pharaohs, were rarely thought to be divine. Each of the cities was seen as the home of one of the major Sumerian gods (Nanna at Ur, Inanna at Uruk) and in the period known as the Early Dynastic (c.3000–c.2340 BCE), the Sumerians began to

build stepped temple towers, or ziggurats, in honor of their deities. The sophisticated palace cultures were supported by specialized administrators, merchants, and scribes, whose need to keep records led to the development of the first full writing system, in a script known as cuneiform.

Conquest and decline

The separate city-states of Sumeria were briefly united around 2400 BCE, when King Lugalzagesi of the city-state of Umma conquered Ur and Uruk and reduced the eastern city of Lagash to dependent status. But within half a century, the whole area had been absorbed into the Empire of Sargon, king of Akkad (*see box, facing page*).

⬇ **The city of Uruk** was the earliest of the Sumerian cities to flourish, and incorporated the sacred precinct of Eanna, the "house of the sky."

Ur

SOUTH OF MODERN IRAQ ⌛ c.3000–c.2000 BCE

One of the city-states of Sumeria (*see facing page*), Ur began to thrive around 2800 BCE, becoming extremely wealthy; the tombs of rulers such as Queen Pu-abi and Meskalamdug have yielded artifacts of great value.

Ur was eclipsed politically during the occupation of Sumeria by Sargon (*see below*), but in around 2050 BCE, Ur-Nammu founded the Third Dynasty of Ur. For 70 years Ur dominated a huge area divided into 20 provinces, stretching from Susa in southwest Iranto Ashur, far to the northwest of the Sumerian heartland. During this time the population increased and cities flourished, supported by a system of forced labor. The city of Ur itself was enhanced with the construction of a great ziggurat. Ur-Nammu's heirs extended the empire, especially under Shulgi (ruled 2094–2047 BCE), but under Ibbi-Sin (ruled 2028–2004 BCE) outlying regions broke away, and invaders from nearby Elam finally ended the Third Dynasty's power.

A Sumerian gaming board, inlaid with shell and lapis lazuli, was among the treasures excavated from the Royal Cemetery at Ur.

The Akkadian Empire

MODERN IRAQ, SW IRAN, SYRIA, LEBANON, SE TURKEY ⌛ c.2300–c.2083 BCE

The northern part of Sumeria, known as Babylonia, gave rise to the earliest successful attempt to unite the Near East when Sargon smashed the power of Lugalzagesi of Umma, securing control over the whole region. His capital at Akkad dominated an empire that became ever more centralized. A calendar was introduced for the whole of Babylonia, new systems of taxation and standardized weights and measures were imposed, and Akkadian became the language of government. Sargon's armies reached as far as the Mediterranean coast, but it was difficult to control the outlying regions. Rebellion broke out in the reign of Sargon's grandson, Naram-sin (ruled 2254–2218 BCE), who took on the title "king of the world" and was worshiped as a god while alive. Naram-sin was victorious, but thereafter the Akkadians were on the defensive; their empire eventually fell during the reign of King Shar-kali-sharri, the son of Naram-Sin.

⟫ SARGON OF AKKAD

Born a commoner, Sargon (ruled 2334– 2279 BCE) rose to power in the city of Kish and took the name Sharru-kin (Sargon), "the king is legitimate." From his new base at Akkad, he sent his armies to establish the world's first empire.

The rise of Babylon

MODERN IRAQ, SE SYRIA **c.1900–1595 BCE**

From around 1900 BCE, the Babylonian kings began annexing states to the north, such as Sippar and Kish, marking the start of the "Old Babylonian" period. They were prevented from further advances by Shamshi-Adad, who held a strong state in upper Mesopotamia.

Babylon under Hammurabi

After Shamsi-Adad's death, Hammurabi of Babylon extended his city-state's reach even further, conquering the whole of southern Mesopotamia

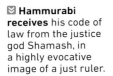

Hammurabi receives his code of law from the justice god Shamash, in a highly evocative image of a just ruler.

> ### HAMMURABI AND HIS LAW CODE
>
> A warrior, statesman, and lawgiver, Hammurabi (ruled 1792–1750 BCE) raised Babylon from the status of a minor city-state to the principal Mesopotamian power. He described himself as "the king who has made the four quarters of the earth subservient" and his law code, containing some 282 legal decrees, was probably more an attempt to portray himself as a supporter of justice than a practical legal document. Its penalties are often harsh and retributive, such as the loss of an eye for blinding a free man.

between 1766 and 1761 BCE. Only further west, in modern Syria, did kings such as Zimri-Lim (ruled c.1775–1762 BCE) of Mari seek to maintain independence. Late in his reign, Hammurabi attacked even Mari and reduced Zimri-Lim to vassalage. Having achieved his territorial ambitions, Hammurabi issued his famous code of law. By the time of Hammurabi's death, Babylon had become the regional superpower.

The Decline of Babylon

Under Samsuiluna (ruled 1749–1712 BCE), Hammurabi's son, Babylon faced a serious rebellion during which cities such as Nippur and Ur broke away from its control. The south of Mesopotamia went into decline, but the Old Babylonian dynasty continued to rule the north until 1595 BCE, when a new group, the Kassites, sacked the city.

> " At the command of the **sun god**... **may my justice become visible** in the land. "
>
> **The law code of Hammurabi, c.1750 BCE**

The Hittites

CENTRAL AND SE TURKEY ⌛ c.1700–c.1200 BCE

The kingdom of the Hittites, called Hatti, was based in central Anatolia around their capital city Hattusa, but constantly shifted its borders, extending at times as far as western Syria in the south and the coasts of the Black Sea and the Aegean in the north and west.

Comparatively little is known of the Hittite Old Kingdom, the first ruler of which, Hattusili, founded Hattusa in about 1650 BCE. Under Hattusili's successor Mursili I (ruled c.1620–c.1590 BCE), Hittite armies campaigned in Syria, but by the reign of Telipinu (c.1525–c.1500 BCE), Hatti was once again reduced to its core territory around the capital.

Under Tudhaliya III (ruled c.1360–c.1344 BCE), the first ruler of the New Kingdom, the Hittites expanded again, defeating the rulers of Aleppo and the Mitanni. Hatti reached its height under

Suppiluliuma I, who conquered northern Syria and threatened Egyptian control over Palestine. Mutawalli II (ruled 1295–1272 BCE) fought the Egyptians in a bitterly contested battle at Kadesh in 1274 BCE, which both sides claimed as a victory. However, the aftermath of the battle firmly cemented Hittite control in Syria. The growing threat from Assyria to the east, and the rebellion of vassal states in the west, rapidly undermined the Hittite kingdom, and in 1207 unknown raiders sacked Hatti again, after which the Hittite state collapsed completely.

》 SUPPILULIUMA I

One of the most militarily successful Hittite kings, Suppiluliuma I (ruled 1344–1322 BCE) conquered Mitanni to the north and parts of Syria. So great was his prestige that Tutankhamun's widow invited one of his sons to come to Egypt as her husband.

⌃ **A statue of a Hittite goddess**, one of a pantheon of deities headed by the storm god Teshub and his female counterpart, the sun goddess Hebat.

⌄ **The Gate of the Lions** at Hattusa (now Bogazköy in Turkey) provided an impressive ceremonial entrance to the Hittite royal capital.

The late Bronze Age collapse

THE NEAR EAST ⌛ **c.1200–c.1050 BCE**

In the late Bronze Age of the Near East, a diplomatic community of empires had maintained a thriving international system based on bronze. Between 1200 and 1050 BCE, records hint at upheaval, as raids and migrations overwhelmed the established powers. The collapse appears to have begun a little before 1200 BCE, when the citadels of Mycenaean Greece (*see p.71*) were destroyed.

The fall of empires

In 1207 BCE, the Hittite capital of Hattusa was sacked and the empire fell. The Egyptians had to fight off invasions by groups they called the "Sea Peoples," which eventually led to the demise of the New Kingdom in 1069 BCE. Elsewhere, the Kassite dynasty of Babylon collapsed around 1154 BCE, while, in Assyria, the archives speak of constant skirmishes. The ensuing "Dark Age," with almost no written sources, would last for 150 years.

⌃ **A group of Philistine captives** taken by the Egyptian pharaoh Rameses III in c.1182 BCE; the Philistines, or "Peleset," were one of the "Sea Peoples."

The Phoenicians

LEBANON, THE MEDITERRANEAN COASTLINE ⌛ **c.1200–146 BCE**

From around 1200 BCE, the coastal cities of Tyre, Byblos, and Sidon, in an area the Greeks called Phoenicia, formed the core of a sea-based trading network. The Phoenicians used maritime power to control a dense web of routes crossing the Mediterranean, with trading links as far afield as Mesopotamia and the Red Sea, supplying a range of goods from rich, exotic fabrics and glass to cedar wood. They also established colonies that included Lixus in Morocco, Gades (Cadiz) in Spain, Motya in Sicily, and, most importantly, Carthage (in modern Tunisia), founded around 814 BCE.

After Phoenicia itself fell to Assyria in the 9th century BCE (and then to Egypt, Babylon, and Persia), Carthage became the principal center of Phoenician politics, conquering its own empire in the western Mediterranean. Carthage ultimately lost the battle for dominance of this region to the Romans, who defeated the Carthaginians in three Punic Wars in the 3rd and 2nd centuries BCE.

◁ **The Phoenicians** were skilled navigators and built many forms of boats, from smaller vessels to multi-oared galleys.

The Assyrian Empire

⟨⟩ MODERN IRAQ, W IRAN, SYRIA, LEBANON, SW TURKEY ⌛ c.2000–c.610 BCE

Assyria came to prominence around 2000 BCE, prospering from the copper trade with Anatolia. During the reign of Assur-Ubalit (1363–1328 BCE), the Assyrians carved out an empire, culminating in the conquest of Babylon in the reign of Tukulti-Ninurta I (ruled 1243–1207 BCE). Assyria then fell victim to invasion by the "Sea Peoples," and it was not until around 1000 BCE that the Neo-Assyrian Empire emerged.

The Neo-Assyrians won fame as fierce warriors, utilizing armies of chariots, infantry, and horseback riders that made ample use of the new iron weaponry. They used terror tactics to suppress their enemies, with mass executions, impalements, and deportations. Assurnasirpal II (ruled 883–859 BCE) and Shalmaneser III (ruled 858–824 BCE) expanded the Assyrians' territory as far west as the Mediterranean. After a brief decline, the Neo-Assyrian Empire revived under Tiglath-Pileser III and his heir Sargon II (ruled 721–705 BCE).

Victory, then collapse

In 689 BCE, in the reign of Sennacherib (704–681 BCE), the Neo-Assyrians sacked Babylon, then, under Assurbanipal (ruled 668–627 BCE), they occupied parts of Egypt. However, the Neo-Assyrians became overstretched, and in 612 BCE a coalition of Medes and Babylonians captured the Assyrian capital Nineveh. By 610 BCE the empire had vanished.

❯❯ TIGLATH-PILESER III

The administrative reforms of Tiglath-Pileser III (ruled 744–727 BCE) strengthened Neo-Assyria. He extended Assyrian control along the Mediterranean coast, becoming king of Babylon and leading an army to the gates of Teushpa, the Urartian capital.

☑ **The reconstructed Nergal gate of Nineveh**, which was one of the chief cities of the Assyrian Empire, and its last capital under Sennacherib and his successors.

The invention of writing

Writing represented a leap forward in the intellectual evolution of humans. Its development occurred independently in five different areas: Mesopotamia, Egypt, India, China, and Mesoamerica. Much of the earliest extant writing is on stone, but many inscriptions survive on papyrus from Egypt and clay tablets from Mesopotamia, and these documents shed precious light on ancient cultures.

⊼ **Cuneiform script**, imprinted on clay tablets, is one of the earliest forms of written expression.

From symbols to script

The development of writing—as the symbolic representation of spoken language—was a gradual process that probably began in the Middle East in the middle of the 4th millennium BCE.

Early writing was made up of pictures, which helped create visual records of trading transactions. Over time, these pictures were simplified into symbols. In Mesopotamia, this process resulted in wedge-shaped cuneiform writing, and, in Egypt, pictorial hieroglyphs were used—from around 3200 BCE—for a period of more than 3,500 years. Many of these early scripts were logographic,

meaning that each symbol represented an entire word or idea. Egyptian hieroglyphic and Mesopotamian cuneiform writing mixed logograms with symbols that represented sounds.

As writing advanced, this combined approach enabled people to reproduce spoken language accurately in written form. Archives such as those at Mari and Ugarit in Syria yield a wealth of information about the dealings of rulers, who used writing to manage information about their estates. From the Mayan kings of Mesoamerica to the Egyptian pharaohs and Chinese emperors, rulers also set up

> **The Rosetta Stone** enabled François Champollion, in 1822–24, to decipher hieroglyphs, because it has parallel texts in hieroglyphic, demotic, and in Ancient Greek, which was already understood.

> " To the **Phoenician people** is due great **honor,** for they **invented** the letters of the **alphabet**. "
>
> **Pliny the Elder (Roman author),** *Natural History*, 1st century CE

monumental inscriptions as a means to record their achievements and inspire awe in their subjects.

Scribes and literacy

The establishment of written archives and governments created a need for a literate class able to produce and read them. In Egypt, the education of scribes—who were elevated to a position of great prestige in society—began in youth, and included mathematics and accountancy. Although literary and devotional texts were produced in Egypt and Mesopotamia, reading them remained the province of the elite members of society.

The alphabet

The concept of an alphabet in which every symbol denotes a particular sound only arose in the late 2nd millennium BCE. The people of Ugarit in Syria developed a cuneiform alphabet around 2000 BCE.

Turquoise miners in Sinai used another early alphabet system shortly afterward, and it may have been this script, with 30 signs, that spread northward through Palestine into Phoenicia, where it evolved into the 22-sign Phoenician alphabet around 1000 BCE. The Phoenicians' trading network, in turn, exported their script throughout the Mediterranean, where it cast its influence in the developing scripts of Greece and Rome.

Egyptian hieroglyphs remained unchanged over centuries, in part because of their religious use, such as in this 20th-century BCE coffin panel.

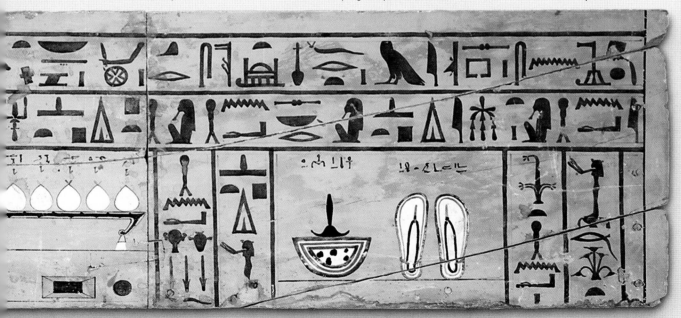

Egypt

Around 3100 BCE, a unified kingdom of Egypt emerged—ruled by a single king, or pharaoh—which occupied the banks of the Nile as far south as Aswan. Under the Early Dynastic period (c.3100–2469 BCE), the Old Kingdom (2649–2134 BCE), the Middle Kingdom (2040–1640 BCE), and the New Kingdom (1550–1069 BCE), Egypt experienced nearly 3,000 years of prosperity and cultural continuity, before foreign invaders occupied it from the 8th century BCE.

» Tomb treasures, such as this effigy of an Old Kingdom official and his family, teach us much about ancient Egypt.

The Old Kingdom

⚑ EGYPT ⌛ 2649–2134 BCE

Around 3100 BCE, the two kingdoms of Upper Egypt (the south) and Lower Egypt (the north) merged into a single state at the hands of a pharaoh named Menes. Then, from 2649 BCE, under the rulers of the 3rd dynasty, the Old Kingdom was inaugurated. Its most striking remains are the great funerary monuments known as the pyramids, but there is also evidence of a centralized state based around the capital at Memphis. A vast political and administrative bureaucracy grew up that included local governors, who oversaw regions called *nomes*. The pharaoh himself came to occupy a central religious role, because he upheld a system that ensured the Nile brought silt-rich annual floods each year and kept the valley fertile. Vast irrigation schemes directed the waters to wide areas of agricultural land, and devices called "nilometers" predicted the rise of the river and the bounty (or dearth) of the subsequent harvest.

Under the Old Kingdom, Egypt first began to project its power abroad, with expeditions during the reign of Snefru (2575–2551 BCE) to Nubia to collect raw materials, and campaigns into Libya by the 6th-dynasty pharaohs (2323–2150 BCE).

During the long reign of Pepi II (2246–2152 BCE), central authority began to dissolve and, within 20 years, the Old Kingdom collapsed, as famine wracked the land and officials in the provinces established their own rule. A century of uncertainty ensued, known as the First Intermediate Period (2134–2040 BCE).

The pyramids

EGYPT c.2600–c.1525 BCE

Early Dynastic pharaohs were buried in mud-brick box-shaped tombs known as mastabas. During the reign of the 3rd-dynasty pharaoh Djoser (2630–2611 BCE) a new, grander structure appeared. His step pyramid at Saqqara was essentially a series of mastabas set one on top of the other, and prefigured a series of massive true pyramids constructed during the 4th dynasty (2575–2465 BCE). Snefru probably built pyramids at Dahshur and Meidum, but under his successor Khufu, the Great Pyramid at Giza, near Memphis, was erected. Containing over two million blocks of stone, each weighing around 2½ tons (2,300 kg), its construction involved a truly prodigious expenditure of precious resources.

Each pyramid was both a tomb and a temple dedicated to the cult of the dead pharaoh. The pyramids were constructed in limestone, with the royal burial concealed in a granite chamber deep in the interior. They were accompanied by funerary temples, smaller pyramids for queens, mastabas for officials, pits in which to bury sacred boats, and a causeway leading to a valley temple, which was the ceremonial entrance to the complex.

The decline of the pyramids

The pyramids of the 5th and succeeding dynasties were sited in places other than Giza, including at Abusir near Saqqara, and were smaller than Khufu's Great Pyramid. The last true royal pyramid built in Egypt was that of Ahmose I (ruled 1550–1525 BCE). The New Kingdom pharaohs chose to be buried in less extravagant tombs located further south in the Valley of the Kings, near Thebes.

⏏ **The courtly elite** were also buried at Saqqara. This Egyptian bas-relief is from the tomb of Hezyre, physician and scribe to the pharaoh Djoser.

❯❯ KHUFU

Surprisingly little is known of Khufu's reign (2551–2528 BCE), except through the existence of the Great Pyramid. The Greek historian Herodotus told of Khufu's cruelty, although this is probably no more than a reflection of the huge force of will that he must have needed to ensure the Great Pyramid's construction. The pyramid's burial chamber was robbed in antiquity, but the first recorded traveler to enter the tomb was British consul Nathaniel Davison, in 1765.

The largest and oldest of the three Giza pyramids, Khufu's Great Pyramid probably took around 20 years to build.

The funerary temple of Hatshepsut at Deir el Bahri, Thebes, is a spectacular monument to one of ancient Egypt's few female rulers. Hatshepsut (ruled 1473–1458 BCE) took on all the trappings of a male pharaoh. On one of the terraces are statues of her as the god Osiris.

The Middle Kingdom

🏛 **EGYPT** ⌛ **2040–1640** BCE

During the First Intermediate Period, the most powerful Egyptian rulers were at Heracleopolis, south of Memphis. From around 2150 BCE, there was civil war between the Heracleopolitan pharaohs and rivals farther south at Edfu and Thebes. Finally, around 2040 BCE, the Theban king Nebhepetre Mentuhotep II (ruled 2061–2010 BCE) was victorious, reuniting Egypt and beginning the Middle Kingdom.

The height of the Middle Kingdom

Amenemhet I (ruled 1991–1962 BCE), the first pharaoh of the 12th dynasty, restored Egypt's vigor. He established a new capital at Itj-tawy near Memphis, and sent expeditions to Nubia (modern Sudan), conquering territory as far south as the Second Cataract of the Nile. The 12th-dynasty pharaohs also mounted campaigns in Syria and Palestine.

The central authority's influence seems to have lessened during the 13th dynasty (1783–1640 BCE), which had a large number of short-lived rulers, but there is little evidence of decline. There are, however, indications of an increased number of immigrants from Palestine, foreshadowing the stresses that would, in time, bring down the Middle Kingdom.

The end of the Middle Kingdom

Toward the end of the 13th dynasty, Egypt came under intensive pressure from Asiatic groups migrating westward, who began to occupy large areas of the Nile delta. Around 1650 BCE, one

🖼 **Colorful wall paintings**, such as this well-preserved example at the Tomb of Sirenpowet II, adorned the walls of Middle Kingdom tombs.

group, known as the Hyksos (a name derived from an Egyptian word meaning "foreign princes"), established their own kingdom in the north of Egypt. Native Egyptian rulers continued to rule in the south from Thebes, while the Hyksos could not be dislodged from their capital at Avaris. This century of political turmoil is referred to as the Second Intermediate Period.

> " Asians will fall to his **sword**, Libyans will fall to his **flame**, rebels to his **wrath**, traitors to his **might**.
>
> **The Prophecy of Neferty from the time of Amenemhet I** "

Egyptian religion

Egyptian religion was immensely complex, with a large number of gods, many of them localized and many appearing with different aspects. Earlier pharaohs associated themselves with the sky god Horus or the sun god Re, but gradually the cult of Osiris, king of the dead, became dominant. The need to ensure the immortality of the ruler's soul after death was the primary focus of Egyptian religious belief.

The cult of the dead

The unification of Egypt under the Old Kingdom rationalized the various local pantheons and, throughout the year, the pharaoh engaged in a series of ritual activities to ensure the fertility of the land and the crossing of the sky by the sun each day.

Most important of all was the cult of the dead. Egyptians believed that, after death, the pharaohs were reborn as the king of the dead, Osiris. A complex mythology surrounded the rites that

ensured this resurrection, when the royal *ka* (or life-force) would be united with his *ba* (the soul, or a person's personality). To ensure the *ka* recognized its former body, and so could reach the afterlife, preserving the corpse through mummification became paramount. Once the pharaoh's soul reached the underworld, a jury of 12 gods would weigh its misdeeds against a feather. If the two weighed the same, the pharaoh was ensured eternal life.

The official cults were only briefly challenged under Akhenaten (ruled 1353–1335 BCE), who tried to establish the worship of the sun disc (Aten) as the state religion—perhaps the first example of monotheism.

⌃ **A "trinity" of Horus**, Isis, and Osiris became the focus of religious belief by the time of the Old Kingdom.

⌃ **To preserve a pharaoh's body**, vital organs were removed, then the corpse was stuffed with linen, soaked with preservatives, and wrapped.

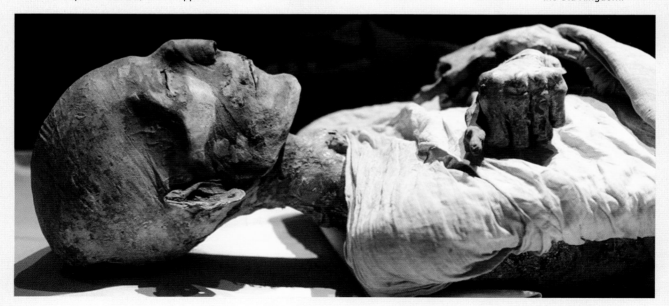

The New Kingdom and after

EGYPT ⌛ **1550–1069** BCE

The Hyksos were finally expelled from Egypt by the Theban ruler Kamose (ruled 1555–1550 BCE) and his successor Ahmose I (ruled 1550–1525 BCE), the first pharaoh of the New Kingdom. This era is often seen as a time of glorious "empire" for Egypt, during which Egypt extended its trade links and refined its skill in diplomacy. It quashed threats to the throne making use of warfare techniques borrowed from the Hyksos.

Imperial and cultural apogee

The early rulers of the 18th dynasty (1550–1307 BCE) sought to establish an Egyptian Empire, first in Palestine and then in parts of Syria. Tuthmosis I (ruled 1504–1492 BCE) campaigned as far as the Euphrates River and there set up a stela—an inscribed standing stone—commemorating his army's achievement. Under the reigns of Tuthmosis II and his widow Hatshepsut, between 1493 and 1458 BCE, the pace of military expansion slowed. Hatshepsut's nephew, Tuthmosis III (ruled 1479–1425 BCE), however, led nearly 20 expeditions into Palestine and Syria, defeating peoples as far-flung as the Mitanni near the Euphrates and extending Egyptian control southward down the Nile.

After a brief period of political weakness following the early death of the boy-pharaoh Tutankhamun (ruled 1333–1323 BCE), the 19th-dynasty rulers reasserted Egypt's control of its overseas empire, beginning with Seti I (ruled 1305–1290 BCE), whose aggressive campaigning brought him into conflict with the Hittites. His son, Rameses II (*see facing page*), continued the war, but in 1274 BCE his army was nearly destroyed near the Syrian town of Qadesh. Thereafter, Egypt's control over Palestine waned. Merneptah (ruled 1224–1214 BCE) fought a series of battles to keep Libyan tribesmen from the Nile Delta, but the respite was short-lived and Rameses III (ruled 1194–1163 BCE) faced a great army of "Sea Peoples," who had rampaged through Syria and Palestine. Rameses defeated them in 1182 BCE, but growing internal dissent, along with a series of weak successors, eventually brought the New Kingdom to an end.

The New Kingdom had been an age of spectacular architectural and artistic achievements, as well as religious ferment. The lavish tomb contents of Tutankhamun were interred and the monumental buildings and statues of Rameses II were erected. Royalty

The lavishness of the golden death mask of Tutankhamun belies the reality of a boy-pharaoh who had very little influence.

were now buried in underground tombs, centered on the Valley of the Kings, near Thebes. Amenophis IV (ruled 1353–1335 BCE) took sun worship to extremes, briefly imposing on his people the cult of Aten—worship of the sun disc alone—and renaming himself Akhenaten in honor of his beliefs.

The Third Intermediate and late periods

For 150 years after the New Kingdom's end, the high priests of Amun and the rulers of Tanis in the Delta contested control of Egypt. Gradually, Egypt fell to foreign rulers, beginning with the 22nd dynasty, founded in 945 BCE by Shoshenq,

a general from Libya. When Egypt was reunited in the 25th dynasty, it was by the Nubian king Shabaqa (ruled 712–698 BCE). Successive periods of Nubian, Assyrian, and Persian rule were punctuated by periods of native dominance, until Egypt had its last years of pharaonic rule under the Ptolemies (304–30 BCE), a dynasty that was Macedonian-Greek in origin.

⚑ **Throughout his reign**, Rameses II dedicated himself to a program of building, most spectacularly these huge statues of the pharaoh at Abu Simbel in Nubia.

» RAMESES II

One of the most celebrated of Egypt's pharaohs, Rameses II (ruled 1290–1223 BCE), succeeded to the throne at the height of Egyptian power. Early on in his reign, he succeeded in campaigns in Syria, but after defeat by the Hittites at Qadesh in 1274 BCE, he struggled to regain the initiative and had to make a treaty in 1258 BCE to end the war. As well as the temple at Abu Simbel, Rameses built a new capital at Pi-Rameses in the eastern Nile Delta, and a great mortuary temple, the Ramesseum, near the Valley of the Kings, close to Thebes.

⚑ **Opulent grave goods**, such as this colorful jeweled scarab chest ornament, were a feature of New Kingdom burials.

Europe

Europe's first civilizations flourished in the southeast, the earliest on the island of Crete, where the Minoans established a highly sophisticated Bronze Age culture. After the collapse of their society by around 1450 BCE, the Minoans were supplanted by the Mycenaeans, incomers from mainland Greece, who adopted many aspects of Minoan culture and occupied its palaces, but who were in turn swept away around 1200 BCE in a period of political turmoil.

Minoan Crete

CRETE **c.2000–c.1450 BCE**

By around 2000 BCE, trading towns on the Cretan coast had expanded to give rise to an advanced civilization centered on a series of palaces, notably at Knossos, Phaistos, Mallia, and Zakros. The Minoans depended on long-distance trade and became skilled seafarers, building up a large fleet that carried their artifacts into the eastern Mediterranean. Minoan rulers seem to have played both a political and a religious role, and many government officials were probably also priests. They kept official archives, but we have yet to decipher their script, known as Linear A. Society was divided into classes, with the court supported by a large class of agricultural laborers.

Craftspeople produced sophisticated goods, such as "Kamáres ware" pottery, with designs in black, white, and red.

The end of the palaces

The reasons for the decline of Minoan culture are unclear. Around 1500 BCE, a massive volcanic eruption on the neighboring island of Thera may have disrupted or destroyed the Minoans' trading network, undermining the basis of their wealth. Around 1450 BCE, aided by an earthquake on Crete that destroyed some of the palaces, Mycenaean invaders delivered the fatal blow to the Minoan city-states, and the civilization collapsed.

The ruins of the palace at Mallia, an important Minoan administrative center which, unlike Knossos and Phaistos, was defended by a town wall.

The Palace of Knossos

KNOSSOS, CRETE **c.2000–c.1200 BCE**

Knossos, near Heraklion, was the most elaborate of the Minoan palaces, so much so that it gave rise to the later legend of the labyrinth within which lurked a monstrous half-human bull. When British archaeologist Sir Arthur Evans excavated the site between 1900 and 1932, he uncovered frescoes that abound in images of bulls, as well as double-headed axes and snakes, and these must all have played an important role in Minoan religious symbolism. Damaged by an earthquake around 1700 BCE, the Knossos palace was rebuilt on an even grander scale, measuring some 45 acres (18 hectares), with a large series of shrines. The palace flourished for a further 250 years, and seems to have survived the wholesale destruction of Minoan sites around 1450 BCE, after which it was occupied for a further two centuries, most probably by Mycenaean invaders.

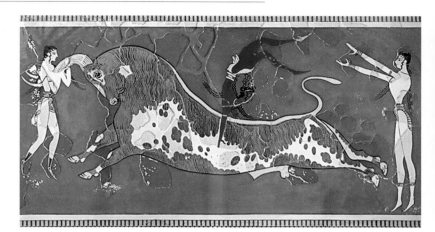

A fresco at Knossos depicts "bull-leaping," which may have been a sport or a religious ritual.

The Mycenaeans

MAINLAND GREECE, CRETE **c.1600–c.1070 BCE**

Beginning around 1600 BCE, the Mycenaean culture grew from southern Greece, reaching as far north as Thessaly within 200 years. By around 1450 BCE, the Mycenaeans also expanded their rule southward, toppling an already weakened Minoan civilization. Although not as adept at or dependent on trade as the Minoans, the Mycenaeans maintained commercial settlements on islands such as Rhodes.

The Mycenaean culture was based around fortified palace sites, such as Mycenae, Pylos, and Tiryns, with massive circuit walls and a central megaron—a square room that was the palace's focal point. Extensive archives, written in a script known as Linear B, have been found at the palace sites, providing a mass of information about Mycenaean social and economic life.

By around 1200 BCE, the Mycenaean culture was in decline, and most of its major centers had been destroyed by fire. Some centers limped on, exhibiting a lower and more provincial level of material culture, but by 1070 BCE the last Mycenaean palaces had been abandoned. Greece had entered its "Dark Age," a period in its history—lasting for centuries—for which no records exist.

A gold death mask, once believed to be that of legendary Greek king Agamemnon, found at Mycenae.

South Asia

A fertile cradle of river-fed land, crossing parts of modern India, Pakistan, and Afghanistan, gave birth to the Indus Valley civilization in the mid-4th millennium BCE. Its impressive, well-planned cities, most notably Harappa and Mohenjo-Daro, housed large populations and produced artifacts of great beauty. However, a deeper knowledge of this fascinating civilization is still tantalizingly out of reach, as the Indus Valley script remains undeciphered.

The Indus Valley civilization

PAKISTAN, NW INDIA, SE AFGHANISTAN **c.3300–c.1600 BCE**

The Indus Valley civilization flourished across a large area of present-day Pakistan, northwest India, and Afghanistan, along the fertile Indus and Ghaggar-Hakra rivers. In common with the civilizations of Mesopotamia and Egypt, the Indus Valley depended heavily on land made fertile by regular floods and on the skilled use of irrigation and water-management techniques.

The "Early Harappan" phase of the civilization (c.3300–c.2800 BCE) saw the Indus Valley peoples grow crops, including peas, sesame seeds, and dates, and domesticate animals, such as the water buffalo. Sanitation systems and the earliest known examples of the Indus script also emerged in this phase.

Cities of the Indus Valley produced refined artifacts, including fine jewelry in gold and fired steatite (soapstone), gold and silver ornaments, and skilfully worked figurines in bronze, terracotta, and glazed ceramics. Such treasures seem to indicate that this was a stratified society with an elite class that was able to commission precious works. The discovery of Indus Valley artifacts elsewhere in the world indicates that the civilization had widespread trading links, particularly with Mesopotamia, Afghanistan, and Iran.

From 2600–1900 BCE the civilization reached its peak, in what is known as the "Mature Harappan" period, when many large, well-planned cities thrived. The cities appear to have suffered from increased flooding from 1700 BCE onward and from increased attacks by unknown outsiders. By 1600 BCE the quality of Indus Valley artifacts had declined and most of the main city sites had been abandoned.

The undeciphered Indus script is found on hundreds of clay seals, along with vivid animal images.

Mohenjo-Daro

⚐ PAKISTAN ⌛ c.2500–c.1600 BCE

Mohenjo-Daro was one of the world's first planned cities and, like Harappa some 300 miles (500 km) to its northeast, was one of the Indus Valley civilization's principal settlements. Set out on a grid pattern, it had broad avenues and narrow side streets lined with spacious townhouses. Wells with high, sealed walls to prevent contamination were built to provide clean water for the inhabitants.

The structure of the city

A higher area set on an artificial mound some 40 ft (12 m) high has been dubbed Mohenjo-Daro's "Citadel," though it is thought to have been a place for public gatherings and an administrative center rather than a fortified strongpoint. Within the citadel, the "Great Bath," an enclosed water tank

❰❰ The "Lower Town" of Mohenjo-Daro is in the foreground, with the city's "Citadel" dramatically rearing up on the mound in the background.

or pool, may have had some ritual purpose. In the western quarter, large granaries indicate a central authority that was able to dictate the storing of surpluses. To the south, the "Lower Town" may have housed skilled craftsmen and the lower classes. What is certain is that the city stood at the center of a network of trade and cultural exchange that reached as far as Tilmun (modern Bahrain) in the Persian Gulf.

Numerous religious artifacts have been found at the site of Mohenjo-Daro, notably images of a mother goddess often found in association with male symbols. These may indicate a fertility cult, although no temples or structures with an overt religious purpose have been identified.

Decline and abandonment

Water was a constant threat to Mohenjo-Daro, which was flooded and rebuilt as many as nine times on the same site during its period of occupation. Around 1700 BCE, the city suffered a major flood from the Indus. A huge protective embankment was built to protect the city, but Mohenjo-Daro was abandoned once and for all within a century.

❰❰ This striking statue has been frequently dubbed the "Priest-King," although there is no evidence that such a figure existed in Mohenjo-Daro's society.

East Asia

From around 4500 BCE, the Neolithic societies centered on the banks of China's Yellow River gave rise to a series of increasingly sophisticated cultures and then the first real towns. China's first centralized state emerged under the rule of the Shang dynasty (18th–11th centuries BCE). The Shang's rich culture of producing art and artifacts, particularly using bronze, is reflected in the artistic traditions of subsequent Chinese dynasties.

Early Chinese cultures

CHINA ⧖ c.4500–c.1800 BCE

⊗ **A Yangshao red vase** from around 2000 BCE. Such pottery has been found in more than a thousand sites in the Yellow River area.

Late Neolithic China gave rise to village cultures of some complexity. The Yangshao culture emerged along the banks of the Yellow River in central China, and more than one thousand sites have been excavated to date. Studies at one of the best-known sites, Banpo, show that Yangshao people cultivated millet, used polished stone tools, and wore hemp and possibly silk. They produced pots made of red clay, often decorated with spiral patterns, and some of the burials found at the village show evidence of belief in a connection with a spirit world. At Longshan in Shandong province, at the lower reaches of the Yellow River, another culture created finer black pottery (some of it turned on a potter's wheel) and stone axes. This culture spread far along the banks of the middle and lower Yangtze to the south.

In 1959, archaeologists discovered the Erlitou culture in the Yellow River valley in Henan province, unearthing palacelike buildings, tombs, and bronze artifacts— the oldest yet found in China. More recent archaeological finds have revealed a variety of late Neolithic cultures outside the Yellow River valley, such as the Majiabang along the Yangtze in Jiangsu province, and the Dapenkeng culture in South China.

Shang China

EASTERN CHINA **c.1750–1027** BCE

The Shang, by tradition the second of China's dynasties, ruled over much of northern and central China from around 1750 BCE. They had several capitals, the last of which was discovered at Anyang on the banks of the Huan in the 1920s. Here, archaeologists have unearthed the remains of the large ceremonial and administrative center of the late Shang state.

By around 1650 BCE, the Shang were established at the capital Zhengzhou, where a massive defensive wall, some 4 miles (6.4 km) long, enclosed a large settlement with buildings constructed of stamped earth.

Shang culture

The most prized archaeological finds from the Shang period are bronze objects, made primarily for ceremonial purposes. Many of the vessels found at Zhengzhou and Anyang had a ritual use, possibly for preparing sacrificial meats or heating wine. Highly stylized forms of bronze containers evolved, which would be produced for many centuries. The Shang also continued the production of jade discs, which had begun in Neolithic times. Often decorated with ornate carving, the discs' exact function remains a mystery, but they may have been buried with the dead. Shang tombs have yielded large numbers of "oracle bones," the shoulder bones of cattle, which were used for telling the future. Inscriptions on the oracle bones provide the earliest evidence of Chinese writing.

The Shang dynasty came to an end in around 1050 BCE when revolt, led by the Zhou, broke out in the west of the Shang territory. The Zhou, who had extended their influence throughout the present Shaanxi and Gansu provinces, finally overpowered the Shang emperor and became the dominant power.

This mask is characteristic of the high level of bronze craftsmanship under the Shang dynasty.

In Shang tradition, when an important person died, his chariot, charioteers, and horses were buried with him, as in this example from a village near Anyang.

The Americas

From the mid-2nd millennium BCE, advanced societies began to develop in the Americas in two separate areas, Peru and Mesoamerica. The earliest civilizations in those regions were those of the Chavín and the Olmecs respectively. Both built large ceremonial centers and both followed a cult of the jaguar in their systems of religious beliefs, but they left little or nothing in the way of written records, and their political history is almost impossible to reconstruct.

The Chavín of Peru

⚑ **PERU** ⌛ **c.1250–c.200** BCE

By about 1250 BCE, village life based on the production of corn and pottery had spread throughout Peru's coastal and highland regions. However, it was not until around 900 BCE that the first identifiable culture spread across much of Peru. Centered on the great temple of Chavín de Huántar, at the confluence of the Wacheqsa and Mosna rivers, the Chavín culture touched all parts of Peru save the extreme south. As there is no evidence of fortresses, armies, or any of the other paraphernalia of empire, the culture's spread was probably not by force.

Chavín site and collapse

The site at Chavín de Huántar reveals its people's great engineering and architectural expertise. The Old Temple was built around 900 BCE on a massive terraced pyramid. From the central platform projected a series of fearsome fanged monsters, while at the temple's center stood the Lanzón, a 15 ft (4.5 m) high granite stela—or stone slab—which may have been a devotional image. The site also includes a courtyard, perhaps an assembly place for ritual processions. Chavín wealth was used, at some time after 500 BCE, to build a New Temple twice the size of the old one. The power of the culture was waning, however, and outlying regions broke away. By 200 BCE, the Chavín period was over.

≫ **Chavín art** was characterized by images of snarling animals, such as these fierce jaguars from a staircase at Chavín de Huántar.

The Olmecs

GULF COAST OF MEXICO **c.1800–c.400 BCE**

The Olmec culture established itself in the lowlands of southern Mexico shortly after 1800 BCE. By around 800 BCE, their influence had spread over an extensive area of Mesoamerica, underpinned by a simple agricultural economy that was based on corn.

Olmec centers

The first important Olmec center was San Lorenzo in southern Mexico, which was at its height between 1200 and 900 BCE. The city seems to have had an advanced drainage system and its buildings, erected on earthen mounds and arranged around open plazas, included a temple and houses made of poles and thatch. There were also many monuments, such as giant carved heads, altarlike structures, huge sculptures of seated people, and depictions of a variety of animals, notably the jaguar.

Near the San Lorenzo site, at Cascajal, archaeologists have found a stone dating from around 900 BCE. It bears symbols that may be Olmec writing, and thus might represent the first writing system in Mesoamerica.

◄◄ **An Olmec relief** of a priest making an offering to a deity, in the form of a feathered, crested rattlesnake.

There is evidence of widespread destruction of monuments around 900 BCE, when the center of San Lorenzo seems to have come to an end. The other major Olmec center was the city of La Venta, near the border of modern Tabasco and Veracruz states, which had a much larger population than San Lorenzo. Thriving between 900 and 400 BCE, La Venta effectively took over from San Lorenzo as the principal Olmec settlement. As at San Lorenzo, colossal stone heads and jaguar figures and imagery have been found, as well as ceremonial and temple complexes, including a giant pyramid.

The major buildings at the site were all precisely aligned, perhaps linked with ideas about astronomy. By around 400 BCE, the Olmec culture was in decline, although its influence persisted in regional cultures, especially that of the Zapotecs of Monte Albán (*see p.129*).

◄◄ **An Olmec stone statue**, from La Venta, known as the "Governor." His elaborate dress implies that he was a ruler.

The Classical
World

The world in 700 BCE–600 CE

The millennium that followed 750 BCE saw much of the world's population incorporated into the great Classical civilizations of Eurasia—Greece, Rome, Persia, India, and China. These empires went on to reach unparalleled levels of sophistication and military effectiveness, and set models for administration and scholarship

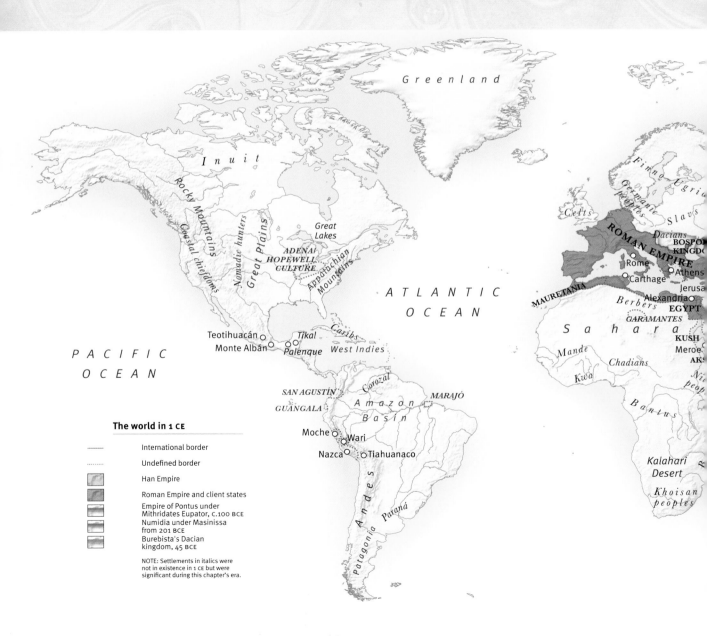

The world in 1 CE

———	International border
·········	Undefined border
	Han Empire
	Roman Empire and client states
	Empire of Pontus under Mithridates Eupator, C.100 BCE
	Numidia under Masinissa from 201 BCE
	Burebista's Dacian kingdom, 45 BCE

NOTE: Settlements in italics were not in existence in 1 CE but were significant during this chapter's era.

that would be followed for many centuries. In Central and South America, Africa, and Japan, new civilizations also emerged, in many ways equally as advanced, but with a much smaller reach than those of Eurasia. The Classical era also saw the birth of some influential religions—Buddhism, Judaism, and Christianity.

The Classical world in 1 CE

By 1 CE, the Greeks—who had earlier controlled an empire that stretched to India—had been conquered by the Roman Empire, which jostled for power with the Parthian (Persian) Empire. China, unified in 221 BCE, was now ruled by the Han dynasty, while India was fragmented after the fall of the Mauryan Empire in 185 BCE.

⬆ **The Roman Empire** had conquered the whole of the Mediterranean coastline by 1 CE, and had also extended into Asia Minor (in modern Turkey), Gaul (modern France), and parts of Germany. Over the next century it would take Britain, Dacia (Romania), and parts of Mesopotamia, reaching its maximum area.

Persia

From provincial beginnings, a dynasty of Persian kings—
the Achaemenids—emerged to exert power across Asia from the
Mediterranean to northwest India. Two centuries after a failed attempt to
subdue Greece in the 5th century BCE, the tables turned when Alexander
the Great's Macedonians overthrew Achaemenid rule. Persian power
re-emerged under the Parthians and Sassanids, who, from the 220s CE,
struggled bitterly with the Romans until the 7th century CE.

The Achaemenid Empire

W ASIA, EGYPT **550–330 BCE**

According to Persian tradition, Cyrus (ruled
559–530 BCE), founder of the Achaemenid Empire,
had been a vassal of Astyages, ruler of the Median
kingdom to the north of the Persian homeland.
Cyrus defeated Astyages in 550 BCE, securing
dominance over eastern Iran, and then captured
Babylon in 539 BCE. His heir, Cambyses (ruled
530–522 BCE), extended the empire
to Egypt, before a revolt by
his brother Bardiya led
to his assassination. In
the following years, the
influential king Darius I
(ruled 522–486 BCE)
occupied parts of
Libya and northwestern
India, and also tried
to invade Greece, but

a coalition of Greek states defeated him
in 490 BCE. A decade later, in 480–478 BCE,
Xerxes (ruled 486–465 BCE) failed in a similar
enterprise, and the Achaemenid rulers' impulse
for expansion waned.

Vulnerability and fall

The 4th century BCE was dogged by bitter dynastic
struggles that undermined the power of later
rulers. The empire was increasingly reliant
on foreign mercenaries and, because
of its vast size, vulnerable
to revolt and invasion.
It ended in the 330s BCE,
when Alexander the Great
(*see pp. 96–7*) defeated
the last Achaemenid
emperor, Darius III.

>> **The tomb of
Cyrus** was built at
Pasargadae, where
he had established
the first Achaemenid
royal capital sometime
before 550 BCE.

Persepolis

The royal capital of the Achaemenid Empire was Persepolis, founded by Darius I around 518 BCE and connected to an efficient system of royal roads. While the administration of government usually took place at the palace at Susa to the west, Persepolis lay at the heart of the Achaemenids' regal power.

A city of treasures

Darius founded his new capital on a high plain around 50 miles (80 km) southwest of the old Persian center at Pasargadae. Builders leveled an artificial terrace of 33 acres (135,000 sq m) on which to erect a series of palaces and chambers. Largest of these was the *apadana*, a reception hall that may have been able to

hold up to 10,000 people. On the stairway to the *apadana*, a series of reliefs depicted tribute-bearers from the empire's 20 provinces bringing offerings to the Persian ruler, for Persepolis may also have acted as the Achaemenids' central treasury. A huge Throne Hall was built under Darius I, and additions to the complex were still being made in the reign of Artaxerxes III (ruled 358–338 BCE). In 331 BCE, Alexander the Great captured Persepolis, and the next year a fire razed it to the ground.

⬀ **A golden griffin bracelet** that forms part of the Oxus Treasure, a fabulous hoard from the Achaemenid era found in 19th-century Afghanistan.

⬇ **Dignitaries from Medea** bearing tribute approach the Council Hall at Persepolis. The ruined city is now a UNESCO World Heritage site.

Persian religion

IRAN 🕮 **c.1000 BCE–7TH CENTURY CE**

At the heart of the Persian religious system lay a fusion between traditional Iranian religions and the teachings of the prophet Zoroaster, who lived either around 1000 BCE or in the 7th century BCE. He preached a dualist faith in which the supreme god Ahura Mazda, the personification of good, engaged in a constant struggle with the spirit of darkness, known as Angra Mainyu. The Achaemenids may not have been pure Zoroastrians, and they revered other Persian deities, too. Their successors, the Parthians, set up Zoroastrian fire altars throughout the empire, on which a flame burned constantly as a symbol of purity.

Under the Sassanids (*see facing page*), from the 3rd century CE, Zoroastrianism began to take on the characteristics of a state religion, and followers of other faiths, which had previously largely been tolerated, suffered persecution.

⟩⟩ **A bas-relief sculpture** of two *fravashis*. In Zoroastrian belief, these winged guardian spirits guide and protect people throughout their life.

Parthian Persia

IRAN, IRAQ 🕮 **247 BCE–224 CE**

In the 3rd century BCE, the Greek successors of Alexander the Great, the Seleucids (*see p.98*), controlled Persia, but their hold slipped, and in 247 BCE, the Parthians began to throw off Greek rule. They took control of the silk routes from China, and then under Mithridates I (ruled 171–138 BCE) pushed westward to annex most of the Seleucid lands in Mesopotamia. Parthia, though, was politically divided and its princes often established near-independent fiefs, undermining further attempts at expansion.

Made up of expert cavalrymen, the Parthian army was almost invincible and at Carrhae in 53 BCE, crushed a Roman army, starting a long period of tension with Rome, particularly over Armenia. Pretenders to the Armenian throne often sought Roman support against the Parthians, and it was one such appeal that almost led to the Roman emperor Trajan's conquest of western Persia in 116–117 CE. The Parthians survived only to succumb to an internal revolt in the southern province of Pars in the 3rd century CE.

⟨⟨ **A valiant Parthian king** hunts a lion with bow and arrow on this decorated silver bowl.

Sassanid Persia

IRAN, IRAQ 📅 **224–651 CE**

Parthian Persia (*see facing page*) collapsed in 224 CE as a result of internal revolt. Persia's resurgence came under the Sassanids, whose first king, Ardashir I, ruled from 224 to 241 CE. The Sassanid kings, ruling from a capital at Ctesiphon on the banks of the Tigris, established a more centralized state than the Parthians, and easily held their own against the Romans to their west. By 238 CE, they had taken the border cities of Nisibis and Hatra, and under Shapur I (ruled 241–272 CE), dealt the Romans a double blow, first defeating the emperor Gordian III in 244 CE, then Valerian in 260 CE. Shapur looked set to overrun the eastern Roman provinces, but the local Arab ruler of Palmyra, in Syria, held him back.

Over the next three centuries, the pendulum swung between Roman and Sassanid advantage in a region thickly defended by fortified frontier cities. Then, in the early 7th century, Khusrau II Parviz (ruled 591–628 CE) finally broke the deadlock, taking Roman Syria, Palestine, and Egypt by 619 CE. Yet the Byzantine (eastern Roman) Empire fought back, undoing all of Khusrau's victories by 627 CE. The exhausted Sassanids then fell prey to Arab-Muslim armies invading from the south and west. Defeated at Qadisiya in 637 CE and at Nehavand in 642 CE, the last Sassanid king, Yazdegird III (ruled 632–651 CE), retreated eastward and died a fugitive at Merv in Central Asia.

⟫ SHAPUR THE GREAT

Having fought for his father Ardashir against the Parthians, Shapur I succeeded to the Sassanid throne in 241 CE while in his mid-20s. Almost immediately, he faced a Roman invasion, but this collapsed, and the emperor, Gordian, was murdered. This disaster forced the remnants of the Roman army, now under Philip, to sue for peace. Shapur's victory over the Romans near Carrhae in 260 CE was even more spectacular. Shapur captured the emperor Valerian, and later had his body flayed, stuffed, and mounted as a grisly trophy.

◳ **A rock-cut relief** at Naqsh-e Rustam, near Persepolis, shows a mounted Shapur I lording it over the defeated Roman emperors Philip and Valerian.

Greece

From unpromising beginnings in a collection of small and quarrelsome city-states, the Greeks entered an era of unparalleled creativity and surprising military success, seeing off the might of the Persian Empire and establishing colonies throughout the Mediterranean and Black Sea. Under Alexander the Great, the Greeks held political sway over most of the Near East, and even after Alexander's death, their cultural influence remained powerful there for centuries.

Archaic Greece

◳ **GREECE** ⌛ **700–500 BCE**

We know little about the era following the collapse of Greece's Mycenaean civilization in 1070 BCE (*see p.71*), because no written records survive. But by around 750 BCE, scattered clusters of villages throughout the Greek mainland, islands, and Ionia (Greek-settled Asia Minor) had grown into city-states, or *poleis*. Rivalry between the *poleis* was fierce, and fighting frequent; by 600 BCE, Sparta, Thebes, Corinth, and Athens were dominant. Governing systems varied from *polis* to *polis*. At first, monarchy was most common, but in the 7th century BCE, some city-states overthrew their kings and instituted "tyrannies": rule by autocrats from new families, such as the Pisistratids at Athens. A basic form of democracy emerged side-by-side with this in Athens (*see p.90*), beginning with the reforms of the great law-giver Solon in around 594 BCE.

Despite continuing rivalry, some cultural factors united the *poleis*: belief in common deities and participation in common cultural events, such as the pan-Hellenic games at Olympia. Philosophers, mainly in Ionia, began to speculate on the nature of the universe, while a rich legacy of poetry includes probably the first written versions of Homer's *Iliad* and *Odyssey*.

» **Rows of marble lions** on the island of Naxos were dedicated to the god Apollo in the 7th century BCE.

The Greek–Persian wars

GREECE, THE AEGEAN, W ASIA MINOR ⌛ **499–449** BCE

In 499 BCE, the Ionian cities of western Asia Minor, with some assistance from Athens, staged a revolt against Persia, which had conquered the region in 546 BCE. The Persians were victorious, suppressing the rebels in 493 BCE, after which the Persian king Darius I (*see p.84*) resolved to teach the Greeks a lesson. This was a mistake of epic proportions. Having easily occupied the Greek islands and found ready collaborators among certain of the northern Greek cities, Darius's army landed near Marathon (a small town on the coast of Attica, northeast of Athens) in late summer 490 BCE. There, a phalanx of Athenian citizen-soldiers—with shields locked together to form a united front—and their allies from the city of Plataea kept the Persians in check, despite being greatly outnumbered. Although Marathon was a minor setback, the damage to Persian prestige was profound and they withdrew.

The second Persian invasion

The Persians were not to give up and the fight was renewed under Darius's successor, Xerxes, in 480 BCE. A shaky coalition of Greek city-states formed to combat the invasion, but despite heroic resistance by the Spartan king Leonidas at Thermopylae (in which all the Spartans perished), the Persians soon won over the important state of Thebes to their side and had Athens at their mercy. The city was put to the torch, but Themistocles, a politician, had by then persuaded his fellow Athenians to finance a naval fleet.

This policy bore fruit in the naval defeat of the Persians at Salamis, with Themistocles at the helm, also in 480 BCE. A further victory on land at Plataea (in 479 BCE) stiffened Greek resolve and forced the retreat of the main Persian force, and this signaled the end of Persian ambition on the Greek mainland. Although the war continued on in Ionia and the Aegean until 448 BCE, the Greeks, by defending their independence, had in effect already emerged as the victors.

◀ **Leonidas**, the Spartan king, led an army of only 300 Spartans against Persian forces at the battle of Thermopylae.

Athens and democracy

ATHENS 594–338 BCE

The oldest and most stable democracy in ancient Greece developed in Athens, invoking the right of all citizens—a category excluding women, children, slaves, and foreigners—to participate in political decision-making.

At the start of the 6th century BCE, the reforms of the Athenian statesman Solon had diluted the aristocrats' power in favor of the citizen assembly (*ekklesia*), but it was only under the magistrate Cleisthenes (c.570–c.507 BCE) that the Athenian constitution began to approach its final form. He divided Athens into about 140 voting districts (*demes*), which were grouped together into 10 tribes. Each of these supplied 50 members annually to a council of 500, and this group supplied the 50-member group of council leaders (*Prytaneis*) to administer the government's daily affairs.

The assembly

The composition of the *Prytaneis* changed regularly so that no one held power for too long. The full *ekklesia*—with a quorum of 6,000 people—convened around 40 times a year, meeting on the Pnyx, a hill near the Acropolis, to vote on important matters, including the election of the city's generals (*strategoi*). Pericles (495–429 BCE), the most brilliant orator in 5th-century BCE Athens, consolidated the power of the masses by compensating the poor for the time they spent attending the assembly.

> ❝ A man who takes **no interest** in **politics** has **no business** here at all ❞
>
> **Pericles, 495–429 BCE**

Democracy and empire

As Athens' power waxed, the attractions of holding office grew. Ostracism—a vote by the *ekklesia* to exile over-mighty politicians—aimed to curb the abuse of power by a few. Athenian defeats in the Peloponnesian War (*see p.94*) twice suspended democracy, which, although later restored, became a shadow of its former glory by the time the Romans took over Greece in the mid-2nd century BCE.

The Porch of the Caryatids, on the Acropolis of Athens, had to be rebuilt after being burned down by the Persians in 480 BCE.

Greek colonization

From the late 9th century BCE, **the Greeks** dramatically expanded their world by dispatching colonists from cities in Greece to all corners of the Mediterranean and the Black Sea. This process continued for more than three centuries. Exactly why colonization was so important is unclear, but it may have been both a catalyst for trade and a pressure valve for excess population or political difficulties in Greece itself.

The acquisition of lands

Although the Greeks had set up foreign trading posts, such as at Al Mina in Syria, their new colonies were fully fledged citizen communities. Among the earliest were those in eastern Sicily, including Syracuse, founded around 733 BCE. Shortly after this, colonization began in southern Italy, with cities such as Rhegium, Sybaris, and Croton springing up in a network so dense that the area came to be known as Magna Graecia ("Greater Greece").

The movement spread far to the south and west, founding Cyrene in North Africa around 630 BCE, and Massilia (modern Marseilles, in France) around 600 BCE. The Greeks first reached the Iberian Peninsula—at Tartessus in modern Spain— in around 640 BCE. In the east, colonies spread up the coast of the Black Sea, from Byzantium to the Crimea, and to Trapezus (modern Trabzon) on the northern coastline of the Anatolian peninsula.

By the late 6th century BCE, the Greek impetus for colonization had faded, and as the system of city-states in Greece itself came under strain, future Greek expansion would come largely under the patronage of Alexander the Great's Macedonian empire and its successor states.

≪ **A silver coin from Catana** (modern Catania), a Greek settlement in Sicily that was colonized around 720 BCE.

▽ **The city of Ephesus**, a Greek colony located on Turkey's western coastline, was established in an 11th-century BCE wave of Greek expansion.

The Parthenon, the great temple to the goddess Athena, was built at Athens in the mid-5th century BCE. The project was initiated by the city's leading statesman Pericles, and the work was partly overseen by Phidias, one of Classical Greece's greatest artists. It was completed around 432 BCE.

The Peloponnesian War

📍 GREECE, W TURKEY, SICILY ⌛ 431–404 BCE

The Peloponnesian War, a bitter 30-year struggle, arose from the rivalry between the two most prominent Greek city-states, Athens and Sparta. Unlike the democratic constitution of its rival (*see p.90*), Sparta was governed by kings and a small military elite, moderated by five annually elected magistrates (or *ephors*). The mass of the population were *helots*, effectively serfs, with no political rights. In the mid-5th century BCE, Athens established an empire based on its maritime strength, bringing it into conflict with Sparta's land-based power.

🔼 **A helmet typical** of the protective gear of the hoplites, the heavy infantry of the Greek armies.

The stages of war

The initial pretext for war was the attempt in 432–431 BCE by Potidaea, an Athenian client-city in northern Greece, to break away from the Athenian empire. Sparta and its allies came to Potidaea's aid, but the Athenians initially held the upper hand. Sparta fought back, winning a great victory at Amphipolis in 422 BCE, and both sides agreed to observe a 50-year truce.

Hostilities broke out again in 415 BCE, when the Athenians, encouraged by the extremist anti-Spartan statesman Alcibiades, sent a great fleet to Sicily, intent on absorbing Syracuse into their empire. The Spartans reacted by supporting the Syracusans, and Athens was sucked into a debilitating and ultimately unsuccessful siege of the city.

⟫ THUCYDIDES

One of the first true historians, Thucydides (c.460–c.404 BCE) wrote a *History of the Peloponnesian War*, recounting events he had lived through. The speeches he put in the mouths of the protagonists are some of the masterpieces of Greek literature.

In 413 BCE, the Spartans destroyed the Athenian armada in Sicily, but still the war dragged on. Finally in 405 BCE, at Aegospotami on the Hellespont, the Spartans captured most of the Athenian fleet while it was beached on shore. Deprived of their naval support, the Athenians could not resist a Spartan blockade, and in 404 BCE, they surrendered, agreeing to the destruction of their defensive walls. Athens would never again be such a dominant force among the Greek city-states.

🔽 **The Athenians' naval fleet** included oared warships known as triremes. These vessels were fast and maneuverable, and were able to ram enemy ships.

Classical Greek culture

The Classical Greek city-states of the 6th to 4th centuries BCE gave birth to a civilization of extreme creativity, remarkable both for its uniformity of belief and culture, and its diversity of political systems. It has given us philosophers, artists, and playwrights whose works we still celebrate today.

▲ **The art of vase painting** reached new heights during the Classical period of Greece, often depicting scenes from myth.

Religion, art, and philosophy

The possession of a common religion was a hallmark of "Greekness," and temples, shrines, and oracles to the principal gods—Zeus, their king; Hera, his wife; Apollo, the sun god—sprang up throughout Greece and the Greek colonies.

Cult centers such as Olympia and Delphi became important pan-Greek gathering places and at some, in particular at Olympia, the Greeks held games in honor of the gods. The temples the Greeks built to their gods are among the most breathtaking relics of the Classical age, and include the great marble temple of the Parthenon built on the Athenian acropolis between 447 and 432 BCE. Sculptors such as Phidias (born 490 BCE), who created the great cult statue of Athena for the Parthenon, are among the world's earliest named artists. The Greeks excelled in the dramatic arts, too, with tragedies by Aeschylus, Sophocles, and Euripides, and comedies by Aristophanes, being performed at an annual religious festival, called the *Dionysia* in honor of the god Dionysus.

Of equally profound and lasting influence was the work of Greek philosophers such as Socrates (c.469–399 BCE), Plato (c.427–347 BCE), and Aristotle (384–322 BCE), the first to apply rigorous logic in an attempt to understand the world, whose works were valued into the Middle Ages and beyond.

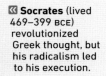

◀◀ **Socrates** (lived 469–399 BCE) revolutionized Greek thought, but his radicalism led to his execution.

The conquests of Alexander the Great

📖 **GREECE, THE NEAR EAST** ⏳ **336–323** BCE

In the 4th century BCE, Greece saw a struggle for power between several city-states, with first Sparta and then, from 371 BCE, Thebes emerging as the victor. From the early 350s BCE, the northern Greek state of Macedonia began to expand under an energetic and ruthless new king, Philip II. In 338 BCE, Philip, aided by his 18-year-old son Alexander, gained victory against the Thebans and their allies at Chaeronea. The other Greeks then rapidly submitted to Macedonian overlordship.

The young Alexander was not Philip's only son, and his succession to the throne was by no means assured. Philip's assassination in 336 BCE has long been suspected to be at Alexander's prompting.

Once his father was dead, Alexander moved with brutal speed to put down rivals and, in 335 BCE, suppress a Theban revolt.

The invasion of Persia

Now secure on the Macedonian throne, Alexander embarked on an enterprise of staggering ambition: the invasion of the Achaemenid Persian empire. In 334 BCE, he led an army of some 50,000 across the Hellespont into Asia Minor—modern Turkey— with the initial intention of liberating the Greek cities there from Persian control. Disputed successions and rebellions had weakened the Achaemenid empire in the 4th century BCE,

📷 **A Roman-era mosaic** showing Alexander riding his horse Bucephalus into battle, possibly at Issus in 333 BCE.

but its ruler, Darius III, could still call upon resources vastly superior to those of Alexander. Nonetheless, Alexander, with tactical and strategic brilliance, and with more than an eye for his image as an all-powerful ruler, defeated a large Persian force at Granicus in 334 BCE, and then the next year bested Darius III himself at Issus in Syria.

Utilizing the professionalism and maneuverability of his smaller forces against the vast, cumbersome Persian armies, he seemed unbeatable. Pausing to visit Egypt, he defeated Darius one final time at Gaugamela on the banks of the Tigris in 331 BCE. The fugitive Persian king was murdered the following year and Alexander took on the trappings of an oriental potentate, adopting Persian court dress and protocol and moving to secure all the former provinces of the Achaemenid empire.

Final campaigns and death

Alexander spent 329 and 328 BCE suppressing revolts in the eastern provinces of Bactria and Sogdia, after which he pushed on into northwestern India, defeating the local ruler Porus at Hydaspes in 326 BCE. Finally, even his loyal Macedonians refused to go further. A long and grueling return across desert terrain to reach central Persia, and the perceived influence of native Persians in Alexander's entourage, fueled a series of mutinies.

Then, in 323 BCE, aged only 32, the conqueror of the known world died of a fever at Babylon. His embalmed body was sent to Egypt, and his generals plotted to seize power for themselves, since, as he was still relatively young at the time of his death, Alexander had not chosen a successor.

> " His friends asked: '**To whom do you leave the kingdom**?' And he replied '**To the strongest**'.
>
> Diodorus Siculus on the death of Alexander (*Library of History*, XVII, 117)

The successors of Alexander

⚑ EGYPT, SYRIA, MACEDONIA ⚔ 323–31 BCE

Alexander the Great's death in 323 BCE led to a long struggle for control of his empire. This began almost at once, for Alexander's wife Roxana was pregnant, and the army split between those wanting to see if she bore a son and those who supported the severely disabled half-brother of Alexander, Philip Arrhidaeus. In the end, the child was born male and as Alexander IV he ruled jointly with Arrhidaeus, who became Philip III.

However, this only masked the deep divisions between the generals, who then proceeded to carve out their own territories: Ptolemy in Egypt; Antigonus in Asia Minor; Lysimachus in Thrace; Eumenes in Cappadocia; and Seleucus in Persia. A series of wars between these *Diadochoi* (or "successors") erupted, which between 323 and 279 BCE gradually eliminated the weaker contenders.

⬇ **The Greek city of Corinth** in the Peloponnese was taken by the Romans in 146 BCE, marking the end of mainland Greece's independence.

Decline and fall

By 301 BCE, three main successor states survived—the Antigonids based in Macedonia, the Seleucids in Mesopotamia and Syria, and the Ptolemies in Egypt—together with a constellation of smaller statelets that fed off warfare between the big three. After Antigonus I of Macedonia was defeated by the others at Issus in 301 BCE and the other weaker states had been eliminated, the tensions diminished and the three Greek kingdoms survived until they were successively swallowed up by the Romans: Macedonia in 168 BCE, a much-reduced Seleucid kingdom in 64 BCE, and finally, Egypt in 31 BCE.

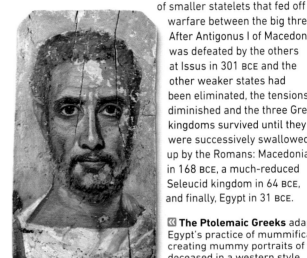

◀ **The Ptolemaic Greeks** adapted Egypt's practice of mummification, creating mummy portraits of the deceased in a western style.

Hellenistic Culture

Alexander's conquests left a large part of western Asia and North Africa in Greek hands. As part of his efforts to solidify his hold over this enormous territory, Alexander himself encouraged the foundation of Greek cities in the newly conquered lands, including most notably Alexandria in Egypt. These became the focus for the diffusion of Greek culture, known as Hellenism, throughout the East.

The Hellenistic city

Greek-speakers were a definite minority in Alexander's empire and the successor states, but everywhere the cities bore the hallmarks of the mother country. These included temples built in the Greek fashion, a central marketplace and meeting space (or *agora*), and the gymnasium, which was not merely a place of exercise, but acted as a center for Greek-style education where young men could study classic authors and obtain a sense of Greek culture.

Divergence and dissolution

Although united by the Greek language, the Hellenistic cities and kingdoms did absorb eastern influences, notably in Egypt where the Greek-speaking kings ruled as pharaohs. Hellenistic art styles also traveled far to the east, influencing the Buddha figures of the Indian state of Gandhara in the 2nd century BCE. In science and literature, the Hellenistic Greeks continued the Classical tradition of creativity. The mathematicians Euclid (c.300 BCE) and Archimedes (287–212 BCE), the comic playwright Menander (342–293 BCE), and the historian Polybius (c.200–c.118 BCE) are a few of the influential figures whose work was absorbed by the Romans during their conquests of the Hellenistic lands, ensuring that Greece's cultural legacy lived on.

» **Antiochus I of Commagene** (ruled 70–38 BCE) was ruler of a Hellenistic kingdom near Armenia and had this spectacular funerary monument built to himself in the Greek style.

Rome

From inauspicious beginnings as a small hilltop settlement in central Italy in the mid-8th century BCE, Rome survived turbulent early centuries to conquer the entire Italian peninsula—and then created an empire encompassing the whole of the Mediterranean world, parts of the Near East, and northwestern Europe. Rome's military and administrative strength allowed it to endure several crises until, finally, waves of barbarian invaders brought about its fall.

Early Rome

⚐ **CENTRAL ITALY** ⌛ **753–509** BCE

According to tradition, Rome was founded on April 21, 753 BCE, by Romulus, said to have been the son of the god Mars. Like most of the traditions associated with Rome's earliest days, it is hard to disentangle truth from myth.

Rome under the monarchy

The first settlement, atop the Palatine Hill overlooking the Tiber River, was almost indistinguishable from the area's myriad small 8th-century BCE villages. Crucially, Rome seems to have been more receptive to outside influences than its rivals, and particularly to that of the more developed Etruscan civilization that flourished in central Italy.

Some of Rome's early kings—there were seven by tradition—may have been Etruscan. The story goes that the second king, Numa Pompilius, established many of Rome's religious traditions, while Ancus Marcius in the 7th century BCE expanded the territory of the fledgling city-state through a series of localized struggles against the neighboring Latin tribe.

From the reign of Tullus Hostilius (673–642 BCE) comes the first evidence of a Roman senate, in the form of the Cura Hostilia building. The accession of Tarquinius Priscus—probably an Etruscan—in 616 BCE brought a new dynamism to Rome. However the next king, Tarquinius Superbus, was a tyrant, and his unpopular rule led to his deposition in 509 BCE by a group of aristocrats. From this point onward Rome was a republic.

◀ **In this Renaissance mosaic**, Romulus, the legendary founder of Rome, and his twin brother Remus suckle from the she-wolf said to have raised them.

The Roman Republic

ITALIAN PENINSULA ⏳ **509 BCE–c.250 BCE**

When Rome became a republic in 509 BCE, it retained some of the elements of the old monarchical system, including the Senate—an amorphous group of elders with decision-making powers. Every year, a citizen assembly elected two consuls, whose dual authority was an attempt to prevent despotism.

The structure of society

The early Republic was dominated by the conflict between two groups of citizens, the patricians (elite landowners) and the underclass of plebeians. The patricians monopolized political power, and provided all the members for the Senate. Plebeian resentment of this hierarchy led to a series of violent conflicts, which in 494 BCE resulted in the creation of a plebeian assembly with two elected tribunes (who later came to have a veto over laws passed in the Senate). The codification of Roman laws in the "Twelve Tables" in 450 BCE eased other restrictions on the plebeians; and in 366 BCE the first plebeian consul was elected.

The expansion of Rome

After a Roman victory against a league of Latin neighbors in 496 BCE, a series of "colonies" of Roman citizens set out from Rome, gradually forming a network of Roman-controlled or -inclined cities throughout central Italy. In 396 BCE, the Romans captured the leading Etruscan city of Veii, and by the early 3rd century BCE had also defeated the Samnites to begin the extension of their power into south-central Italy.

▷▷ **A statue of a lictor**, who carried the fasces, the bundle of rods and axes that symbolized the power of the Republic's magistrates.

◁ **The Temple of Castor and Pollux** (*center right*), in the Forum at Rome, was where the patricians met to discuss the government of the early Republic.

The Punic Wars

📖 **ITALY, SPAIN, N AFRICA** ⏳ **264–148** BCE

Rome expanded its influence through the Italian peninsula during the first half of the 3rd century BCE, gradually creating conflict with other powers in the Mediterranean. Most notable among these adversaries were the Carthaginians, who, from their capital in modern Tunisia, North Africa, controlled an empire that included Sicily.

War broke out with Rome in 264 BCE over a quarrel between Carthaginian-allied Syracuse and the Mamertines of Messana, also in Sicily, who appealed to the Romans for help. The fighting—known as the First Punic War—dragged on for 23 years, involving land battles and sieges that generally went the Romans' way, and more decisive naval battles ending in a Roman victory at the Aegates Islands in 241 BCE. Carthage was stripped of its territories in Sicily, but compensated by going on to form a new empire in Spain.

A Second Punic War broke out in 218 BCE, when the Spanish city of Saguntum, fearing absorption by the Carthaginian general Hannibal, appealed to the Roman Senate for aid. The Romans demanded Hannibal's surrender; the latter responded with an invasion. Crossing the Alps—with an army that

📧 **A romanticized view** of the battle of Zama in 202 BCE, where Scipio finally defeated Hannibal and destroyed his last army—20,000 Carthaginians died.

We have been **defeated** in a **great battle**.

MARCUS POMPONIUS ANNOUNCING THE DISASTROUS ROMAN DEFEAT AT LAKE TRASIMENE, 217 BCE

included war elephants—in the winter of 218 BCE, he soon defeated the Romans at Ticinus and Trebia, in the north of Italy.

Hannibal's Italian campaigns

After this victory, many Cisalpine Gauls—Celts settled around Milan—flocked to Hannibal's cause. A further Roman defeat at Lake Trasimene, in central Italy, in 217 BCE led to the deaths of around 15,000 Romans. The next year the Romans suffered an even greater disaster farther south at Cannae, where their general Varro rashly allowed his army to be outflanked and encircled by the Carthaginian cavalry, and then massacred.

Many cities then defected from the Roman cause, but General Fabius Maximus kept Hannibal away from Rome and halted the momentum of his earlier victories. In 207 BCE, Hasdrubal, the brother of Hannibal, was defeated and killed at Metaurus, northeast Italy, and five years later a Roman counter-strike by Scipio forced Hannibal to return to Africa.

The end of the Punic Wars

In October 202 BCE, the Carthaginians were defeated, stripped of their Spanish territories, and reduced to a small territory around Carthage. Yet Rome was not satisfied, and in 149 BCE used a pretext to begin a Third Punic War. Carthage was besieged, and then stormed in 146 BCE. The Romans razed the city, deported its people, and finally annexed its remaining territory.

❯❯ HANNIBAL

Born c.247 BCE, Hannibal became Carthage's leading general during the Second Punic War and commander-in-chief in 221 BCE. His plan to lead an army across southern Gaul (modern France) into Italy was a bold one, and he showed tactical genius in a string of victories against Rome. Yet he lacked strategic vision and became bogged down once Roman resistance stiffened. After the war, he was chief magistrate of Carthage, but Roman fears of a Carthaginian revival led to his exile in 195 BCE. He died in c.183 BCE.

⬈ A Carthaginian stela from the tophet, or graveyard, at Carthage. The horn-shaped symbol is for Tanit, a moon goddess.

The end of the Republic

📍 **ITALY, GAUL** ⏳ **137–44** BCE

During the 2nd century BCE the political situation in Rome became increasingly tense. Then, in the 80s BCE, the city was hit by a political and military struggle for power between Marius, the reformer of the Roman army, and Sulla, a politician who, after Marius's death, became Dictator, or sole ruler, in 82 BCE.

Pompey and Caesar

That year, Sulla killed more than 500 of his opponents and packed the Senate with his supporters. After Sulla's death in 78 BCE, another popular general, Pompey, rose to power. For 15 years Pompey excelled at his political role, and bolstered his military reputation with several victories in the East. Yet, in 60 BCE, increasing factional violence led him to broker a three-way alliance, called the "First Triumvirate," with the rich financier Crassus and a rising military star—Julius Caesar. This collapsed in 49 BCE and led to civil war between the factions of Caesar and Pompey.

The first civil war

Caesar pushed Pompey out of Italy and, in 48 BCE, defeated him at Pharsalus in Thessaly. Pompey was murdered in Egypt, but his partisans fought on until, in 46 BCE, Caesar triumphed, becoming Dictator (first for ten years, then for life). Fearing Caesar would make himself king, a group of republicans, including Marcus Brutus, assassinated him. However, their murderous act failed to save the Republic from collapse.

》 JULIUS CAESAR

Born in 100 BCE, Caesar became Roman consul in 59 BCE. He created a new province for Rome in Gaul from 58 to 52 BCE and this brought him great political power and popularity—which ultimately led to his murder in 44 BCE.

◿ **The assassination of Julius Caesar** was carried out by only a small group of senators; most fled or waited to see what actions the assassins would take next.

The first emperor: Augustus

ITALY, THE MEDITERRANEAN | **44 BCE–14 CE**

After Julius Caesar died in 44 BCE, his chief lieutenant Mark Antony, attempting to manipulate public opinion, allied himself with Octavian—Caesar's 18-year-old adoptive son—in order to exploit his family connections and gain political support. Antony miscalculated, for Octavian, although young, was even shrewder than Caesar. He remained in alliance with Antony and Lepidus—who played the role of financier in this "Second Triumvirate"—for only as long as it took to defeat the armies that had been raised by Brutus and Cassius, Caesar's murderers.

In 32 BCE, war broke out among the Second Triumvirate. At Actium the following year, Antony was defeated, and both he and his mistress, the Egyptian pharaoh Cleopatra, committed suicide. Octavian did not seek immediate revenge against Antony's partisans. Nor did he have himself made Dictator, as Caesar had done. Instead, he manipulated Republican politics to acquire supreme power without seeming to usurp the Senate's authority.

From general to emperor

In 27 BCE, Octavian was granted a special form of authority, known as *proconsular imperium*, for 10 years, which in effect allowed him to act as he chose in all provinces where the army was currently based. In the same year, he took the title "Augustus." In 23 BCE, Augustus acquired the permanent power of a tribune of the plebeians, making him invulnerable to legal action. Although he did not refer to himself as an emperor, this was the position he now held.

> ** Wars**, both civil and foreign, I **undertook**, both **on sea** and on **land**!
>
> Inscription of Augustus (the *Res Gestae Divi Augusti*) from Ankara, Turkey, c.14 CE

Military expansion

Augustus secured the empire's borders along the Danube River and sent armies into Germany, which he was about to conquer when a disastrous defeat in 9 CE caused a retreat from the Elbe River back to the Rhine. His last years saw a defensive stance along existing frontiers.

During Augustus's reign (27 BCE–14 CE), the production of images of the emperor, such as this statue from Turin, Italy, became a vital part of imperial propaganda.

The government and army

⚑ ROMAN EMPIRE ⏳ 27 BCE–c.200 CE

The empire over which Augustus assumed rule in 27 BCE was very different from the Rome of the early republic. Now ruling over territories that stretched from the Iberian peninsula in the west to Syria and Armenia in the east—as well as large parts of North Africa—the Roman government faced far greater challenges than the old, informal systems could manage.

Government and the provinces

At the center of Roman government, the role of the emperor remained ambivalent. Certain emperors, such as Claudius (ruled 41–54 CE), liked to flatter the old senatorial class with the fantasy that the emperor was just a superior sort of senator; others, such as Nero (ruled 54–68 CE), tended to much more direct, despotic, and capricious rule.

The early empire had little in the way of a public service, and many important roles, such as running the imperial treasury, were assumed by freedmen (former slaves). Provincial governors, however, who administered Rome's imperial territories, were almost all senators. The Roman government raised its revenue mainly through indirect taxes on sales or death duties. Some was

▲ **The legions' superior equipment** and training made them more than a match for non-Roman enemies.

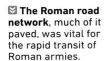

▽ **The Roman road network**, much of it paved, was vital for the rapid transit of Roman armies.

spent on the upkeep or building of Roman roads, which linked the main cities of the empire, but as much as 80 percent was spent on the army.

The Roman legions

Augustus had inherited 80 legions, which he cut to 28, each comprising around 5,000 men. Supporting them, and directly answerable to the emperor, were infantry and cavalry regiments of noncitizens (called "auxiliaries"). The total manpower may have been around 300,000.

The legions formed a formidable strike force, almost irresistible in open combat. Their engineering expertise meant they could also conduct siege warfare expertly and take on large-scale construction projects, such as roads and fortifications. Over time the army formed its own power base, through the imperial guard (the Praetorians) based in Rome and the legionary frontier garrisons, and became as much a cause of internal instability as a guardian against outside threat.

The early empire

ROMAN EMPIRE ⚔ **14–69** CE

Augustus died in 14 CE, having chosen Tiberius, the son of his wife Livia by her first marriage, as his heir. Tiberius was 55 when he came to the throne, having proved himself a capable general and administrator, yet he was never truly popular and, in the middle period of his reign, became dominated by Sejanus, the prefect of the Praetorian guard. In the last seven years of his life, Tiberius shut himself away in his palace on the island of Capri, leading to an atmosphere of frustration and stagnation in Rome.

The post-Tiberian emperors

Tiberius's rule gave way to a new, young emperor, Caligula (ruled 41–54 CE), who the governing class welcomed with open arms. However, Caligula's patent instability and dangerous temper led to his assassination and replacement by a man the Praetorians thought would be a pliant weakling: Claudius (ruled 41–54 CE). Yet Claudius proved shrewd; he sponsored large-scale public works that included a new port at Ostia and, although not a military man, ordered the conquest of Britain from 43 CE. Claudius was succeeded by the mercurial Nero (ruled 54–68 CE), who, unsuited to power, became mired in corruption. When an army revolt broke out in Spain in 68 CE, civil war erupted, leading to four emperors in a single year, until finally Vespasian (ruled 69–79 CE), a tough-minded general, emerged triumphant.

⬆ **A cameo showing Augustus's wife Livia** and her son Tiberius, who became the second emperor of the Julio-Claudian dynasty (27 BCE–68 CE).

« **The Colosseum**, the empire's largest amphitheater—begun under Vespasian and completed by his son Titus—housed spectacular gladiatorial shows.

The empire at its height

ROMAN EMPIRE **69–180 CE**

Vespasian's accession in 69 CE inaugurated a new dynasty, the Flavians, during which stability at first seemed to return to the empire. Vespasian's economic reforms filled the treasury, and new territory was occupied in northern Britain and parts of Germany and Asia Minor. But Vespasian's son Titus, succeeding him in 79 CE, was to die after just two years. Titus's younger brother Domitian (ruled 81–96 CE) made a promising start, but degenerated into tyranny and was assassinated, possibly on the orders of the Senate itself.

The "golden age"

The Senate then put forward one of their own as emperor, a 70-year-old, much-respected senator named Nerva. To ensure the succession, Nerva adopted the talented governor of Upper Germany, Trajan, as his son, beginning a practice that would see the next emperors, Hadrian, Antoninus Pius, and Marcus Aurelius, all adopted by their predecessor. This gave the empire a golden age—a century of stability.

Trajan and Hadrian

Nerva died after just two years, and Trajan soon began to enlarge the empire's frontiers, seizing Dacia (modern Romania) in two wars between 101 and 106 CE; the mercantile kingdom of Nabataea (largely in modern Jordan) in 106 CE;

⬆ **A marble frieze**, from Ephesus showing emperors Hadrian, Marcus Aurelius, and Lucius Verus. Hadrian has a beard, a Greek fashion he made popular at Rome.

and much of Mesopotamia (now Iraq) from 115 to 117 CE. These victories brought massive booty that helped fill the treasury. Yet the eastern territories were not secure, and when Trajan died in 117 CE they were already in revolt.

It was perhaps this that persuaded Trajan's successor, Hadrian, to be more cautious. He started no new wars of expansion and built defensive works in Germany and Britain.

⬇ **Hadrian's Wall** is a monumental barrier stretching 80 Roman miles (117 km) across northern Britain, built to defend the province against barbarian incursions.

Hadrian traveled widely, seeing more of his domains than any emperor before him, and established a permanent imperial council that reduced the importance of the senate.

The later Antonines

Hadrian adopted the elderly Antoninus Pius (ruled 138–161 CE), intending the latter's young protégé Marcus Aurelius to succeed him quickly. Yet Antoninus lived for another 23 years in a tranquil reign that saw few revolts.

When Marcus Aurelius finally succeeded in 161 CE, ruling jointly with Lucius Verus—another of Hadrian's circle—he faced a series of crises. A plague between 168 and 169 CE killed thousands, including Lucius Verus, and the empire became entangled in the Marcomannic Wars against barbarians on the Danube.

Before his death in 180 CE, Marcus had chosen his own son Commodus to succeed him, the first son ever born to a ruling emperor. However, like Domitian's, Commodus's rule was unstable and would spell the end of Rome's golden age.

›› TRAJAN

Trajan (ruled 98–117 CE) was from an Italian family that had moved to Spain, making him the first emperor with strong non-Italian roots. He made his name while fighting under Domitian along the Rhine in the 80s CE and as governor of Upper Germany. Popular with the army, he was an obvious choice to succeed Nerva. He showed astonishing energy in expanding the empire's frontiers, an achievement he celebrated in Trajan's Column, which was built beside the new Forum that Trajan commissioned in central Rome.

> ❝ He was the **first** to **construct a wall**… which was to **separate barbarians and Romans**. ❞
>
> The *Historia Augusta* on Hadrian's building of the Wall

Crisis and reform

ROMAN EMPIRE ⧗ **180–305 CE**

The emperors of the late-1st and 2nd centuries BCE had handpicked their successors. Marcus Aurelius was the first emperor for a century to have an adult male son, Commodus—but he proved a lesson in the weakness of hereditary succession.

Commodus was rash and fickle. His behavior sparked a series of military revolts that led finally to the triumph of Septimius Severus (ruled 193–211 CE), the governor of Upper Pannonia (in modern Hungary). A firm and active ruler, Severus seemed set to restore confidence in the empire. He divided large provinces into two, to avoid any one governor having too much military power,

and he conquered territories in Mesopotamia. Yet his successor Caracalla (ruled 211–217 CE) proved more capable of making enemies than ruling—he murdered his brother and co-emperor Geta. Caracalla himself was murdered in 217 CE near Carrhae (in modern Turkey) by an army faction fearful that he would execute them.

The beginning of the end

For a while the empire teetered between hope and farce. Emperor Elagabalus (ruled 218–222 CE), who was a Syrian high priest of dubious morality and Septimius Severus's

⟫ **The detailed carving** on this imperial Roman marble sarcophagus shows Roman soldiers battling the Goths during the 3rd century CE.

great-nephew, scandalized and alienated Senatorial opinion. His cousin Severus Alexander, brought in to replace him, lost the support of the army and was murdered in Germany in 235 CE. This ushered in a half-century of chaos, when emperors, brought to power and then murdered by their own soldiers, rarely lasted more than a few years.

For 20 years, Gaul broke away to be ruled by its own emperors. More dangerously, after the Persians captured the emperor Valerian (ruled 253–260 CE) in 260 CE, the city of Palmyra in Syria established its own eastern empire under Queen Zenobia and her son Vaballathus. To add to the official empire's woes, new groups of barbarians, including the Goths, pressed down from eastern and central Europe toward the Rhine and Danube frontiers. Aurelian (ruled 270–275 CE) finally defeated Zenobia and brought Gaul back into the empire, but he had to abandon Dacia, and still barbarians such as the Franks and Alamanns raided Gaul, and the Goths pillaged across the Danube. It was all too much for a single emperor to deal with.

⬆ **This Roman coin** from c.218 CE bears a depiction of the controversial emperor Elagabalus.

The tetrarchy

Nominated by the army as emperor in 284 CE, Diocletian chose an old military colleague, Maximian, to rule jointly with him. In 293 CE, he further subdivided the imperial office by selecting two junior emperors (or "Caesars") to reign with the two senior ones (or "Augusti").

Now that there were, in effect, four emperors—in a system known as the Tetrarchy—facing a challenge in one area of the empire no longer meant abandoning problems elsewhere. Diocletian also reformed the army, recruiting smaller legions better adapted to combat the barbarian incursions. In an unprecedented act, in 305 CE Diocletian abdicated voluntarily due to ill health, and retired to his palace at Spalatum (modern-day Split, Croatia).

" This man… **overturned** the whole **order of things**: For **he chose three** other **men** to **share** the **imperial government** with him.

Lactantius, speaking of Diocletian,
De Mortibus Persecutorum

Constantine and the new Christian Empire

ROMAN EMPIRE ⌛ **306–337 CE**

When Emperor Diocletian retired in 305 CE, his system of four rulers (the Tetrarchy; *see p.111*) fell apart. The new college of four emperors excluded Maxentius, the son of Diocletian's colleague Maximian, and Constantine, the son of a Caesar in the Tetrarchy. The result was chaos, and by 310 CE there were no fewer than seven competing emperors. In the civil war that followed, Constantine won out, first defeating Maxentius at the Battle of Milvian Bridge in 312 CE, and then finally, in 324 CE, becoming the unchallenged sole emperor.

Constantine's reforms

Constantine divided the army between a mobile field force (the *comitatenses*) and the frontier garrisons (the *limitanei*). The bureaucracy became much more formal, hierarchical, and efficient, headed by a praetorian prefect. The new emperor also founded a new capital city at Constantinople (now Istanbul), modeled on Rome with its seven hills, from which to administer the eastern empire.

Constantine and Christianity

Constantine is best known for his support of Christians, following their persecution under Diocletian. He decreed freedom of worship by the Edict of Milan in 313 CE, sponsored the first large churches in Rome, and allowed bishops to take an increasingly important role in politics.

›› CONSTANTINE

Born in the 280s BCE, Constantine took a long road to Christianity. He claimed to have received a vision before the Battle of Milvian Bridge in 312 BCE, and after this he honored the Christian god. He was finally baptized on his deathbed in 337 CE.

☑ **Constantine (right)** gives the symbols of imperial rule—the Phrygian bonnet, canopy, and Lateran Palace—to Pope Sylvester I in this 12th-century fresco.

The fall of the Roman empire

ROMAN EMPIRE ⌛ **337–476** CE

Following the end of the reign of Constantine (*see facing page*), the Roman Empire became overwhelmed, by an increasingly complex and inflexible political and bureaucratic system; by pressure from barbarians along the frontier; and by a series of ineffective rulers in the western empire. A division between eastern and western empires meant that after 395 CE, no one ruled both halves together as sole emperor. No longer able to absorb the outsiders pressing against its frontiers, by the mid-4th century the empire was on the defensive, and the catastrophic destruction of the eastern field army by the Goths at Adrianople in 378 CE almost led to a total collapse.

The empire fragments and falls

The barbarians moved from raids to seizing land on which to settle, reducing the number of citizens the empire's central authorities could tax and put to work. Much of the eastern empire was shielded from this— it was the western half that lost much of Spain and Gaul to the Visigoths and the Franks in the first part of the 5th century CE, and the grain-rich provinces of North Africa to the Vandals between 429 and 439 CE. Britain broke away from the empire in 410–411 CE, and Rome itself was sacked—the first time it had fallen to a foreign enemy in almost 800 years—by the Goths in 410 CE. The westward movement of the Huns from the 430s meant that the empire was facing challenges on too many fronts, and

◀ **The barbarians** fought the Romans with primitive weapons, such as this francisca, a Frankish throwing ax.

the ineffective rules of Honorius (393–423 CE) and Valentinian III (424–455 CE) did nothing to stem the tide. A series of short-lived western emperors became the puppets of the conquering German chieftains.

In 476 CE, the Germanic general Odovacar demanded land in Italy for his soldiers. When the boy-emperor Romulus Augustulus defiantly refused, he was deposed. Odovacar did not bother to appoint a new emperor, ruling as a king himself, and as a result, the Roman Empire in the west was at an end.

✉ **A Roman legionary** fights a Germanic warrior. Almost invincible at its height, the Roman army later suffered a decline in resources that left it vulnerable.

> ❝ The **Imperial city**… was delivered to the **licentious fury** of the **tribes** of **Germany** and **Scythia**. ❞
>
> Edward Gibbon, *The Decline and Fall of the Roman Empire*, on the sack of Rome by the Goths, 410 CE

Celtic and Germanic Europe

Although it is through the Romans that we know much of the history of the peoples who bordered their empire, many of these groups had rich traditions of their own. The Celts thrived in central and western Europe until the Romans conquered Gaul and Britain, while the Germanic tribes migrated west and south, finally conquering much of the western Roman empire in the 4th and 5th centuries CE.

The Celts

CENTRAL AND W EUROPE 500 BCE–83 CE

Fierce warriors and skilled ironworkers with a love of feasting, the Celts swept across large areas of Europe from around 500 BCE, dominating much of the center and west of the continent by 200 BCE. Although they were not one cohesive people, they displayed a uniform culture (known in its later phase as the La Tène culture).

It was typified by organization into tribes or clans, village or nomadic life, and a strong warrior tradition, with warfare common between tribes. Tribes or even individual families occupied hill forts—hilltops encircled by a ditch and bank—for protection.

Beliefs and decline

The Celts relied on oral transmission of culture through bards and poets; their religion, governed by the priestly class (the Druids), had a complex pantheon. Metalworking was a speciality and was used to embellish objects from household utensils to battle chariots.

From the 50s BCE, the Romans pushed the Celts to the margins of Europe: tribes in Gaul were conquered by Julius Caesar, and the British Celtic kingdoms were subdued between 43 and 83 CE. Only in Scotland and Ireland did Celtic culture survive.

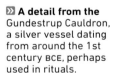
A detail from the Gundestrup Cauldron, a silver vessel dating from around the 1st century BCE, perhaps used in rituals.

Successor states to Rome

W AND S EUROPE ⏳ **418–774** CE

As the power of Rome waned, barbarian groups began to put down permanent roots on former Roman territory and establish more settled forms of government. The most successful of the new states to emerge was the kingdom of the Franks.

At first a confederacy of Germanic tribes in the area of modern Belgium and Holland, the Franks were united under the leadership of Clovis (ruled 481–511 CE), who conquered most of the old Roman provinces of Gaul. Clovis also converted to Catholicism, a sharp divergence from the practice of many other Germanic kings, who had adopted a new form of Christianity called Arianism (after the 4th century priest Arius), which was regarded as heretical by other Christians. Clovis's descendants, the Merovingians, ruled France until the 8th century CE.

≪ Alaric, whose name means "king of all," was the Goths' greatest war leader. He led his tribe in a sack of Rome in 410 CE.

The Goths, who had threatened the Roman empire in the late 4th and early 5th centuries CE, split into two groups: Visigoths and Ostrogoths. The former settled in southwest France under Theoderic I, but in 507 CE were pushed out by the Franks, finally settling in Spain. The Ostrogoths, having stayed in the Balkans, moved to Italy in 488 CE at the urging of Zeno, the eastern Roman emperor, who wanted revenge against Odovacar—the deposer of the last western emperor, in 476 CE. By 493 CE Zeno was king of Italy, beginning a dynasty that lasted until the eastern Romans completed their reconquest of Italy in 554 CE.

⊠ The Battle of Tolbiac, recreated in this 19th-century painting, saw the Frankish king Clovis emerge victorious against a group named the Alamanns.

People of the steppes

The steppes—grasslands that stretch from Eastern Europe to China—have been home to nomadic and semi-nomadic groups for millennia. The history of the steppe people has been influenced by geography, while their migrations brought clashes with a range of powers, from the Romans in the west to the Parthians, Sassanids, and India's Mauryan empire in the east.

The Scythians

◴ **CENTRAL ASIA**   ⌛ **6TH CENTURY** BCE–**2ND CENTURY** CE

First mentioned in historical sources in the 6th century BCE, the Scythians seem to have migrated from central Asia to southern Russia at about that time. Their warriors fought with bows, arrows, and axes, and most often on horseback. They sported felt caps, and, except for some members of the aristocracy, wore little or no armor.

Culture and wealth

The Scythians possessed sizeable territories at different periods, although tracing them is made difficult by the tendency of Greek and Latin authors to refer indiscriminately to groups from the steppes as "Scythians."

One group, the "Royal Scyths," controlled an area around southern Russia, where stunning grave finds of gold artifacts point to a well-developed culture. By the 2nd century CE, the Scythians had been marginalized by Sarmatians—Iranian-speaking newcomers—who were in turn defeated by the Huns (*see facing page*) in the 4th century CE.

The Scythians have left a large number of pyramid-shaped burial mounds, known as *kurgans*, in the south Russian steppes, particularly at Pazyryk. In these they buried the mummified bodies of rulers, together with their horses and lavish grave-offerings of gold.

≪ **A gold comb** from a grave at Socha kurgan, depicting Scythians in battle; the mounted warrior bears equipment far superior to that of the soldiers on foot.

❝ Having **neither cities nor forts**, and **carrying** their **dwellings with them**… [the Scythians are] all **accustomed** to **shoot from horseback**.

Herodotus, *Histories*, c.430 BCE ❞

The Huns

S RUSSIA, CENTRAL EUROPE, THE BALKANS ⏳ **4TH AND 5TH CENTURIES** CE

First mentioned in the 370s CE, the Huns, who became the most feared and loathed of Rome's barbarian enemies, were most likely a composite group whose numbers were swelled by those they defeated.

In 434 CE, the Hunnish king Rua died and his nephew Attila initiated an increasingly aggressive policy, ravaging much of the Balkans and sacking a string of cities in 441–442 CE and again in 447 CE. In 451 CE, the Huns turned west toward the rich lands of Gaul, but were defeated by a last-ditch alliance of Romans under the general Aëtius and his barbarian allies.

Undaunted, Attila moved into Italy the following year, but was deflected from an attack on Rome, possibly by an outbreak of plague. After their father's death the year after that, Attila's sons failed to keep the empire together, and within 10 years the Huns had almost disappeared as an organized group.

⟫ ATTILA

Attila (ruled 434–453 CE) was known as "The Scourge of God" because he devastated swaths of Christian Roman territory. A ruthless warrior, he died as a result of overindulgence at his wedding feast.

The Kushans

CENTRAL ASIA, N INDIA ⏳ **1ST CENTURY** BCE–c.350 CE

Possibly originating in a nomadic group known to the Chinese as the Yuezhi, the Kushans (or Kusanas) dominated a region of northern India around the Punjab from the early 1st century CE.

The Kushan empire reached its zenith under Kanishka (c.78–100 CE), who ruled virtually all of northern India, including the great cities of Ujjain and Pataliputra. Under great pressure from the Sassanid Persians (see p.87) from the 220s CE, the Kushan empire fragmented and the rise of the Guptas to their south in the 320s CE finally put an end to their rule. Kushan art, influenced by Greece and Buddhism (to which they converted), is most notable for its elegant statues.

✉ **Although influenced by Zoroastrianism**, the Kushans converted to Buddhism and built temples such as this 4th-century CE example at Takht-i-Rustam, Afghanistan.

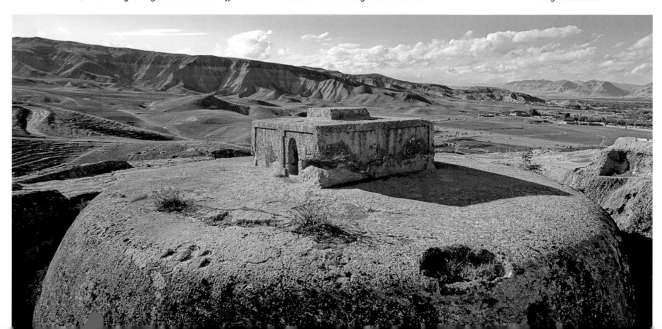

India

From the 4th century BCE, northern and central India came to be dominated by a series of empires, beginning with the Mauryan, which reached its greatest cultural flowering under the rule of Ashoka, a great promoter of Buddhism. After an interlude of Kushan rule, the Guptas then emerged to dominate India for 150 years, before attacks by the barbarian White Huns led to the region reverting to a collection of smaller kingdoms.

Chandragupta and the rise of the Mauryans

N AND CENTRAL INDIA c.321–185 BCE

Around 321 BCE, Chandragupta Maurya (ruled c.321–298 BCE) toppled the Nanda dynasty of Magadha, the most prosperous state in north India, to found the Mauryan empire.

Mauryan rule

By 303 BCE, Chandragupta had defeated the Seleucids, rulers of Persia, and had secured areas around modern Herat and in Baluchistan. He presided over a thriving agricultural state backed by a powerful army. His son Bindusara (ruled c.298–272 BCE) may have extended the Mauryan empire into south India, and his successor Ashoka (ruled c.268–232 BCE) conquered Kalinga (in modern Orissa) in 261–260 BCE. On Ashoka's death, the empire broke into western and eastern parts and, despite a brief reunification around 223 BCE, was gradually reduced to its heartland in Magadha. The assassination of the last emperor, Brihadratha, in 185 BCE brought the Mauryan era to an end.

✉ **The cave complex at Ajanta** in Maharashtra contains paintings that span the period of time from the 2nd century BCE to the Guptas in the 6th century CE.

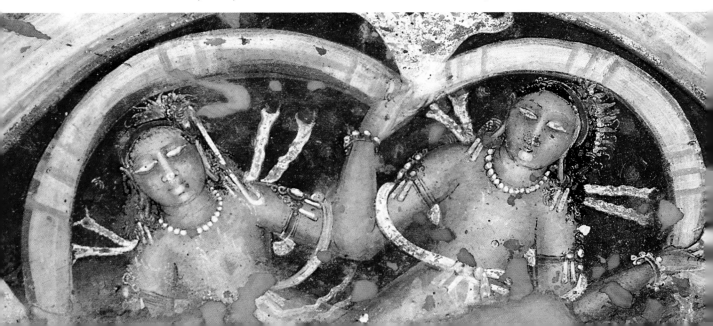

Ashoka and Buddhism

INDIA ⌛ **268–232** BCE

After a particularly bloody battle at Dayala in the state of Kalinga, where the rivers ran red with the blood of the slain, the Mauryan ruler Ashoka (*see facing page*) is said to have been stricken with remorse and converted to Buddhism. In 259 BCE, he toured his domains, spreading the Buddhist message of *dhamma*, or moral principles, and ordered the construction of stone pillars bearing edicts that promoted the Buddhist creed. He also sent missionaries abroad. Although Ashoka's reign was a period of peace and prosperity, subsequent Mauryan rulers were more concerned with war than with religion.

» **A metal relief of a symbol**—a group of four lions—that Ashoka chose to top many of the inscribed pillars he erected during the tour of his empire.

Gupta India

INDIA ⌛ **c.320–c.570** CE

After the Mauryans (*see facing page*), the Sungas briefly ruled central India until 73 BCE. Thereafter, save for a century of Kushan dominance in the late 1st and early 2nd centuries CE, no one group dominated as large an area as the Mauryans, until Chandragupta I (ruled c.320–330 CE) captured the old imperial capital of Pataliputra, resulting in the emergence of the Gupta empire around 320 CE.

Under Chandragupta II (ruled c.376–415 CE), the empire reached its greatest extent, defeating the Saka satraps (governors) who had ruled western India, and expanding eastward into Bengal. Under Kumara Gupta (ruled c.415–455 CE), incursions by the Hephtalites (or "White Huns") undermined the empire. By the mid-6th century CE, it was reduced to a small area around Magadha and then, around 570 CE, it disappeared entirely.

⌃ **Carvings from the temple complex** at Udayagiri in Orissa, India. Possibly begun in the 2nd century CE, the temples were in use into the Gupta period.

This 18th-century Indian miniature painting shows a conversation on the theme of righteousness between the god Krishna and Arjuna (in the central chariot), which forms the core of the Hindu devotional poem the *Bhagavad Gita*.

World religions

From the first millennium BCE, religions spread across huge areas. Hinduism and Buddhism made their way across Southeast Asia, while the Middle East saw the expanding influence of Judaism, followed by Christianity and Islam. By the 7th century CE, Hinduism and Buddhism were in retreat, and Christianity and Islam had taken root throughout the Roman and Sassanid Persian empires.

Hinduism

By the 6th century BCE, the ancient religion of India focused on three main gods: Brahma the creator; Vishnu the preserver; and Shiva the destroyer. Around 500 BCE, the main form of worship was Brahmanism, and about this time great epics such as the *Mahabharata* and *Ramayana* were composed. Hindu beliefs spread as far as Java (where they gave rise to the lavish temple complex at Prambanan in the 9th century CE), Bali (where they survive still), Angkor in Cambodia, and Champa in modern Vietnam.

◄ **Reverence for Shiva the destroyer** became one of the principal expressions of Hinduism, especially in southern Asia.

Buddhism

A royal prince born in northeast India around 563 BCE, Siddhartha Gautama turned his back on his wealth to develop Buddhism. Promoting an ascetic way of life and a set of moral values rather than belief in a god, Gautama (the Buddha) taught that the only way to escape *samsara*, the cycle of death and rebirth, was to achieve moral perfection. Initially finding great success under the Mauryan ruler Ashoka in the 2nd century BCE, Buddhism became almost extinct in India, but spread into China and Japan, becoming established there from the 7th century CE.

Monotheistic faiths

Judaism, the first monotheistic religion to spread widely, evolved from an older, ritualistic form attributed to Moses. By the time of the Roman empire, Jewish communities had become dispersed throughout the Mediterranean. Despite severe persecution, Judaism has never lost its status as a world religion. Christianity began as an offshoot of Judaism in the 1st century CE, but then became a distinct faith focused on the belief that Jesus Christ, the Son of God, died to atone for human sin. It endured waves of repression, notably under the Roman emperors Domitian in the late 1st century CE and Diocletian in the early 4th century CE. Yet once Emperor Constantine (ruled 306–337 CE) decreed its toleration in 313 CE, it became the empire's official religion and spread throughout the Roman world, reaching Germany, Russia, and Scandinavia by the 10th century.

The last principal monotheistic religion to emerge was Islam in Arabia in the 7th century CE, spread by the prophet Muhammad. His supporters proclaimed that he had received a divine revelation, encapsulated in the Qur'an. Arab armies inspired by Islam swept through the Near East and North Africa, reaching Spain by 711 CE.

⌃ **This 4th-century** Christian artifact is a bronze lamp in the form of a boat carrying St. Peter and St. Paul.

⌄ **The stupas and Buddha images** constructed around 800 CE at Borobodur in Java are among the world's most expressive images of Buddhism.

China

By the 5th century BCE, China had disintegrated into a number of competing kingdoms known as the Warring States. The state of Qin conquered these one by one, and had defeated them all by 221 BCE under Qin Shi Huang, the first emperor of a united China. He brought a period of stability and prosperity to China, but the Qin dynasty did not survive for long. Around 200 BCE the Han seized power, and would rule China for some four centuries.

The warring states

CHINA   475–221 BCE

The Zhou dynasty that followed the Shang (see p.77) was the last of the pre-imperial dynasties. The Zhou lasted longer than any other dynasty in Chinese history, but from around 722 BCE, it disintegrated into a number of independent states. From 475 BCE, China entered the Warring States period, when a series of conflicts between the minor territorial overlords led to a process of gradual consolidation. By the 3rd century BCE, there were just seven competing states, the most powerful of which was the state of Qin.

In 356 BCE, the chief minister of Qin, Shang Yang, established a new political philosophy—known as Legalism—based on rule of law, with a new legal code that diluted the power of the nobles and increased that of the ruler. The whole power of the state was directed toward warfare, with all adult males registered for military service. By about 230 BCE, Qin was ready to begin the conquest of its remaining rivals.

◁ **A bronze lei, or wine vessel**, from the Warring States period. Despite the political chaos that characterized this time, it also saw cultural achievements.

The First Emperor

CHINA ⏳ 246–206 BCE

In 246 BCE, Qin Shi Huang ascended to the throne of Qin. An energetic and ruthless ruler, from 230 BCE he set about the absorption of all the other Chinese states, completing the process with the conquest of Qi in 221 BCE. Having secured his position as the "First Emperor," Qin Shi Huang began a series of reforms to consolidate his rule.

The First Emperor's reforms

Under the guidance of his chief minister Li Si, Qin Shi Huang put into place Legalist reforms, abolishing feudal fiefs and decreeing the adoption of a standardized written script and the establishment of official measurements for weights and lengths. In 213–212 BCE he ordered the burning of books that criticized his policies, and conducted a purge of scholars, executing some 450 of them. Qin Shi Huang reinforced

China's frontiers: his general Meng Tian constructed a defensive wall in the Ordos region of Inner Mongolia (the forerunner of the Great Wall of China); and he also had the Straight Road built, which ran 500 miles (800 km) from the capital Xianyang to the Ordos region, to allow for the rapid transport of troops. He also sent troops to conquer new lands in Guangdong.

The end of Qin

Eventually, Qin Shi Huang's energies waned and he became obsessed with securing his own immortality. By the time the First Emperor died in 210 BCE, China was afflicted by popular uprisings and factional plotting at court. Although Qin Shi Huang had claimed his dynasty would last for endless generations, by 206 BCE Xianyang had been burned and Ziying, the last Qin emperor, had been deposed.

◀ **Near the burial chamber** of Qin Shi Huang's mausoleum stood an army of terracotta warriors, intended to defend the First Emperor in death.

Han China

🏴 CHINA ⧖ 206 BCE–220 CE

The fall of Qin was accompanied by a complex civil war from which Liu Bang, who had captured the Qin capital of Xianyang in 206 BCE, finally emerged victorious after a decisive battle four years later at Gaixia (in modern Anhui province). He assumed the imperial title of Gaozu and began the Han dynasty, which went on to rule China for some 400 years.

The rule of Gaozu

Gaozu established a new capital at Chang'an, simplified court ritual, and, as a counterpoint to the old regime's political philosophy of Legalism (*see p.124*), encouraged the rise of Confucianism, with the emperor becoming the center of a state cult. He also strengthened central rule with the

◀ A later Han glazed ceramic model of a watchtower, displaying precise architectural detail. Such pieces were often intended for the tombs of important personages.

organization of commanderies (military districts) intended to avoid any return to the chaos of the Warring States. Gaozu did, however, tolerate the existence of ten semi-independent kingdoms to the north and east. Han China retained a strong bureaucracy, with a formal hierarchy established by the end of Gaozu's reign, in a decree of 196 BCE.

The height of the Han

Under Wudi (ruled 141–87 BCE), the Han reached the height of their dominance. Wudi cut down the remaining powers of the aristocrats, relying on a hand-picked civil service; in 124 BCE an academy was inaugurated for future officeholders. In 115 BCE he also established state granaries to keep prices under government control.

Wudi expanded the borders of the Chinese empire, fighting a long series of wars against the nomadic Xiongnu in the north from 114 to 91 BCE, but achieving greatest success in the northeast,

where he established four commanderies in Korea after 128 BCE, and in the south, where he occupied parts of Guangdong, Guangzi, and north Vietnam from 111 BCE. Yet the latter part of the emperor's reign was marred by his increased introspection and his search for immortality. His successors were generally feeble and the court became dominated by eunuchs. The economy was undermined by financial mismanagement and the state weakened by widespread tax evasion.

Wang Mang and the later Han

In 9 CE, Wang Mang, the regent for a succession of child emperors, usurped the Han throne. He ordered large private estates to be broken up and began a program of reforms, including restrictions on slavery. But a catastrophic famine that had begun when the Yellow River changed its course in 11 CE led to widespread peasant uprisings, and in 25 CE the Han were restored under Guang Wudi. A new capital was set up at Luoyang, but it took 11 years to put down a series of pretenders who claimed the right to succeed

» LIU BANG

Born into poverty, Liu Bang was initially a supporter of Xian Yu, an aristocrat opposed to Qin rule. Yet he managed to build his own army and capture the Qin capital Xianyang in 206 BCE. He never learned to read, and distrusted court protocol, making him popular outside court circles.

Wang Mang. The Han never regained its former power. A revolt by the Yellow Turban religious sect from 184 to 186 CE, and the brutal massacre of hundreds of court officials by a ruling eunuch clique in 189 CE, fueled the chaos. In 196 CE, the general Cao Cao assumed power, ruling through a Han puppet, but after his death in 220 CE even this pretense was dropped and the dynasty ended.

China's first emperor had sought to protect a unified China within a protective wall, but internal conflicts became a greater threat in the centuries to follow.

The Americas

During the "Classic" period, from around 200 BCE, several cultures flourished in Central America. The Olmecs were superseded by a number of new groups, including the inhabitants of Teotihuacán, the Zapotecs of the Mexican Gulf coast, and, especially, the Maya civilization, which spread throughout southern Mexico, the Yucatán, and Guatemala. In South America, regional cultures, including Moche, Nazca, and Paracas, succeeded the Chavín of Peru.

Teotihuacán

CENTRAL MEXICO   2ND TO 7TH CENTURY CE

The greatest Classic period Mexican city was Teotihuacán. From the 2nd century CE, this enormous urban area was laid out on a grid pattern, its major axis (the "Avenue of the Dead") running 3½ miles (6 km) roughly north–south. At the center of the axis was a large palace complex, and at its northernmost reach the great Pyramid of the Moon. At its southern end was the Pyramid of the Sun, built with some 42 million cubic feet (1.2 million cubic meters) of sun-dried bricks and stone.

By the 4th century CE, Teotihuacán's population was as high as 200,000, and its influence spread throughout Mexico. Its wealth derived from its control of the resources of the fertile Valley of Mexico and domination of trade routes as far as the Gulf and Pacific coasts of Mexico. Teotihuacán ware has been found as far afield as the Maya city of Kaminaljuyu in Guatemala.

The end of Teotihuacán

At some time during the 7th century CE, Teotihuacán's palaces were burned and its temples defaced. What crisis precipitated the vandalism is unknown. The abandoned city was thereafter treated by successive Mexican cultures, including the Aztecs, with almost reverential awe.

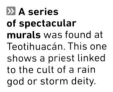

» A series of spectacular murals was found at Teotihuacán. This one shows a priest linked to the cult of a rain god or storm deity.

The Zapotecs

⚑ VALLEY OF OAXACA, MEXICO ⚒ c.500 BCE–c.900 CE

Around 500 BCE, a powerful new regional culture, the Zapotecs, arose in the Valley of Oaxaca near Mexico's Gulf coast, based around the city of Monte Albán. Built on a leveled hilltop site, the city flourished for more than 1,000 years.

One of the city's most evocative monuments is the Temple of the Danzantes, containing hundreds of carvings of men in distorted postures, their disarticulated limbs and closed eyes probably indicating that they represent not dancers ("Danzantes") as was once thought, but the chiefs of rival cities killed by Monte Albán's rulers. Carved glyphs on the Danzantes stones reveal that the Zapotecs used a sophisticated calendar and writing system.

⏵⏵ A Zapotec deity is depicted on an urn dating from Monte Albán's Classic period, around 200 to 350 CE.

The Classic period and decline

By its Classic period, from 200 CE, Monte Albán had a population of about 25,000, with a series of satellite settlements on the lower ground surrounding the city. Around 170 subterranean tombs of nobles have been found from this period.

Between 150 BCE and 150 CE, the city grew further with the building of a grand main plaza. A series of inscriptions here that feature upside-down disembodied heads are likely to refer to expansion by conquest. But by 900 CE, the urban center of Monte Albán was mostly deserted. No one knows why the site was abandoned, but it was to remain empty until partial reuse by the Mixtec culture in the 12th and 13th centuries CE.

⏷ Most early Mesoamerican cultures played a very similar, ritualized "ball game" on spectacular sloping or terraced courts; this is the court at Monte Albán.

Classic Maya culture

CENTRAL AMERICA 🗺 **c.300–c.900 CE**

At its height (some 600 years referred to as the "Classic" period) the Maya culture flourished over a wide swath of Central America, especially the Yucatán peninsula and Guatemala's jungle-clad lowlands. At its heart stood a number of important cities. Originally ritual centers, many grew into populous city-states. The Maya built huge, often pyramidal stone temples, such as those at Tikal in Guatemala, and showed a great talent for carved stone and stucco (plaster) reliefs, with some especially fine examples at Palenque in Mexico.

Maya culture

Maya cities featured palaces, open plazas, and terraces, as well as courts where the Maya people played their sacred ball game. Religious ritual played a major part in Maya life.

The Maya practiced a form of "auto-sacrifice," in which they pierced their own body parts to release blood as an offering to the gods, but more extreme reports of human sacrifice seem to be unfounded. The Maya developed a sophisticated writing system using some 800 characters, or glyphs. They also had a complex calendrical system, featuring a 260-day sacred year and a 365-day solar year.

Maya history

Before Maya glyphs were deciphered in the 20th century, little was known of the history of the various city-states, such as Tikal and Palenque. But the glyphs have revealed an area riven by constant war, with unstable dynasties making rapid conquests and then vanishing into obscurity. The city of Yaxchilán, for example, produced one of the greatest Classic-period kings, Bird Jaguar IV (ruled 752–768 CE), who conquered a number of neighboring lords and erected many new buildings, but within a generation of his death the city had stagnated.

▽ **One of the pyramidal Maya temples** at Palenque in Mexico, a city whose power reached its zenith under the rule of K'inich Janaab' Pakal from 615 to 683 CE.

Early South America

PERU ⌛ c.500 bce–c.600 ce

(see p.78)

⟨⟨ **Perhaps the most famous** of the Nazca Desert images (or geogylphs), the spiral-tailed monkey is reminiscent of the spider monkeys found in Peru's jungles.

From around 500 bce, a number of regional cultures began to supplant Peru's Chavín culture (*see p.78*). The Paracas people, who flourished in southern coastal Peru between 500 bce and 200 ce, adopted many elements of Chavín iconography, including the feline representations that appear on their pots. The dry climate, which allowed bodies to be mummified, also preserved beautiful textiles, lavishly decorated with mythical creatures and more earthly animals. The largest cache of mummies, around 430, was found at Wari Kayan on the Paracas peninsula, all wrapped in textiles and accompanied by grave goods such as gold ornaments.

The Nazca

The Nazca culture flourished in the south of Peru from around 200 bce to 500 ce. While largely a village-dwelling people, the Nazca did construct some imposing architectural complexes, such as the monumental religious center at Cahuachi, which dates from around 100 ce. Although their textiles, metalwork, and pottery are of high quality, they are better known for the vast drawings that they made in the desert. They created a range of animal pictures and abstract representations by clearing stones from the desert surface and exposing the subsoil to create lines. The patterns, some of them many miles long, can be fully seen only from the air. Spectacular examples include a depiction of a hummingbird sucking nectar, a plant, and a monkey with a coiled tail. Their precise purpose is unknown.

The Moche

In Peru's northern valleys, the Moche came to dominate from around 100 ce. Talented craftsmen, they constructed large pyramids, known as *huacas*, and are particularly noted for their fine textiles, metalwork, and pottery. From great centers such as Huaca del Sol, with its flat-topped pyramids, the Moche rulers held sway over a predominantly agricultural society. Then, from around 300 ce, larger urban centers arose, the Moche expanded into southern regions, and indications of large-scale warfare appear (often depicted on the pottery). In the late 6th century ce, environmental disasters such as drought and flooding seem to have undermined the Moche's stability, and their culture collapsed.

⌃ **Typical Moche cups**, this one in the form of a fox-headed human, feature a "stirrup" handle/spout.

The Medieval World

The world in 600–1450

Following the collapse of the western Roman Empire in the 5th century CE, civilization in Europe fell behind the rest of the world for almost a thousand years. In this period China proved to be politically strong and technologically innovative under the Tang and Song dynasties, while much of the Middle East and

The world in 1300

———	International border
·········	Undefined border
	Byzantine Empire
	England and possessions
	Aragon and possessions
	Venetian Republic and possessions
	Denmark and possessions
	France
	Castile
	Portugal
	Mongol Empire on death of Genghis Khan 1227 controlled by Khwarizm Shah 1219
	Holy Roman Empire

NOTE: Settlements in italics were not in existence in 1300 but were significant during this chapter's era.

North Africa was united under an Arab Empire inspired by the new religion of Islam. The Americas, India, and Southeast Asia were also dominated by distinctive cultures. However, from the late medieval period movements began to emerge in Europe that would ultimately lead to European domination of the globe.

The medieval world in 1300

By 1300, large parts of Eurasia were dominated by the Mongols. Areas of northern India, North Africa, and the Middle East were controlled by various Muslim rulers, such as the Mamluks in Egypt. In Mexico, the empire of the Aztecs was just beginning to expand, while the Incas had only just settled around Cuzco in Peru.

⌃ **The feudal monarchies** of England and France had consolidated into large regional states by 1300, but conflict between popes and emperors prevented this process in the rest of Europe. In Spain, the Christian states of Castile and Aragon had reconquered much of the peninsula from Muslim emirates, leaving only Granada outside their control.

East and Southeast Asia

The early Middle Ages saw the rise of sophisticated new cultures and centralized states in East and Southeast Asia: Japan, Korea, Angkor (Cambodia), Pagan (Burma), and Dai-Viet (Vietnam) all flourished under new kingdoms. China, after a period of disunity, reunited under the Tang dynasty in 618 (and their Song successors from 960), and reached astounding technological and artistic heights.

China disunited

CHINA | **221–618 CE**

In 221 CE, the Han dynasty that had ruled China for 400 years (*see pp.126–7*) collapsed amid a welter of uprisings. China split into the Three Kingdoms: the Wei in the north, the Shu in the southwest, and the Wu in the southeast. Their rivalry is recounted in the great 14th-century Chinese novel *The Romance of the Three Kingdoms*, but in truth there was little romance about it, and the struggle left China debilitated by warfare.

The rise of the Sui

The Wei conquered the Shu in 264 CE and, under a dynasty called the Western Jin, overcame the Wu in 280 CE, but the period of unity was brief. Under pressure from northern nomadic groups called the Xiongnu and Xiangbei, the Western Jin buckled, their capital Luoyang was sacked, and China fell apart, with the Sixteen Kingdoms ruling the north, and the Six Dynasties holding sway over the south. Finally, the north of China was united in 577 CE, and in 588 CE Yangdi—first emperor of the Sui dynasty—launched an invasion of south China. Only a matter of months later, the last Southern Jin emperor surrendered his capital at Jiankang (modern Nanjing), and China's three centuries of disunity was over.

◀ **A guardian deity** at the Jinci temple, Shanxi province. The temple was restored and enlarged during Wei rule.

Tang China

CHINA ⚊ **618–907**

In 617, Li Yuan, a frontier general, rose up against the Sui dynasty (*see facing page*), which was exhausted following an ill-fated invasion of Korea. Capturing the Sui capital Chang'an late that year, by 624 Li Yuan had secured all of China and ruled as Gaozu, the first emperor of the Tang. The dynasty is associated with prosperity, especially under Gaozu's successor Taizong (ruled 626–649).

Tang rule

Taizong set up state schools and colleges and reintroduced the Han system of examinations for those wanting to work in official positions. Tang armies expanded into central Asia, defeating the Turks at Issyk Kul, in modern-day Kyrgyzstan, in 657 and advancing as far west as the borders of Persia.

China attained a new level of cultural influence, with Chang'an, the terminus of the Silk Road, bringing in traders from across Asia, while painting and literature reached greater heights of sophistication. Late in the reign of Xuanzong (712–756), however, aristocratic factionalism led to a large-scale rebellion led by An Lushan in 755. Although this was finally put down in 763, the Tang never regained their authority, and in 907 the last Tang emperor, Ai, was killed by one of his generals. China split apart once more.

⟫ GAOZU (LI YUAN)

From a noble family, Li Yuan served as a general during the Sui attack on Korea in 613. When Emperor Yang was killed in a military coup in 618, Li Yuan took advantage of the chaos to push aside the last Sui emperor and seize power himself.

> **❝** Have I not heard that **pure wine makes a sage**, and even **muddy wine** can make **a man wise**? **❞**
>
> From *Drinking Alone in the Moonlight*, by Tang "god of poetry" Li Bai, c.710–762

⟪ The head of a colossal Buddha statue, some 233 ft (71 m) tall, carved on a cliff near Leshan around 713 during the early Tang dynasty.

Song China

CHINA ⌛ **960–1279**

⌃ **A Song Yaozhu-style** vessel, delicately carved in a fashion typical of the dynasty.

The first half of the 10th century was a period of disunity for China. A succession of Five Dynasties ruled the north, while the south fragmented into Ten Kingdoms. Zhao Kuangyin, a general under the Later Zhou, the last of the Five Dynasties, usurped the throne in 960 to found the Song dynasty.

Song prosperity

Under the Song, China was reunited and entered a period of economic achievement, introducing the first paper currency in 1024 and developing new methods of rice farming that doubled output.

A series of waterways improved China's infrastructure, and a fairer system for awarding the *jinshi* degree for officials overhauled the bureaucracy, so that a wider range of people could rise through the ranks.

The decline of the Song

In 1068, the emperor of the time, Shenzong, entrusted his minister Wang Anshi with the task of implementing radical reforms. Wang Anshi needed to raise money. He imposed a government monopoly on tea and challenged wealthy families who evaded taxes. To reduce the cost of the standing army, he ordered every household to supply men for a local militia. This measure was highly unpopular and Wang Anshi was dismissed, but the dynasty was weakened.

Then in 1125, the Jurchen, semi-nomads from Manchuria, captured the capital Kaifeng and the Song court fled south. The southern Song emperors, based at Hangzhou, could never regain control over the north. The dynasty was culturally dynamic, developing Neo-Confucianism—which stressed self-cultivation and conformity to Confucian ideals—but it was enfeebled politically and militarily.

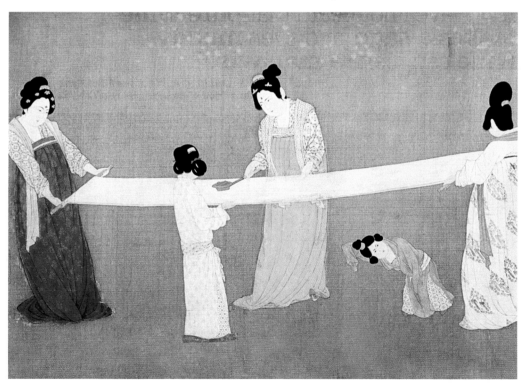

≫ **Ladies of the Song court** are shown ironing silk in this painting by the eighth Song emperor Huizong, a patron of the arts and an accomplished artist himself.

Mongol and Ming China

CHINA **1279–1644**

In 1279, the southern Song were overrun by the Mongol armies of Kublai Khan (*see pp.142–3*). The Jin of northern China had already been pushed aside by the Mongols in 1234, so China became united under the Mongol rule of the Yuan dynasty. The Mongols imported a military elite whose cultural differences from the native Chinese hindered integration. By the 1350s, dissatisfaction with Yuan rule led to a series of revolts, including, from 1351, that of the Red Turban Army. From the ranks of this army rose Zhu Yuanzhang, who outfoxed his rivals in a complex civil war to seize power as the first Ming emperor, known as Hongwu, in 1368.

China under the Ming

The Ming ruled China for some 250 years, presiding over the growth of a vigorous urban culture. Emperor Hongwu reformed the army and the taxation regime, instituting a system of secret agents to cement his rule. In 1403, Emperor Yongle transferred the capital from Nanjing to Beijing, and dispatched a number of ambitious maritime expeditions, led by the eunuch Zhen He, that reached as far as east Africa. Later emperors, however, were weaker and the reforming instinct of the first rulers gave way to inactivity and conservatism. By the mid-17th century, the Ming's hold on power had become brittle.

⌃ **The Pavilion of Myriad** Springs in the Imperial Garden of the Forbidden City, Beijing, which was built in 1535 under the Ming dynasty.

⟫ THE EMPEROR YONGLE

The third emperor of the Ming dynasty, Yongle ascended the throne after overthrowing his older brother Jiangwen in 1403. He oversaw an expansive phase in Ming history, sending expeditions north to smash the remnants of the Yuan, and in 1406 dispatched an army south that crushed the rulers of Vietnam and absorbed it as a Chinese province. At his new capital of Beijing, Yongle also constructed the vast palace complex of the Forbidden City.

>> **The Forbidden City**, situated in Beijing, China, was constructed under Emperor Yongle of the Ming dynasty between 1406 and 1420. For almost five centuries, until the fall of the Qing dynasty in 1912, it served a dual role as the home of the emperor and the center of Chinese government.

The Mongols

◾ CENTRAL ASIA, E EUROPE, CHINA, SE ASIA ◾ 1206–1405

Before the early 13th century, a number of nomadic groups to the north and west of China periodically entered the settled regions. Some were defeated in battle, others contained, and others still assimilated into Chinese culture. The Mongols were one of these groups, but they were hopelessly disunited until the leadership of Temüjin, who took the title Genghis Khan in 1206. Proclaiming his supreme rule, he welded together the Mongol clans, whose domination of the steppes and neighboring lands would continue for more than a century.

The Mongol conquests

By 1218, Genghis had overcome the Kara Khitan khanate of central Asia, and he then unleashed a devastating three-year campaign against the Khwarezmid empire that controlled much of modern Iran and Afghanistan. It was during this time that the Mongols earned their reputation as merciless fighters, sacking the Silk Road cities of Samarkand and Bukhara and slaughtering the populations of any town that dared resist. The Mongols, excellent horsemen who were highly mobile and able to strike with speed, proved formidable enemies even for well-organized states.

Genghis died in 1227, and in 1229, Ogedei—who had inherited the title of "Great Khan"—sent the Mongol armies into China, pushing the Jin (*see p.139*) out of the north of the country by 1234. Ogedei then dispatched his horde westward, overrunning almost the whole of Russia, including Kiev, its most important city, by 1240. Still the Mongol appetite for territorial aggrandizement seemed unabated, and the following year their defeat of a Polish-German army at Legnica, Poland, struck terror in those farther west, who thought their turn would come next. The death of Ogedei in 1241, however, caused the Mongol army to withdraw while the Mongols chose a successor.

Later Mongol rulers

Mongke, who was selected as Great Khan in 1251, campaigned in northern China and against the Abbasid caliphate (*see p.155*) in the Middle East, sacking Baghdad in 1258. Shortly after his death in 1260, the Egyptian Mamluks (slave

⬙ A set of Mongol knives, part of the arsenal of weaponry with which Genghis Khan's army spread terror as it swept aside all opposition.

> ❝ In **military exercises** I am always in **front** and in time of **battle** I am **never behind**. ❞

Words attributed to Genghis Khan by a Chinese monk, c.1224

soldiers) defeated a small Mongol army at Ain Jalut, puncturing the Mongols' reputation for invincibility. In the 1270s, Kublai Khan concentrated his attentions on southern China (*see p.139*), and the Mongols ruled China until 1368. They dominated central Asia for a century after that, but the only real resurgence in their power came under Tamerlane, from 1370 to 1405, who united a large part of central Asia and very nearly destroyed the Ottoman Turkish empire (*see p.157*).

▽ **The citadel of Aleppo in Syria**, which was captured by the Mongols in spring 1260, marking the high point of their success in the Near East.

❯❯ GENGHIS KHAN

Born in 1162 as Temüjin to a family of minor chieftains, Genghis Khan spent much of his childhood as a precarious semi-outlaw. He earned a military reputation in minor skirmishes against the Chinese, eventually securing a leading position among the tribes. In 1206, he was proclaimed Genghis Khan, or "universal ruler," going on to command a feared army of more than 200,000 men. He is thought to have died following a riding accident in 1227, and was buried according to custom in an unmarked grave in Mongolia.

Early Japan

JAPAN ⌛ **5TH CENTURY** BCE **TO 551** CE

The earliest recognized Japanese culture, the Jomon—who were predominantly hunters and fishermen—transformed under Chinese influence into the Yayoi culture around the 5th century BCE. Yayoi people lived in small farming communities in square or circular pit dwellings with thatched roofs. They were expert potters and stonemasons, and began a long tradition of Japanese metalworking, especially in bronze.

From around the middle of the 3rd century CE, the Yayoi began to build large stone burial chambers and huge earthen tomb mounds (or *kofun*). Paintings found within these tombs, showing warriors wearing elaborate armor, indicate a powerful aristocracy.

The Yamato

Japan's villages gradually coalesced into larger communities and, in the 4th century CE—possibly under the influence of Korean refugees fleeing from a Chinese invasion in 369—a larger kingdom emerged in southern Japan, on the Yamato plain. From then until the 6th century CE, the Yamato kings unified Japan.

Terracotta figures or *haniwa* were ritually placed around Yayoi burial mounds.

The Asuka and Nara periods

JAPAN ⌛ **552–794**

The arrival of Buddhism in Japan in 552 CE marks the beginning of the Asuka period. The regent Shotoku Taishi (574–622) founded the great monastery at Horyuji, and promoted Chinese models in politics, art, and religion.

In 710, the Japanese capital was fixed at Nara, and Buddhism became more dominant in court life, especially during the reign of Shomu (724–749), who ordered the erection of the Great Buddha figure inaugurated at Nara's Todaiji temple in 752. Shomu was the first emperor to retire and become a Buddhist monk. Buddhism became so powerful that in 784, anti-Buddhist factions moved the imperial court north to Nagaoka to distance it from the old capital's monasteries. A decade later, it moved again, this time to Kyoto.

The Gojunoto (five-storied) pagoda in the Horyuji temple complex, founded by Shotoku in the 6th century, is the oldest wooden pagoda in Japan.

The Heian period

JAPAN ⏳ 794–1185

In 794, the Japanese court moved to Kyoto, and the 400 years that followed is known as the Heian period. It was marred early on by a struggle to put down a rebellion in northern Japan. The rebellion was finally crushed around 801 by Tamura Maro, who was consequently honored with the title *sei tai-shogun* ("barbarian-crushing general"), the first holder of the title in Japanese history. In 858, Fujiwara Yoshifusa became regent for the young emperor Seiwa, beginning a domination of the court by the Fujiwara family that would last for more than 300 years.

◀ **A painted scroll** illustrating a scene from *The Tale of Genji*, a novel of Japanese courtly life.

Japan under the Fujiwara

The most powerful of the Fujiwara regents was Michinaga, who held sway from 995 to 1027, assisted by the marriage of four of his daughters to successive emperors. The Fujiwara period saw great cultural achievements, among them the *The Tale of Genji*—written, unusually, by a female author, the Lady Murasaki Shikibu—which encapsulates beautifully the refined aesthetic taste of the period.

After Michinaga, the Fujiwara's power declined somewhat and an emperor named Go-Sanjo briefly managed to dispense with a Fujiwara regent. Under his successor, Shirakawa (ruled 1073–1087), the curious practice of "cloistered emperors" (*insei*) emerged, whereby the emperor would abdicate in favor of a child successor and retire to a monastery but still, to some extent, direct affairs from there. This did nothing to temper the growing powers of warring clans, who were rivals to the Fujiwara. The tensions erupted into the Gempei Wars (1180–1185), a bitter struggle for dominance between the powerful Minamoto and Taira families.

▲ **This fine sculpture** of a fierce guardian king, created during the Fujiwara period, is typical of the high level of craftsmanship of the time.

The Kamakura and Muromachi shogunates

JAPAN ⏳ **1185–1573**

In the early 1180s, the Gempei Wars racked Japan until Minamoto Yoritomo triumphed after a great naval victory at Dan-no-Ouro in 1185. However, peace did not come until the early 1190s, as Yoritomo—who in 1192 became "shogun" (or military dictator)—subdued or killed any remaining lords who seemed to threaten his authority, including his longtime ally Yoshitsune, the victorious general at Dan-no-Ouro.

The samurai and shogun power

From the factionalism of the Gempei Wars emerged the samurai, originally rough fighting men who evolved into a striking mix of the savage and the refined. The ideal warrior was as capable of dashing off a poem as he was of slicing off an enemy's head with his two-handed sword. He subscribed to an austere code of honor and, rather than face defeat, would commit ritual suicide (*seppuku*) by disemboweling himself. The emperors of the time, although occasionally seeking to assert themselves, were largely powerless. Instead, the shoguns, based from 1185 to 1336 at the Minamoto center of Kamakura, acted through a council and judicial board of enquiry that largely bypassed the imperial court at Kyoto. For much of the 13th century, the power of the shogunate was itself subverted by the regent, a position that was held by ten successive generations of the powerful Hojo clan.

» ASHIKAGA TAKAUJI

Among the most ruthless samurai, Ashikaga Takauji was employed by the Hojo regent to crush the revolt of Emperor Go-Daigo in 1333, but changed sides and restored imperial power. After 1335, he broke also with the imperial court and declared himself shogun.

» **A scene from the** *Tamamo-no-mae*, written during the Muromachi era, which tells of a beautiful courtesan who turns out to be the spirit of a malevolent fox.

The end of Kamakura power

Attempts by the Mongols to invade in 1274 and 1281 were the only real threat to Japan during this time. The samurai pushed back the first attack, and a great storm, called the *kamikaze* ("divine wind"), ended the second. In 1333, Emperor Go-Daigo tried to impose his direct rule, attracting some support from the nobility. The Kamakura shogun sent general Ashikaga Takauji to punish this presumptuousness, but the general defected and captured Kyoto in the name of the restored emperor. Kamakura was burned and the last Hojo regent deposed.

Go-Daigo's rejoicing did not last long, as his two generals Takauji and Nitta Yoshisada quarreled. The emperor supported Yoshisada, but Takauji won the power struggle. While Go-Daigo established an alternative court in the Yoshino mountains south of Kyoto, Takauji appointed a new emperor—Komyo—and declared himself shogun, the first of the Ashikaga period.

The Muromachi shogunate

The Ashikaga shogunate (from 1392 referred to as the Muromachi) ruled Japan for 240 years. It took nearly 60 years of intermittent war before Yoshimitsu, the third Ashikaga shogun, suppressed Go-Daigo's rival court at Yoshino and restored the imperial regalia to Kyoto. Then, for five decades, Japan experienced peace and a cultural renaissance. However, peasant risings followed famine and plague in the 1420s, and when Shogun Yoshimasa retired in 1467, civil war (the Onin War) broke out over the succession. A tense peace was restored in 1477, but central authority was disrupted, and real power rested with the regional *daimyo* (warlords). This led to a Japan that was unified in theory, but wholly disunited in practice.

» **The curved samurai sword** or *katana*, the samurai's badge of office, was made of hard layers of tempered steel that gave it an extremely sharp cutting edge.

Gunpowder weaponry

Europe adopted gunpowder in the 14th century, but it was not a European innovation—the Chinese had used it for centuries. It was, however, in Europe that its rapid spread and refinement led to a revolution in military tactics, and, ultimately, to the development of handheld weapons and field artillery of massive power with which European armies would come to dominate the battlefield.

⏫ **This early Chinese** gunpowder weapon fires a volley of arrows from a bamboo launching tube.

Early gunpowder

The earliest recipe for gunpowder was recorded in China around 1040, and the Chinese may have used gunpowder offensively in "fire-lances" as early as 1182. Yet, it was not until the Ming dynasty, in the 14th and 15th centuries, that the Chinese began to use gunpowder weapons on a wider scale, with innovations such as the deployment of dragoons, or mounted gunners.

By then, the technology had been exported to Europe. The English first used cannons at Crécy in 1346, but these early firearms were liable to overheat or explode. More reliable mobile artillery came with the introduction of iron—rather than stone—cannon balls, which meant that the guns could be smaller, and the development of faster-burning gunpowder around 1420. The French defeat of the English at Castillon in 1453 was the first example of a battle won through the use of such artillery.

Handguns

The 1450s saw the development of the first handguns. Called arquebuses, these muzzle-loaded weapons were fired by a matchlock mechanism, which allowed for reloading during combat. These firearms were able to pierce plate armor. However, reloading was slow, and the

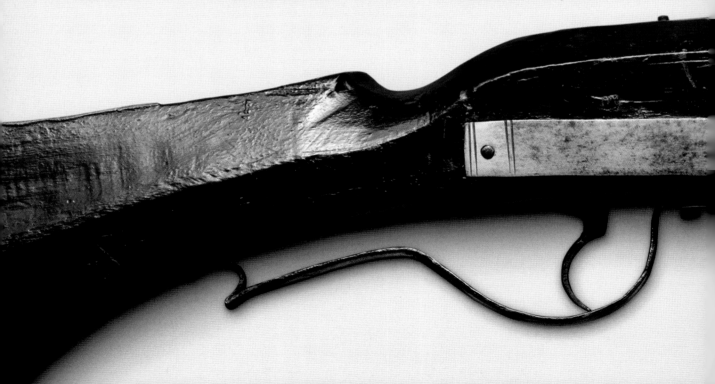

arquebusiers, as they were called, therefore needed to be protected by groups of pikemen (in a formation known as the Swiss phalanx).

Artillery

By the early 16th century, technological advances had boosted the capabilities of artillery. Trunnions—protrusions from the barrel of the gun—allowed it to be raised or lowered easily, vastly improving aim. Cities that had previously been protected by thick walls became vulnerable, and warfare returned to a pattern of field engagements.

The spread of firearms

During the Italian Wars (1494–1559), gunpowder weapons came of age. At the Battle of Ravenna in 1512, a two-hour artillery duel opened the fighting. Arquebusiers played a vital role in the decisive Imperial victory at the Battle of Pavia in 1525. New weapons appeared, notably the musket, which, although heavier than the arquebus and requiring a stand to allow the musketeer to fire it, had greater force and range. Although firearms were most advanced in Europe at this time, Asian

The French army bombards a city's walls using new cannon weaponry during the Hundred Years' War (1337–1453).

powers, such as China, had also continued their development. The Chinese, for example, devised a primitive form of machine gun in the 16th century.

Firearms spread into Japan and India, too, so that by the end of the 16th century, wherever there was conflict, it was almost bound to involve the use of gunpowder weaponry. Those cultures without firearms, such as the Aztecs and Incas in the Americas, and most sub-Saharan African peoples, became relatively easy prey once the gun-wielding Europeans arrived.

Matchlock muskets were a huge technological advance, and were effective at ranges of up to 330 ft (100 m). Their simple design meant that they were used in Europe up until the 18th century.

Medieval Korea

KOREA 108 BCE–1910 CE

The Korean peninsula was subject to Chinese influence from very early times. In 108 BCE, it was conquered by Han armies (*see p.127*), who established a series of commanderies there. With the decline of the Han from the 1st century BCE, three rival kingdoms vied for control of Korea: Silla in the southeast, Baekje in the southwest, and Koguryo in the north. A small group of city-states known as Kaya also flourished in the southeast from around 40 to 532 CE, escaping the grasp of their larger neighbors.

The unification of Korea

The protracted struggle for supremacy between Silla, Baekje, and Koguryo lasted until 668 and is known as the Three Kingdoms period. Silla, founded in 57 BCE, emerged as the most powerful of the three. Under King Beophung (ruled 514–540 CE), who adopted Buddhism,

> ## ⟩⟩ WANG GEON
>
> The founder of the Goryeo dynasty, Wang Geon (ruled 918–943) had been a general to the anti-Silla rebel Gung Ye, who created the state of Taebong with Wang Geon as prime minister. When Gung Ye's rule grew tyrannical, Wang Geon deposed him.

the Silla encroached on Baekje's territory. Baekje had been a conduit for Buddhism into Korea in the 4th century, thanks to close ties to Japan and China. After the kingdom's eventual fall to Silla in 660, many Baekje nobles fled to Japan, becoming ancestors of several *daimyo* (warlord) clans.

Koguryo suffered frequent Chinese intervention, with its capital at Wandu destroyed several times. Yet the kingdom recovered, and under Gwanggaeto

⊠ **The Bulguksa temple** in South Korea. King Beophung founded the first temple on this site around 528.

◀◀ **Fierce guardian spirits** of the north and the south protect Korea's great Buddhist temple at Bulguksa.

> **Baekje** is at full moon, **Silla** is at half moon.

Prophecy of the decline of Silla and rise of Baekje, 659

(ruled 391–413) conquered most of the Korean peninsula. However, internal strife, pressure from Baekje and Silla, and conflict with Sui and Tang China (*see pp.136–7*) in the early 7th century led to Koguryo's decline and, in 668, it, too, fell to Silla, completing the unification of Korea under the Silla king Munmo.

Attempts under the unified Silla state to impose a Chinese-style bureaucracy and generally enhance royal authority foundered in the face of aristocratic resistance, and in the late 9th century, Korea broke up again. Civil war ensued, but Korea was united once more in 935 by Wang Geon, founder of the Goryeo dynasty. Although generally prosperous, the country suffered civil wars in the 12th century, and in the 14th century fell under the control of the Mongol Yuan dynasty of China. Goryeo finally collapsed in 1392, after a rebellion by the general Yi Songgye.

Choson Korea

Yi Songgye founded the Choson dynasty, which would rule Korea into modern times, only finally being deposed in 1910. Yi's son Sejong implemented a series of Neo-Confucian reforms, which aimed to harmonize all aspects of human behavior with an underlying universal order. To this end, Sejong instituted a civil service examination system along Chinese lines and created a new phonetic alphabet (called *hang'ul*) for the Korean language. He also encouraged the advancement of science, particularly in astronomy and meteorology, and agricultural reforms to increase the yields of the countryside.

Rivalries among scholar-officials who vied for positions in the state bureaucracy plagued Sejong's successors. This sapped Korea's strength, and the country was unprepared when Japan invaded in the 1590s. Two invasions in six years devastated Korea, but the Japanese were finally repelled. Choson recovered in the 17th century, and the reigns of Yeongjo (1724–1776) and his successors brought peace until the end of the 19th century, when Korea was drawn into rivalry between Japan, Russia, and China (*see pp.274–7*), finally becoming a Japanese protectorate. The Choson were eventually removed from the throne in 1910.

⌃ **This *maebyong* wine vessel** (from the Chinese for "vase for plum blossom") is characteristic of Korea's Goryeo period.

The Khmer Empire

CAMBODIA 889–1431

Around 800, King Jayavarman II (ruled 802–850) consolidated small central Cambodian kingdoms to establish a state called Kambujadesa, marking the start of the Khmer Empire. Its culture was strongly influenced by India, and Jayavarman ordered the construction of Indian-style Hindu temples near Siem Reap. Under Yasovarman I, who became king in 889, a capital was established at Angkor, which grew to become a vast ceremonial complex. Angkor reached its peak under Suryavarman, who from 1011 reunified Cambodia after a period of civil war.

◩ The Angkor Wat temple was founded by the Khmer king Suryavarman II (ruled 1113–1145).

Empire and decline

In 1177, the Chams (*see facing page*) sacked Angkor, but four years later were in turn defeated by Jayavarman VII, Angkor's greatest ruler, who then extended the empire to include parts of modern Thailand and Vietnam. Jayavarman VII was a Buddhist and, after his death in 1215, a Hindu reaction set in during which all the images of Buddha at Angkor were defaced. The empire then went into decline and became a localized power. It disappeared entirely after the sack of Angkor by the Thais in 1431.

Pagan Burma

BURMA 849–1287

Burmese chronicles give 849 as the date when King Pyinbya founded the city of Pagan, which would become the center of Burma's first powerful state. Later, under King Anawrahta (ruled 1044–1077), Pagan emerged as a real power, conquering the Mon city of Thaton, a center of Indian civilization, in 1057.

Anawrahta also annexed parts of Thailand, Arakan on the border of India, and Nan-chao in southern China, creating an empire that would last into the 13th century. The density of temples in Pagan itself was such

that by the early 13th century, the empire established a new center several miles to the east.

Under Kyaswa (ruled 1234–1250), Pagan fell into decline, as the king confiscated the lands of Buddhist monasteries, an unpopular policy that undermined royal authority. The despotic ruler Narathihapate (ruled 1254–1287) dared invade the Mongol vassal state of Kaungai in 1277, only for the Mongol armies to retaliate and sack Pagan in 1287. Narathihapate fled from Burma and in the aftermath, Pagan's subjects rose up and its empire collapsed.

Champa

S VIETNAM | **192–1471**

The kingdom of Champa may have had its origins in the state of Lin Yi, founded around 192, but by the 7th century was independent, with its own culture. Successive capitals of Champa were destroyed by Javan attacks, before King Indravarman II (854–893) founded a new center at Indrapura (in modern Quan-nam province). In 979, an invasion of Dai Viet (*see right*) led to a long struggle that ended only in 1471 with the Dai Viet capture of Vijaya, the last Cham capital.

» **Stylized sculptures** of fearsome guardians and mythical animals adorned Champa temples.

Dai Viet

N VIETNAM | **938–1528**

Dai Viet ("Great Viet") was established in 938 as an independent state in northern Vietnam by Ngo Quen, after a revolt against Chinese overlordship. Under Dai Viet's Li dynasty (1009–1225), a series of wars broke out with Champa to the south (*see left*) over disputed border provinces. From 1225, during the Tran dynasty, Dai Viet fought off three Mongol invasions, and finally, under Le Thanh-Ton (ruled 1460–1497), succeeded in conquering Champa. After 1528, Dai Viet broke up and was not reunited until the early 19th century.

Srivijaya

JAVA | **7TH–14TH CENTURIES**

From the 5th century, the island peoples of Sumatra and Java set up prosperous trading communities rivaling the coastal states of the Southeast Asian mainland. By the 7th century, the Srivijaya Empire controlled most of Sumatra and the Malay peninsula. The earliest account comes from a Chinese Buddhist pilgrim in 671, who remarked that there were a thousand Buddhist monks at the court, and Srivijaya clearly acted as a center for the diffusion of Buddhism in the region.

Srivijaya faced many rivals, including the Sailendra kingdom of central Java—which constructed the vast temple at Borobodur around 800—and its hold began to weaken in the 11th century. By 1400, it had been replaced by newer maritime powers, especially the Malay Majapahit Empire.

✉ **A gallery of Buddha statues** from Wat Phra Borom in Chaiya in southern Thailand, which was a regional capital of the Srivijaya Empire.

The Middle East and North Africa

In the early 7th century, the emergence of a new religion, Islam, changed the shape of the Middle East forever. The new faith inspired unprecedented unity in the tribes of the Arabian peninsula, and Arab armies carried Islam through the Middle East and North Africa. Despite fragmentation in the Islamic world in the 8th century, Islamic empires, such as the Seljuk and Ottoman, still rose to prominence.

The rise of Islam

ARABIA, THE NEAR EAST ⏳ **610–661**

The prophet Muhammad was born around 570 in the prosperous central Arabian trading town of Mecca. Around 610, he received the divine revelation that would form the basis of the religion of Islam, and began to gather a group of followers.

The spread of Islam in Arabia

Although some in Mecca accepted Muhammad's new creed, others were threatened by it and, in 622, Muhammad was forced into exile in Medina. The citizens of Medina were longtime rivals to Mecca and willingly accepted Muhammad and his teachings, providing him with many converts. This led to a bitter struggle with the Meccans, which finally ended with the capture of Mecca in 630.

From there, Muhammad directed the conquest of much of the rest of the Arabian peninsula before his death in 632. Abu Bakr was appointed caliph (or successor); under his rule (632–634) anti-Muslim uprisings in Arabia were put down and Arab armies began to penetrate Sassanid Persia (see p.87) and Byzantine-held Syria (see p.178). Under the next caliph, Umar (ruled 634–644), the Islamic empire expanded far beyond Arabia.

Early expansion and civil unrest

The Arabs smashed the Byzantine field army at Yarmuk in 636, leading to the capture of Jerusalem in 637 and the occupation of Egypt in 641. The Sassanid Persian empire also fell to

the caliphate after the defeat of the Persian *shah* (king), Yazdegird III, in 642. Increasing disputes over the succession, especially after the murder of the third caliph, Uthman, in 656, finally led to a civil war and the assassination of 'Ali, the fourth caliph and Muhammad's cousin, in 661.

⬧ **Alam standards**, carried in Shia religious processions, were intended to represent the sword of 'Ali. Holy names are carved along the blade.

The Umayyad and Abbasid caliphates

MIDDLE EAST **661–1258**

After the assassination of the fourth Muslim caliph 'Ali, Mu'awiyah—the governor of Syria and a distant relative of Muhammad—seized power, installing himself in a new capital at Damascus. Mu'awiyah founded the Umayyad dynasty, which borrowed heavily from Byzantine and Persian institutions to build a strong central authority for the Islamic state. The Umayyads extended their rule in North Africa, capturing the Byzantine stronghold of Carthage (in Tunisia) in 698, and swept into Spain in 711.

From Damascus to Baghdad

Despite these Ummayad successes, in 750 a number of anti-Umayyad factions joined in a successful revolt against them led by 'Abbas, who claimed the caliphate and moved the seat of government to Baghdad. His descendants, the Abbasids, would be caliphs until 1258. Initially 'Abbas presided over a golden age, in which art, science, architecture, and Islamic jurisprudence

flourished. In 756, however, Spain broke away under a line of the Umayyad family, and North Africa followed with the foundation of a rival Fatimid caliphate in Egypt in 969. By the 11th century, the Abbasid caliphs controlled little beyond the suburbs of Baghdad and were firmly under the thumb of the Seljuk Turkish emirs (*see p.156*). In 1258, even this pitiful flame of independence was snuffed out when the Mongol Hulegu sacked Baghdad (*see p.142*) and had Al-Musta'sim, the last caliph, trampled to death by horses.

⟫ HAROUN AL-RASHID

The greatest of the Abbasid caliphs, Haroun (786–809) turned Baghdad into the most prosperous city of its day. He defeated the Byzantines in 806, and was a fine diplomat, exchanging ambassadors with the Frankish ruler Charlemagne.

◀ **A mosaic from the Umayyad mosque** in Damascus, a beautiful Islamic-Byzantine building constructed under the caliph al-Walid between 706 and 715.

The Seljuk Turks

TURKEY, SYRIA ⌛ **1038–1306**

Throughout the 9th century, groups of Turkish-speaking nomads migrated westward from central Asia. In the 10th century, they reached Persia, where many of them took service in Muslim armies and converted to Islam.

The first Seljuks

One group, the Seljuks, led by Tugrul Beg, initially served the Kara-Khanid emirs of Bukhara in Persia, but became so powerful that in 1038, Tugrul declared himself sultan in the city of Nishapur in northeastern Iran. From here, his armies moved westward. In 1055, Tugrul became involved in a power struggle between the Abbasid (see p.155) caliph Al Qa'im and his Egyptian Fatimid rival, who had taken Baghdad.

Tugrul took Baghdad for the Abbasid caliphs in 1060, but then reduced them to little more than figureheads. Tugrul's successor, Alp Arslan, conquered Georgia and Armenia in 1064, and in 1071 defeated the Byzantine emperor Romanus IV, leading to Turkish occupation of much of central Anatolia (in modern Turkey). The administrative reforms of Alp Arslan's Persian official Nizam al-Mulk supported the sultan's military victories and cemented Seljuk stability.

Decline of the Seljuks

Alp Arslan's son Malik Shah I (ruled 1072–1092) consolidated Seljuk rule in Anatolia, but a revolt by his cousin Suleyman in 1086 led to the rival Seljuk Sultanate of Rum, which controlled much of the west of Alp Arslan's former domain.

By the 12th century, Malik Shah's Seljuks had disbanded; pressure from the Mongols in the early 13th century and competition with more vigorous Muslim emirates put the Rum Sultanate into decline, and after 1306, it disappeared entirely.

》 ALP ARSLAN

Initially a Seljuk governer, Alp Arslan succeeded to the sultanate in 1064. His first invasion of the Byzantine empire in 1068 failed, but after his victory against the Byzantines in 1071, Anatolia would always remain largely Turkish-occupied.

《 **The main gateway** of the Ince Minare *medrese* (school of theology) in Konya, Turkey, built by the Seljuks around 1267.

Rise of the Ottomans

TURKEY **MID-13TH CENTURY–1481**

In the 12th century, Turkish Seljuks dominated Anatolia (*see facing page*), but their influence weakened in the 13th century and rival Turkish groups vied for power. Among them was a small band led by Osman, after whom the Ottoman empire would be named. Osman's group took advantage of a strategic position on the eastern approach route to Constantinople (now Istanbul) to secure possession of many Byzantine cities in western Anatolia (*see p.179*). This provided them with resources for further expansion.

Blue tilework graces many Ottoman-era mosques at Iznik, an early Ottoman conquest.

into Europe to occupy Gallipoli. From this bridgehead, the Ottomans spread through eastern Thrace and across the Balkans. Murad I (ruled 1362–1389), as well as expanding Ottoman land in eastern Anatolia, captured the great city of Adrianople (Edirne) in Thrace in 1369, which thereafter became the Ottoman capital.

The early sultans

Osman's son Orhan (ruled 1324–1362) took the major city of Prusa (Bursa) and established it as his capital, marking the effective establishment of the Ottoman empire. By the late 1330s, the Byzantines were confined to just a few settlements close to Constantinople. In 1352, aided by the Byzantine emperor John VI Kantakouzenos, who was locked in civil war with his rival John V Palaiologos, Orhan crossed

Rise and fall

The Ottomans began to exert pressure on the other Christian regions of the Balkans, capturing Sofia (in Bulgaria) in 1385 and destroying the army of Prince Lazar of Serbia in 1389. It seemed only a matter of time before Constantinople would fall, but in 1402, the Mongol Tamerlane smashed the Ottoman army outside Ankara (*see p.143*). The Turkish emirates that the Ottomans had conquered over the previous century broke away, and it took 50 years under Mehmet I (ruled 1413–1421) and Murad II (ruled 1421–1451) to regain the Ottoman position in Anatolia and the Balkans.

» MEHMET II

Known as "the Conqueror," Mehmet II (ruled 1451–1481) was the Ottoman sultan who, in 1453, finally took the Byzantine capital Constantinople. Having constructed a series of fortresses to throttle the city's communication lines, he laid siege in early spring, using cannons to pound the city walls. In 1456, he failed to repeat his success at Belgrade, but he successively conquered Serbia (1458), Bosnia (1463), most of Albania (1478), and even, in the last year of his life, oversaw the capture of Otranto in the heel of Italy.

India

Kingdoms and empires rose and fell in India in the Middle Ages. Following the demise of the Guptas, in 606 Emperor Harsha established a powerful state across much of northern India, but after his death the empire fragmented into small kingdoms, only really to be united under the Delhi Sultanate in the 13th century. Southern India saw similar struggles, with rival states fighting bitterly until the emergence of the Cholas in the 9th century.

Chola India

SOUTH INDIA c.850–1279

▶▶ **A statue from** the 11th-century Brihadishwara temple in the Chola capital of Thanjavur.

Between the 7th and 9th centuries, the Pallava and the Chalukya kingdoms contested the right to rule southern India until the rise of the Cholas, around 850. They were to sweep away the two rivals to establish a new state that would dominate the area until around 1200.

Rise and fall

The Chola kingdom overthrew the Pallavas around 897 under Aditya, but then suffered a century of decline at the hands of the rival Rashtrakuta kingdom. Then, under Rajaraja I, who came to the throne in 985, Chola was on the rise once more, conquering all south India and even intervening as far north as Bengal. Rajaraja and his son Rajendra I built magnificent temples at Thanjavur and at Gangaikondacholapuram, a Hindu riposte to the growing power of Islam in northern India. Rajendra I also projected Chola power overseas, conquering Sri Lanka and exercising some influence, if not control, over the Srivijaya empire of Indonesia and the state of Kadaram (around Penang in modern Malaysia).

Back in south India, however, the Cholas fell into difficulties. Sri Lanka was lost in 1070, and around 1118, a resurgent Chalukya kingdom took much territory around Mysore. Beset by civil strife and faced with the threat of the Pandyan Empire on his borders, Rajendra III, the last recorded Chola ruler, struggled on until 1279, after which his kingdom disappeared.

The Delhi Sultanate

NORTH INDIA ⚊ **1206–1526**

In 1193, the armies of Muhammad of Ghur (from modern Afghanistan) sacked Delhi, carving out an empire from a number of weak and fractious Rajput Hindu principalities. After Muhammad's death in 1206, his most trusted general, the former slave Qutb-ud-din Aibek (ruled 1206–1211), gained control of his territories and established the Delhi Sultanate.

A fragile rule

The rule of Aibek's successors was precarious. The nomadic tribes who made up the nobility did not have a strong tradition of hereditary kingship, and during the rule of the Slave Dynasty (1206–1290), at least five of the 11 sultans were assassinated. Then, between 1299 and 1307, Sultan Alauddin Khilji launched a series of successful military strikes against the rich kingdoms south of Delhi. By 1321, much of the south was under the control of governors appointed by the sultan, and Sultan Muhammad ibn Tughluq even moved the capital and its whole population 700 miles (1,100 km) south to Devagiri. Although Delhi was reinstated two years later, so many of its people had died in the two moves that travelers reported it to be a "ghost town."

The sultanate's strength was now waning, and the establishment of the Hindu Vijayanagar empire in central India in the 1330s ended its rule there. The Delhi sultans, declining in policial force, limped on until 1526, when they were finally supplanted in Delhi by the Mughals.

>> **MAHMUD OF GHAZNI**

In 997, Mahmud of Ghazni succeeded his father as the ruler of a minor state around Ghazni, in modern Afghanistan. From here, he created a vast empire encompassing large parts of Afghanistan, Iran, Pakistan, and northwest India before dying in 1030.

The Qutb Minar mosque in Delhi has a minaret that is 240 ft (73 m) tall. It celebrates Sultan Aibek's victories.

> When I entered **Delhi** it was almost a **desert**... Its **buildings were very few** and in other respects it was **quite empty**.

Arab traveler Ibn Battutah, visiting Delhi in 1334 after Sultan Muhammad deported its population

Sub-Saharan Africa

Buoyed by trading links with Asia and Islamic North Africa, from the 8th century, a number of prosperous empires and commercial centers formed in Africa to the south of the Sahara Desert, including the Mali and Songhay empires in West Africa and Great Zimbabwe in south-central Africa. The spread of Islam across north and east Africa helped create routes through the desert that became the first trading networks to encompass the sub-Saharan regions.

The Mali Empire

⚑ WEST AFRICA ⌛ c.800–1545

In West Africa, between the 8th and 11th centuries, the Ghana Empire grew powerful on the trans-Saharan gold trade. Yet by the 12th century, it was in decline, and was supplanted by the Mali Empire, founded in 1235 by Sundiata Keita. Like Ghana, the Mali Empire was based in the Sahel, the savanna region along the Sahara's southern border. From here, it, too, exploited the Saharan trade routes, exchanging desert-mined salt for gold.

Wealth and collapse

Mali reached its peak in the 14th century under Sundiata Keita's grand-nephew Mansa Musa (ruled 1312–1337). He is most noted for his spectacular "Pilgrimage of Gold" to Mecca in 1324–1325, when he spent or gave away so much gold that the inflation it caused damaged the economy of North Africa for a decade. Mansa Musa extended Mali's territory and built up the city of Timbuktu into a wealthy commercial hub and a center for scholarship.

In the early 15th century, Mali's subject states, notably Songhay, based at Gao some 250 miles (400 km) downriver from Timbuktu, broke away. Having lost control of the crucial trade routes after a disastrous defeat by Songhay in 1545, Mali's Empire collapsed.

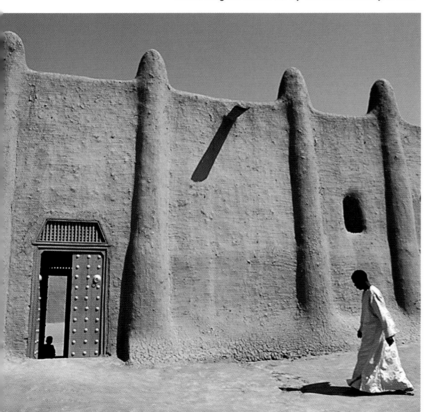

◤ **The walls of the Great Mosque** at Djenné, a trading city conquered by Sonni Ali, first great king of the Songhay Empire which rose to overcome Mali.

Ife and Benin

NIGERIA   **c.700–1500**

The Ife kingdom developed among the Yoruba people of southwestern Nigeria around 700. At its height, between 900 and 1200, this kingdom had grown to dominate a large area of western Africa. The capital, Ife, was the center of this sophisticated empire, most notable for its production of high-quality bronze heads. However, in around 1400, the Ife were supplanted by the Empire of Benin, which grew up to their west.

A bronze Ife head, cast in a beautiful naturalistic style that has made the culture's artistic production justly famous.

Under Ewuare—the first great *oba* (ruler) of Benin, from 1440—the capital was fortified with a great moat and armies sent out that ultimately dominated an area of some 31,000 sq miles (80,000 sq km). Like their Ife predecessors, the people of Benin produced superb terracotta and bronze heads, and they grew rich from a monopoly on contacts with European newcomers—initially the Portuguese—in the later 15th century, profiting from trade in ivory, palm oil, gold, pepper, and slaves.

Great Zimbabwe

SOUTHERN AFRICA   **11TH–15TH CENTURIES**

One of the greatest urban centers of sub-Saharan Africa grew up from the 11th century at Great Zimbabwe (from which the modern state of Zimbabwe takes its name). The huge settlement sprawls over 3 sq miles (7 sq km), with a number of stone enclosures containing some 300 structures. Great Zimbabwe was in a strategic position to control trade—including in gold—from the interior to the east coast of Africa. It was also home to a thriving agricultural economy. With a population of around 15,000 people, Great Zimbabwe served as the center of the Mwenemutapa Empire. However, possibly as a result of overcultivation of the surrounding land, in the mid-15th century, Great Zimbabwe was abandoned.

The 13th-century Great Enclosure is the most impressive of the stone structures at Great Zimbabwe. Its 82 ft (25 m) walls may have enclosed a royal palace.

Europe

Around the early 5th century CE, Germanic barbarian tribes settled on the former territory of the Roman Empire. But by around 600, the chaos had resolved itself, and what had once been the Roman Empire was now a series of successor states. A Christian culture emerged in Europe, in part based on a form of social and political structures known as feudalism, which would persist through wars and crises into the mid-15th century.

Ostrogoths and Lombards in Italy

ITALY **493–774**

Between 488 and 493 CE, Theodoric I, ruler of the barbarian Ostrogoths (*see p.115*), conquered Italy. His kingdom drew deeply on Roman forms of administration, yet opposition to his rule drove him to execute Boethius, a leader of the old Roman Senate, in 525 CE.

After Theodoric's death in 526 CE, his daughter Amalasuintha acted as regent for his young grandson and designated heir, Athalaric. Dissent among the Ostrogoth nobles led to the whole state unraveling. Amalasuintha appealed to the Byzantine emperor Justinian (*see p.178*) for help, and after her murder (possibly on the orders of her cousin) in 535 CE, Justinian took the opportunity to intervene, setting off the Gothic Wars. By 554 CE, after hard and bitter campaigning, Justinian's forces emerged the masters of a devastated Italy.

Lombard Italy

In 568 CE, the barbarian Lombards invaded Italy from the northeast under Alboin (ruled c.565–572 CE). In 572 CE, they reached Pavia and carved out a kingdom in northern Italy. This soon split into 35 dukedoms, but was reunited under Authari (ruled 584–590 CE) and, from 589 CE, held off Byzantine advances. Under Agilulf (ruled 590–616 CE), the Lombards became Catholic, controlling northern Italy until the Frankish Charlemagne (*see p.165*) deposed their last king, Desiderius, in 774.

⌃ **An Ostrogothic brooch** from around 500 CE, showing a vibrancy far removed from Roman art forms.

Visigoths in Spain

SPAIN ☒ **469–711**

The Visigoths, who settled in southwestern Gaul in 418 CE as allies of the Romans, began from 469 CE to conquer territory in Spain. In 507 CE, when the Franks defeated them in a great battle at Vouillé, near Poitiers, the Visigoths fell back on these Spanish territories.

The Visigothic kingdom

Under Agila (ruled 549–554 CE), the Visigoths lost territory in southeast Spain to a resurgent Byzantine Empire. From its capital at Toledo, however, the Visigothic state recovered, reaching its apogee under Leovigild (ruled 568–586 CE), a great organizer and legislator. Leogivild was succeeded by his son Reccared, who in 589 CE converted to Catholicism, abandoning the kingdom's previous Arian form of Christianity. The Visigothic kingdom finally came to an end when, weakened by a civil war after the accession of Roderick in 711, it easily fell to invading Muslim armies (*see p.154*).

⏵⏵ **The church of San Pedro de la Nave** at Zamora, built under the Visigothic king Egica (ruled 687–701) toward the end of Visigothic rule in Spain.

Anglo-Saxon England

ENGLAND ☒ **411–1066**

Britain was under Roman administration until 411 CE, and in the little-understood period that followed, Germanic invaders—Jutes, Angles, and Saxons—began to settle on the island, displacing the native Romano-Celtic population. By the 7th century, these had coalesced into a number of small states, conventionally known as the "Heptarchy."

Expansion of Wessex

Principal among these states were Wessex in the southwest, Mercia in the Midlands, and Northumbria in the north. In the long struggle between them, it was Wessex that would emerge victorious. Danish invasions in the 9th century sapped the remaining power of Northumbria and Mercia, whose last great king, Offa, died in 796. Alfred the Great fended off the Danish conquest of Wessex with several victories in the 870s, but it was not until the time of Edward the Elder (ruled 899–924) that England was united under a single Anglo-Saxon monarchy.

⏵⏵ **ALFRED THE GREAT**

As well as saving Wessex from Danish invasion in 878, Alfred (ruled 871–899) restored Wessex's defenses by building a series of burhs (fortified towns), revising the legal system, and overseeing the first major translations of books into Anglo-Saxon.

Merovingian and Carolingian France

FRANCE 511–987

After the fall of the Roman Empire, Europe fragmented into many states, the most successful of which was the Kingdom of the Franks. A confederacy of tribes originating from the area around modern Belgium and Holland, the Franks, under their leader Clovis (ruled c.481–511), conquered most of the old Roman province of Gaul.

The Merovingians

Clovis overcame the Roman general Syagrius (who controlled large parts of northern Gaul) in 486, saw off rival Frankish kings, crucially converted to Catholicism in 496, and expelled the Visigoths from Gaul in 507. On his death, the kingdom was divided between his four sons, establishing the Merovingian dynasty. This dynasty continued to expand, taking the rest of Gaul (except Brittany and Septimania) by 536 and dominating northern Italy in the 540s and 550s.

However, in the 7th century, after Dagobert I (622–639), the power of the Frankish kings declined. Several died young and rival aristocratic factions started to vie for power. In the early

☑ **The Baptistery of Saint-Jean,** Poitiers, constructed around 360 and restored by the Merovingians in the early 6th century.

> ## A **chief** in whose shadow the **Christian people** repose in **peace** and who **strikes terror** into the **pagan nations**.

Alcuin of York, in a letter describing Charlemagne c.796

8th century, one of these factions, the Carolingians, emerged as dominant. Beginning with Pepin II (d.713), they developed their office as "mayor of the palace" to become the real power in the land.

The Carolingians

In 754, Pepin III (ruled 747–768) obtained papal approval to depose the last Merovingian ruler and become the first king of the new Carolingian dynasty. Under his son, Charlemagne, the Frankish kingdom reached the height of its power, initiating a series of aggressive overtures against its neighbors. Charlemagne's military campaigns resulted in conquests in Saxony, the annexation of the Lombard kingdom of Italy in 774, and victories as far afield as the lands of the Avar Empire in Pannonia, on the Danube (modern Hungary), in the 790s.

Charlemagne presided over a glittering age of cultural achievements, which earned it the label "the Carolingian Renaissance." In order to reform the Frankish church, he ordered the importation of works of liturgy and church law from Italy. The kingdom's administration and legal system was thoroughly overhauled. These changes were overseen by the *missi dominici*—the personal envoys of the king.

Carolingian decline

Charlemagne had himself crowned "Emperor of the Romans" in 800, but his successors struggled to equal his prowess. When Charlemagne's son, Louis the Pious, died in 840, the empire was divided between his three sons. Their quarrels, and the further subdivision of the empire among their heirs, sapped the dynasty's strength. The growing threats of Viking raiders (*see p.168*) from the north and of Magyar incursions from the east further

helped to undermine the Carolingians' authority. Hugh Capet, a Frankish aristocrat, deposed the last Carolingian king, Louis V, in 987, to form a new dynasty, the Capetians.

⟫ CHARLEMAGNE

Initially ruling with his brother Carloman (d.771), Charlemagne (ruled 768–814) faced few internal challenges to his authority, enabling him to embark on a bold program of expansion abroad and reform at home. He built up a sumptuous new capital at Aachen, Germany, and his court was Europe's most important center of learning in the 9th century. Charlemagne modeled aspects of his rule upon the Romans, crowning himself emperor and appearing on coins wearing the military cloak and laurel crown of a Roman ruler.

An ornate water jug gifted to Charlemagne by Haroun al-Rashid, Caliph of Baghdad, in a gesture of diplomatic friendship.

Feudalism

The term feudalism describes the system of relationships between kings and nobles in northern and western Europe during much of the medieval period, and by extension to the wider society and economy in which these elites operated. At the heart of the feudal system lay the obligation that noblemen (and, in turn, their retainers) would provide military service in return for the holding of land.

Feudal Europe

The feudal system, although extremely complex, was never arranged into written law. Much of what is known about feudalism therefore comes with the benefit of historical hindsight. Feudalism contained elements of Germanic custom, mixed with the late-Roman practice of gifting land to barbarian groups in return for military service.

It evolved during Carolingian times into the practice of a ruler assigning a parcel of land (known as a "fief") to a nobleman. In return for the land, the nobleman (who was known as a "vassal") swore his loyalty to the king—or another lord—and promised to perform various duties, particularly military

A **14th-century French view** of the investiture of a knight. The new knight kneels before his lord, pledging loyalty in exchange for privileges.

service, for a set number of days each year. Many nobles further apportioned parts of their fiefs to subtenants, who in turn performed military duties and swore allegiance. It was not unusual for vassals to have allegiances to more than one lord. A hierarchy of obligations thus developed, helping to link together a country's web of lordships, but doing little to bolster the central authority of the king.

Knights and castles

The backbone of medieval European armies were the knights, heavy cavalry who by the 11th century represented an elite caste of warriors that fought on behalf of their feudal lord. Their status was confirmed through symbols and ceremonies, such as the "accolade"—the king touching his vassal on the shoulders with a sword to confer knighthood.

> The **faithful vassal** should… **counsel** and **aid** his lord.
>
> **Fulbert of Chartres in a letter to Duke William of Aquitaine, 1020**

A castle was a fortified base from which a feudal lord could dominate the countryside—as well as being his dwelling place and the seat of the local court of justice. Once ensconced inside, an uncooperative nobleman was extremely difficult for anyone, including the king, to dislodge.

Changes in feudalism

Toward the 14th century, a new variant, known as "bastard feudalism," arose in which vassals substituted their military obligations for monetary payments. This was a sign of a changing society. As feudal ties weakened and monarchs tried to assert direct control over their realms, the age of feudalism was coming to a close, finally ending in the 16th century.

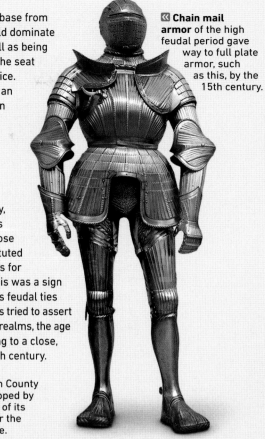

Chain mail armor of the high feudal period gave way to full plate armor, such as this, by the 15th century.

The Rock of Cashel in County Tipperary, Ireland, is topped by a great castle, evidence of its feudal lord's power over the surrounding countryside.

The Vikings

SCANDINAVIA, NW EUROPE, NEWFOUNDLAND ⚔ **793–1069**

In the late 8th century, possibly propelled by overpopulation in their Scandinavian homelands, a wave of shipborne raiders, the Vikings, began a reign of terror over northwestern Europe.

Taking advantage of divisions in the Carolingian empire (*see pp.164–5*), Anglo-Saxon England, and Ireland, the Vikings first attacked soft targets, such as the island monastery of Lindisfarne in northeast England, in 793. But these fiercely effective warriors were capable of great mobility, even sailing up rivers, and moved on to dominate the territories they had previously pillaged.

In England in the late 9th century, they colonized a large part of the Midlands and north, which became known as the Danelaw. They explored new lands in the Atlantic, too, settling Iceland from 870, Greenland in the late 10th century, and even North America in about 1000.

▶ **This replica Viking ship** is modeled on a ship that was excavated in Oseberg, Norway. Dating from 815–820, it was built for ceremonial rather than practical purposes.

Kievan Rus

UKRAINE, RUSSIA ⚔ **C.800–1043**

From the early 9th century, Viking Scandinavians, mainly Swedes, began to settle in trading towns in the north of modern Russia and Ukraine, principally at Staraya Ladoga on the Volkhov River.

The conquest of Kiev

At first, the Vikings sought to control trade rather than plunder or conquer, establishing a trading network that extended as far as the Islamic world. In the mid-9th century, however, these merchants seem to have expanded their lands, setting up bases farther down the Volga and Dniepr rivers. Then, around 850, trade turned to conquest, and tradition relates that in 862, the people of Novgorod invited a Viking group (the Rus) led by Riurik to defend them.

In 879, Riurik's son Oleg traveled south to seize Kiev and established a Viking dynasty there, which would give rise to many medieval Russian principalities. Kievan Rus became Christian around 988, when its ruler Vladimir was baptized and, although it raided Constantinople in 1043, it became merely another eastern European principality.

The Normans

NORMANDY, ENGLAND, S ITALY   911–1087

Viking raids affected Carolingian France (*see pp.164–5*) badly, and in 911, the Carolingians gave the leader of one band, Rollo, extensive territories in modern Normandy as a "pay-off" in exchange for defending it from other marauders.

The Norman conquests

Rollo's descendants, the Dukes of Normandy, rapidly absorbed French culture to create a hybrid Norman state. In 1066, Duke William the Bastard (later called "the Conqueror") took advantage of a disputed succession in England to launch an audacious invasion and seize the English throne himself. The newly Norman kingdom of England imported French cultural and administrative practices and established the strongest centralized monarchy in Europe.

WILLIAM THE CONQUEROR

With a distant claim to the English throne through a great-aunt, in 1066, William invaded to usurp Harold Godwinsson as king of England, defeating him at Hastings in October of that year. William ruled England until 1087.

England was not the only place the Normans sought to satisfy their desire for expansion. From the 1040s, under Robert Guiscard, they conquered southern Italy and Sicily, founding a kingdom that lasted until the German emperor Henry VI suppressed it in 1194.

> They are a **race** inured to **war**, and **can hardly live without it**.
>
> William of Malmesbury, from *Deeds of the Kings of the English*, describing the Normans, 12th century

This scene from the Bayeux tapestry, commissioned to celebrate the Norman victory at Hastings, shows the Norman army gaining the upper hand.

⊼ **The Benedictine monastery** of Mont St. Michel lies off the Norman coast of France and was occupied by monks from 966 until the late 18th century.

Monasticism

⚑ **EGYPT, EUROPE** ⌛ **c.350–1229**

From the time of the early Christian church, men and women had chosen to devote themselves to a life of spiritual dedication as monks or nuns. Gradually communities arose with fixed codes of conduct, such as the "Rule" of St. Benedict of Nursia (c.480–547) in Italy.

The new monastic orders

Early monasticism became especially strong in the Celtic lands and above all in the Carolingian empire (*see pp.164–5*) of France, with wealthy monasteries such as that of Cluny (belonging to the Benedictine order) the frequent target of Viking raiders. Disenchantment with the materialistic approach these abbeys took, and a general desire for a more spiritual observance, led to the founding of new religious orders from the 11th century, beginning with the Carthusians, founded by Bruno of Cologne around 1082. The Cistercians followed in 1098, insisting on a rigorous life of manual work and prayer. Yet by the 13th century, the reformist zeal of even these communities had ebbed, and further new monastic orders sprang up, most notably the Franciscan and Dominican friars.

They were known as mendicants, from the Latin word for "beggars," for they renounced personal property and were not attached to richly endowed abbeys. To support themselves they depended on charity, bringing them closely in touch with ordinary people. In particular, the Franciscan friars, founded by St. Francis of Assisi in 1210, sought a return to the simplicity and poverty of the early church, while the Dominicans became committed to education and the fight against heresy. The popularity of the new orders was also at the root of their undoing, for they, too, received bequests, grew wealthy, and became complex organizations far removed from the ideals of their founders.

❝ Where there is **charity and wisdom**, there is neither **fear nor ignorance**. ❞

St. Francis of Assisi, *Admonitions*, c.1220

Popes and emperors

FRANCE, GERMANY, ITALY 1049–1122

The collapse of the Roman Empire in the west in the 5th century did not spell the end for Christianity, as the Franks in Gaul soon became Catholics, with the Visigoths (*see p.163*) following in the late 6th century. Under the Frankish emperor Charlemagne, church and state enjoyed a close relationship, and Charlemagne often used the church's spiritual authority to enhance his own.

Papal reforms and the investiture controversy

In the 11th century, relations between the secular rulers and the church broke down. Pope Leo IX (ruled 1049–1054) tried to limit practices such as clerical marriage and simony (the purchase of positions in the church hierarchy).

His protégé Pope Gregory VII sought to expand the influence of the church, even if this meant clashing with the authority of kings and princes. In 1075, a dispute broke out over investiture (the right to appoint bishops), which the Pope declared his own, but to which the emperor had historically laid claim. The German emperor

>> **POPE GREGORY VII**

Known as Hildebrand, Gregory served as papal legate to France and Germany before becoming pope. His papacy (1074–1085) was consumed by the struggle with the German emperor Henry IV over investiture (*see right*). In the end Henry won out, occupying Rome in 1084 and exiling Gregory to southern Italy.

Henry IV persuaded his bishops to declare Gregory deposed, and the Pope excommunicated the emperor in response. His authority undermined, and faced by a rebellion of German princes, Henry was forced into a humiliating climb-down, and at Canossa in Italy in 1077 had to do four days of public penance, after which he received absolution.

Continued conflict

The conflict was only finally settled by the Concordat of Worms in 1122. Disputes over the borderline between papal and secular authority never really dissipated, and fed into the discontents that would fuel the Reformation (*see p.218*).

On the imperial crown of Otto I (Holy Roman Emperor 962–976) the biblical Solomon symbolizes the wisdom of kings, illustrating how secular rulers used Christian imagery to bolster their authority.

The Crusades

⚐ LEBANON, SYRIA, PALESTINE, ISRAEL ⏳ 1095–1291

The capture of Jerusalem by Muslim armies in 637 had long rankled in Europe, seeming to cut off Christianity from its wellsprings in the Holy Land. Nevertheless, for a long time Christian pilgrims were in fact able to make the journey to Jerusalem, but in the 11th century the expansion of the Seljuk Turkish Sultanate (see p.156) threatened to prevent access to non-Muslim travelers. In 1095, Byzantine emperor Alexius I sent envoys to the West to plead for assistance. They found a willing listener in Pope Urban II. That November, in a field outside the cathedral at Claremont in France, the Pope called for a military expedition to liberate the Holy City of Jerusalem from Muslim rule. The crowd erupted with cries of "It is the will of God," and thousands of crusaders, as these soldiers became known, "took the cross" to join the military pilgrimage to the Holy Land.

The First Crusades

The first of the armies to cross the Balkans into Anatolia was a rag-tag assortment of peasants, some knights, and religious zealots, all under the doubtful leadership of a charismatic preacher, Peter the Hermit. They were soon cut to pieces by the Turks. The force that followed them was far more professional: a largely Frankish army with a strong aristocratic component. Motivated by a mix

》 The crusaders' sea voyage to the Holy Land was fraught with danger, but avoided a trek across Anatolia, with its threat of Turkish attack.

It is the **will of God**.

Response of the crowd to Pope Urban II's preaching of
the First Crusade, at Claremont, November 1095

of religious idealism, eagerness to acquire new lands, and the simple attraction of a sanctioned fight, the crusaders skirted Constantinople, then beat the Seljuk Sultan Kilij Arslan at Dorylaeum in July, forcing the Turks to stand aside and let them march into the Holy Land. After besieging it for eight months, they took Antioch in June 1098 and then marched on the ultimate prize of Jerusalem. After another prolonged siege, the city fell amid horrific bloodshed, as the crusaders slaughtered Muslims and Jews alike.

Changing fortunes

The crusaders established a series of small states along the coastline of Palestine and inland in Syria, chief among them the Kingdom of Jerusalem. They formed military orders of knights—the Templars and Hospitallers—who were sworn to monastic-type vows, but defended the Holy Land with swords, not prayers.

However, the Muslim forces regrouped, and they began to eat away at the crusader states, taking Edessa in 1144. A Second Crusade was launched in 1145, but it met with limited success. In the 1180s, most of Syria and Palestine united under the Muslim Sultan Saladin, who smashed the crusader armies at Hattin in 1187, and a

few months later seized Jerusalem itself. The Third Crusade, led by the German emperor Frederick Barbarossa and the English and French kings Richard the Lionheart and Philip Augustus, checked Saladin's progress but did not regain Jerusalem.

Thereafter the crusading movement declined: the Fourth Crusade in 1204 was unable to even reach the Holy Land, the participants content to sack the fellow-Christian city of Constantinople and dismember the Byzantine Empire; while later the Fifth (1217–1221) and subsequent crusades were sidetracked in Egypt. One by one the crusaders' fortresses fell, until in 1291 the Mamluk Sultan al-Ashraf Kalil stormed Acre, their last stronghold. Although the crusaders launched more expeditions, they were hopelessly unsuccessful, and the age of the crusades was over.

》 SALADIN

Founder of the Ayyubid dynasty and unifier of the Muslim states in the Middle East, Saladin ruled as sultan of Egypt from 1138 to 1193. Despite his victory against the crusaders at Hattin, they considered him an honorable and chivalrous leader.

⬆ **This sumptuous cross** is a sign both of the crusaders' wealth and the lavishness with which they adorned religious symbols.

The German Emperor Frederick Barbarossa is shown here defeating the Seljuk Turks at the Battle of Iconium, in May 1190 during the Third Crusade. Shortly afterward, Barbarossa drowned while crossing a river, undermining the Crusade's leadership.

The Black Death

EUROPE, THE MIDDLE EAST 1346–1351

Although Europe had experienced many serious outbreaks of disease (the first recorded being the great pestilence that struck Athens in 430–429 BCE), the most devastating of all struck in the mid-14th century, killing between one-third and half the continent's population.

The plague strikes

Known as the Black Death, the plague may have spread to Europe from central Asia. Theories abound on what caused the disease, although it is widely supposed to have been *Yersinia pestis*, a bacterium carried by fleas on rodents. The bacterial infection is transferred to humans when the fleas feed on human blood.

> ## So many died that all believed it was the **end of the world**.
>
> **Italian chronicler Agnolo di Tura on the Black Death in Siena, c.1350**

The infection has three variants: bubonic plague, which is characterized by buboes, or swellings, of the neck, groin, and armpits; pneumonic plague, which infects the lungs; and septicemic plague, or blood poisoning.

The plague was transmitted via Constantinople in 1347 and reached most parts of Europe during 1348 and 1349. It caused widespread terror and panic, and most attempts to fight its spread were useless. Macabre outbreaks of religious fervor accompanied the progress of the disease, and the *Danse Macabre*, or "dance of death," became a common artistic motif of the afflicted times.

By 1350, the Black Death had largely run its course, but with somewhere between 25 and 50 million Europeans dead, a sudden shortage of labor may have contributed to profound social changes. The peasantry found their diminished numbers led to a greater demand for their services, which meant that their living conditions and legal rights greatly improved.

✉ **Physicians used leeches** to try to cure patients. As the leech drew blood, so "noxious vapors" causing the disease might be removed from his or her body.

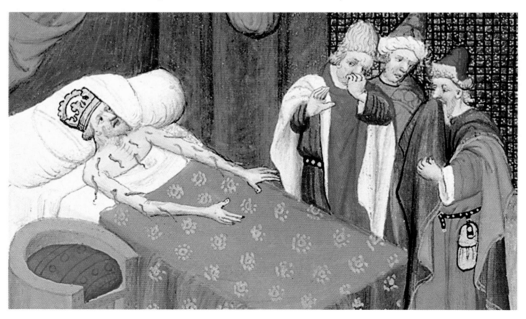

The Hundred Years' War

FRANCE ⌛ **1337–1453**

In the 12th century, the Plantagenet kings of England acquired territories in France. This sparked hostility between the English and French, eventually leading to the Hundred Years' War.

War breaks out

In 1328, Edward III of England sought to assert his claim to the French throne by right of his grandfather, Philip IV of France. Once rebuffed, Edward prepared for war. Open conflict broke out in 1337, culminating in an English invasion of northern France in 1346. Edward was victorious at Crécy (1346) and Poitiers (1360), leading to the Treaty of Brétigny, by which England was left in possession of much of northern and western France. From 1369, under the French king Charles V, war broke out again when the French pushed back the English, who responded with a series of devastating raids (or *chevauchées*). However, the English failed to recover the lost ground.

Henry V of England relaunched the war in 1415, gaining victory at Agincourt and securing almost all France north of the Loire. Inspired by Joan of Arc, a dejected France recovered to take the last English outposts in Gascony in the 1450s. After a final defeat at Castillon in 1453, the English were left with almost no territory in France, save Calais.

≪ Henry V led England to a decisive victory at Agincourt, northern France, in 1415.

≫ JOAN OF ARC

Born in 1412, Joan of Arc claimed she had seen visions that inspired her to come to the aid of France. She reinvigorated the French to defend Orléans in 1429, but she was allowed to fall into the hands of the English, who burned her as a heretic.

Byzantine Empire

After 395 CE, the Roman Empire was divided into two halves, and its eastern portion, which survived the fall of Rome, is known as the Byzantine Empire. With their capital at Constantinople, the Byzantine emperors experienced centuries of barbarian invasions, periods of resurgence and reconquest, and Muslim-Arab invasions that cut away half their territory. Then, finally, 1,000 years after Rome's fall, they succumbed to the Ottoman Turks in 1453.

The early Byzantine Empire

NEAR EAST, ANATOLIA, BALKANS, N AFRICA   395–717

In the 5th century CE, barbarian rulers invaded part of the eastern Roman Empire, but the Byzantines weathered the storm, maintained their position, and, under Justinian (ruled 527–565 CE), even managed to reconquer many of the lost provinces in North Africa and Italy.

These were brittle victories, however, and many of the devastated territories produced little tax revenue, or loyalty. In 568 CE, the Byzantines lost much of Italy to the Lombards (*see p.162*), and exhausting wars with the Persian Empire, which ended in a Byzantine victory in 628, left both

realms severely weakened. The invasions by Muslim-Arab armies from the 620s led to the fall of Jerusalem in 637, of Alexandria (and Egypt) in 640, and finally of Carthage in 698, spelling the end of Byzantine North Africa. When Arab armies besieged Constantinople in 717, it looked as if the empire was finished.

⊟ **A mosaic depicting Justinian** from the Church of San Vitale, Ravenna, Italy. Justinian's legal reforms made him a hugely respected emperor.

Byzantine survival and fall

NEAR EAST, ANATOLIA, BALKANS 717–1453

The Byzantine emperor Leo III (ruled 717–741) fended off Arab invasion in 717 with the aid of the Bulgarian *khan* (ruler). In the mid-8th century, Leo III weakened the empire by causing uproar when he banned religious icons, claiming they were tantamount to idol worship.

From the 9th century, under the Macedonian dynasty, the empire began to recover. Nicephorus Phocas (ruled 963–969) won a string of victories in Syria, and John Tzimiskes (ruled 969–976) defeated the Bulgar tsar Boris II, thereby securing the empire's position in the Balkans, and reconquered large parts of Syria.

The revival peaks and falters

Under Basil II, "the Bulgar-Slayer" (ruled 963–1025), the revival of the empire seemed to be complete. The Bulgars were smashed at the Battle of Kleidion (1014), and much of southern Italy was retaken. But Basil neglected the empire's eastern frontier and his successors ignored the army, allowing the Seljuk Turks (*see p.156*) to make incursions into the empire, massacring the Byzantine army at Manzikert in 1071. Much of Asia Minor was lost by 1080, and only the energy of Alexius I Comnenus (ruled 1081–1118) staved off disaster.

Nevertheless, Byzantium's fatal decline had now set in. Newly assertive enemies such as the Normans chipped away at Byzantine Italy and, in the Balkans, the Slav kingdoms grew ever stronger. Against the relentless pressure of the Seljuk and Ottoman Turks, even the most energetic emperors could do little more than slow the pace of collapse. By the early 15th century, Byzantium controlled just a few territories and Constantinople had become an

⌂ A view of Constantinople, from a late 15th century German history, shows the city as imagined a short time after its fall to the Ottoman Turks in 1453.

isolated, beleaguered outpost. On May 29, 1453, the army of the Ottoman Sultan Mehmet II stormed the city walls and the Byzantine Empire came to an end.

» BASIL THE BULGAR-SLAYER

The greatest of the Macedonian emperors, Basil ascended the throne as an infant in 963, but did not rule in his own right until 976. In 995, he rampaged through the Near East, sacking a string of Arab cities and securing control of northern Syria. From 1000, he won his greatest triumphs against the Bulgars, culminating in the victory at Kleidion in 1014, after which he is said to have blinded all but one man in every 100 of his prisoners, sending the stumbling mass back to the Bulgarian Tsar Samuel, who died of shock and shame.

The Americas

During the 9th century, the lowland Maya city-states were abandoned, leading to the end of the Classic era in Central America, but the Maya did continue to flourish in the northern Yucatán. In Mexico, the Toltecs built ceremonial centers and then, in the 14th century, the Aztecs established a great empire. In the 15th century in South America, the cultures of Tiwanaku and Wari gave rise to the greatest and most advanced empire Peru had yet known, that of the Incas.

The Toltecs

⛩ CENTRAL MEXICO ⏳ c.900–c.1180

Around the 9th century, Mexico gave birth to new, more militarized cultures, well placed to take advantage of the persistent warfare of the region. Among them were the Chichimecs, nomadic invaders from the north, and a more advanced culture known as the Toltecs, from whom the Aztecs claimed descent.

The Toltec capital

The Toltecs first entered Mexico in the early 10th century and, under their ruler Topiltzin Quetzalcoatl, made a capital at Tollan (modern-day Tula). From here, between 950 and 1150, they held sway over a portion of the valleys of Mexico, Puebla, and Morelos. The racks at Tula that held the skulls of dead enemies, and the sacrificial motifs prevalent in its reliefs, speak of a warrior culture. Around 1180, outsiders invaded Tollan, burning the city and ending Toltec dominance in central Mexico.

《 One of the Atlantes—monumental columns carved in the form of Toltec warriors—that expressed the Toltecs' militaristic ideology in stone.

The Maya

MEXICO, GUATEMALA c.800–1697

The vivid murals from Bonampak (near Yaxchilán) date from the late 8th century and are some of the finest surviving examples of Maya painting.

Historians have proposed many explanations for the sudden collapse of the lowland Maya city-states during the 800s—from natural causes, such as disease or climate change, to soil exhaustion, war, or loss of control by the ruling classes. However, no theory has yet been proven absolutely.

After c.900, all the main Maya centers were in the northern part of the Yucatán. One, Chichen Itzá, had been founded in the second half of the 8th century by a confederation of various Maya lowland groups and the Itzá people.

Chichen Itzá

The city, which experimented with new rituals and forms of shared government, was a thriving community in the 9th to 11th centuries, but collapsed thereafter. The architecture of the city bears a striking resemblance to that of the Toltec capital Tollan, which flourished around the same time. It is unclear what form of contact took place between Chichen Itzá and Tollan, but there must have been extensive cultural and trade links across Mexico.

After Chichen Itzá's collapse, Mayapán took over as the leading Maya city, ruling a confederacy of peoples that lasted until the arrival of the Spanish in the 16th century. Maya resistance to the Spanish was fierce, and independent Maya states lasted until the conquest of the final Itzá capital of Nojpeten (Tayasal) in 1697.

This limestone carving from the Mayan city of Yaxchilán depicts a bloodletting ritual.

The Aztecs

⚑ **MEXICO** ⌛ **c.1168–1520**

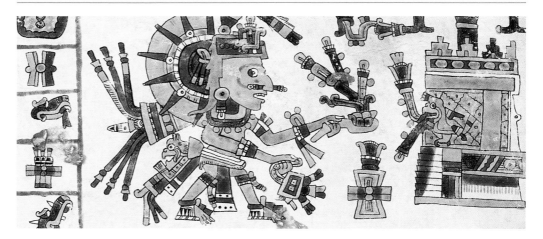

⟫ **Detail from the Codex Cospi**, an illustrated Aztec divinatory calendar, made from thin strips of plant fibers covered with whitewash.

The Aztecs, or the Mexica as they called themselves, began as an insignificant group in the Valley of Mexico, an area racked by constant warfare in the 13th century and ruled by petty kingdoms. They grew to be, by the 15th century, the most powerful people in Mesoamerica.

The Aztec empire

Aztec tradition relates that their peoples migrated from a land in the north named "Aztlán" in 1168, and in 1375, they appointed their first *tlatoani* (king), possibly from a family of Toltec origin.

He ruled from Tenochtitlán (modern Mexico City), at the time the largest and most powerful city in Mesoamerica. In the vast marshes that surrounded Tenochtitlán, the Aztecs built dams to trap the fresh water from the rivers that flowed into the lake. They also grew crops on *chinampas*, artificial islands created in the shallow lake. In 1429, the fourth Aztec ruler, Itzcoatl (ruled 1428–1440),

brokered a triple alliance that united his city with the cities of Texcoco and Tlacopan. In time, though, the Aztecs exploited their allies and went on to conquer all of Mexico. By 1500, even parts of Guatemala and El Salvador paid tribute to the Aztec empire. Yet soon after the Spanish arrived in Mexico in 1519 (*see p.209*), the Aztec civilization collapsed.

Aztec religion

The Aztecs had a large number of gods related to the creation of the cosmos, to the sun, and to fertility, death, and war. The two main temples of Tenochtitlán were dedicated to Huitzilopochtli, the god of war, and Tlaloc, the god of rain and water. Another important god, Quetzalcoatl, was the feathered-serpent god of wind, creativity, and fertility. The Aztecs believed that if they did not satisfy the gods with sacrifices of blood, the sun would not continue its journey across the sky.

☑ **Sacrificial knives**, such as this Aztec priest's knife with an ornately carved handle, were used to dispatch thousands of people at the temples each year.

Early North American cultures

⚐ **SW AND MIDWESTERN USA** ⌛ **c.700–c.1450**

In southwest North America, small villages subsisting on corn gradually merged into three principal cultures—the Hohokam, the Mogollon, and the Anasazi—by 700.

By 900, the Hohokam, the earliest of the three traditions, had built canals up to 9 miles (15 km) long and a sophisticated irrigation network that allowed them to grow two crops a year. Strongly influenced by Mexico, in their major settlements at Snaketown and Pueblo Grande they constructed ballcourts and platform temples in the Mesoamerican style. From the 10th century, the Mogollon, to the southeast of the Hohokam, lived in large adobe-built complexes (*pueblos*), and from earliest times were expert potters.

The most widespread culture of the three was the Anasazi, which reached its height between 900 and 1100. Around 1100, the Anasazi left their *pueblos* and began to take refuge in cliff-dwellings sheltered by canyon walls. By 1300, however, most of these were abandoned, possibly because of crop failure.

Mound-dwellers

Farther to the east, a separate group of cultures emerged in the Middle Mississippi Valley. Here, at the turn of the 8th century, sizeable towns appeared, most featuring large, rectangular mounds. The towns served as administrative and ceremonial centers for the Adena and Hopewell peoples.

The greatest was Cahokia, at the confluence of the Mississippi and Missouri rivers. By the 13th century, Cahokia had a population of 30,000, with more than a hundred flat mounds containing high-status graves. By 1450, however, Cahokia was abandoned, possibly after an epidemic of disease.

⬆ **This ornamental gorget** from the Mississippian culture was worn over the chest with a hide thong.

⬇ **"The Cliff Palace"** at Chapin Mesa is one of the largest Anasazi cliff-dwellings. It housed some 100 people between about 1190 and 1280.

⌃ **The great Gateway of the Sun**, Tiwanaku's largest monumental portal, with its semi-subterranean temple in the foreground.

⌃ **A feather hat** from Peru's highland Wari culture, richly decorated with ferocious stylized animal heads.

Early cultures of South America

⌖ **PERU AND BOLIVIA** ⌛ **c.650–c.1470**

From around 650, the highlands of the central Andes in South America came to be dominated by a series of empires.

Tiwanaku and Wari

The earliest of these empires was Tiwanaku. Its capital was positioned on the high altiplano of Bolivia. By 500 CE, its influence had spread into parts of the southern Andes and, at its peak, the city had around 50,000 inhabitants. The city was characterized by great monolithic portals, dedicated to a solar "gateway god."

The Tiwanaku rulers ordered large agricultural complexes of terraced fields to be built and controlled a thriving trade in textiles, pottery, and gold. In the end, it was probably a drought that saw Tiwanaku abandoned around 1000.

Around 435 miles (700 km) northwest of Tiwanaku, the city of Wari emerged around 600. Its culture was characterized by large high-walled enclosures, scattered throughout Peru, where the Wari elite lived, dominating the local people by force. The empire seems to have been established

rapidly, with most of the satellite colonies appearing around 650. Around 900, the Wari Empire dissolved, possibly because of internal revolts that broke the bonds of a domain held together by military strength.

The Chimú

The collapse of the Moche culture around 800 (*see p.131*) left a political vacuum in coastal Peru. After the brief flourishing of a people known as the Sican, this void was eventually filled by the Chimú, who established their capital at Chan Chan near the Pacific coast around 900.

Characterized by vast *ciudadelas* (palace compounds), at its height Chan Chan covered some 5,000 acres (20 sq km) and had a population as high as 35,000. The *ciudadelas* formed the enclosures of the Chimú lords, who from 1150 embarked on the conquest of the north coast of Peru. Ultimately, around 1370, this brought them into conflict with the growing power of the Incas (*see facing page*), who a century later finally conquered Chan Chan.

The Inca Empire

PERU AND BOLIVIA ☒ **c.1300–1532**

The Incas first settled high in the Peruvian Andes around modern Cuzco about 1300. However, in 1438, under their leader Pachacuti ("transformer of the earth"), the Incas' expansion began in earnest, until the culture dominated much of modern Peru and Bolivia—an area they called Tawantinsuyu, "the Land of the Four Quarters." Around 1470, the Inca Empire absorbed its most dangerous rival, conquering the Chimú capital of Chan Chan, and by 1493, Inca rule reached north to Quito in Ecuador.

Hierarchy, administration, and religion

Pachacuti and his son Tupac Inca created a federal system consisting of four provinces, each overseen by an Inca governor. At the top of the empire's social hierarchy was the Sapa Inca, whose rule was absolute in political and religious affairs. A complex bureaucracy administered his empire but, being absolutely dependent on him, the whole system crumbled when the Sapa Inca fell into the hands of Spanish invaders in the 1530s (*see p.209*).

The empire was linked by a network of roads, many of them paved, which connected the outlying regions to the capital Cuzco. The Incas had no horses, nor had they discovered the use of the wheel for transport, so relays of runners carried messages, while llamas served as pack animals.

Lacking a developed system of writing, the Incas kept records on *quipus*, collections of colored threads that were knotted to calculate taxation, keep records of livestock, and pass on simple messages. The Inca built large temples, many of them to the sun-god Inti. The most important of these was the Qorikancha, which lay close to Cuzco's

❯❯ PACHACUTI

The ninth Sapa Inca, Pachacuti (ruled 1438–1471) vastly extended the Inca Empire, sending his armies north almost to Quito, and south nearly to Sucre in Bolivia. He rebuilt Cuzco in the shape of a puma and strengthened the cult of the sun god Inti.

central plaza and in which the Spanish conquistadors would find an entire replica garden of precious materials, including "corn" with stems of silver and ears made from gold.

❯❯ **This gold disc** representing the sun god Inti is one of the few Inca artifacts that the Spanish conquerors failed to melt down.

The city of Machu Picchu was constructed in the mid-15th century, probably by the Inca ruler Pachacuti. Dramatically situated, it most likely served as a religious center rather than a defensive one, and was abandoned a short time before the Spanish conquest of 1532–1533.

Polynesia

Beginning around 200 BCE, the Polynesian people began a major expansion and by approximately 1000 CE, settlers had explored and settled all corners of the South Pacific, achieving astonishing feats of long-distance navigation. At their farthest extent, they reached New Zealand and Easter Island, and established a diverse range of cultures, making the Polynesians the most widely dispersed ethnic group of the time.

Polynesian expansion and navigation

⚐ **POLYNESIA** ⌛ **c.200 BCE–c.1000 CE**

The Polynesian people are likely to have descended from a southeast Asian group, possibly from modern Taiwan, and have genetic affinities to a people indigenous to Melanesia, a group of islands north of Australia. This cultural mix gave rise to the Lapita culture, whose fine red pottery dates back to around 1600 BCE.

The great Polynesian expansion

The Lapita people used stone adzes and cultivated yam and taro, as well as coconut, breadfruit, and bananas, and they domesticated pigs and chickens—all elements that would form an important part of later Polynesian culture.

Excellent navigators, they used outrigger canoes to traverse great distances. To guide them, they used the stars, birds, winds, currents, and tides, and may also have used charts made of sticks. They reached the Marquesas Islands around 200 BCE; Easter Island, Tahiti, and Hawaii in about 400 CE; and finally New Zealand around 1000. At each they established chiefdoms, which led to the growth of sophisticated and hierarchical societies.

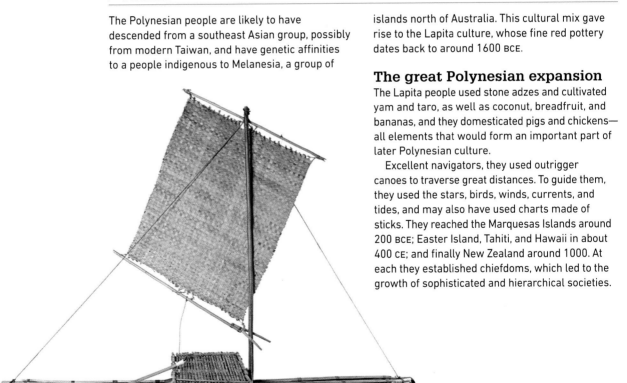

◅ **This model of a Polynesian canoe** shows the double hull that lent the necessary stability for ocean voyages.

The Maori

[symbol] **NEW ZEALAND** [symbol] **c.1000–1840**

New Zealand was the last major area to be settled by the Polynesians, who reached it around 1000. Its climate is very different from tropical Polynesia, which led to changes in established Polynesian ways of life. Of the traditional Polynesian crops, only the sweet potato took hold. Much of South Island was not viable for agriculture, promoting a culture based on fishing, hunting, and gathering. Around 1300, the Maori, as the descendants of the original settlers are known, did turn more to agriculture, probably because food for hunting became scarce.

The population on North Island increased significantly, and the period after 1350, known as the Classic era, saw the building of massive earthwork forts, with rich burials. There appears to have been an upsurge in warfare between competing Maori groups, with the building of even larger forts (*pa*) with complexes of terraces and ditches. Despite their strikingly rich culture, the Maori never united politically, putting them at a disadvantage when European colonists arrived in the 19th century.

[symbol] **Maori *tiki* talismans** were traditionally worn for good luck, and by women to guard against infertility. This one is made in greenstone.

Easter Island

[symbol] **EASTER ISLAND** [symbol] **c.400–1868**

Easter Island (or to give it its Polynesian name, Rapa Nui) is one of the most isolated islands in Polynesia. It lies 1,290 miles (2,000 km) from its closest neighbor and may have been settled by Polynesians around 400.

Between 1000 and 1200, the trees on Easter Island began to disappear. This seems largely to have been triggered by the colonists' obsessive construction of giant stone heads, called *moai*. They were carved in one piece from compressed volcanic

ash and required enormous use of resources to move from the stone quarries and erect. Eventually, some time after 1600, when the last trees were cut, the islands' ecosystem collapsed as soil erosion leeched the land of its ability to bear crops, and there was no more wood to build boats for fishing. In the ensuing social turmoil, the *moai* were deliberately thrown down beginning in the early 18th century, so that by 1868, none were left intact.

[symbol] **Re-erected *moai*** statues on Easter Island are believed to embody revered ancestors.

The Early
Modern World

The world in 1450–1750

Europe underwent a cultural revolution—the Renaissance—in the 15th and 16th centuries, in which much of the continent's ancient learning was rediscovered. A spirit of scientific inquiry arose that provided key technological advantages over the rest of the world, and voyages of exploration soon became tidal waves of colonization,

The world in 1700

——	International border
·······	Undefined border
	Ottoman Empire
	Russian Empire
	Safavid Empire
	Mughal Empire
	Qing Empire
◆	England and possessions
◆	France and possessions
◆	Denmark and possessions
◆	Spain and possessions
◆	Portugal and possessions
◆	Netherlands and possessions
	Hohenzollern possessions
	Sweden and possessions
	Venetian Republic and possessions
	Austrian Habsburg territories
	Japan
——	Holy Roman Empire

reaching most parts of the globe. By the mid-18th century, several European countries were global powers, though their rise was not unopposed. Ming and Qing China, Mughal India, Safavid Persia, and the Ottomans resisted Europe's expansion, but their resources were overwhelmed by superior technology and organization.

The early modern world in 1700

By 1700, most of Central and South America (except Brazil) was controlled by Spain, with large British and French colonies in North America. Muslim empires were at their height in Persia, India, and modern Turkey. The Russian empire had expanded eastward to Siberia, while the Qing held sway in China.

☖ **The Thirty Years' War** (1618–1648) ravaged much of central Europe. In 1700 Germany remained divided and weak, but the Austrian Habsburgs held extensive territories and had begun to make inroads into Ottoman control of the Balkans. Expansion by the Russians brought them into conflict with Poland–Lithuania and Sweden.

Asia

The period from 1450 to 1650 was a time of great turmoil for Asia. China saw the collapse of the Ming dynasty and its replacement by the Qing, a dynasty that originated from Manchuria, in the northeast. In Japan, meanwhile, a series of bitter civil wars ended with unification under the Tokugawa shoguns. In western Asia, three Muslim empires arose to dominate the region: the Mughals in India, the Ottomans in Turkey, and the Safavids in Persia.

Decline of the Ming

CHINA 🕮 1449–1644

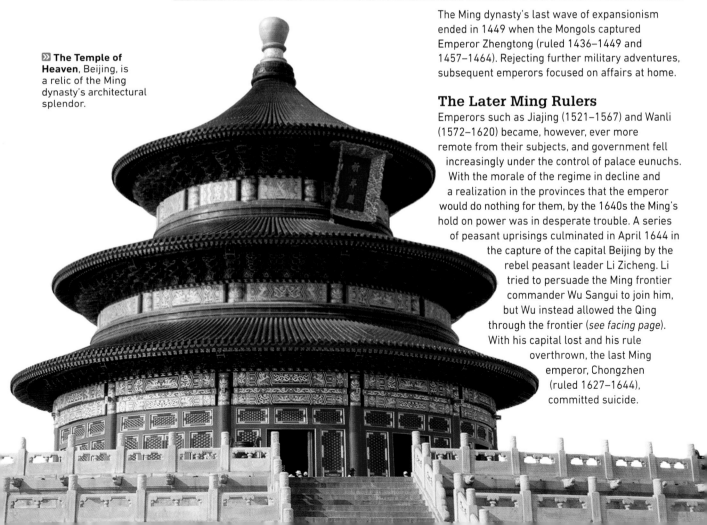

》 **The Temple of Heaven**, Beijing, is a relic of the Ming dynasty's architectural splendor.

The Ming dynasty's last wave of expansionism ended in 1449 when the Mongols captured Emperor Zhengtong (ruled 1436–1449 and 1457–1464). Rejecting further military adventures, subsequent emperors focused on affairs at home.

The Later Ming Rulers

Emperors such as Jiajing (1521–1567) and Wanli (1572–1620) became, however, ever more remote from their subjects, and government fell increasingly under the control of palace eunuchs. With the morale of the regime in decline and a realization in the provinces that the emperor would do nothing for them, by the 1640s the Ming's hold on power was in desperate trouble. A series of peasant uprisings culminated in April 1644 in the capture of the capital Beijing by the rebel peasant leader Li Zicheng. Li tried to persuade the Ming frontier commander Wu Sangui to join him, but Wu instead allowed the Qing through the frontier (*see facing page*). With his capital lost and his rule overthrown, the last Ming emperor, Chongzhen (ruled 1627–1644), committed suicide.

The rise of the Qing

⚑ CHINA ⌛ 1616–50

In northeastern China, an area that lay outside Ming control, a group called the Jurchens, descendants of the Jin dynasty (1115–1234 CE), began, in the late 16th century, to absorb their neighboring peoples. In 1616 their leader Nurhaci founded the Later Jin dynasty and formally organized both his people and the Mongol tribes of the region.

The population was enrolled into four military units called banners, each identified by the color of its standard. Nurhaci's successor Huang Taiji (ruled 1626–1643) introduced Chinese-style institutions among the Jurchen, changing the name of his people in 1636 to Manchu, and restyling the dynasty in 1637 as Qing. In 1644, expanding into territory farther south, the Qing took control of the Ming capital Beijing from rebel forces (*see facing page*) and installed six-year-old Shunzhi as emperor (ruled 1644–1661). Qing forces went on sweeping south, crushing any resistance. By 1650, apart from isolated holdouts such as Taiwan, Qing control over China was complete.

◀ A mounted warrior, typical of the Qing fighters who fought sporadic Ming resistance in the 1640s.

China under the Qing

⚑ CHINA ⌛ 1644–1795 CE

The Qing bureaucracy in China retained many features of the earlier Ming system, but caused resentment by decreeing that all Chinese men adopt the traditional Qing hairstyle—a shaved forehead and long, braided ponytail or queue. The successors of Shunzhi (*see above*)—Kangxi (ruled 1661–1722), Yongzheng (ruled 1722–1735), and Qianlong (ruled 1736–1796)—presided over the period of greatest expansion. The Qing absorbed Outer Mongolia, and claimed Tibet as a protectorate in 1750. This was also a time of influences from outside China. Kangxi passed an "edict of toleration" that enabled the spread of Christian Jesuit missions, while exports of tea, silk, and ceramics to Europe burgeoned.

◀ A sinuous dragon coils around a panel from the Dazheng Hall of the Shenyang Palace in northeast China, the original residence of the Qing rulers.

⌃ Toyotomi Hideyoshi was one of Nobunaga's chief generals, with considerable military talent.

Japan united and the Tokugawa shogunate

JAPAN ⏳ 1560–1800

In the mid-1500s, Japan was fragmented into many semi-independent domains, each ruled by a separate *daimyo* (warlord), while the shogun (ruler of the military), and even more so the emperor, were powerless to exert their authority.

Gradually, groups of *daimyo* clustered together and, in 1560, the leader of one group, Imagawa Yoshimoto, tried to take control of the royal capital, Kyoto. To do so he had to cross the lands of Oda Nobunaga, who cut his forces to pieces. Nobunaga then entered Kyoto himself, beginning a 40-year process of Japanese unification.

Nobunaga and Hideyoshi

By 1577, Nobunaga had conquered central Japan; he then moved against more distant *daimyo*. His chief general, Toyotomi Hideyoshi, was engaged in a bitter struggle against the powerful Mori clan of northern Honshu when Nobunaga was assassinated in 1582. Hideyoshi broke off the conflict in order to take over Nobunaga's mantle as head of the unification drive. He had still to overcome six major *daimyo* groupings, finally forcing the capitulation of the most powerful, the Hojo of Odawara, in 1590.

Ieyasu completes the unification

Hideyoshi died in 1598, and a power struggle immediately broke out, from which Tokugawa Ieyasu emerged the victor, smashing his opponents' armies at Sekigahara in 1600. Confiscating vast

≫ TOKUGAWA IEYASU

Born Matsudaira Takechiyo in 1542, Tokugawa Ieyasu was a claimant to succeed Oda Nobunaga as shogun in 1582, but was outmaneuvered by another general, Toyotomi Hideyoshi. Only once Hideyoshi had died, and Ieyasu had won a decisive victory over other rivals at the battle of Sekigahara, did he finally take over the shogunate. His reforms stabilized the power of the Tokugawa shogunate, strengthening it against challenges from regional *daimyo* (warlords). He died in 1616, leaving Japan's unification as his legacy.

tracts of land from the defeated *daimyo*, he established himself as shogun, but with an unparalleled monopoly on power. Ieyasu made Edo (Tokyo) the new, military capital of Japan. The emperor and his court, although revered, retained only ceremonial stature at Kyoto, and Japanese society became more structured. Extensive legislation established a hierarchy of four classes: samurai, farmer, artisan, and merchant.

Japan turns inward

Under the Tokugawa, Confucian doctrines began to exert a greater influence in Japan. With its emphasis on loyalty to the political order and social stability, Confucianism suited the regime

⚅ **The Japanese tea ceremony** (*chanoyu*) was refined in the Tokugawa era, becoming a symbol of the delicate etiquette that held together the society of the age.

well, and went hand-in-hand with a closing inward of Japan. In 1612, Tokugawa Hidetada (ruled 1605–1623) confirmed a policy of national seclusion (known as *sakoku*) and, in 1614, foreign trade was restricted to the cities of Nagasaki and Hirado in southern Kyushu. By 1639, the Portuguese traders had been expelled and the Dutch confined to a small island off Nagasaki. Tokugawa rule brought Japan two centuries of relative peace and tranquility, as well as a cultural flowering.

Many of the elements recognized as the keystones of Japanese traditional culture emerged during this period, such as *haiku* poetry, flower arranging, the tea ceremony, the final form of *Noh* theatre, and *Ukiyo-e* ("pictures of the floating world") prints. Yet, for all its unchallenged authority, the later Tokugawa regime was inflexible. Its seclusion from the outside world made Japan ill-prepared to face a resurgent and industrialized Europe in the 19th century that was very different from the Europe it had turned its back on.

⏩ **A Japanese mask** used in *Noh* theatre. The restraint and elegance of *Noh* appealed to upper-class Japanese Edo society.

India under the Mughals

⚐ INDIA ⌛ 1526–1739

Ultimately one of the most powerful states of the 17th century, the Islamic Mughal Empire had much more modest beginnings in the efforts of Babur, an ambitious Central Asian princeling who wanted to carve himself a territory near Samarkand. In 1504, Babur seized Kabul in modern Afghanistan and the next year he launched his first raid into India.

Babur and Humayun

In 1519, Babur launched a concerted bid to unseat the Lodi sultans of Delhi (see p.159). In April 1526, at Panipat, Babur crushed the army of Ibrahim Lodi. He then marched on and took not only Delhi but also Agra, where the Lodi treasury was lodged.

Moving west, at Khanwa the following year he defeated a huge army raised by Rana Sangha of Mewar (in modern-day Rajasthan). By the time of his death in 1530, Babur had consolidated his position as master of the rich cities of northern India. His son Humayun, however, met with less success. By 1540, he had lost his father's kingdom to the Afghan ruler Sher Shah Suri, and was in exile at the Safavid court in Persia. In 1555, with the support of the Persians (see pp.204–5), he restored Mughal rule by pushing aside Sher Shah's feeble successors. He died soon after, leaving the empire to his 12-year-old son Akbar.

≫ BABUR

Founder of the Mughals, Babur (ruled 1526–1530) was descended from the Mongol conqueror Tamerlane, who had raided Delhi in 1328. Babur outdid him by capturing the city and becoming the first Mughal emperor.

◄ **A Mughal miniature** of the Battle of Panipat (1526) clearly shows the cannons, part of the arsenal of firearms that was instrumental in Babur's victory.

The reign of Akbar

At first under the tutelage of the capable regent Bairam Khan, Akbar oversaw a vast extension of Mughal territory. In his lifetime Mughal dominion expanded to reach from Kashmir in the north and Afghanistan in the northwest to Bengal in the east and the Deccan plateau in the south. To consolidate his position, Akbar established a centralized system of government, administered by warrior-aristocrats (*mansabdars*). The most senior of these were paid with land grants (*jagirs*), and held the right to collect tax from this land. Akbar promoted a policy of religious tolerance. He reduced the influence of the Muslim scholars (*ulama*) on government policy, abolished taxes on non-Muslims (*jizya*), and replaced the Muslim lunar calendar with a solar one. He thereby avoided dissension among his many non-Muslim subjects.

Akbar's reign also saw a cultural renaissance. A new style of north Indian classical music flourished, as did an enormously productive school of Mughal painting that combined Persian and Indian styles.

Jahangir and Shah Jahan

Akbar died in 1605, and was succeeded by his son Jahangir, who had already tried several times to depose him. In turn, Jahangir faced a rebellion in 1623 by his third son, Khurram, which ended only a year before Jahangir's death in 1627. A civil war instantly erupted among Jahangir's four sons over the succession.

The victor, Khurram, who took the name Shah Jahan (ruled 1628–1658), contributed some of the Mughal Empire's greatest surviving monuments, including a new capital at Delhi—which he called

⏏ **Akbar ordered a lavish** new capital at Fatehpur Sikri, 28 miles (45 km) from Agra. The word *fateh* means "victory," commemorating Babur's triumphs.

Shahjahanabad—centered on the Red Fort and the Jama Masjid; and the majestic Taj Mahal at Agra. These huge projects were symbols of Mughal wealth gained from flourishing agriculture and trade. In 1657, Shah Jahan fell gravely ill. Without waiting to see the outcome of their father's illness, his sons threw themselves with great gusto into a vicious and damaging civil war, from which Aurangzeb, the third son, emerged victorious in 1660. Shah Jahan had by now recovered, but Aurangzeb locked him away in the palace at Agra, where he died, neglected and bitter, in 1666.

Aurangzeb and the decline of the empire

Aurangzeb oversaw the expansion of the empire to its greatest extent, yet he also sowed the seeds of its decline. He was often away on campaigns, and his efforts to defeat the Maratha confederacy of Shivaji in the south, which was seeking to build an empire of its own, met with little success. He was also intolerant in religious matters, reimposing taxes on Hindu pilgrims and, in 1670, reinstating the *jizya* tax on all non-Muslims. All these moves polarized opinion of him and undermined his support among the vast numbers of Hindus and Sikhs in the Mughal Empire.

Aurangzeb died in 1707 and a rapid succession of weak rulers further undermined Mughal power. In 1739, Nadir Shah, the ruler of Persia, sacked Delhi and seized the Mughal treasury. As a serious political force, the Mughal Empire was now dead.

⏏ **The Mughal court** excelled in decorative arts, architecture, and producing miniatures.

The Taj Mahal, at Agra, is Mughal emperor Shah Jahan's stunning mausoleum for his wife Mumtaz Mahal, who died in childbirth in 1631. It is the ultimate Mughal garden tomb, representing paradise on earth, and took from 1632 to 1654 to complete. Shah Jahan is buried there, too.

The Ottoman Empire

⬛ TURKEY, NEAR EAST, BALKANS, N AFRICA ⬛ 1453–1739

After their conquest of the Byzantine Empire in 1453 under their Sultan Mehmet II (*see p.179*), Ottoman armies surged forward into the Balkans. However, failure to capture Belgrade (then in Hungary) in 1456 put a temporary halt to westward expansion. The remnant of Hungary, and a fiercely independent Albanian principality under the rule of the warrior-prince Skanderbeg, kept a watchful eye on their new Turkish neighbors. The Ottomans turned their attention east, where the growing power of Safavid Persia (*see pp.204–5*) threatened to stem or even reverse the Ottoman tide.

The height of Ottoman power

It was not until the Battle of Chaldiran in 1514 that Selim I (ruled 1512–1520) was able to best the Safavid dynasty. The Ottomans then pushed rapidly forward, capturing the holy sites in Jerusalem, and in 1517 overthrowing the Mamluk rulers of Egypt by capturing Cairo. In 1520, Suleyman, Selim's son, took charge. In 1523, he captured the island of Rhodes, which was the stronghold of the Knights of St. John, a military order of the crusader era.

Having stabilized the situation in Egypt with a new law code in 1525 that appeased local resentment, Suleyman turned once more to war with an attack on Hungary. At Mohács in 1526, he cut to pieces the army of Louis II of Hungary, resulting in the division of the kingdom between the Ottomans and the Austrian Habsburgs. In 1529, Suleyman attempted to take by siege the Habsburg capital of Vienna, but this marked a watershed in his territorial ambitions, and after only three weeks his army, frustrated, retired into Hungary.

The beginning of decline

Suleyman's personal life was less fortunate. His two favorite sons, Mustafa and Bayezid, were accused of conspiring against him.

To save his throne, Suleyman was forced to have them both executed (in 1553 and 1562), casting a shadow over the rest of his reign. He died on a final Hungarian campaign in 1566

⬛ Ottoman forces equipped with cannons tried to capture Vienna in 1529, but Suleyman's army was unable to dislodge the city's defenders.

》 SULEYMAN I

Known in the West as "the Magnificent" and to Islamic writers as *Kanuni* ("the lawgiver"), Suleyman (ruled 1520–1566) was one of the greatest Ottoman sultans and believed himself to be the spiritual heir of Alexander the Great (*see pp.96–7*) and Julius Caesar (*see p.104*). By the time of Suleyman's death, the Ottomans controlled large parts of southeast Europe, the North African coast, and the Middle East.

and the throne fell to his third son Selim, nicknamed "the drunkard," whose rule was of a very different nature. Selim's formative experiences were in the enclosed world of the harem of the Topkapi Palace in Istanbul.

He had little or no military training, and like subsequent sultans, relied on viziers (ministers) to control the empire. Lacking the sultan's controlling hand, the empire fell prey to competing elements in the government: the Diwan (supreme court); the Grand Vizier (chief minister); and the janissaries (elite army units).

The demise and the Tulip Age

In the 1650s, Mehmet Koprülü, the Grand Vizier to Mehmet IV (ruled 1648–1687), began a systematic attempt to root out corruption.

He also planned a resumption of Ottoman conquest, but died in 1661 before his plans could come to fruition. His brother-in-law

Kara Mustafa continued Koprülü's ambitions, besieging Vienna in 1683. Once again, however, the Turks were forced to abandon the siege. A steady European encroachment on Ottoman lands began, spearheaded by the Habsburgs. Belgrade and Serbia were lost by the Treaty of Passarowitz in 1718, but Mahmud I (ruled 1730–54) brought respite by negotiating the Treaty of Belgrade in 1739.

Amazingly, though the Ottomans were militarily enfeebled, racked by revolt, and faced constant threat from, or actual secession of, its borderlands, the empire still experienced a golden cultural age in the late 17th and 18th centuries. A refined court culture—the "Tulip Age"—belied the reality of a state that, within 150 years, would lose most of its European lands.

▢ **Decorative tilework**, often created using recycled material from older structures, was a feature of Ottoman architecture.

> ❝ I am **God's slave** and **sultan of this world**… in Baghdad **I am shah**, in Byzantine realms the **Caesar**, and in Egypt **the sultan**. ❞
>
> **Inscription of Suleyman the Magnificent on the citadel of Bender, Moldavia, 1538**

Safavid Persia

PERSIA ⏳ **1501–1736**

Following the collapse in 1335 of the Mongol Il-khanate, which had ruled Persia since the 1250s, the country dissolved into a collection of successor states. Then, from the 1370s, Tamerlane, a steppe conqueror in the tradition of Genghis Khan (*see p.143*), built a vast Central Asian empire that, from the 1380s, included much of Persia. After Tamerlane's death in 1405, his descendants continued to rule eastern Persia, while the western portion of the country fell to a group made up of Turkmen dynasties known as the Aq Qoyunlu and Kara Qoyunlu.

The rise of the Safavids

Beset by civil war in the late 15th century, the Aq Qoyunlu were overcome by a new group that had grown up around the Safavids, a Sufi order of Muslim mystics. In 1501, the 14-year-old Safavid shah Ismail I (ruled 1501–1524) defeated the Aq Qoyunlu at Shirur, and by 1507 all of western Persia had fallen to the Safavids. Pushing farther west still, Ismail's armies met the Ottomans. A protracted struggle culminated at Chaldiran

⌈⌈ **The Masjid-e Shah** (or Imam Mosque), begun by Shah Abbas I in 1611, forms an imposing centerpiece in Isfahan's Maydan Square.

in 1514, where the Ottoman Sultan Selim I defeated Ismail and prevented the absorption of eastern Anatolia into the Safavid empire.

The height of power

By 1513, Ismail had created a stable frontier to the east that restrained his Central Asian Uzbek neighbors. With further westward expansion blocked by the Ottoman Empire, Ismail turned his attention to making profound reforms within the Persian state. He imposed a new official faith on the country, a variety of Shia Islam that was to dominate Persian religious life into the modern era.

Ottoman and Uzbek aggression and incursions dogged Ismail's descendants until the reign of Shah Abbas I, under whom Safavid rule reached its peak. Between 1587 and 1607 he recaptured lost territories, and in 1598, he moved the capital from Qazvin to Isfahan, where he ordered the construction of a dazzling array of new buildings, centered on the grand Maydan Square.

Abbas I's character had a dark side. In 1615, he had his (probably innocent) heir, Safi Mirza, executed on suspicion of treasonous plotting, and for similar reasons had his other two sons blinded, disqualifying them from succeeding him. On Abbas's death in 1629, it was his grandson, Safi I, who became shah.

> **Now** that **I am king** we are going to **forget** about the practice of **Sultan** Muhammad Shah; **the king** is going to **make the decisions** now.

Safavid ruler Shah Abbas I on his accession to the throne in 1587

The fall of the Safavids

Despite the loss of Baghdad to the Ottomans in 1638, Safi's able minister Saru Taqi ensured financial stability and the reign of Safi's son Shah Abbas II (1642–1666) was peaceful and prosperous. However, his successor Sulayman presided over a gentle decline, as he retreated to the harem and ceased to exert effective power.

By 1720, faced with multiple revolts, the Safavid regime fell apart and in October 1722 Shah Husayn surrendered Isfahan to an army led by the rebel Afghan leader Mahmud Ghilzai. Ghilzai did not last long as shah, being murdered in 1725. The country then fell under the control of another tribal leader, Nadir Khan. Ruling through Safavid puppets until 1736, he then declared himself shah and set about an ambitious military program that included the reconquest of western Persia from the Ottomans and the sacking of Delhi, the Mughal capital, in 1739. However, his cruelty and extortionate tax regimes to fund his campaigns made him deeply unpopular; he was killed in 1747, and Persia once more descended into chaos.

》 SHAH ABBAS I

Aged only 16 when he came to the throne, Shah Abbas I (ruled 1587–1629) proved a determined and able ruler. He embarked on a program of building that would lead his reign to be regarded as a golden age for Persia.

⬣ An 18th-century hunting scene reflecting the cultured elegance of the later Safavid court, more inclined to the pursuits of leisure than war.

Voyages of discovery

At the start of the 15th century, Europeans' knowledge of the world beyond their own continent was limited, and based largely on the cartography of Ptolemy, a Greek polymath who had died 13 centuries earlier, in about 168 CE. Yet, in little over a century, European horizons expanded massively as their navigators set sail, opening up new sea routes to India and the East and discovering the continent of America.

The first routes

The Portuguese were early pioneers in endeavors at sea, concentrating first on southward voyages around the African coastline. In 1486, Diogo Cão explored the Congo River, before making his final landfall at Cape Cross in what is now Namibia. Two years later, Bartolomeu Dias rounded the Cape of Good Hope and sailed into the Indian Ocean, while in 1498 Vasco da Gama crossed over the Indian Ocean to Calicut in southern India.

◄ **King Manuel I of Portugal** gives his blessing to Vasco da Gama as he sets out in 1497 on the voyage that would discover a sea route to India.

◄◄ **Black pepper** was one of the precious commodities that Europeans sought in pioneering new routes to Asia.

The incentive for these expeditions was largely a desire to find a sea route to the sources of the lucrative spice trade in eastern Asia. Not wishing to be outdone by their Portuguese rivals, the Spanish sought an alternative, westerly route to Asia and, in 1491, the Genoese-born Christopher Columbus was able to persuade Queen Isabella of Castile to support a voyage across the Atlantic.

The Americas

Columbus set sail in August 1492 with three ships (*see overleaf*). He accepted Ptolemy's calculation of the world's size and so when he sighted land, he believed it to be eastern Asia, not a new continent ripe for expansion.

Even a further three voyages did not shake this conviction. Further explorations followed rapidly; within five years, in 1497, John Cabot sailed into North American waters off Newfoundland, while the voyage of Jacques Cartier in 1534 took the French to the Gulf of Saint Lawrence. The Portuguese, meanwhile, began to occupy their own area of the Americas, following the discovery of the Brazilian coastline by Alvares Cabral in 1500.

The first circumnavigation

The lure of trade routes to Asia continued to motivate European monarchs and the sailors they funded. In 1519, the Portuguese explorer Ferdinand Magellan set out to sail to the Spice Islands (the Moluccas in Indonesia). He died in 1521 and his deputy completed the voyage; he and his crew were the first Europeans to sail around the world.

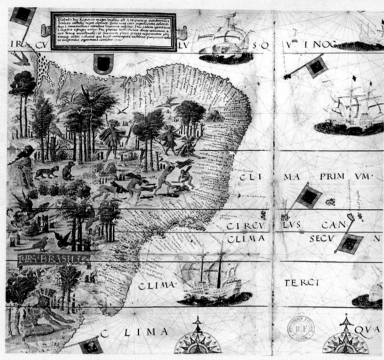

⌃ **An atlas** from c.1519 shows details of the coastline of Brazil—a Portuguese discovery.

The Americas

Soon after Columbus landed in the Americas in 1492, new Spanish expeditions occupied a series of Caribbean islands and toppled the Aztec empire of Mexico and the Inca rulers of Peru. Spain's authority in the New World was soon challenged by other European countries, notably France and England—both of which secured large territories in North America—and Portugal, which gained control of Brazil.

Columbus lands in America

🏴 **THE CARIBBEAN** ⏳ **OCTOBER 11, 1492**

In 1491, Christopher Columbus won the backing of Queen Isabella of Castile for a voyage that he planned to make to eastern Asia, after an eight-year search for a sponsor. On August 3 the following year, he set sail from the Spanish port of Palos in a small flotilla made up of the *Santa Maria*, *Pinta*, and *Niña*.

San Salvador

After an arduous voyage, on October 11, one of Columbus's men finally caught sight of land. Columbus named the island—whose exact location is now uncertain—San Salvador, claiming it for Spain. He called the local Arawak natives "Indians" in the firm belief that he had reached the coast of Asia. Three days after reaching San Salvador, Columbus departed, sailing to Cuba and then to Hispaniola, where he established a small colony, the precursor of the massive Spanish settlement to come.

✉ **Christopher Columbus** landed in the Americas after five weeks at sea. He had wrongly calculated that Asia was just 2,800 miles (4,500 km) west of Europe.

Spain conquers Mexico

MEXICO ⌛ **1519–1521**

Once the Spanish were established in the Caribbean, they learned of the rich Aztec culture on the Mexican mainland. In February 1519, the conquistador Hernán Cortés sailed from Havana, Cuba, to find it. Having forced his way through the Yucatán peninsula, on August 16, he moved inland with 15 horsemen and 400 infantry. He secured native allies in the Tlaxcala, bitter enemies of the Aztecs.

The capture of Tenochtitlán

In November 1519, Cortés reached Tenochtitlán, the Aztec capital, where the ruler, Moctezuma, received the Spanish cordially. But Cortés soon had Moctezuma put under house arrest and, when the Spanish massacred a number of Aztec nobles, Tenochtitlán descended into chaos. Moctezuma was killed by his own people, while the Spanish fought their way in hand-to-hand combat out of the city. Undaunted, in spring 1521, Cortés returned with fresh reinforcements to begin a new siege of Tenochtitlán. This ended in August of the same year with the capture of the new Aztec ruler, Cuahtemoc, and the total dissolution of the Aztec empire.

❯❯ HERNÁN CORTÉS

After conquering the Aztecs, Hernán Cortés became governor of Mexico, but suffered successive attempts by the Spanish authorities to remove him or curb his power. In 1547, he died, wealthy but embittered, in Seville.

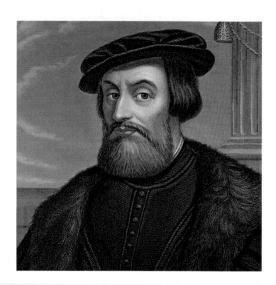

Spain conquers Peru

PERU ⌛ **1527–1572**

In 1527, a small Spanish expedition, in search of the rich land of "Birú" (Peru), led by Francisco Pizarro, landed at Tumbes, an outpost of the Inca empire. Pizarro returned in 1531 with 180 men. He found the Incas recovering from a civil war, which allowed him to cross the Andes freely to reach Cajamarca, where the Inca leader Atahualpa was camped.

The fall of the Inca empire

Luring the Inca ruler into a meeting, Pizarro took him hostage and then, in July 1533, had him executed. The Spanish marched on the capital Cuzco, which they took in November. The prestige of the Inca nobility was severely damaged by their failure to protect Atahualpa, and they

mounted little coherent opposition. Yet in 1536, Manco Capac, installed as a puppet ruler, began a rebellion. Although the Spanish soon retook Cuzco from the rebels, Inca resistance continued on the fringes of Peru until 1572, when their final stronghold of Vilcamaba fell, and Titu Cusi, the last Inca ruler, was executed.

❯❯ ATAHUALPA

With control of the imperial army in Quito, Atahualpa was able to triumph over his brother Huascar to seize power of the Inca realm in 1532, ending Peru's civil war. By the time of this victory, the Spanish had arrived; they executed Atahualpa in 1533.

The Spanish Empire in the New World

CENTRAL AND SOUTH AMERICA · **1523–1700**

⌃ **The two hemispheres** of the world on this 1744 silver coin symbolize the global nature of Spanish conquests.

The Spanish faced grave problems governing their vast territories in the Americas, because they lay so far from Spain itself. From 1523, a formal body, the Council of the Indies, was set up to formulate policy for the new colonies. Unfortunately, very few of its members had actual experience in the Americas, and the distances involved led to an unresponsive form of government.

New World silver

Later in the 16th century, the Spanish replaced the crown's representatives in the Americas—the governors or captain-generals—with a system of viceroyalties (provinces). That of New Spain supervised the territories to the north of Panama, and that of Peru had authority over the lands to the south.

The native Americans in the Spanish colonies suffered under the *encomienda* system, which made them the personal "possessions" of Spanish landowners. The obligation on the natives to pay

⌄ **With Spanish** colonization of the Americas came Catholicism and magnificent church architecture.

increasing tributes, while at the same time their population was shrinking, caused terrible hardships. The Spanish Empire's real economic wealth came, though, from a huge mountain of silver ore discovered at Potosí in Bolivia in 1545, which delivered enormous revenues. Up until 1660, some 17,600 tons (16,000 tonnes) of the metal were shipped to Seville, permitting Philip II of Spain and his successors to conduct a series of long (and expensive) wars.

Challenges to Spanish rule

Spanish control of America was never complete. In eastern South America, Spain competed with Portuguese (and later Dutch) settlements in Brazil; and in the Caribbean, various islands were seized by the French and English. In North America, where Spanish control extended into Florida and California, the growing might of France and England put a definitive end to the hopes of an all-Spanish Americas.

 Roanoke island, site of the first English colony (often called the "lost colony"), lies within a chain of barrier islands on which several supply ships came to grief.

European colonies in North America

NORTH AMERICA ⚙ **1584–1724**

Although the Spanish had bases in Florida to protect their silver-bullion fleets, it was the English who first attempted to colonize the eastern seaboard of North America. In 1584, English adventurer Sir Walter Raleigh dispatched a fleet to establish a settlement on Roanoke Island in Virginia, but the colony disappeared in 1590. After the English defeat of the Spanish Armada in 1588 (*see p.223*), weakening Spanish domination in the North Atlantic, the English made new attempts to colonize North America.

English rule and its competitors

In 1607 the Virginia Company of London established a colony at Jamestown. In 1620, the English established a further settlement at New Plymouth in Massachussetts, spearheaded by a group of Puritans—religious dissenters—who sailed to the New World on the *Mayflower*. From these tiny beginnings, English control spread throughout the eastern seaboard, with colonies established in Maryland in 1634, Rhode Island in 1636, and Pennsylvania (named for its Quaker founder William Penn) in 1681. Farther south, the English crown took a more direct role, including establishing a colony in the Carolinas in 1663.

Other Europeans joined the scramble, with the Dutch West India Company establishing Fort Orange (now Albany) on the Hudson River in 1623, and a Swedish colony founded in Delaware in 1638. These were eventually swept away by the more powerful English, who, by 1724, controlled the east coast from New England to Georgia. Only in modern Canada to the north were the English challenged— by French colonists. The French had founded Québec in 1608, and by 1712 controlled a vast area from eastern Canada to the Rocky Mountains, and extending as far south as Louisiana.

> " We **went by the shore** to **seeke** for their **boats**, but could **find none**…
>
> **Captain John White, on finding the English colony at Roanoke abandoned and the settlers vanished, 1589**

Trading empires

Parallel to their endeavors of exploration and colonization, many European nations developed large trading empires between the late 15th and 18th centuries, stretching to Africa, Asia, and the Americas. Those established by Spain, Portugal, and France tended to be extensions of monarchical control; by contrast, the maritime empires of England and the Netherlands were more mercantile in nature.

European trade

Portugal's experience in pioneering sea routes to the East was matched by its acquisitions there. Forts at Goa (1510), Malacca (1511), and Ormuz (1515) in the Indian Ocean, established by Admiral Afonso da Albuquerque, ensured Portuguese control of the Persian Gulf and the major trade routes leading east. Macau (in southern China)

>> **An Indian cotton wall-hanging** from the late-16th century provides an early example of local impressions of European traders.

followed in 1517, and by the 1560s, half the spice and three-quarters of the pepper traded in Europe was imported by Portugal. Spain's American empire yielded vast revenues from silver, shipped to Europe and China for trade. France, while it benefited from the Canadian fur trade, regarded its empire as a means for the state to assert power and limit English ambitions, rather than as an enabler of trade.

The Dutch and the English

The empires of Holland and England had their basis in commerce. The Dutch East India Company, or VOC, was founded in 1602 and established its first outpost at Bantam (in Java) in 1604. It expanded to possess a string of factories stretching from Galle in Sri Lanka to southern India, Bengal, Malacca, Taiwan, and

Nagasaki in Japan—all controlled from Batavia in northwestern Java. However, from the mid-17th century, trade with Japan waned, and the cost of defending the empire rose. The English encroached on VOC territory with their own East India Company, while internal corruption drained finances, and by the middle of the 18th century, the VOC had become a shadow of its former self.

The English founded its counterpart, the British East India Company, in 1600. After 1615, this company's foothold in Bengal gave it access to crucial resources and allowed it to found bases in Bombay (1668) and Calcutta (1690) in India. In 1694, it was granted a monopoly on trade with India, cementing the company's position and affording it political power. Yet by the mid-19th century the English East India Company was also on the decline, brought down by the costs of military adventures and the heavy burden of corrupt practices—the very problems that had brought down its Dutch rival.

≫ **The insignia** of the VOC, or Dutch East India Company, established to trade with Asia.

⊠ **The establishment of Fort St. George** (the future Madras) in 1639 gave the English East India Company a vital toehold in southeastern India.

Europe

By the mid-15th century, Europe, devastated by plague and warfare, had fallen behind other parts of the world both culturally and politically. Yet at this very time a remarkable artistic and literary revolution began in Italy that would resound for centuries to come, while increasingly centralized monarchies emerging in England, France, and Spain were soon ready to build global empires.

Humanism

⚑ **EUROPE** ⌛ **c.1450–c.1550**

❯❯ ERASMUS (c.1466–1536)

The Dutch humanist Gerhard Gerhards (c.1466–1536)—known as Erasmus—was an ordained priest, but lived as a scholar. In works such as *In Praise of Folly* (1509), he criticized the corruption of the Church, advocating a life of firm moral and religious principles. His critical scholarship of Biblical texts helped pave the way for the Reformation (*see pp.218–9*).

By the 15th century, education and literature in Europe had been dominated for hundreds of years by the needs and preoccupations of the Christian Church. Although great Classical authors such as Aristotle had formed part of the curriculum taught in universities, their works had been interpreted very much in the light of Catholic teachings.

In the mid-15th century this began to change, as scholars in Italy became interested in a wider range of Classical literature, and especially works with a more secular bias that predated the rise of Christianity.

The spread of humanism

New Latin works were unearthed, such as those of Vitruvius, whose treatise on Roman architecture profoundly influenced 15th-century Florentine architects such as Filippo Brunelleschi; while other, previously neglected authors such as Cicero and Virgil enjoyed a new vogue.

The movement became known as "humanism" for the degree to which its scholarship placed humankind, rather than God, at the center of its worldview. From Italy, the movement spread northward, producing such towering figures as the Dutch humanist Erasmus and the English statesman Thomas More.

The Renaissance

EUROPE 1450–1550

The European Renaissance ("rebirth") refers to a broad movement, beginning in Italy in the early to mid-15th century, that drew inspiration from a new interest in the Classical world to produce astonishing developments in art, architecture, and literature. A prosperous mercantile class became the patrons of the new arts, giving greater freedom to the artists, while the advent of printing enabled the rapid dissemination of ideas.

Architecture and art

In architecture, a mix of civic pride and firm ambitions to rival the achievements of Roman architecture provided the impetus for remarkable works such as the dome built for the cathedral of Florence (completed in 1436) by Filippo Brunelleschi. In painting and sculpture, the influence of ancient Greece and Rome was even more apparent; for there was a great interest in the nude human body, as seen especially in the works of Michelangelo Buonarroti. The roll call of Italian artists of this time is awe-inspiring, including such geniuses as Raphael and Leonardo da Vinci. Meanwhile, in literature, the Renaissance produced such famous works as *The Prince* (1532), Machiavelli's eminently secular handbook for rulers.

» LEONARDO DA VINCI

Outstanding among the great geniuses of the Renaissance, Leonardo (1452–1519) was apprenticed in 1466 to the sculptor Andrea del Verocchio. He showed a precocious talent in painting, but also embraced engineering and theorized a number of military devices. His artistic works include the innovative *Last Supper*, a mural at the church of Santa Maria delle Grazie in Milan, and the enigmatic portrait *Mona Lisa*.

Sandro Botticelli's *The Birth of Venus* (c.1486) clearly shows the 15th century's new preoccupation with subjects from Classical mythology.

The ceiling of the Sistine Chapel in the Vatican is a masterwork of the Florentine Michelangelo Buonarroti (1475–1564). Commissioned by Pope Julius I in 1508, the ceiling frescoes depict scenes from the Old Testament and took four years to complete, with the artist working from a scaffold.

The Reformation and Counter-Reformation

GERMANY, SWITZERLAND, FRANCE, SCANDINAVIA, BRITAIN **1517–63**

On October 31, 1517, Martin Luther (1483–1546), a priest who had become professor of theology at Wittenberg University, Germany, posted a document, his "95 Theses," on the door of the town church. In essence it was a public protest against the sale by priests of "indulgences" (pardons for sins), a practice widely criticized as an abuse of clerical power. This single act was the catalyst for a movement calling for reform of the Catholic Church that was to transform Europe.

Luther went on to attack other precepts of the Church, including the core Catholic dogma of transubstantiation (the belief that the bread and wine at communion transform into the body and blood of Christ) and, crucially, papal supremacy. Attempts were made to reconcile

⌃ **Martin Luther translated** the Bible into German, a project he undertook to give the German people more direct access to the scriptures.

Luther with the religious authorities, until in 1521 he was summoned to present his views at an imperial assembly (*Diet*) at Worms before the Holy Roman Emperor Charles V. Luther refused to recant and, in response to the Emperor's outlawing of him and his views, began an autonomous church.

The spread of Protestantism

Luther's teachings appealed to German princes opposed to imperial dominance; they wrote a public letter of protest to the emperor on Luther's behalf, from which the term "Protestantism" was born. Throughout the 1520s, the German states of Saxony, Hesse, Brandenburg, and Brunswick one by one took up Lutheranism. Political struggle turned into outright war, and although the emperor defeated the Lutherans in battle at Mühlberg in 1547, he could not overcome them politically. Charles V was forced to compromise with the Peace of Augsburg in 1555, by which he tolerated Lutheranism in areas where the local prince espoused it.

While never recanting his views, Luther abhorred the violence the reform movement had engendered (and indeed had supported

⟪ In the *Raising of Lazarus* (1558), by Lucas Cranach, Luther (in the foreground, left) stands among other Protestant reformers.

⌃ **The coronation of Charles V** as Holy Roman Emperor in 1519. He would preside over a huge empire that marked the pinnacle of Habsburg power.

the crushing of a revolt in Germany, in 1524, by peasants influenced by his own ideas). But he was followed by more radical reformers, most notably John Calvin (1509–1564). Calvin stressed predestination (God's control over all human actions) and a direct relationship with God, devoid of priestly or papal interference. Calvinism took hold in Scotland, the Netherlands, and large parts of France. Lutheranism had meanwhile spread from large areas of Germany into Scandinavia, and was a factor in English king Henry VIII's break with Rome in the 1530s. The Roman Catholic Church faced crisis.

The Counter-Reformation

Yet Catholicism saved itself. Meeting in three sessions at Trent in the Italian Alps from 1545–63, the Catholic hierarchy strengthened both the Church's theology and its political

≫ **EMPEROR CHARLES V**

Holy Roman Emperor Charles V (ruled 1519–1558) united the Habsburg dominions in Austria with Spain and Burgundy (and later Spain's colonies) to rule over a vast European realm. His reign was troubled by religious strife, with the outbreak of the Protestant Reformation. Charles was the nephew of Spanish princess Catherine of Aragon, who became English king Henry VIII's first wife. Fear of the Emperor's wrath is likely to have been a factor in Pope Clement VII's refusal to annul this marriage, which prompted England's split from Rome.

position. Poland, Austria, and Bavaria were won back from Protestantism, although a series of religious wars in Europe from the 1550s paid for further gains. The Catholic Church also reformed old religious orders and created new ones, most notably the Jesuits, who went on to establish influential schools and missions under the guidance of their founder Ignatius Loyola (1491–1556).

⌃ **St. Ignatius Loyola** served as a soldier in Spain until, in 1522, he took up a more spiritual life.

Printing

⌃ Printed pamphlets were produced as propaganda during the German Peasants' War of 1524 (*see p.219*).

Although printing using reusable and moveable blocks appeared in China as early as 1040, the first effective press for printing books using moveable metal type and oil-based ink emerged in 15th-century Europe. Its invention is attributed to a German craftsman and entrepreneur, Johannes Gutenberg (c.1398–1468). The first book printed on this new type of press was the Bible, in 1455.

The spread of print

Gutenberg's printing techniques soon spread across Europe. By 1470, there were seven presses in Germany, and this grew to more than 50 by 1499. The first printed book in Italy was produced in 1467; presses were established in Paris by 1470, and in London (by William Caxton) in 1476. The most prestigious early printer, Aldus Manutius, set up the Aldine Press in Venice in 1495 to specialize in Greek, Latin, and early Italian classics.

By 1500, some 35,000 different books were in print. Much cheaper than handwritten works, printed books revolutionized the diffusion of knowledge. The numbers of booksellers and publishers increased, and in the late 15th century, book fairs were held in Lyons, Leipzig, and Frankfurt. As printing became more commonplace, so the types of publications widened. In 1609, the first "news books" (forerunners of newspapers) appeared in Strasbourg (then German), and the first picture book for children was produced in Nuremberg, Germany, in 1658.

Johannes Gutenberg shows the first proofs of his 1455 Latin Bible. There were some 150 different Bible editions printed in the 15th century.

The Italian Wars

ITALY 1494–1559

In 1494, Ludovico Sforza of Milan encouraged Charles VIII of France to invade Naples, an act that led to six decades of international warfare over territory in Italy involving France, Spain, and England, as well as the Holy Roman (Habsburg) and Ottoman empires. A Habsburg defeat of the French at Pavia in 1525 seemed to promise an end to the conflict, but led only to the Papacy joining a pro-French alliance. In return, Rome was brutally sacked in 1527 by German mercenaries in the pay of the Habsburgs. Peace of a sort was restored by the Treaty of Cateau-Cambrésis in 1559, by which Henri II of France renounced all claims to Italy, leaving most of the peninsula under the influence of Spain.

The Battle of Pavia was the first engagement in which handheld firearms played a crucial role.

The French Wars of Religion

FRANCE 1559–1598

By the mid-16th century, the Protestant community in France, known as Huguenots, had grown considerably and included many nobility. The weakness of the French crown during the reigns of the heirs of Henri II (who died in 1559) left effective power in the hands of the ducal house of Guise, fanatical anti-Protestants bent on the extermination of the Huguenots.

The powerful house of Bourbon favored the Protestants, and war broke out between the two in 1562. A brief pause in 1563–1567 was followed by a further bout of bloodshed in 1568–1570, and the St. Bartholomew's Day Massacre of thousands of Protestants in Paris in 1572. More civil strife followed, and nothing seemed able to reconcile the two parties, until the death of Henri III in 1589 left Henri de Bourbon, Protestant king of Navarre, as heir to the throne. To accede as king of France,

Henri became a Catholic. This action, and his guaranteeing of rights to Protestants in the Edict of Nantes (1598), cooled tempers and finally brought an end to France's Wars of Religion.

» HENRI IV

A Huguenot supporter, in 1589 Henri of Navarre (1553–1610) had to fight a Catholic attempt to block his succession to the French throne. In 1593, he converted to Catholicism, undermining his opposition, to rule as Henri IV.

The rise of Spain

⊞ SPAIN ☖ 1492–1598

As Europe emerged from the medieval era, Spain was politically and religiously disunited, divided between several competing kingdoms, with many of its territories occupied by Muslim emirates since the 8th century (*see p.155*).

The emergence of a great nation

In 1469, Queen Isabella of Castile married King Ferdinand of Aragon, uniting the two most important Spanish kingdoms, and in 1492 the royal couple completed the Reconquista—the reconquest of the Muslim-held lands in Spain—with the capture of Granada. The subsequent discovery and conquest of the Americas (*see pp.208–10*) enabled the Habsburg Charles V,

⬆ **The magnificent El Escorial** near Madrid was built in the reign of Philip II as a monastery, royal residence, and burial place for the monarchs of Spain.

the Holy Roman Emperor who became King Charles I of a united Spain in 1519 (*see p.219*), to muster sufficient finances to thrust Spain to the forefront of European politics. When he died in 1556, the Habsburg realms were split and Philip II inherited Spain and the Netherlands.

The Spain of Philip II

Under Philip II (ruled 1556–1598), Spain projected its power in all directions. Its naval force defeated the Turks at Lepanto in 1571, annexed Portugal in 1580, fought a long war in the Netherlands, and sent a great fleet against England in 1588 (*see facing page*). Yet by the 1590s, the flow of silver from the New World was slackening and competition from the French and English in North America and the Caribbean was stifling Spain's routes of commerce. In Spain itself, a plague in 1599–1600 wiped out around 15 percent of the population. Although still Europe's most powerful country, the Spain that Philip III inherited in 1598 was dangerously overstretched.

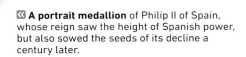

◀ **A portrait medallion** of Philip II of Spain, whose reign saw the height of Spanish power, but also sowed the seeds of its decline a century later.

The Spanish Armada

ENGLISH CHANNEL · 1588

From the mid-16th century, tensions between Europe's Catholic and Protestant rulers threatened to erupt into warfare. Philip II of Spain (*see facing page*) had long been irritated by the interference in Spain's affairs by England's Protestant queen Elizabeth I (ruled 1558–1603), especially her support for an anti-Spanish revolt in the Netherlands (*see below*).

In 1588, he ordered a great fleet, the Spanish Armada, commanded by the Duke of Medina Sidonia, to begin an invasion of England. Setting out in May, 130 Spanish ships reached the English coast in late July. English blocking actions, led by Francis Drake and Lord Howard of Effingham, achieved little, until on August 7–8 English fire-ships broke up the Armada and left it vulnerable to an attack that inflicted enormous human casualties on the Spanish. This proved to be Elizabeth's finest hour: Sidonia took the remains of the Armada on a long and costly retreat around Scotland and Ireland back to Spain.

Elizabeth I of England, a powerful Protestant monarch, posed a constant threat to Spain's Philip II.

The Dutch revolt

BELGIUM, THE NETHERLANDS · 1568–1648

Ruled by the Dukes of Burgundy in the 15th century, by the 16th century the Netherlands had fallen into the domains of the Habsburg Empire. While its ruler Charles V was perceived as sympathetic to Dutch interests, his successor Philip II of Spain spoke neither Dutch nor French, and was more intolerant of Dutch Protestantism.

In 1567, an attempt by the Habsburg governor, the Duke of Alba, to repress religious unrest led to open revolt the following year. Although initially suppressed, the revolt flared up again in 1572. In 1579, a union of provinces loyal to Spain (the Union of Arras) was formed in the south of the Netherlands.

This was countered by the Union of Utrecht in the north which, under William of Orange, became, in effect, independent from Spain. Although the Spanish general Parma retook the largest city of the Utrecht union, Antwerp, in 1585, the Spanish could not make any more headway to the north. This was acknowledged in a 12-year truce starting in 1609, and, though the Spanish tried again to recapture the rebellious provinces during the Thirty Years' War (*see p.224*), at its end in 1648 Spain was finally forced to officially recognize Dutch independence.

>> WILLIAM OF ORANGE

In 1558, Philip II of Spain made William the Silent, Prince of Orange, stadtholder (governor) of Holland. But William led the Protestant rebels against Spain in the Dutch Revolt and was assassinated in 1584 by a French Catholic agent.

» **Albrecht von Wallenstein** was the Catholic side's most able general, delivering a string of victories in the early 1630s, until he was murdered in 1634.

The Thirty Years' War

⚐ **GERMANY** ⌛ **1618–48**

In central Europe at the beginning of the 17th century, a watchful calm followed the turmoil of the Reformation (*see pp.218–9*). However, in 1617, Ferdinand of Styria, a devout Catholic, was named king of Bohemia, a mostly Protestant territory. The Bohemian nobility rebelled, and in 1618 threw Ferdinand's representatives from the windows of Hradschin Castle in the "Defenestration of Prague." The nobles then appointed Frederick V as king of Bohemia, but were overcome by an army raised by Catholic German states at the Battle of White Mountain in 1620, and Bohemia reverted to Catholic Habsburg control.

The war spread as other European powers, notably France, the Dutch Republic, and Sweden, tried to thwart Catholic ambition. In the end, fighting dragged on for three decades.

The final stages

The Swedes under Gustavus Adolphus II won a string of battles that seemed to promise victory to the Protestants, but his death at Lützen in 1632 swung power back to the Catholics. The Peace of Prague in 1635 nearly ended the war, but France, displeased with the terms, set it off once more. Only in 1648, by the Peace of Westphalia, was harmony finally restored, with the borders of European states temporarily stabilized, and the Habsburgs' wings firmly clipped.

> **❝ Germany** is a place of **dead men's skulls**… and a **field of blood. ❞**
>
> Edward Calamy,
> English preacher, 1641

The English Civil War

ENGLAND, SCOTLAND, IRELAND   1642–51

During the late 16th and early 17th centuries England had evolved a strong parliament with the right to veto taxation. Charles I (ruled 1625–1649), a firm believer in the "Divine Right" of monarchs to rule without being limited by any constitutional pact with their subjects, sought to outflank his troublesome parliament by simply suspending it for 11 years from 1629. He then raised revenue through extraordinary measures such as "Ship Money"—a levy imposed on all the counties of England to fund the navy.

The first civil war

In order to raise the funds necessary to quell a Calvinist revolt in Scotland, Charles was forced to recall parliament in 1640. Relations between king and assembly soon deteriorated into open hostility and, in January 1642, the king entered parliament with an armed force to arrest his leading opponents. The attempt failed and, fearing for his own safety, Charles retired north from London to raise an army.

The ensuing conflict continued for four years: an initial inconclusive engagement at Edgehill was followed by victories for either side during 1643. The following year, however, the royalists'

A clash of swords, following a cavalry charge, was often the deciding factor in battles of the English Civil War, despite widespread use of firearms.

fortunes waned, and the involvement of the Scots in the anti-royalist coalition further dented the king's cause. Parliamentary victories at Marston Moor in 1644 and Naseby in 1645 finally led to the king's surrender to the Scots in 1646.

The royalist collapse

The war was not over, however. The king made a deal with the Scots to adopt their Presbyterian form of church government in England in return for aid in restoring him to power. In July 1648, war broke out again, but the Scottish army was easily crushed at Preston, dashing Charles I's hopes of victory. The king was tried and executed on January 30, 1649, and England became a republic or "Commonwealth." However, there were more battles to be fought: Charles I's son (later Charles II) was still at large, and only his defeat at Worcester in 1651 brought an end to the final phase of the English Civil War.

» OLIVER CROMWELL

Member of Parliament for Huntingdon from 1628, Oliver Cromwell (1599–1658) gradually aligned himself with those seeking constitutional reform in England. Fighting for the Parliamentarians against the king in the English Civil War, his instinctive leadership ability and shrewdness allowed him to rise in the ranks until, by 1645, he was the preeminent parliamentary commander. The Parliamentarians won the Civil War in 1651 and Cromwell was made Lord Protector—in effect, military dictator—of England in 1653.

The emergence of Muscovy

RUSSIA 1462–1725

In the 14th century, the territory of modern Russia, led by the principality of Muscovy, threw off decades of Mongol rule (*see pp.142–3*). Initially occupying a tiny enclave around the city of Moscow itself, Muscovy expanded hugely during the long reign of Ivan III (1462–1505), absorbing almost all of the other Russian principalities.

Ivan the Terrible

Ivan IV "the Terrible" (ruled 1533–1584) consolidated Moscow's power still further. He reformed local government, tightened royal control over the church, curbed the power of the *boyars* (nobles), and established a more professional army. His military campaigns expanded Muscovy's borders along the Volga River—taking the khanate of Astrakhan—and in the Baltic, where his armies

seized much of Livonia. Yet the latter part of his reign descended into tyranny, marked by the slaughter of vast numbers of the nobility. After Ivan's death and the reign of his son Feodor (ruled 1584–1598), Muscovy was rocked by famine, civil war, and invasions from Poland that nearly caused its dissolution. Recovery came under a new dynasty, the Romanovs, who would rule Russia for three centuries from 1613.

The Romanovs

The early Romanovs gradually restored Muscovy's power and in 1667 regained most of the territory in the west that had been lost to Poland. Peter the Great built on these foundations, reconstructing the state according to western models, vastly increasing tax revenues, and waging successful wars against the Ottoman Empire (*see pp.202–3*). By the end of Peter's reign in 1725, Russia was one of the most powerful European nations.

≪ **The Ivan the Great Bell Tower** in the Kremlin is a fortified palace complex that has acted as the seat of the rulers of Russia from the 14th century.

≫ PETER THE GREAT

Peter the Great (ruled 1682–1725) was aged only nine when he became tsar of Russia. For the early part of his reign, his half-sister Sophia exercised power, and then his mother Nataliya took control until her death in 1694. Finally able to rule in his own right, Peter set about a program of modernization. This bore fruit during the Great Northern War with Sweden (*see facing page*) in Russia's victory at Poltava in 1709. As well as his military and political reforms, Peter established a new Russian capital at St. Petersburg in 1703.

> " The **Grand Duke leaves** his men **little rest**. He is **usually** at **war**...
>
> German diplomat Sigismund von Herberstein
> on the Grand Duchy of Muscovy, 1549

Poland–Lithuania

POLAND, LITHUANIA 1386–1672

In 1386, Jogaila of Lithuania converted to Christianity to marry the Catholic Queen Jadwiga of Poland, loosely joining the two countries. In 1569, by the Union of Lublin, the federation became the formal "Commonwealth of the Two Nations." Its assembly, the Sejm, had the right to elect monarchs, but the custom of the *liberum veto*, by which a single Sejm member could veto any measure, led to stagnation. In 1667, the Commonwealth lost much eastern territory to Russia and was thereafter largely at the mercy of the Austro-Hungarian Habsburg monarchy to the west and the Russian tsars to the east.

» **The Polish eagle** is part of the coat of arms of the Polish–Lithuanian Commonwealth, which united the two countries from 1572 until its dissolution in 1792.

The rise of Sweden and the Great Northern War

SWEDEN 1523–1719

Gustav Vasa's election as king of Sweden in 1523 marked the start of the country's rise as a great power. Gustav instituted a hereditary monarchy, centralized the bureaucracy, and imported the Reformation (*see pp.218–9*), claiming church lands and so enriching the royal treasury.

After Gustav's death in 1560, Sweden underwent a period of turbulence until the reign of Gustavus II Adolphus (1611–32). His death in the Thirty Years' War (*see p.224*)—during which Sweden gained territories on the southern Baltic—did not lead to an immediate crisis, yet, with a weak economy compared to its European rivals, Sweden's military successes were brought to an end in the late 17th century.

In 1700, King Charles XII (ruled 1697–1718) sparked off the Great Northern War with Russia. It ended in disaster, as Charles was defeated at Poltava in 1709, spent five years in exile in the Ottoman Empire, and then died during a siege near Oslo in 1718, leaving Sweden vulnerable to a Russian counter-invasion in 1719.

« **Charles XII of Sweden's** defeat by Russia dashed Sweden's hopes of becoming a military power.

17th-century France and absolutism

⚑ FRANCE ⌛ 1603–1715

⏏ **Louis XIV**, known as "The Sun King," spent lavishly to enhance France's military and cultural prestige.

The death in 1603 of Henri IV (who had brought religious peace to France), left his nine-year-old son Louis XIII (ruled 1610–1643) on the throne. The capable governance of Cardinal Richelieu steered France through the perils of the Thirty Years' War (*see p.224*), and laid the foundations for the great reign of Louis XIV (ruled 1643–1715). Only four years old at the time of his accession, Louis was very much under the sway of his chief minister, Cardinal Mazarin, until Mazarin died in 1661.

The rule of Louis XIV

Instead of appointing another minister in the mold of Richelieu or Mazarin, Louis chose to rule in his own right as an absolute monarch. He began a series of wars to secure France's frontiers. From 1688 to 1697, he was at war against a "Grand Alliance" that included England and Holland. After only a brief pause, in 1700

Louis moved to put a French prince on the throne of Spain, unleashing the War of the Spanish Succession, as other powers sought to avoid the two countries becoming united. The war dragged on until 1714, when the military brilliance of the English general Marlborough thwarted Louis's plans, leading to a peace in which a French prince became king of Spain, but without uniting the two countries.

Domestically, the wars required a vast improvement in the collection of taxation revenues, which was supervised by Jean-Bapiste Colbert, the director of finances; while Louis enhanced the prestige of the court by establishing a dazzling new palace at Versailles.

▽ **The Palace of Versailles**, built on the site of a simple royal hunting lodge, was commissioned by Louis XIV in 1669. It became the home of the royal court in 1682.

The rise of capitalism and the slave trade

EUROPE, AFRICA, THE AMERICAS ⚓ **c.1600–1865**

The birth of businesses such as the English and Dutch East India companies in the early 17th century (*see pp.212–3*) formed the basis for modern capitalist-style economies.

These companies enjoyed a much more long-term and independent existence than their precursors, and could build up capital and make longer-term investment plans. Specialized traders now emerged, who arranged the buying and selling of "stock" in the companies (shares in their ownership), making it easier to raise new funds. In Amsterdam, the Amsterdamsche Wisselbank (Amsterdam Exchange bank) was founded in 1609 as a center for the sale and exchange of stocks, while in London the first listing of share and commodity prices was published in 1698.

The slave trade

Among the many profitable commercial ventures the new capitalists engaged in was the slave trade. Slaves were gathered, largely in West Africa—often with the cooperation or connivance of local rulers—and were shipped under inhuman circumstances to the New World. Here, they were exchanged for commodities such as sugar, tobacco, and cotton, which would in turn be sold at a great profit in Europe.

The "Middle Passage," or transit of slaves over the Atlantic, saw some 78,000 slaves a year transported in the 1780s, with up to 600 slaves

packed into each ship. They were shackled together in cramped spaces between deck and hold, where disease, damp, and hunger exacted a terrible toll in deaths. The slave trade was abolished in the British Empire only in 1807, although slavery persisted in the US until 1865.

⬆ **Edward Lloyd's coffee house** in London became a center for merchants to discuss investment. It would evolve into the modern-day Lloyds insurance market.

⬇ **A model of the slave ship *Brookes***, showing the positions into which more than 500 slaves were crammed for the harrowing transatlantic voyage.

The scientific revolution and the Enlightenment

EUROPE ⏳ **16TH–18TH CENTURIES**

The 16th and 17th centuries saw a metamorphosis in European thinking about the natural world. Just as the Renaissance had transformed art, and the Reformation had loosened the shackles of religious dogma, so now a third revolution produced a new view of the universe.

Improvements in technology began to undermine many long-held theories, the most celebrated casualty being the ancient Earth-centered model of the universe. In 1543, the Polish priest and astronomer Nicolaus Copernicus published a proposal for a sun-centered system with the Earth and five other planets in orbit around it. In 1610, the Italian astronomer Galileo Galilei, using a new, improved telescope, discovered four moons in orbit around Jupiter, thereby definitively showing that the Earth was not, as previously believed, the center of all motion in the universe.

Advances in medicine

In other areas, too, scientific endeavors made rapid progress. In anatomy, the discovery of a lost text by the Roman medical writer Galen convinced the Flemish scholar Vesalius that Galen had never actually dissected a human body, spurring him to

Copernicus's revolutionary view of the solar system put the Earth in orbit around the sun.

publish his great atlas of anatomy *De Humani Corporis Fabrica* in 1543. Further advances in medical science yielded the first accurate description of the circulation of blood in 1628 by William Harvey, personal physician to Charles I of England. His theory was confirmed in 1661 by the direct observation of capillaries using the recently invented microscope.

The Enlightenment

Just as this scientific revolution had grown from a new freedom in scientific thinking, so the Enlightenment, a radical current of intellectual thought, liberated philosophy.

René Descartes (1596–1650), the "father of modern philosophy," was both thinker and mathematician, arguing that only through reason could mathematical and universal truths be discovered. In the 18th century, thinkers known as *philosophes* applied ideas from the advances in science to challenge the way people thought about government and society, seeking to replace superstition, tyranny, and injustice with reason, tolerance, and equality. "What does it mean to be free?" asked François-Marie Arouet (known

❯❯ ISAAC NEWTON

In 1609, Johannes Kepler showed that the planets orbited the sun in an elliptical, not a circular, motion, but he could not explain why. The answer was provided by the English polymath Isaac Newton (1643–1727), who realized that the force of "gravity" found on Earth, which caused objects to fall when released, might extend into outer space and be generated by all objects possessing mass. Newton published this theory in his *Principia Mathematica* of 1687, one of the most influential works in scientific history.

⌃ **René Descartes** argued that logical deduction should be trusted more than sensory perception.

as Voltaire), answering: "To reason correctly and know the rights of man." Jean-Jacques Rousseau railed against moral decadence and inequality in his essays on the *Arts and Sciences* (1749) and on *Equality* (1755), arguing that social progress had helped corrupt human nature.

The spread of ideas

The most influential tool for spreading Enlightenment values was Denis Diderot's 28-volume *Encylopédie*, which boasted an impressive array of contributors, including Voltaire and Rousseau. Its aim was to assemble all existing knowledge in clear, accessible prose.

A favorite target for the *philosophes* was royal absolutism. Montesquieu's celebrated treatise *Spirit of the Laws* (1748) proposed a limited monarchy based on a three-way division of powers between the executive (the king), the legislature (parliament), and the judiciary. Such intellectual notions greatly added to the ferment that would, within the next half-century, give rise to both the American and French revolutions.

≫ **Jean-Jacques Rousseau** wrote that "Man is born free, and is everywhere in chains," profoundly influencing later French revolutionaries.

❝ The **consent** of the people is the **sole basis** of a **government's authority**.

Jean-Jacques Rousseau, *Social Contract*, 1762 ❞

The World of Empires

The world in 1750–1914

The American and French Revolutions transformed Western political expectations. Though the results were contradictory—the US emerged as a fully functioning democracy, while France was destabilized for almost a century—demands for political liberation echoed throughout the 19th century. A wave of nationalist uprisings

The world in 1850

- —— International border
- ········ Undefined border
- Qing Empire
- Ottoman Empire
- Britain and possessions
- France and possessions
- Denmark and possessions
- Spain and possessions
- Portugal and possessions
- Netherlands and possessions
- Prussia
- Russian Empire
- Japan
- Austrian Empire
- Persia
- United States of America
- Napoleon's French Empire 1812
- Muhammad Ali's possessions 1840
- United Provinces of Central America 1823–38
- Great Colombia 1819–30

brought independence to much of Latin America and unification to Italy and Germany. Elsewhere, however, colonial nations continued to dominate much of the globe, stifling local political development. Even independent regions, such as China and Japan, suffered from significant interventions or interference by European powers.

The world of empires in 1850

By 1850, the US spanned the breadth of North America, while most of Latin America had thrown off Spanish and Portuguese rule. Only a few colonies existed in Africa, but India had almost entirely become a dominion of the British, who also settled in Australia and New Zealand. A weak Qing dynasty ruled China.

⏶ **Many of the European powers** had suffered nationalist revolutions in 1848, but territorially they remained largely unchanged. By 1850 Italy and Germany, still divided into a number of small states, were just two decades away from unification. In the Balkans, the Ottoman empire still held most of the region, but had lost control of Greece.

The Americas

By 1750, virtually the whole of the Americas was occupied by the Spanish, Portuguese, French, or British, with the remaining few islands and enclaves occupied by lesser European powers. In contrast, by 1914, only a few areas remained as European colonies, the rest having experienced around a century of independence. In the case of the United States and Spain's American colonies, this was won from the mother country through revolutionary wars.

Europeans in the Americas

NORTH AMERICA, CARIBBEAN 1750

By the middle of the 18th century, most of the territory of eastern North America had been carved up among the European nations. The British occupied the Thirteen Colonies, an area of the eastern seaboard of what would become the United States, as well as Nova Scotia and an area around Hudson's Bay in modern Canada.

The French position

Britain's principal opponents in North America were the French, who held much of modern eastern Canada (or "New France") from their main fortress at Québec. From here, the French had crept south down the Great Lakes and the Ohio River as far as Detroit (founded in 1701), and by 1750 they had a string of fortified positions along these waterways. The goal was to link with their existing possessions around New Orleans in the south to create a north–south corridor of French territory from which to put pressure on the British. At about the same time, British colonists began to move into Ohio, escalating the potential for conflict between Britain and France. Adding to the volatile mix—and so the likelihood of war in eastern North America— were the long-held Spanish positions in Florida and the Caribbean, which they had occupied since the early 16th century.

>> **From forts such as San Felipe** on Puerto Rico in the Caribbean, Spain defended an arc of territory from seaward invasion.

The French and Indian War

E NORTH AMERICA   **1754–1760**

Britain and France had sparred for decades for control of the crucial waterways of the Ohio and Mississippi rivers. In 1754, a skirmish near Fort Duquesne between the French and Virginian colonial troops prompted the dispatch of a British expeditionary force, led by Major-General Edward Braddock, who attempted to seize the French fort. With the help of their Native American Iroquois allies, the French routed the British. Native forces were to play a major part on both sides in what became known as the French and Indian War.

The war spreads

A series of French victories was halted only by a setback at Lake St. George in September 1755, which saved the Hudson Valley for Britain. By 1756, the conflict had become global (as the Seven Years' War; *see pp.246–7*), and the British began to see that North America was an arena in which they could damage French interests and force France to divert resources from Europe.

In 1758, the British launched campaigns to thrust north from New York, seize Louisbourg, and march on the French capital in North America, Québec.

The end of New France

The French commander, Marquis de Montcalm, fought a series of able blocking actions, but the British took Louisbourg and pushed up the St. Lawrence River, so that by June 1759 Montcalm was confined to Québec. General Wolfe's British force took the city, although both commanders were killed in the engagement. In September 1760, the Marquis de Vaudreuil surrendered the last French stronghold at Montréal, ending the North American phase of the Seven Years' War and handing the territories of "New France" over to Britain.

🔽 **The Marquis de Montcalm** was mortally wounded in the defeat of his forces on the Plains of Abraham outside Québec.

🔼 **A medal struck** to commemorate the British capture of Québec in modern Canada from the French in 1759.

The Revolutionary War

E NORTH AMERICA ⚓ **1775–1783**

The British colonies in North America were liable to pay tax to Britain, but without receiving the benefit of representation in parliament, which rankled greatly with the colonists. A series of measures passed from 1763, aimed at raising money for the British government, caused further discontent, and the Stamp Act, a direct tax on paper, provoked riots. In 1773, a group of Bostonians, disguised as Native Americans, threw a cargo of highly taxed East India Company tea into Boston Harbor. Their slogan—"no taxation without representation"—struck a deep chord with most colonists.

The outbreak of war

In response, the British passed a series of laws in 1774, which the Americans dubbed the "Intolerable Acts." These measures were intended to restore order, but served only to unite the colonies in further protest. A colonial Continental Congress in Philadelphia in September 1774 demanded the repeal of the Intolerable Acts. The appeal fell on

⊼ **The "Boston Tea Party"** protest in 1773, against Britain's three-penny tax on tea, saw American colonists hurl crates of tea into Boston Harbor.

deaf ears and the British government called on General Thomas Gage, commander of the British forces in Boston, to arrest the colonists' troublesome leaders. The first skirmish, described later as "the

» **George Washington** crossed the Delaware River into New Jersey in December 1776, at a time when his army was under severe British pressure.

⟫ GEORGE WASHINGTON

Born to a family of Virginia landowners, George Washington (1732–1799) served on the British side in the French and Indian War (*see p.237*), experience that led Congress to appoint him commander of the American military forces in 1775. He came to command widespread respect for his morality and tenacity and, after independence, was president of the Constitutional Convention that drafted the US constitution in 1787. In 1789, he was elected first president of the USA, a position he held for two terms, until 1797.

shot heard round the world," occurred at Lexington, Massachusetts, on April 19, 1775. Besieged in Boston, Gage then bungled an attempt to dislodge rebel positions at the Battle of Bunker Hill in June, a success that bolstered the Americans' morale. Soon afterward, George Washington became commander of the newly formed Continental Army. Despite setbacks, including the British capture of New York, in July 1776 the Americans made a decisive break with Britain. After a series of difficult negotiations among themselves, the American colonies agreed

on a Declaration of Independence, thanks largely to the intellectual force and literary skills of Thomas Jefferson (1743–1826), later to become the third president of the United States.

The American victory

The British fought on, but Washington's victory at Saratoga in October 1777 stirred the interest of the French, still stinging from their expulsion from Canada (*see p.237*), who formed an alliance with the colonists. The signing of a treaty between the Americans and the French in February 1778 marked a major turning point in the war.

All hope of a British victory ended on October 19, 1781 when Lord Cornwallis was forced to surrender the last major British army at Yorktown, Virginia, after an 18-day siege. The British suspended any further military operations against the Americans. In November 1782, they signed a provisional agreement recognizing American independence, a decision ratified by the Treaty of Paris in 1783. George Washington became the first president and John Adams the first vice president of the new United States of America, which at the time was often also referred to as "the Union."

⌃ **The Declaration of Independence** was adopted on July 4, 1776. Its signatories included John Adams and Thomas Jefferson, both later US presidents.

The expansion of the United States

USA ⚍ **1783–1867**

After the Treaty of Paris in 1783, the new US (the Union) had frontiers along the Mississippi River to the west, where it faced remaining French possessions, and along the Great Lakes to the north, where it bordered British Canada. The US did not remain confined to these boundaries for long, however. Expansion across the Mississippi began with the 1803 Louisiana Purchase, by which Napoleon, abandoning plans to rebuild a French New World empire, ceded a vast territory that doubled the size of the US for a mere $15 million.

The frontier moves west

A conflict with Britain (the War of 1812) ended in a stalemate and an agreement in 1818 to demarcate the US's northern border with

》 **MERIWETHER LEWIS**

Secretary to President Jefferson, in 1803 Meriwether Lewis (1774–1809) was sent to explore the region acquired by the Louisiana Purchase. He and his men reached the Pacific coast in 1805, making them the first Europeans to traverse the width of the US.

Canada along the 49th parallel (line of latitude). To the south, the US acquired Florida from Spain in 1813–1819. In 1846, Oregon Country was split with the British, again along the 49th parallel, providing a Pacific frontier.

Texas had become independent from Mexico in 1836, but was annexed by the US in 1845, which led to war with the Mexicans. In 1848, a victorious US acquired California, Nevada, Utah, and New Mexico. The Gadsden Purchase in 1853, which added further land from northern Mexico, and the purchase of Alaska from Russia in 1867 completed the growth of the continental Union.

Land of opportunity

As the young nation expanded, large numbers of settlers traveled west to the newly acquired lands. The 1862 Homestead Act, which offered farmers ownership of 160 acres (65 hectares) of land after they had farmed it for five years, accelerated the migration, as did the completion of a transcontinental railroad in 1869.

The expansion of the settlement frontier, however, was accompanied by the displacement— often by force—of Native American tribes. The death of General George Custer at Little Big Horn in 1876 was one of the rare conflicts in which Native Americans were the victors.

◄◄ **A memorial to the volunteers** who died in 1836 at the Alamo, the most famous battle in Texas's fight for independence from Mexico.

The slide to civil war

US 1820–1861

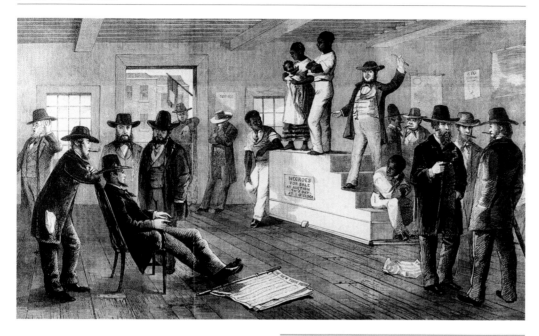

Slave auctions were commonplace in the southern US; the largest, in Georgia, involved the sale of over 430 slaves.

The Constitutional Convention of 1787 had allowed individual member states of the new US (the Union) to retain slavery if they wished. The northern states abolished slavery, while a roughly equal number of southern states kept it, leading to constant friction.

The slavery debate

The admission of new "free" states—which outlawed slavery—to the Union threatened to upset its equilibrium. In the so-called "Missouri Compromise" of 1820, slavery was forbidden in much of the West, but this was overturned by the Kansas-Nebraska Act of 1854, while a Supreme Court decision in 1857 further strengthened slavery's status. Still, the increasing numbers of free territories jostling for statehood alarmed supporters of slavery.

After an armed raid in 1859 by anti-slavery militant John Brown to free slaves at Harper's Ferry, Virginia, this concern turned into active opposition. In November 1860, the first Republican Party president, Abraham Lincoln, was elected on a platform of opposition to slavery's expansion.

ABRAHAM LINCOLN

Kentucky-born Abraham Lincoln (1809–1865) helped found the anti-slavery Republican Party in 1854. Selected as a compromise Republican candidate in the 1860 elections, his victory in the northern states provoked states in the south to leave the Union. However, his determination saw the Union through the ensuing Civil War. In 1865, Lincoln signed a resolution on the abolition of slavery; he was assassinated just as the war ended.

The southern states had opted for a pro-slavery Democrat, John Breckenridge, and on December 20, 1860, South Carolina voted to leave the Union. By February 1861, six more states had also withdrawn, creating a new body known as the Confederacy. With tensions between north and south running so high, it was only a matter of time before hostilities would break out.

The American Civil War

⚑ USA ⏳ 1860–1865

By the spring of 1861, seven states had seceded from the Union (see p.241) to form the pro-slavery Confederacy. On April 12, Confederate forces bombarded Fort Sumter in Charleston Harbor, South Carolina, eventually forcing the surrender of its Union troops. The first shots of the Civil War had been fired.

The two sides were ill-matched; the Union had vast economic resources and its population was far larger, at 22 million. Even when a further four states joined the Confederacy after the Fort Sumter attack, its population numbered only 9 million, of whom 3.5 million were slaves.

The Confederacy's strategy was to defend itself from attack long enough to force recognition from the Union government. The skill of some masterful Confederate battlefield commanders enabled it to resist, in fact, for far longer than could be predicted from its military resources.

The effort devoted by each side to the war was prodigious. Conscription (a military draft) was introduced by the Confederacy in 1862, and by the Union in 1863. By the conflict's end, some 50 percent of the eligible population of the Union had been mobilized, and around 75 percent in the Confederacy.

☑ **Abraham Lincoln** (*right*), US President during the Civil War, was seen as the bringer of liberty to the slaves of the south.

❝ Government of the **people**, **by** the **people, for** the **people**.

Abraham Lincoln, 1863 ❞

The early course of the war

Superior Confederate generalship led to early success, with "Stonewall" Jackson's two victories at Bull Run, Virginia, seriously endangering the Union's capital at Washington, DC. A further attempt by the brilliant Confederate general Robert E. Lee to invade the Union ended in disaster at Gettysburg in a three-day battle in July 1863. This marked the turning point of the war.

On the western front, Union general Ulysses S. Grant won a costly victory at Shiloh, Tennessee, in April 1862 and then thrust down the Mississippi River, taking a strategic position at Vicksburg in April 1863 before pushing further south to cut the Confederacy in two—isolating Arkansas, Louisiana, and Texas from the other states. In the fall of 1864, Union general William Sherman began his "March to the Sea," moving from the Mississippi to cut a destructive swath through the Confederacy as far as Atlanta on the eastern seaboard.

Confederate surrender

In Virginia, meanwhile, Lee sparred for months with Grant, the Confederate general maneuvering his forces both to evade capture and to shield the Confederate capital at Richmond. In the end, despite brilliant rearguard actions, his resources were simply drained, his army reduced to barely 8,000. After Richmond finally fell on April 3, 1865, Lee surrendered to Grant at Appomattox Court House on April 9. Early the following month, the last Confederate forces surrendered in Carolina and Alabama, and the war was over.

It had cost the Union side 110,000 battlefield deaths, the Confederacy 93,000, and each side many more from disease or exhaustion. The main outcome was the emancipation of the southern slaves; Lincoln had issued a proclamation to

A Union soldier's portable desk. A remarkable number of letters and memoirs, written by ordinary soldiers, survive from the Civil War.

Soldiers pose for the camera at Fair Oaks, Virginia; the Civil War was one of the first conflicts to be recorded in photographs.

this effect on January 1, 1863, and the US adopted the 13th Amendment, enshrining this in the Constitution in December 1865.

Reconstruction

After the war, the southern states underwent a process of "Reconstruction" intended to prepare them for readmission to the Union. Former Confederate officials were banned from holding public office, and veterans were required to pledge allegiance to the Union. It was a harsh regime that bred resentment in the southern states. Georgia was the last state to be readmitted to the Union, in July 1870, but Reconstruction continued until 1877, when a deal (known as the "Compromise") was struck to allow the withdrawal of the final Federal forces from the south.

Latin American independence

CENTRAL AND SOUTH AMERICA ⌛ **1808–1920**

In 1775, Spanish and Portuguese control of their Latin American empires seemed unchallenged. Yet the outbreak of the American and French revolutions provided inspiration for those seeking independence for Central and South America and offered avenues for seeking aid for those already struggling to gain autonomy.

When Napoleon turned on his Spanish allies in 1808 during the Peninsular War (see p.254), events took a disastrous turn for Spain. With the Spanish king Charles VI and his son, Ferdinand, taken hostage by Napoleon, rebels bent on independence exploited the power vacuum to jostle for power across Spanish America.

The liberation of Spanish America

Revolutionary forces rose from opposite ends of the continent. From the south, José de San Martín, a former Spanish military officer, led 5,000 troops across the Andes from Argentina

✉ **Pancho Villa** (center) was a key figure in the Mexican Revolution and the last to lay down his arms, only giving up the fight in 1920.

⟫ SIMÓN BOLÍVAR

Hero of South America's struggle for independence from Spain, Simón Bolívar (1783–1830) began his revolutionary career in Venezuela in 1813. Known as *El Libertador* ("the Liberator"), his hopes of a grand union of the newly independent states were dashed, as the early Republic of Gran Colombia fell apart into its component countries (Columbia, Panama, and Ecuador) shortly before he died of tuberculosis in 1830.

to strike at a weak point in Chile in 1817. San Martín then liberated the Spanish stronghold of Peru. From the north came Simón Bolívar, whose forces entered Venezuela in 1813; they waged a ferocious campaign, but with limited results. However, in 1817 a larger, revitalized movement for independence emerged to complete the struggle for the north. In 1821, Bolívar was named president of Gran Colombia—a union of Colombia, Panama, and Ecuador.

By 1821 further campaigns had wrested New Granada and Venezuela from Spanish control. In the central Andes, the southern and northern armies crushed the remaining loyalist strength. Peru, which the Spanish had recaptured, regained its independence in 1824.

In Mexico, meanwhile, a movement emerged in 1810, led by a radical priest, Miguel Hidalgo y Costilla, who built up an untrained force of 80,000

> ❝ **All** who have **served** the **Revolution** have **plowed the sea**.
>
> **Simón Bolívar, 1830**

◀ **A monument, nicknamed El Ángel** ("The Angel"), was built in Mexico City in 1910 to commemorate the centenary of the start of Mexico's liberation struggle.

indigenous fighters. Although Hidalgo was captured and executed in 1811, he had badly shaken Spanish control of Mexico, and the country achieved independence in 1821.

In Brazil, the colonial upper classes, reliant on African slavery, wanted to maintain ties with Portugal. Then, in 1808, the Portuguese court fled to Brazil to escape Napoleon. King John returned to Lisbon in 1821, leaving his son Pedro in the colony. In 1822, Pedro declared Brazil independent and himself Emperor.

The Mexican revolution

While Brazil retained its integrity, the former Spanish America split into more than a dozen republics. However, internal fighting caused the first constitutional governments to fall and Latin America in the mid-19th century was plagued by instability, leading to the rise of military strongmen (*caudillos*).

In 1876, one of these, General Porfirio Díaz, seized power in Mexico and established a dictatorship. Resentment toward him exploded in the Mexican Revolution of 1910, which overthrew Díaz in 1911. His replacement, Francisco Madero, failed to fulfil the expectations of more radical revolutionaries such as Emiliano Zapata and Francisco ("Pancho") Villa, leading the civil war to rumble on until 1920.

》 JOSÉ DE SAN MARTÍN

Argentinian national hero José de San Martín (1778–1850) joined South America's struggle for independence in 1812. In 1817 he crossed the Andes to overthrow Spanish control of Chile, and won definitive independence for Peru in 1824. He died in France.

Europe

When France overthrew its monarchy in 1789, the new regime seemed bent on exporting democracy throughout Europe, but after two decades of Revolutionary and Napoleonic wars the European status quo remained largely intact. However, Europe was then shaken by a violent upsurge in 1848, fed by new ideals of nationalism that ultimately led to the unifications of Italy and Germany and to independence for a string of Balkan countries.

The Seven Years' War

EUROPE ⌛ **1756–1763**

In 1756, Frederick II of Prussia signed a treaty with Britain to protect British rule in Hanover (in modern Germany). Maria Theresa of Austria used this as a pretext with which to effect a "diplomatic revolution," in which she allied with her former enemy France and firmed up ties with Empress Elizabeth of Russia, making Prussia vulnerable to invasion.

Striking first, Frederick sought to occupy Saxony, but was unsuccessful. In 1757, however, he did triumph over the French at Rossbach in Saxony, and then crushed the Austrians in Silesia before inflicting a defeat on the Russians at Zorndorf in 1758. The tide turned strongly against Frederick in 1760 and 1761, but the succession of the pro-Prussian Peter III in Russia in 1762 brought a new ally.

Prussian victory at Freiberg, Saxony, in 1762 meant that in 1763 the Treaty of Paris, which brought an end to the Seven Years' War in Europe, restored the status quo.

⟫ FREDERICK II

A military genius, Frederick II "the Great" of Prussia (ruled 1740–1786) reformed the Prussian army and used it to fight a series of campaigns aimed at gathering the disparate possessions of Prussia into a united state.

The first global war

The Seven Years' War broke out in 1756 between Prussia on one side and Austria, France, and Russia on the other. The involvement of Britain, through its holding of Hanover, meant that the war soon gained a global dimension, as France and Britain extended the conflict to their overseas colonies. In the Americas, fighting had erupted in 1755 (*see p.237*), a year before the main war actually began in Europe.

The war in India

In 1756, the *nawab* (ruler) of Bengal sparked hostilities in India by capturing the British base at Calcutta, and putting his prisoners in the "Black Hole"—a small, dark cell in which many died. The victory of Robert Clive over the *nawab* in June 1757 dramatically revived British fortunes in India (*see p.270*). The failure of a French siege of Madras in 1759, a British victory at Wandiwash in 1760, and the fall of the main French base in India at Pondicherry the following year meant the end of the Indian phase of the Seven Years' War.

The war elsewhere

In the other main non-European theaters of the war, the British generally had the better of the fighting, capturing Senegal from the French in 1758, seizing the French islands of Guadeloupe and Martinique in 1762, and briefly occupying the Spanish forts at Havana in Cuba and Manila in the Philippines in 1762–1763. By the Treaty of Paris, which ended the war, Britain ceded back many of its conquests, but retained French Canada, Spanish Florida, and some French outposts in West Africa.

>> **A Prussian war banner** displaying the imperial eagle and the motto "for glory and fatherland."

The British fleet captured Havana in 1762. The occupation was short-lived, as the Treaty of Paris in 1763 gave Florida to Britain in exchange for the city.

The French Revolution

FRANCE **1789–1796**

France's costly involvement in the American Revolutionary War (*see pp.238–9*) put financial reform at the top of the country's political agenda. Bad harvests in 1788–1789 aggravated social tensions and fueled resentment of the *ancien régime*—a system by which 40 percent of the land was owned by the nobility and clergy, who made up a mere 3 percent of the population and who were exempt from taxes.

The Estates-General

After the nobility blocked his attempt to raise revenue, Louis XVI (ruled 1774–1792) was forced, in May 1789, to convene the Estates-General— a parliament made up of clergy, nobility, and

☑ **Louis XVI was executed** by guillotine on January 21, 1793, on the site that is now the Place de la Concorde in Paris.

commoners. The third estate, representing the commoners, insisted on greater voting rights. These were refused and the commoners broke away and took power as a National Assembly— the first step to revolutionary change. Rioting in July 1789 led to the capture of the Bastille prison (*see pp.250–1*), a huge blow against the oppressive forces of the *ancien régime*.

Revolutionary reforms

On August 4, the National Assembly abolished feudal privileges, sweeping away an entire system of property ownership. For the next two years, the National Assembly passed reforms that further undermined the *ancien régime*, including the "Declaration of the Rights of Man," as well as army reforms, and forced the clergy to take a civic oath to the state. In June 1791, Louis XVI, having schemed to

undermine the Assembly, attempted to flee abroad, but was captured at Varennes, east of Paris. This apparent abandonment of his people crucially undermined regard for the monarchy.

In April 1792, the Assembly declared war on Austria and Prussia, who were sympathetic to the king, but this caused panic in Paris, and on August 20 a mob stormed the Tuileries palace and deposed the king. In the aftermath, a more radical assembly (the Convention) was elected, and France was declared a Republic in September. In January 1793, the king was charged with crimes against the French nation, convicted, and executed.

The Terror

Faced with mounting military and economic problems, the Convention established a Revolutionary Tribunal to mete out instant justice, and a Committee of Public Safety (CPS) to wield central power, which it did with mixed success. Internal conflict was rife, and on June 2, 1793, the

moderate Girondin faction was expelled from the Convention and the extremist Jacobins seized power under Robespierre. The Jacobins unleashed the "Terror" on France, aimed at purging any remaining anti-Revolutionaries and pro-royalists. In 10 months from September 1793, they executed some 20,000 people, and the Revolution seemed to be consuming itself in violence.

A decisive military victory over Austria in June 1794 eased political pressures and Robespierre and his henchmen were finally toppled in an anti-Jacobin backlash. In 1795, the CPS was replaced by a five-man Directory, which set about the task of restoring faith in the Revolutionary regime.

A membership card for the Convention, under whose rule France was declared a Republic and Louis XVI was executed.

》 ROBESPIERRE

Maximilien Robespierre (1758–1794), a lawyer, was mocked for his high voice, but respected for his pure principles, which earned him the nickname "The Incorruptible." When he came to power in 1793, his extremism unleashed terror on France, and ultimately led to his execution.

▶▶ **By July 14, 1789, the Bastille prison** in Paris housed just seven inmates, but also held vast stores of gunpowder. Weakly defended by a party of *invalides*—troops unfit for active service—it was stormed by a revolutionary mob and its governor, de Launay, was stabbed to death.

France under Napoleon

FRANCE **1799–1815**

The rule of the Directory (1795–1799) was a time of great instability and mounting corruption in France. The division of power between five Directors and a two-chamber parliament led to chaos, inaction, and disenchantment with the political process.

Into this gap stepped the rising young military star Napoleon Bonaparte. His successes in the Italian campaign of the 1790s lent him an aura of steadiness and invincibility that the fractious Revolutionaries badly needed. In November 1799, having abandoned his army in Palestine, Napoleon arrived back in France to answer his nation's call.

From First Consul to Emperor

The Coup of 18 Brumaire (November 9, 1799) saw Napoleon and his backers overthrow the Directory, and he became First Consul in the new leadership.

His two fellow consuls were soon reduced to powerless nonentities, and in 1802 Napoleon had himself declared First Consul for life. Intelligent, determined, and energetic, Napoleon set to sweeping away the ramshackle

⌃ **A new civil code for France** was one of Napoleon's most enduring legacies, enshrining in law some of the freedoms fought for in the French Revolution.

amalgam of Revolutionary and feudal systems that had evolved since 1789. In December 1804, he had himself crowned Emperor. Presiding over the ceremony was Pope Pius VII, for Napoleon had made peace with the Catholic Church the previous year in a Concordat that recognized limited papal authority over Catholics in France.

Domestic reforms

Napoleon's reforms left few spheres of French life untouched. He founded a Bank of France in 1800, and issued a new currency centered around a gold coin, the *napoleon*. He ordered that the educational system be reformed and radically revised the French administrative system, rationalizing the network of *départements* set up in 1790.

A committee of legal experts was formed to bring order to the chaos of legislative codes and temporary expedients. By 1804 it had completed a new civil code that would survive Napoleon's demise as the centerpiece of France's legal system.

The cost of warfare

The universal conscription and punitive taxation necessitated by Napoleon's constant warfare (*see pp.254–5*) were not popular in France. As victory turned to stalemate, then retreat, after the disastrous 1812 campaign in Russia, support for Napoleon steadily ebbed away. When enemy armies reached Paris in 1814, his power base proved brittle; even long-standing loyalists such as Marshal Ney did nothing to prevent his being deposed.

Yet the new Bourbon regime of Louis XVIII was little loved either, and residual affection in France for Napoleon enabled him to return from exile on the Italian island of Elba in May 1815. A final flourish, the "Hundred Days," ended in his defeat at the battle of Waterloo and permanent exile to Saint Helena, an island in the South Atlantic.

> ❝ I have **tasted command,** and I **cannot** give it up. ❞
>
> **Napoleon Bonaparte, 1798**

⟫ NAPOLEON BONAPARTE

Born into an impoverished Corsican noble family, Napoleon Bonaparte (1769–1821) became a junior artillery officer aged just 16. His subsequent career was characterized by superb opportunism and a tactical brilliance in battle that marked him out from other commanders of the age. It brought him high political office, but the scale of his own ambitions and those of his foreign enemies ultimately brought about his deposition.

☑ **At the Committee of Lyon** in 1802, Napoleon created the Repubblica Italiana; in 1805, this became the Kingdom of Italy, with the new emperor as its king.

The Napoleonic Wars

🄟 **EUROPE** ⚔ **1802–1815**

The French Revolutionary Wars (1792–1802) had been intended to protect France's borders from other European powers eager to stop the spread of revolution. They turned gradually into a more aggressive foreign policy, as France's armies met with a series of successes that stoked its hunger for exporting revolution and acquiring land.

The Peace of Amiens, which Napoleon struck with Britain in 1802, promised an end to the wars, but it lasted only a year. By 1805 Britain managed to build an alliance of countries fearful of Napoleon's expansionism—the First Coalition. This was the

🔼 **Napoleon wore** a hat in a bicorn (two-horned) style that incorporated a badge bearing the French Revolutionary colors of red, white, and blue.

🔼 **Wellington leads his army** from an indecisive encounter at Quatre Bras, in 1815, to the final victory at Waterloo two days later.

first of seven such groupings, whose shifting membership would seek to oppose the French emperor and be repeatedly defeated by his armies.

The first great victories

Napoleon's great victories in 1805 against Austria at Ulm and an Austro-Prussian army at Austerlitz placed him at the summit of his power. He was thwarted only by naval defeat at Trafalgar (off the southwest coast of Spain) against the British admiral Nelson in October, which scuppered his plans to invade England.

However, his insistence on an economic blockade by all the nations under his control as an alternative means to cripple England caused great resentment among the other European countries. Napoleon went on to attack Prussia in October 1806, and within three weeks had defeated its armies at Jena and Austerstädt. He then forced peace on Tsar Alexander I of Russia at Tilsit in July 1807.

The downfall of Napoleon

Napoleon's decision to invade Spain and Portugal in 1808, starting the Peninsular War, led to the diversion of badly needed resources into a difficult

> ## History is a **set of lies**… people have **agreed upon**.
>
> **Napoleon Bonaparte,**
> *Memoirs*, **published in 1823**

struggle against local guerrillas who were being aided by British expeditionary forces. From 1809, the British forces, under the Duke of Wellington, gradually fought their way forward in a bitter struggle, finally invading southwest France in 1813–1814.

Meanwhile, in 1812, Napoleon's decision to invade Russia was similarly misjudged. The Russian army simply retreated further eastward, and, although Napoleon's Grande Armée did take Moscow in September, the victory was hollow. The French were forced to pull back in a harrowing winter retreat during which, harassed by the Russians, they lost more than half a million men.

Both of these campaigns left Napoleon vulnerable to a renewed Coalition against him and, in a massive battle at Leipzig in 1813, he suffered his first major battlefield defeat. Though Napoleon fought a brilliant short campaign to block the Coalition advance toward Paris, there was little political will to support continued resistance and, betrayed by defections among his senior officers, he was forced to abdicate.

Napoleon was exiled to the island of Elba, but returned the following year, and many flocked back to his standard. The restoration of his regime depended on early, decisive victories, so defeat by the Prussians and British at Waterloo in June 1815 led to his definitive abdication and the end of the Napoleonic Wars.

›› THE DUKE OF WELLINGTON

In 1808, Arthur Wellesley, 1st Duke of Wellington (1769–1852), was placed in command of a British force dispatched to aid Portugal against France. For the next six years he fought his way through the Iberian peninsula, before invading France itself in late 1813. Despite his professed disdain for the common soldier, Wellington had a clear ability to win battles, which inspired great loyalty in his soldiers. After his defeat of Napoleon at Waterloo in 1815, he took to politics, including stints as British prime minister in 1828–1830 and 1834.

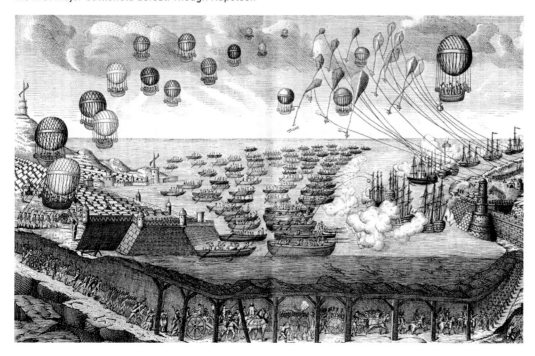

◄ **An artist's view** of Napoleon's planned invasion of England in 1805 shows French forces attacking by sea, air, and tunneling under the English Channel.

Nationalism and revolution

⊕ EUROPE ⌛ 1804–1878

The Congress of Vienna, which met from 1814 to 1815 to settle the terms by which the Napoleonic Wars would be concluded, ended by sealing a return to more or less the same system of European powers that existed before the French Revolution. For the next quarter-century, the "Congress System"—in which the "Concert of Powers" (Britain, Austria, Russia, and Prussia) met periodically to determine political issues—cast a stifling blanket over any aspirations for change.

Growing in strength all this time were feelings of nationalism—the view that ethnic groups had the right to political self-determination and the right to their own independent states. This was a particular problem for the Austro-Hungarian Empire, which boasted many such groups,

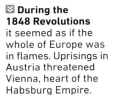

≪ Milan Obrenovic's accession as Serbia's first king in 1882 sealed the country's independence.

including the Austrians, the Hungarians, and the Czechs. It also posed a threat to the integrity of the Ottoman Empire, a similarly multiethnic state.

Nationalism in the Ottoman Empire

As the Ottoman sultans were decidedly not included in the European Concert of Powers, it is scarcely surprising that it was in their domains that nationalism won its earliest successes. A revolutionary uprising broke out in Greece in 1821, supported by foreign (mainly English) intervention—including the picturesque involvement of the English poet Lord Byron. The

⊠ During the 1848 Revolutions it seemed as if the whole of Europe was in flames. Uprisings in Austria threatened Vienna, heart of the Habsburg Empire.

◀ **Eugène Delacroix's** *Liberty Leading the People* was inspired by the uprising that brought Louis-Philippe to the French throne in 1830, only to be deposed in 1848.

revolutionaries won a great naval victory at Navarino in 1827 and finally forced the Ottomans to recognize Greek independence in 1832. In Serbia, a revolt sparked by the reformers Vuk Karadjic and George Petrovic in 1804 secured Russian aid and drove the Ottomans out of the province by 1807. On the defensive after defeat in Greece, the Ottoman sultan finally accepted Serbian autonomy in 1830.

The 1848 revolutions

In central and western Europe, poor harvests in 1846–1847 had resulted in appalling hardship for the peasantry. Combined with nationalist frustrations at the seeming impossibility of political change, this produced an astonishing outbreak of revolutionary movements in 1848 that touched almost all parts of Europe. In France, it led to the overthrow of the monarchy of Louis-Philippe and the establishment of the Second Republic.

In the Austro-Hungarian Empire, a more obviously nationalist series of uprisings almost overthrew Habsburg power to set up a number of new, ethnically based states. In the end the existing regime won out by offering concessions to the Hungarians, the most significant non-German component of the empire. They established the "Dual Monarchy," in which the ruler was emperor in Austria, but king of a theoretically separate Hungarian state. Popular uprisings in Italy and Germany, which seemed to promise statehood, were similarly premature, and ended in brutal suppressions.

The decline and rise of nationalism

With this almost total restoration of the status quo, it seemed that the Concert of Powers would continue to run Europe with a conservative fist much as it had done since 1815. Yet within 20 years, the disparate states of Italy and Germany were united as independent countries (*see pp.258–9*), while the dismemberment of the Ottoman empire continued at the Congress of Berlin (1878), which finally recognized the independence of Serbia, Montenegro, and Romania, and began to establish a separate Bulgarian state.

>> **Wilhelm I** was proclaimed first Kaiser (emperor) of the German Empire in the Hall of Mirrors at the Palace of Versailles.

The unification of Germany

⚐ GERMANY ⚔ 1864–1871

At the time of the 1848 Revolutions (*see p.257*), Germany was a loose confederation of states, the most powerful among them being Prussia. From 1862, Prussia's Minister-President, Otto von Bismarck, sought to secure the supremacy of Prussia within central Europe by encouraging the other German states to unify under its leadership.

The process began in earnest in 1864, when Prussia joined forces with Austria to annex the duchies of Schleswig and Holstein from Denmark. Two years later, war broke out between Prussia and Austria, and a Prussian victory at Königgrätz in 1867 allowed Bismarck to exclude Austria from the German Confederation, and from any say in the constitutional course of the German principalities.

The German Empire

Bismarck was well aware that Napoleon III of France (*see p.260*) would never willingly accept a unified German state on his borders. He attempted to place a German Hohenzollern prince on the throne of Spain to encircle the French.

As a result, Napoleon III declared war on Prussia and its German allies. Napoleon was captured after the Battle of Sedan in September 1870, and, though the French continued to resist under a new

Republic, Bismarck soon had the victory he desired. In a humiliation of the French, the German Empire was proclaimed at the Palace of Versailles on the outskirts of Paris on January 18, 1871, with the Prussian ruler Wilhelm as its first emperor. The new Germany was in principle a federation of 25 states, but there was no doubt that Prussia and Bismarck—champion of the unification—were very firmly in charge.

>> OTTO VON BISMARCK

Prime Minister of Prussia from 1862, Otto von Bismarck (1815–98) wanted to unite Germany under Prussian leadership. His skilful conduct of wars against Denmark and Austria in the 1860s helped secure the infant state; then victory in the Franco-Prussian War (1870–1871) persuaded the other German states to join Prussia to form an empire, of which Bismarck became the first chancellor. Though a conservative leader, he did introduce some social reforms aimed at reducing the growing appeal of socialism (*see p.267*).

The unification of Italy

ITALY · 1831–1871

The Congress of Vienna in 1814 (*see p.256*) confirmed the division of the Italian peninsula into a patchwork of states. A revolutionary society known as the *Carbonari* (coal-burners) began to agitate for unification, and organized a series of insurrections.

In 1831, the Italian patriot Giuseppe Mazzini formed the movement known as "Young Italy," which called for one Italian nation, "independent, free, and Republican." Italian statesmen were quick to grasp their opportunities. Camillo Cavour, the prime minister of Piedmont in northern Italy, provoked a war against Austria in 1859, and his victory enabled Piedmont to take control of most of northern Italy.

The next year, Giuseppe Garibaldi invaded southern Italy with an army of thousands of volunteer "Red Shirts" and occupied Sicily and Naples. In 1861, Piedmont established a "Kingdom of Italy" with Victor Emmanuel of Piedmont as its first monarch. The process of Italian unification was completed with Italy's seizure of the Veneto from Austria in 1866 and, following Napoleon III's withdrawal of the French garrison to fight the Franco-Prussian War, the occupation of Rome in September 1870. Rome officially became the capital of Italy the following year.

> **" A people destined to achieve great things for the welfare of humanity must one day or other be constituted a nation."**
>
> **Giuseppe Mazzini, Italian revolutionary and patriot, 1861**

》 GIUSEPPE GARIBALDI

Having participated in a failed *Carbonari* insurrection in Piedmont in 1834, Giuseppe Garibaldi (1807–1882) was forced to flee Italy to South America. In 1849, he returned to command a Roman army established in the wake of the 1848 Revolutions (*see p.257*), but on its suppression fled once more. In 1860, defying more cautious mainstream nationalists, he captured most of southern Italy. Sidelined thereafter, he fought his last battles in French service during the Franco-Prussian War (*see p.260*).

France under Napoleon III

FRANCE ☰ **1848–1870**

On the restoration of the Bourbon monarchy in France in 1815 (*see p.253*), all members of the Bonaparte family were sent into exile. Napoleon I's nephew, Charles-Louis Napoleon, thus grew up in Switzerland and Germany. However, after the collapse of the "July Monarchy" of Louis-Philippe in 1848, Charles-Louis returned to France, and he was elected president later that year. Then, in 1851, Charles-Louis engineered a coup that resulted in his becoming emperor the following year, as Napoleon III (ruled 1852–1870).

Despite his imperial position, Napoleon III saw himself as a social and economic reformer, encouraging the large-scale renovation of Paris—according to a plan devised by the civic planner Baron Haussmann—and overseeing a massive expansion in France's rail network.

Napoleon III's foreign policy

Napoleon III joined the British side in the Crimean War against Russia (1853–1856), aided the cause of Italian independence by going to war with Austria in 1859, acquired France's first Southeast Asian colony (Cochin-China) in 1862, and intervened in Mexico (1862–1867) to place a Habsburg emperor on the throne there. It was, however, his quarrel with the German chancellor Otto von Bismarck that led to his defeat and deposition in 1870 during the Franco-Prussian War (*see below*). He died in exile in England in 1873.

The Franco-Prussian War

FRANCE ☰ **1870–1871**

In autumn 1870 France, provoked by plans by German chancellor Otto von Bismarck (*see p.258*) to put a German prince on the Spanish throne, declared war on Prussia. A brief occupation of the Rhineland town of Saarbrücken in August 1870 was France's sole success, and a bloody defeat at Gravelotte on August 18 was followed two weeks later by disaster at Sedan, where Napoleon III was forced to surrender. Although France established a Government of National Defense to continue the country's resistance, its armed forces were shattered, and on January 28, 1871, Paris was forced to surrender.

France was left in chaos: most of its politicians were discredited; Paris fell briefly under the power of the radical Commune government; and peace with Prussia involved the surrender of Alsace-Lorraine.

◀ **On January 25, 1871,** frustrated by Paris's continued resistance, Bismarck ordered the city to be bombarded with heavy Krupp guns.

Victorian England

ENGLAND **1837–1901**

◀◀ **The Great Exhibition**
of 1851, held in the
Crystal Palace in Hyde
Park, London, was an
imperial showcase for
the "works of industry
of all nations."

When Queen Victoria ascended to the British throne in 1837, Britain had not yet enjoyed the fruits of its early industrialization (*see p.264*), nor recovered from the loss of its American colonies in 1783 (*see p.239*) or the costs of the Napoleonic Wars (*see pp.254–5*). Yet when she died in 1901, Britain's preeminence as an industrial power was unchallenged, the British flag flew in outposts around the globe, and a cultural self-confidence that grew out of this prosperity had molded a characteristically "Victorian" Britain.

Expansion abroad, reform at home

The demise of the East India Company in 1858 (*see p.213*) left the British Crown in control of large swaths of India. With the acquisition of colonies in Africa, Britain had truly become an imperial power, and in 1877 Victoria took the title "Empress of India."

At home, there was a rise in reformism: a great increase in urbanization inspired a will to tackle the social problems it caused. The repeal of the Corn Laws—which had raised the price of food— in 1846, the passing of the Factory Acts restricting the working hours of children, and the foundation of the Salvation Army in 1865 to encourage charity to London's slum-dwellers were just a few of the social developments of Victoria's reign.

> **We are not interested in the possibilities of defeat.**
>
> **Queen Victoria to
> Arthur Balfour MP, 1899**

》 **QUEEN VICTORIA**

Victoria (ruled 1837–1901) was 18 when she came to the throne, and in 1840 she married her German cousin Prince Albert. Their children married into so many of the royal families of Europe that Victoria was known as the "grandmother of Europe."

Russia in the 19th century

RUSSIA 🔒 **1801–1905**

At the accession of Alexander I in 1801, the Russian Empire already stretched from eastern Siberia to Poland, a vast distance that posed almost unsurmountable governance problems to the tsarist administration. Its mainly rural population, largely serfs, labored under primitive conditions, and although the country had begun to industrialize, it failed to match its western European rivals.

Alexander I and Nicholas I

Russia continued to expand in the early 19th century, acquiring Finland from Sweden in 1809, Bessarabia from Turkey in 1812, and the much-diminished state of Poland in 1815. Further acquisitions in the Caucasus, where the Russians finally suppressed a bitter resistance after the surrender of the guerrilla leader

⬆ **An early Colt revolver** shipped to Russia from the US and used to help the Russians fight the Crimean War.

Shamil in 1859, meant that the Russian Empire was roughly half as large again as it had been under Peter the Great (*see p.226*). It was not a territory that lent itself to central administration: until 1830 there was not even an all-weather road between Moscow and St. Petersburg, and the first railroad followed only in 1851.

The reigns of Alexander I (1801–1825) and Nicholas I (1825–1855) were dogged by the issue of serfdom, and whether the serfs should be

⬇ **A dramatic scene of fighting** during the Crimean War between Russia and Turkey and its allies, the first conflict recorded by both artists and photographers.

emancipated. Alexander, although liberal in theory, even declaring the need for a Russian constitution, did little in practice, while Nicholas was a more straightforward autocrat who ceded little ground.

He suppressed a revolt in Poland in 1830 and sent aid to the Habsburgs in 1848 to put down the revolutions in Austria and Hungary. His reign ended in disaster, when his ambitions to acquire territory from the Ottoman Empire led to a humiliating defeat at the hands of Britain and France in the Crimean War (1853–1856).

Attempt at reform

Alexander II (ruled 1855–1881), who presided over the expansion of the Russian Empire into Central Asia, instituted a series of liberal reforms, finally emancipating the serfs in 1861. Legal reforms enhanced the independence of the judiciary, while in 1864 a system of local government with elected bodies, the *zemstvos*, was set up.

Yet it was also in Alexander II's reign that there were the first revolutionary rumblings, among peasants unhappy that emancipation had not led to prosperity and intellectuals who despised the tsarist system as an oppressive tyranny. One such dissenting group, the "People's Will," finally assassinated the tsar in March 1881.

Repression and revolutionaries

Under Alexander III (ruled 1881–1894), a campaign of police terror smothered the revolutionaries, while reforms in 1889 in part backpedaled on serf emancipation. When Nicholas II came to the throne in 1894, frustration was at boiling point, and the first Marxist party (*see p.267*) was founded in 1898.

△ **Vladimir Makovsky's** *Death in the Snow* shows the suffering caused by tsarist authorities during the crushing of the 1905 Revolution.

Russian defeat in the Russo-Japanese War (1904–1905) increased the clamor for reform to deafening levels, and a wave of revolutionary protest broke out. In response, the tsar allowed the establishment of a state Duma (parliament), and granted basic civil rights. Having satisfied the moderates, he crushed the extremists, ending the Revolution of 1905.

« **Nicholas II** reversed many of the reforms of previous tsars, but this fostered rather than extinguished radical sentiment.

" The late **Emperor did not anticipate** this end, and thus did **not train me in anything**.

Tsar Nicholas II, 1894 "

The Industrial Revolution

From the late 18th century in Britain, a wave of industrialization swept across Europe and North America. It transformed the Western world from a rural society into an urban one, and set the foundations for modern capitalism. This "Industrial Revolution" spurred profound social changes, as well as giving rise to innovations in technology that were to fuel vast economic growth.

» **Romanticized depictions** of the conditions in the new factories did nothing to stem social unrest.

British beginnings

Abundant natural materials such as iron and coal, and a growing middle class eager to invest, allowed Britain to take full advantage of new developments in technology. In the 1770s, James Watts developed an improved steam engine, which could provide the necessary power for various industrial uses, from pumping mines to running machinery in the factories and mills of the early 18th century.

Textile production mechanized particularly rapidly—by 1835 there were more than 120,000 power looms in textile mills—leading men, women, and children to flock to the towns where the factories were situated. There they endured appalling conditions, working long hours for low pay, until the rise of trade unionism (*see p.266*) began to curb the excesses of factory owners.

The Revolution spreads

The new industrial techniques spread outward from Britain, taking hold first in Belgium in the 1820s, then spreading fast during the "Second Industrial Revolution" (1840–1890) when the new railroads in Germany, Switzerland, and the US made it easier to move labor and commodities.

In Europe, the abolition of serfdom—in France during the 1790s, in Germany between 1811 and 1848, and in Russia and Poland in the 1860s—assisted industrialization by creating a more readily available workforce. In the US, large-scale immigration provided the new factories with their employees.

In 1856, Englishman Henry Bessemer invented a new process for making iron into steel—a stronger, more versatile metal than wrought iron. This provided the raw material for new railway lines, improved ships, and more powerful armaments. Demand for steel was almost insatiable—by 1910, Krupp, the leading German steel manufacturer, employed some 70,000 people; in 1846 its workforce had been just 122.

The third wave

From the 1890s, a third wave of industrialization occurred in Russia, Sweden, France, and Italy. This saw the industrialization of chemical and electrical engineering. The Germans now dominated industrial and weaponry production, as Britain's initial lead ebbed away. Fear of what this might mean led Russia, France, and Italy to accelerate investments in arms manufacturing, while

⊡ **George Stephenson's** "North Star" steam engine served on Britain's Great Western Railway, one of the great Victorian rail companies.

Russia improved its rail network specifically for transporting troops. It would be just a few years before Europe would begin fighting the first truly industrialized war—World War I (1914–1918)—a war that would destroy those infrastructures that had been so improved by industry.

⊡ **Developments in engineering** technology enabled the building of triumphant monuments to the modern age, such as the Eiffel Tower in Paris.

Industrialization and the labor movement

EUROPE, THE USA   c.1800–1868

Labor practices in the factories of the Industrial Revolution (see pp.264–5) ranged from neglectful to abusive. From the early 19th century, British workers organized themselves into groups to protect their interests, but these "combinations" were illegal and employers often repressed them.

Trade unionism

In 1824–1825, the British government repealed the anti-Combination laws and, for the first time, trade unions became lawful. In 1829, John Doherty established the Grand General Union of the Operative Spinners of Great Britain and Ireland, the first attempt at a national union—starting a trend that was followed in the 1830s by other trades. Repression was still commonplace—

the deportation of the "Tolpuddle Martyrs," organized agricultural workers, to Australia in 1834 being only the most famous example.

Rapid economic progress in the 1840s strengthened the hand of the unions, and in 1868 the forerunner of Britain's modern Trades Union Congress was founded. Meanwhile, the movement spread overseas to the US, and establishment of unions in continental Europe followed the 1848 Revolutions (see p.257).

⊠ **A German socialist banner** from the 19th century calls on the workers of the world to unite.

⊠ **At the Peterloo Massacre** in 1819, British troops fired on unarmed workers protesting at working conditions and lobbying for reforms.

Socialism and Marxism

The Industrial Revolution inspired political groups to organize workers and improve their lot. A philosophy called socialism arose that argued that wealth should be shared by putting it in the hands of its creators. Similar sentiments had inspired the German Peasants' Revolt in 1532–1534 and had also caused unrest in England after the Civil War (*see p.225*), but the industrialized Europe of the 19th century provided the first arena for these ideas to be put into practice.

Early 19th-century socialists included Robert Owen, a Welsh industrialist, who proposed a society in which property was owned collectively. In France, Henri Saint-Simon advocated a society in which there was equal opportunity for all, while his followers wanted an end to private property. By the early 20th century, many European countries had established socialist parties, including the Labour Party in Britain (1900) and the Socialist Party in France (1902).

▶ **Karl Marx**, with Friedrich Engels, wrote *The Communist Manifesto* (1848), setting out a revolutionary socialism.

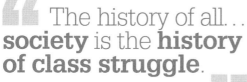

> The history of all... **society** is the **history of class struggle**.
>
> Karl Marx, *The Communist Manifesto*, 1848

Marxism and revolution

More radical still were the ideas of the German-born philosopher and economist Karl Marx (1818–1883), who viewed history as a series of class struggles that would lead to the end of capitalism. Distrusting the compromises of more moderate "Social Democrats," Marx helped establish the International Working Men's Association in 1864, which acted as a platform for the dissemination of his revolutionary theories. Although he believed that the full revolution would break out in France or Germany, it was in the relatively underdeveloped Russia that Marxists would finally seize power, in 1917.

Scientific advances

The Industrial Revolution (*see pp.264–5*) was accompanied by an explosion in technology, leading to huge developments in transportation (the car and airplane), communications (telephone and radio), and even in domestic life (the electric light bulb and gramophone, or record player). In science, British naturalist Charles Darwin overturned previous understanding of the world by developing the theory of evolution.

Scientific discoveries

Few men had a greater impact on life in the 19th century than English physicist Michael Faraday, who discovered that moving a magnet through a coil of wire produced an electric current.

His experiments in electricity in the 1830s led to dramatic progress in the sphere of communications, with the patenting of the electric telegraph in 1837, and the invention of the telephone by the Scottish-born American scientist Alexander Graham Bell in 1876. In 1906, the Italian Guglielmo Marconi built on earlier theoretical work by the German scientist Heinrich Hertz to transmit speech wirelessly over the airwaves using radio transmissions. The appearance of the internal combustion engine, patented by Karl Benz in 1879, led to the development of the first practical automobiles by the mid-1880s.

The first powered, sustained, heavier-than-air flight by the Wright brothers in 1903 further revolutionized transportation. Other innovations of the 1890s, such as the gramophone and moving

Karl Benz, seated on his 1885 Benz Motorwagen, the first automobile to be available for sale to the general public.

pictures (the latter pioneered by the French inventors the Lumière brothers), were only available at first to small groups, but within decades the refinement and expansion of these technologies made them accessible to almost everyone.

The theory of evolution

The long-held notion that animal species had been created by God and remained essentially unchanged was shaken by the publication of Charles Darwin's

≫ **The microscope** that Charles Darwin took with him on his 1831–1836 voyage to the Galápagos Islands in the Pacific.

On the Origin of Species in 1859. Darwin's observation of finches on different islands in the Galápagos group showed they had developed characteristics to suit their particular environments. Darwin argued that through "natural selection" individuals in a species had competed against each other and those stronger or more able survived to pass on their genes. In *The Descent of Man* (1871), Darwin argued that humankind had descended from an apelike ancestor. Initially bitterly contested, Darwin's theory survived to become scientific orthodoxy.

⌃ **Alexander Graham Bell**, the inventor of the telephone, made the first long-distance call, from New York to Chicago, in 1892.

> **Man** with all his **noble qualities**… **still bears** in his bodily frame the **indelible stamp** of his **lowly origin**.
>
> Charles Darwin, *The Descent of Man*, 1871

Asia

The countries of Asia had to contend in the 19th century with increasingly aggressive interventions by European powers, with varying degrees of success. Most of India had fallen under British control by the 1850s, while China had been fatally weakened by the Opium Wars, also fought against Britain. Only Japan had shown that it was more than able to hold its own, by seizing opportunities made possible by industrialization.

The Battle of Plassey

BENGAL, INDIA   JUNE 23–24, 1757

The British East India Company, which had first established a firm base in Bengal at Calcutta in 1690, struggled for the next half-century with local rulers who were eager to minimize its presence in their territories. In 1756, a major crisis erupted when Siraj-ud-Daula, the new *nawab* (ruler) of Bengal, demanded that the British hand over his wealthy subject Krishna Das, who after embezzling government funds had taken refuge in Calcutta.

The fall of Calcutta

Siraj-ud-Daula further demanded that the British demolish the walls of the city, and when they refused, the Bengali army stormed the rather run-down fortifications in June 1757. Some 146 British captives were allegedly then confined in the "Black Hole," the cell of the company barracks, from which it was said only 23 emerged alive. Although exaggerated, the story helped prompt a severe reprisal from the British.

Clive wins at Plassey

The British dispatched soldier and statesman Robert Clive and his troops from Madras to punish the *nawab*. After capturing the French headquarters at Chandernagore, Clive defeated Siraj-ud-Daula in a two-day battle at Plassey on June 23–24. Mir Jafar was made nawab, Clive received 28 million rupees on behalf of the East India Company from the royal treasury, and the Company's position in Bengal appeared secure.

Robert Clive (1725–1774) secured the British position in India as a result of his victory at Plassey.

The British in India

INDIA **1757–1885**

Clive's victory at Plassey in 1757 (*see facing page*) had seemed to cement British power in India. But trouble soon erupted again with Bengal's next *nawab*, Mir Kasim, and on his defeat in 1764, the British East India Company effectively annexed west Bihar. From then on, the British became increasingly entangled in Indian affairs, and as they defended their established interests, they gained more and more territory.

Through the Anglo-Mysore Wars (1767–1799) and the Anglo-Maratha Wars (1775–1818), the Company extended its domains into the south of India to complement its near-monopoly of power in the north. It annexed Sindh in 1843, and conquered the Punjab in two tough wars in 1845–1846 and 1848–1849.

The British Raj

The British, under the Governorship of Lord Dalhousie, now began to unify the administration of all these disparate territories. In the meantime, they acquired more territories by the doctrine of "lapse," which meant that the lands of Indian princes who died without direct heirs simply fell into British possession. This was most unpopular with the native rulers, and Britain's growing power fed into the resentment that sparked the Indian mutiny in 1857 (*see p.272*). Once the British had suppressed the mutiny in 1858, the rights of the East India Company were transferred to the British Crown.

The next half-century of British rule in India, known as the Raj, was peaceful, though the Indian National Congress, which called for greater political rights for Indians, was founded in 1885. But India was the "jewel in the crown" of the British Empire, and the British long resisted making meaningful concessions to the Indian nationalists.

◪ **Duleep Singh**, the last maharaja of the Punjab, was deposed by the British when they annexed his kingdom in 1849.

◪ **The British Raj** built the spectacular Victoria Terminus of the Indian Peninsular Railway in Mumbai.

The Indian mutiny

INDIA **1857–1858**

In the 1850s the British East India Company imposed a variety of measures on its *sepoys*—native Indian soldiers—that caused great resentment. Early in 1857, the British introduced a new Enfield rifle into service in India, and the firing drill required the *sepoys* to bite off the tip of the cartridge. Rumors flew that the tip was smeared with animal (pig or cow) fat, offending the religious sensibilities of both Muslim and Hindu troops.

A mutiny erupted at Meerut in May 1857, which soon spread to units throughout northern India. The involvement of the aged Mughal emperor Bahadur Shah II seemed to promise the revival of native Indian power, but the British fought back and, by September 1857, had recaptured lost Delhi, although the last rebels were only suppressed in July the following year.

Indian mutineers massacred their British prisoners at Cawnpore in July 1857, fueling a desire for revenge among British troops.

The Burmese Wars

BURMA **1824–1885**

Early relations between the British in India and the neighboring kingdom of Burma centered on the East India Company's attempts to open trade links. However, when a common frontier was established between Bengal and the Burmese state of Arakan in the late 18th century, tensions led to three wars between the two countries.

The British invasions

During the first war (1824–1826), the East India Company gained territory in Manipur, Arakan, and Tennasserim. The second Anglo-Burmese War (1852), provoked by minor Burmese violations of the treaty that had settled the first conflict, ended with Burma's loss of Pegu, the northern section of the country, which the British established as the colony of Lower Burma.

For the next 25 years, the Burmese king Mindon Min (ruled 1853–1878) fended off further British advances, but his successor Thibaw (ruled 1878–1885) was less able, and in November 1885 a dispute over payment for timber concessions flared up into war. The British advance was swift, and by the end of the month they had captured Thibaw's capital at Mandalay and deposed him.

A 19th-century Burmese silver dagger, clearly a highly prized weapon, but of little use against the Enfield rifles of the British.

Turkish reform movements

TURKEY **1789–1923**

Reform in the Ottoman Empire began with attempts by Selim III (ruled 1789–1807) to institute a *Nizam-I cedid*, or "New System" of bureaucratic organization, aimed at countering the inaction that had contributed to the Ottoman loss of lands in Serbia and Hungary. His successor Mahmud II (ruled 1808–1839) went on to restore authority to the central government, which had been usurped by powerful local interests.

The Young Turks

Mahmud's successor Abdülmecid (ruled 1839–1861) embarked on a program of modernizing reform that would become known as *Tanzimat* ("reorganization"). However, under Abdul Hamid II (ruled 1876–1909) the Ottoman Empire suffered a disastrous setback: defeat by the Russians in 1878 deprived the empire of most of its European territories, and then, in 1882, it lost Egypt to the British.

Under pressure, Abdul Hamid continued to make educational and military reforms, but this was not sufficient to satisfy radical opinion, and in 1902 a meeting in Paris brought together the leadership of the "Young Turks," a coalition of fervent nationalists who wished to rescue Turkey from its ruinous position. In 1908, the Young Turks joined a rebellion in Macedonia and formed the Committee of Union and Progress (CUP). They forced Abdul Hamid to agree to grant a constitution and establish a parliament.

The empire collapses

The leader of the CUP, Enver Pasha, pushed forward the reform process—opening schools to women, for example. Yet in matters of foreign policy the Young Turks chose unwisely, entering World War I on the side of the Germans. After Germany's defeat in 1918, an Allied invasion led to British forces occupying Istanbul by 1920. Turkey was saved by Kemal Mustafa Ataturk, who rallied the country's armies and drove back the Allies in 1922 to become president of a Turkish Republic in 1923.

⟩⟩ ENVER PASHA

An early leader of the Young Turk movement, Enver Pasha (1881–1922) became Turkey's military attaché in Berlin, a posting that contributed to his advocacy of a Turkish–German alliance during World War I.

✉ **The Dolmabahce Palace**, overlooking the Bosphorus at Istanbul, was the residence of the last Ottoman sultans in the late 19th and early 20th centuries.

Qing China

📖 **CHINA** ⌛ **1796–1912**

In 1796, the White Lotus Rebellion—part tax revolt, part mystical movement, part nostalgia for the rule of the Ming (see p.139)—broke out in Qing China. While it was crushed in 1804, the White Lotus weakened the regime of Emperor Jiaqing (ruled 1796–1820) and began a series of debilitating uprisings that would tear China apart.

The opium trade

During Jiaqing's reign, huge amounts of opium began to flow into China, largely smuggled in by British traders, which necessitated the export of large quantities of silver to pay for it.

Opium addiction became rife and, in 1839, the Chinese government appointed a leading official, Lin Zexu, to suppress trade in the southern port city of Guangzhou. Lin confiscated opium stocks, but also detained several British traders, which prompted the London government to dispatch an expeditionary force, sparking the First Opium War.

The Opium Wars

The conflict was hugely one-sided, and the British soon occupied Hong Kong and Shanghai. The Treaty of Nanjing, which ended the conflict in 1842, ceded Hong Kong to Britain, set limits on the external tariffs China could impose, removed Westerners from Chinese jurisdiction, and opened five "treaty ports" to European traders.

Then, in 1856, the Chinese authorities boarded a British trading vessel, the *Arrow*, and the Second Opium War broke out. This time the French joined in, and after a four-year war that featured the humiliating burning of the Qing Summer Palace in Beijing, the western powers (including Russia) were awarded 10 further treaty ports, on top of enormous financial payments, and the opium trade was legalized.

🔼 **During the 19th century**, European demand for decorative Chinese goods such as silks and porcelain soared.

🔽 **The "Thirteen Factories"** (or *hongs*) of Canton (now Guangzhou) were the sole place where foreigners could trade into China until 1842.

The Taiping Rebellion

The surrender of the Qing regime in the Opium Wars contributed to a rising tide of antigovernment protests. Largest of these was the Taiping Rebellion.

In 1836, a Christian teacher, Hong Xiuquan, had a series of dreams that led him to believe he had a mission to bring Christianity to China. He made converts among peasants in Guangzi, south China, and in January 1851 established the *Taiping Tianguo*—the Heavenly Kingdom of Great Peace. In 1853, the Taiping rebels captured Nanjing, and banned gambling and opium smoking. However, in 1860, the Western-trained "Ever-Victorious Army" defeated a Taiping assault on Shanghai, and in 1864 the Qing government recaptured Nanjing. The revolt effectively collapsed.

Social reform

From 1861, the Qing court was dominated by Empress Ci Xi, mother of the Tongzhi emperor. For 47 years she ruled China, encouraging at first the "Self-strengthening Movement," which permitted limited reforms—including China's first railroad and a reorganized army. However, China's dramatic defeat by Japan's army and navy in the Sino-Japanese War of 1894–1895 over Korea (*see p.277*) undermined support for further reforms.

The end of the Qing

Resentment at the growing influence of Christian missionaries in China fed into an uprising by the Boxers, also known as the "Righteous Fists of Harmony," who aimed to expel all foreigners from China. Tacitly supported by Ci Xi, the Boxers marched on Beijing in June 1900, where they besieged the foreign legations for nearly two months. An alliance of eight foreign nations,

From humble origins as a concubine to the Xianfeng emperor, "Lady Yehonala" became Empress Dowager Ci Xi and controlled China for nearly half a century.

including Britain, France, the US, and Japan, sent a relieving force and crushed the rebels. Its credibility compromised, the Qing regime was finally replaced in 1912 by a Republic of China, led by Sun Yat-Sen.

> As long as **China** remains a **nation of opium smokers**, there is **not** the least reason to **fear** that she will **become a military power** of any **importance**.
>
> Lin Zexu, Chinese commissioner at Guangzhou

The Meiji restoration

JAPAN ⏳ **1833–1911**

From the early 17th century, the Tokugawa shoguns kept peace in Japan and the population prospered. Yet from the early 19th century, several disasters occurred. A famine in 1833–1836 killed many thousands, while, partly in response, a wave of rural riots and urban disorder struck the country.

On top of internal problems, Japan faced new threats from abroad. The country had been virtually closed to foreigners for two centuries, but in the mid-19th century several attempts were made to engage with it. In 1853, the US government sent Commodore Matthew Perry to Edo (Tokyo) with four warships. Perry demanded the opening of Japanese ports for trade, and returned the following year with an even larger flotilla. Powerless to resist such a show of force, the Tokugawa shogun signed the Convention of Kanagawa, opening several ports to the Americans.

The emperor restored

Similar treaties followed with Britain, France, the Netherlands, and Russia. Japan gradually lost control over its customs dues, and a dispute arose in 1859–1860, after foreign merchants discovered that they were able to make a healthy profit buying Japanese gold, in the form of relatively undervalued coins, and taking it out of the country.

It seemed as if the Tokugawa were ignoring Japan's best interests, and a resistance movement broke out under the slogan of *sonnō jōi* ("honor the emperor, expel the barbarians"). A group of leading *daimyo* (noble) families began to lobby for the return of the emperor to real power, after centuries of powerlessness in Kyoto. In 1868, a short civil war brought nearly seven centuries of shogun rule to an end: the emperor was restored and a new era, the Meiji (1868–1912), began.

In 1877, enraged traditionalists started a major uprising—the Satsuma Rebellion. A new conscript army defeated the traditional samurai forces (*see p.146*), ending their role in Japanese politics. The emperor set in motion a series of reforms, including the granting of a formal constitution in 1889.

Japan as a major power

Japan industrialized rapidly and made use of its new economic strength to build up its armed forces. In 1894, Chinese intervention in Korea,

⬆ **The Meiji emperor** was restored to power in 1868, leading to the abolition of shogun feudalism.

where Japan claimed a sphere of influence, led the Japanese to declare war. Japanese armies rapidly proved superior, and they seized the strategic naval base at Port Arthur in Manchuria in November. The Treaty of Shimonoseki (1895), which ended the conflict, saw China abandon its Korean interests and cede Taiwan to Japan.

Japan's next military adventure, a clash with Russia in 1904–1905, again over Korea, resulted in an even more resounding success. The Japanese Imperial Navy decimated the Russian fleet at Tsushima in May 1905, forcing Tsar Nicholas II to agree in September to the Treaty of Portsmouth, by which Russia backed out of Korea and Japan gained occupation of the Liadong peninsula. The defeat of a modern European army by an Asian power sent shockwaves through Western military circles. Japan was a force to be reckoned with, and it renegotiated its treaties to secure full customs control by 1911.

◢ **A great victory parade** in Tokyo marked the Japanese victory in the Russo-Japanese War (1904–1905), igniting a burst of patriotic fervor.

◥ **The Satsuma Rebellion** in 1877 was the last (and most serious) of a series of uprisings by traditionalists bent on reversing the reforms of the Meiji Restoration.

Oceania

By 1750, the Europeans had explored only a few coastlines and scattered islands in the Pacific Ocean, their voyages motivated by the search for the hypothetical *Terra Australis* or great Southern Continent, but equally impeded by the vast distances involved. Nevertheless, by the early 20th century, European powers had colonized the Pacific islands, while the two largest countries, Australia and New Zealand, had become self-governing dominions.

Exploration in the Pacific

SOUTH PACIFIC ☐ 1642–1770

The Pacific Ocean was first sighted by the Spanish explorer Vasco Nuñez de Balboa in 1513, and soon Spanish and Portuguese ships were crossing its northern reaches. But while Magellan crossed the South Seas in 1520, he completely missed Australia, undermining belief that *Terra Australis*, the "Southern Continent," actually existed. Eventually, the Dutch East India Company made the first sure sightings and exploration of the coast of Australia, with Willem Janszoon reaching the Gulf of Carpentaria in 1605. In 1642, the Dutchman Abel Tasman first explored the coastline of Tasmania, and also, heading east, made the first European sighting of New Zealand. The Dutch called these lands New Holland, but they did not seek to settle there.

Cook's voyage

The east coast of mainland Australia, however, was first sighted on April 19, 1770, by the British explorer Captain James Cook, whose ship *Endeavour* had been on a voyage tasked with observing the Transit of Venus (a rare astronomical phenomenon), but also motivated by the desire to forestall French ambitions in the South Pacific. On April 29, Cook made landfall on Australia at Botany Bay, and in August formally claimed possession of the new land for the British Crown.

《 Native inhabitants of New Guinea, in a drawing contemporary with the time of Cook's voyages in the 1770s.

The First Fleet

NEW SOUTH WALES, AUSTRALIA ⌛ **1787–88**

The British were at first unsure as to what to do about the territory Captain Cook discovered in 1770 (*see facing page*). Then Lord Sydney, the home secretary, devised the "Heads of a Plan" to solve the twin problems of how to prevent the French from establishing their own colony in the new land, and what to do with the convicts who would once have been deported to the now-independent Americas. The scheme was to ship a batch of prisoners to Australia.

On May 13, 1787, 11 ships (the "First Fleet"), under the command of Captain Arthur Phillip, set off from Portsmouth, England, bearing around 750 convicts, and arrived at Botany Bay on January 20, 1788. Given the name New South Wales, the small colony was reinforced by a Second Fleet in 1790, and a third a year later. At first, survival was the main concern, but within a few years the first settlement, at Sydney Cove, sent out parties to explore their new homeland.

Leg irons and chains shackled the convicts of the First Fleet on their long sea journey.

The exploration of Australia

AUSTRALIA ⌛ **1798–1861**

Charles Sturt (1795–1869), aged 32 when he arrived in Australia, spent 20 years exploring the continent.

As Australia's first colony, in New South Wales, grew—ably led from 1809 to 1820 by Governor Lachlan Macquaherie—there came a desire to explore the new continent. Early attempts concentrated on charting the coastline, and included, in 1798–1799, George Bass and Matthew Flinders' circumnavigation of Tasmania, previously believed to be joined to the mainland. But then explorers began to strike inland.

In 1813, Gregory Blaxland crossed the Blue Mountains for the first time, and in 1828 Charles Sturt explored Murray and Darling, reaching the sea near present-day Adelaide. By the early 1840s, new "free" colonies (to which convicts were not—at least initially—sent) had been founded in Victoria (1803), Western Australia (1829), and South Australia (1836).

Gradually, the explorations edged toward the center of the continent, and in 1845 Sturt reached the fringes of the Simpson Desert. In 1861, John McDouall Stuart, suffering terrible privations along the way, made the first south-to-north crossing of Australia, beginning at Adelaide. His trip established once and for all the continent's extent.

The federation of Australia

AUSTRALIA **1872–1901**

By the end of the 19th century, the Australian colonies had overcome their early travails, which included conflicts with the Aboriginal peoples, who were gradually pushed out of their lands by European settlers. A growing national self-consciousness emerged, which demanded more than the status of a mere colony of the British Crown.

The connection of the six Australian colonies by telegraph in 1872 fueled the sense of a common destiny and demands for "federation" as a single nation grew. A Federal Council was finally established in 1895, but it had no control over revenue. The 1898 Constitution Bill established a much stronger federal system, and on January 1, 1901, today's Commonwealth of Australia came into being.

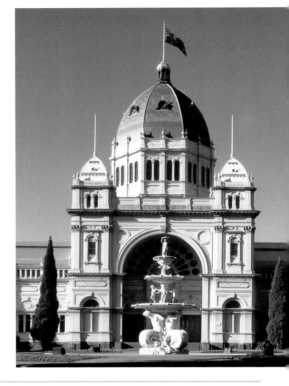

The Royal Exhibition Building in the city of Melbourne housed the first session of Australia's Federal Parliament on May 9, 1901.

European settlement in New Zealand

NEW ZEALAND **1769–1850**

The first contact between Europeans and the Maori of New Zealand (known by the indigenous peoples as *Aotearoa*—the "land of the long white cloud")—ended unhappily when, in 1642, four Dutch crew members sailing with Abel Tasman (*see p.278*) were killed following a dispute. It was not until Captain Cook's "rediscovery" of New Zealand in 1769 that Europeans encroached once more on Maori possession of the land, and only gradually that sealers, whalers, and missionaries began establishing small coastal enclaves.

By 1839, there were probably only 2,500 Europeans on the North and South Islands. The Maori themselves were debilitated by the effects of the epidemic diseases the Europeans brought with them, and by intertribal warfare sparked by the firearms they bought from foreign traders.

Waitangi and European migration

In 1839, a new New Zealand Company set up a formal colony along the lines of those in Australia, and in February 1840 the British and the Maori chiefs signed the Treaty of Waitangi, which (in the British view) ceded Maori sovereignty in exchange for Crown protection. European migration to New Zealand followed, and the settlers founded Auckland and Wellington in 1840, Dunedin in 1848, and Christchurch in 1850. By 1858 the 59,000 Europeans probably outnumbered the Maori.

The New Zealand Wars

ᴘᴜ NEW ZEALAND ⌛ 1840–1873

The Treaty of Waitangi (*see facing page*) did not put an end to friction between the Maori and the British, as the latter sought to expand into new areas. In 1843, open fighting erupted around Nelson, South Island, when armed settlers tried to punish the Maori chief Ngati Toa for resisting further encroachments. The Maori proved competent fighters and beat off the settlers. More fighting erupted on North Island in 1845–1846, in part a Maori civil war, and around Wellington, North Island, in 1846.

The Waikato War

The Maori, making able use of their *pa* (fortified settlements), beat off most European assaults, and for 15 years calm prevailed.

In the 1860s, though, the emergence of a Maori "King Movement," with the selection of the first king Potatau Te Wherowhero, disrupted the balance of power. War flared up again, with the British struggling to break through the Maori network of *pa*. By 1864, a force of almost 14,000 British soldiers had weakened the Maori warriors in the Waikato War, and despite a flare-up in 1872–1873, European military supremacy in New Zealand was thereafter largely left unchallenged.

《 The Maori used wooden war clubs, despite also having European firearms.

Antarctic exploration

ᴘᴜ ANTARCTICA ⌛ 1820–1911

Although the Russian expedition of Fabian von Bellinghausen had sighted the Antarctic continent in 1820, and Briton James Ross had explored part of it (including Victoria Land and the Ross Ice Shelf) in 1839–1843, most of Antarctica remained a mystery in the 1890s. In 1895, the Sixth International Geographical Conference declared the Antarctic the world's last great focus for exploration, and the race was on to discover and chart its secrets.

The race for the Pole

In first place among the objectives was to reach the South Pole. In 1908, Sir Ernest Shackleton's expedition reached 88° 23' south, just 112 miles (180 km) short of the Pole. In 1911, however, the competition reached fever pitch with the simultaneous arrival of a Norwegian expedition, led by Roald Amundsen, and a British one, under Robert Scott. Amundsen's better-planned expedition reached the Pole first, on December 14, beating Scott's group by five weeks.

《 A photograph of Robert Scott's final five-man party for the assault on the South Pole in 1911, all of whom died on the return trip to their base camp.

Africa

In the early 19th century, although Europeans had established settlements at several points along the African coast and North Africa was well known to them, the African interior remained largely uncharted. Yet by 1900, most of the continent had been carved up among European colonial powers, with only a few areas, such as Ethiopia, having been able to resist annexation. Anti-colonial resistance did occur, but in the end European armies always proved too strong.

The early explorers

AFRICA 1805–1871

In 1820, the development of quinine, an effective treatment for malaria, opened up the African interior to proper exploration for the first time. Even so, West Africa was so thoroughly unhealthy for outsiders that it was known as the "White Man's Grave"; Mungo Park's British-sponsored expedition there in 1805 ended in disaster when his party simply disappeared.

In 1828, however, the Frenchman René-August Caillié became the first European to reach the fabled desert metropolis of Timbuktu and return alive, and by 1835, Europeans had mapped most of northwestern Africa.

Charting the great rivers

An expedition in 1858 by Englishmen Richard Burton and John Hanning Speke located Lake Tanganyika and Lake Victoria, although they quarreled over which of the lakes was the source of the Nile. Speke argued (correctly) that it was Victoria, to which he alone had traveled. From the 1840s, the Scottish missionary David Livingstone managed to journey extensively in central and southern Africa. In 1853–1856, he made the first known crossing of Africa from east to west, discovering Victoria Falls on the way, before retiring to a remote station on Lake Tanganyika, where he was in turn famously "discovered" by Henry Morton Stanley in 1871.

By the end of the century, Europeans had charted the courses of the Nile, Niger, Congo, and Zambezi rivers, and the world was well informed of the vast resources that Africa might offer them.

A tropical pith helmet worn by the Scottish missionary David Livingstone (1813–1873) as he explored Africa.

Dr. Livingstone, **I presume?**

Henry Morton Stanley, on finding David Livingstone, 1871

◀◀ **The Ashanti** were one of the few African peoples to offer strong resistance against European imperialism, but were subjugated by the British in 1900.

The Scramble for Africa

📖 **AFRICA** ⏳ **1869–1914**

In 1869, the opening of the Suez Canal, linking the Mediterranean to the Red Sea and thus to Asia, focused European attention on Africa's strategic importance. European colonial presence in Africa was still fragmented. It included Algeria, into which the French had made inroads in the 1830s; a few Spanish settlements; Portugal's territory of Angola; and British and French trading stations in West Africa. Britain administered the Cape Colony, bordered by two Boer (Afrikaners of Dutch origin) states.

The Berlin Conference

In 1884, the German chancellor Otto von Bismarck convened the Berlin Conference to settle rival claims. It was agreed that imperial powers could claim colonies only if they had agreed treaties with native chiefs and had established an administration there (the "Principle of Effectivity"). This led European countries to make effective their claims in areas they feared others might enter, setting off a "Scramble for Africa." By the close of the century virtually all the continent was under European control. By 1914, only two areas remained free: Liberia, which had been settled by freed American slaves; and Ethiopia, which still retained its traditional rulers.

❯❯ CECIL RHODES

Having made his fortune as founder of the De Beers diamond company in South Africa, British businessman Cecil Rhodes (1853–1902) turned to politics. A firm believer in British imperialism, his British South Africa Company made treaties that established a network of control throughout modern Zimbabwe. As Prime Minister of the Cape Colony from 1890, he sponsored the 1895 Jameson Raid, an attack on the independent Boer Republic of the Transvaal. However, the attack failed, ending Rhodes' political career.

Egypt under Muhammad Ali

◫ EGYPT ⌛ 1807–1882

When France and Britain intervened in Egypt during the Napoleonic Wars (*see pp.254–5*) they destabilized the Ottoman regime there, enabling Muhammad Ali—of Albanian origin—to seize

power by 1807. He fought on the Ottoman sultan's behalf against a revolt in Saudi Arabia in 1811–1812, but then absorbed new territory before launching outright war on the sultan in 1832. An agreement in 1840 removed Muhammad Ali's Syrian conquests to restore peace.

Ali reformed Egypt's army and tried to strengthen the economy by establishing state monopolies. His successors, who took the title Khedive, continued this process, but Ismail Pasha (ruled 1863–1879) overreached himself. His ambitious projects bankrupted the country, allowing the British to occupy Egypt in 1882.

◁ **The Suez Canal**, one of Ismail Pasha's hugely ambitious projects, was opened by French Empress Eugenie in November 1868.

The Mahdist movement

◫ SUDAN ⌛ 1881–1898

In 1877, the British military officer Charles George Gordon was appointed governor of the Egyptian-controlled Sudan, a post he held until 1880, when ill health forced him to retire.

Around the same time, a mystical Islamic movement arose under Muhammad Ahmad, who declared himself the Mahdi, promised savior of the Muslim world. The Mahdi's forces annihilated a British expeditionary force under Colonel Hicks at El Obeid, central Sudan, in November 1883. Gordon was sent back to Sudan, but found himself besieged at Khartoum. After prolonged resistance, the city was stormed by Mahdists on January 26, 1885, and Gordon was killed.

Although the Mahdi died in June 1885, his successor, the Khalifa 'Abdallahi, continued to rule Sudan until 1898, when a British force under Lord Kitchener invaded the country, bent on revenge for Gordon's death. At Omdurman on September 2, the British, armed with the new Maxim machine gun, totally destroyed 'Abdallahi's army and the Mahdist state collapsed.

△ **Lord Charles George Gordon** faces down advancing Mahdist rebels on the steps of the British Residence at Khartoum, in 1885.

The Boer Wars

The Dutch were the first Europeans to settle in South Africa, in 1652. From their first colony at Cape Town grew a distinctively Afrikaner, or Boer ("farmer"), society.

By 1815, however, the British had acquired possession of the Cape and, in the 1830s, the pressures of their new colonial masters led the Boers to embark on the "Great Trek" inland. A series of Boer republics grew up, including the Orange Free State and the Transvaal.

In 1877, Britain annexed the Transvaal, but the Boers declared independence again in 1880 and fought a brief and successful war to secure it. In 1895, the Jameson Raid, a botched British attempt to retake the Transvaal, led to a serious escalation in tensions and the outbreak of the Boer War in October 1899.

War breaks out

The Boers struck first and began protracted sieges of Ladysmith, Kimberley, and Mafeking. A British counteroffensive in early 1900, after defeats at Colenso and Spion Kop in December 1899, required vast reinforcements to push the Boers back. Under serious pressure, the Boers turned to a guerrilla campaign, prolonging the war into 1902, while the British employed ruthless tactics, including the use of concentration camps. The Peace of Vereeniging ended the war in 1902, the Boer republics accepting British sovereignty in return for autonomy.

⚑ **The Queen's South Africa medal** was awarded to British troops for service in the Boer War.

⚐ **Guerrilla detachments** drawn from the Boer farming community managed to hold off the British for almost two years between 1900 and 1902.

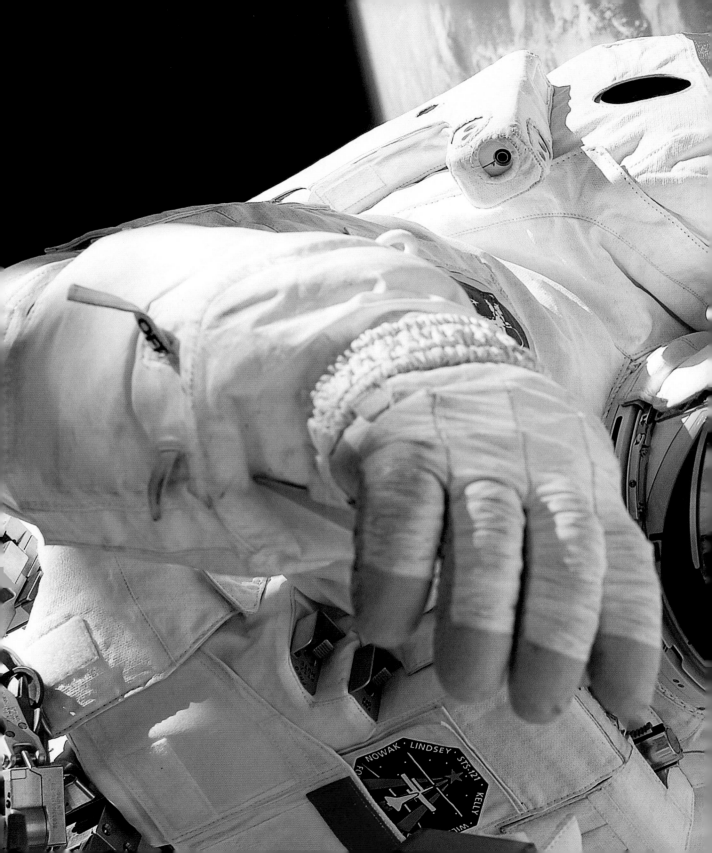

The Modern World

The world in 1914–present

Europe began World War I confidently in command of much of the world's territory. But the conflict's human and economic cost ushered in a period of turmoil that engulfed the continent, and also helped spark the Russian Revolution. In the aftermath of World War II, Europe was forced to abandon most of its colonies and embarked

The world in 1950

	International border
	Undefined border
◇	United Kingdom and possessions
◇	France and possessions
	Denmark and possessions
◇	Spain and possessions
⊙	Portugal and possessions
◇	Netherlands and possessions
	West Germany
	Japan and possessions
	Norway and possessions
	Belgium and possessions
	Italy and possessions
	New Zealand and possessions
◇	Australia and possessions
◇	US and possessions
	Controlled by European Axis powers Nov 15, 1942
	Controlled by Japan Nov 15, 1942

on a process of political unification, while the Cold War—an ideological confrontation between the capitalist USA and communist USSR—took center stage. The end of this struggle in the 1990s briefly promised a new era of peace, but soon gave way to a period of political uncertainty and regional strife.

The modern world in 1950

Though India had regained its independence from Britain in 1947, much of Africa was still under European colonial domination in 1950. However, an ongoing process of large-scale decolonization was about to take place that would leave almost no European colonies in the world by the early 21st century.

⊡ **By 1950, the peace settlement** that ended World War II had left Eastern Europe dominated by the communist Soviet Union, while in capitalist Western Europe a tentative process of political integration began that would lead to the formation of the European Community. In the Middle East, an uneasy truce between Arab states and the new nation of Israel (formed in 1948) marked a brief moment of peace in more than half a century of conflict in the region.

World War I

In 1914, the monarchies that had governed Europe since the end of the Napoleonic Wars a century earlier seemed secure. However, underlying tensions continued to grow, eventually exploding into a war of unprecedented scale and ferocity. In just five years, the war cost the lives of around 10 million soldiers and saw the collapse of the German, Austro-Hungarian, Russian, and Ottoman Turkish empires.

Assassination at Sarajevo

⚑ SARAJEVO, BOSNIA   🕮 JUNE 28, 1914

The Austro-Hungarian Empire struggled to cope with the end of Ottoman Turkish power in the Balkans in the 19th century (*see p.273*), and to deal with nationalists who sought to stop Austria–Hungary's encroachment into lost

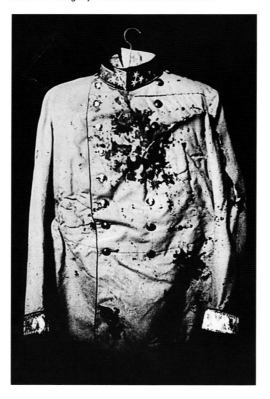

Ottoman territories. In 1908, Austria–Hungary annexed Bosnia, riding roughshod over Bosnia's large Serbian population, which felt that it should be a part of Serbia. The two Balkan Wars (1912–1913), in which Serbia first defeated the Ottomans and then a coalition of other Balkan states, also raised tensions, as Serbia showed it was a formidable military force.

Death in the Balkans

On June 28, 1914, Archduke Franz Ferdinand, heir to the Austro-Hungarian throne, paid an official visit to Sarajevo to inspect military maneuvers. A group of pro-Serbian revolutionaries from the "Young Bosnia" movement lay in wait for him.

As the royal couple drove to an official reception at the town hall, a bomb was thrown into their car, but it bounced off and only caused injuries in the following vehicles. After the reception, the archduke's route was changed, but by ill-fortune a wrong turn took his driver past one of the Young Bosnian conspirators, Gavrilo Princip, a 19-year-old student. He opened fire, killing the archduke and his wife Sophie. The archduke had been the principal proponent of restraint toward Serbia, and his assassination unleashed a confrontation with Austria–Hungary that would soon engulf the whole of Europe.

◀ **The blood-stained jacket** worn by Franz Ferdinand on the day of his assassination in 1914.

Escalation into war

◨ EUROPE ☒ JUNE–SEPTEMBER 1914

Even before the murder of Franz Ferdinand (*see facing page*), there were serious underlying strains between the major European powers. Imperial ambitions, instability caused by a constant repositioning of alliances, and a growing arms race all added to the potentially inflammable situation.

Anger boiled over in the Vienna government after Franz Ferdinand's assassination, and on July 23, 1914, the Austrians issued an ultimatum to Serbia that would, in effect, have ended Serbian independence. Serbia partially accepted the treaty, but the Austrians were not satisfied and both countries mobilized, with Austria declaring war on July 28. Germany had encouraged Austria–Hungary to act, hoping that Britain would remain neutral and that decisive military action would bring a rapid conclusion to the conflict.

The crisis spreads

Russia, fearing that the Austrians might annex its Serbian ally outright, had by now part-mobilized. As a result, the Germans, afraid that Russia might defeat Austria–Hungary, in turn mobilized its own army. Now that Germany might face war with Russia, German military planners thought France could then take advantage and attack Germany's western frontiers.

The simple, but terrible, solution was to strike first, and the Germans developed a plan to cross Belgium into France. Germany declared war on Russia on August 1 and on France two days later. On August 3, German troops crossed the frontiers of Russian Poland and Belgium. The next day Britain entered the conflict on the French side, and World War I had begun.

⌃ **British recruiting posters** featured the image of Lord Kitchener, veteran of the Boer War.

⌄ **German soldiers** travel in a truck mounted on railroad tracks. Such speedy mobilization made the momentum of the July 1914 crisis unstoppable.

The Western Front

W EUROPE ⏳ **1914–1915**

⏶ **An aerial view** of the complex trench system near Fricourt, on the Somme, France.

The shape of the initial fighting in western Europe during World War I was determined by Count Alfred von Schlieffen's German strategic plan of 1905. This called for an attack through Belgium, hooking around French defenses and enveloping Paris, in theory provoking France's swift surrender. Yet when the war broke out in early August 1914, Belgian resistance held up the German timetable, giving the French time to consolidate their defenses and a British force time to arrive to aid them.

In the ensuing First Battle of the Marne, the German thrust reached to within 45 miles (75 km) of Paris before being beaten back. The French and German armies then raced north toward the English Channel, trying to outflank each other. However, the French infantry could not outpace their opponents and, by late fall 1914, the two sides had dug a system of trenches that stretched from the North Sea almost to Switzerland.

War in the trenches

For the rest of World War I, major advances from these trench lines were the exception rather than the rule. Life in the trenches was appalling: epidemics of disease easily took hold, with such horrors as "trench foot" (in which damp and infected flesh simply rotted away) becoming an everyday occurrence.

The trench systems were also increasingly well defended, so that when soldiers went "over the top," they became entangled in barbed wire and were scythed down by fire from machine guns— a relatively recent invention well adapted to conditions on the Western Front. Those who succeeded in reaching the opposition's trench lines found themselves inadequately supported and faced instant counterattack from the enemy's reserve trenches.

Allied French and British attempts to force advances at Neuve Chapelle, Ypres, and Loos in 1915 all failed, with enormous casualties. In an

attempt to break the deadlock, the Germans used poison gas (chlorine) at Ypres in April 1915. This did little but gain a very localized advantage—and at a huge cost, in the suffering inflicted on the soldiers who inhaled this new weapon.

Verdun and the Somme

In 1916, Erich von Falkenhayn, the German Chief of Staff, devised a new strategy of attrition—to "bleed France white" by drawing its armies into a defense of the hugely strategic fortress-city of Verdun. The battle, which pitted an initial 500,000 French defenders against a million Germans, began on February 21, and lasted for 10 months.

The Germans made initial advances, but by December they had lost them all, at the cost of 700,000 casualties on both sides. Further carnage occurred at the

Somme, where, on July 1, an Anglo–French offensive tried to break the German lines with a huge infantry advance. However, the preliminary artillery bombardment had not cut the German lines of barbed wire nor destroyed their trenches, enabling the Germans to inflict appalling casualties on the British: some 57,000 men on the first day alone.

The battle degenerated into a series of costly offensives and counteroffensives that never remotely delivered the hoped-for breakout from the trench lines. The four months of fighting on the Somme cost 300,000 lives in 1916, and yet in 1917, both high commands still planned to win the war through the same sorts of offensives that had failed so miserably the year before.

◀ **Explosives** were often used to detonate mines and so disrupt the enemy's trenches.

▽ **German troops** advancing across open ground, a risky strategy that rarely succeeded without heavy casualties for the attacking side.

The war at sea

NORTH SEA, MEDITERRANEAN, S ATLANTIC   1914–1918

▲ **The German U-boat campaign**, particularly its "unrestricted" phases in 1915 and from 1917, hugely disrupted Allied shipping in the North Atlantic.

Naval warfare in World War I was tentative. Both Britain and Germany had a fleet of "dreadnoughts" (heavily armored battleships) but were eager to avoid a decisive encounter that, if lost, would render them powerless. The British concentrated instead on blockading Germany's North Sea ports to throttle its commerce. The only major fleet-to-fleet encounter, at Jutland (off Denmark) during May 31–June 1, 1916, was indecisive, with both sides suffering significant losses of ships.

Elsewhere, the Germans were initially more adventurous, sending commerce raiders such as the *Emden* to disrupt British and French trade. The German East Asia Squadron, under Admiral von Spee, also threatened trade routes before it was destroyed at the Battle of the Falklands in December 1914. Deprived of more conventional avenues, the Germans turned to submarine warfare, using U-boats to conduct a campaign of "unrestricted warfare" against Allied civilian vessels in 1915. However, the sinking of the passenger liner *Lusitania* in 1915 caused outrage, contributing to the US joining in the war against Germany.

The war in eastern Europe

E EUROPE   1914–1917

During World War I the geography of eastern Europe necessitated different military strategies from those used on the Western Front. More than 930 miles (1,500 km) of front, stretching from the Black Sea to the Baltic, rendered building a defensive trench network impractical, so warfare was more mobile than in the west.

At Tannenberg and the Masurian Lakes in August–September 1914, the Russians reversed the initial German and Austrian advance. In the Gorlice-Tarnów Offensive of May 1915, however, General von Falkenhayn smashed a Russian army, capturing some 140,000 men and securing Galicia. In June 1916, the Russians recovered and were able to launch the Brusilov Offensive, recapturing much lost ground. But the increasing costs of the war and rising social unrest in the army meant that by June 1917, many Russian army units refused to fight, allowing the Germans to transfer reinforcements to the Western Front.

◀ **The German stick grenade** was used to clear out stubbornly defended infantry positions. The British nicknamed it the "potato masher."

Gallipoli

⚐ GALLIPOLI PENINSULA, TURKEY   ⏳ APRIL 1915–JANUARY 1916

After a Turkish fleet attacked Russia's Black Sea ports on October 29, 1914, Turkey allied with Germany. Winston Churchill, British First Lord of the Admiralty, immediately lobbied for an expedition to seize control of the Dardanelles—the strategic straits that linked the Black Sea to the Aegean—to prevent a Turkish blockade that would cut off a vital Russian supply route. But the Allied landings on April 25, 1915, on the Gallipoli peninsula (overlooking the straits) were a disaster. The initial day's objectives were never reached, and a Turkish counterattack, organized by Mustafa Kemal (later Atatürk), confined the Allied forces to enclaves around Cape Helles in the south and Anzac Cove in the north. In mid-December, the Allies evacuated Anzac Cove, and then withdrew from Cape Helles. By January 9, 1916, their withdrawal was complete.

Palestine and the Arab Revolt

⚐ N SAUDI ARABIA, PALESTINE, JORDAN, ISRAEL, IRAQ   ⏳ 1915–1918

Aside from the Gallipoli campaign, initial British moves against the Ottoman Empire in World War I concentrated on seizing control of Mesopotamia.

After the disastrous surrender of a British army at Kut (in Iraq) in April 1916, the focus shifted to a wider area. The British attempted to instigate an Arab uprising against Ottoman rule in northern Arabia and the Transjordan, and to link this with a more conventional military campaign to take control of Palestine. Persuaded by T.E. Lawrence, Sharif Hussein ibn Ali of Mecca raised a revolt against the Ottomans in June 1916, causing enormous disruption in Sinai and Palestine. General Allenby's British army entered Jerusalem in December 1917, and inflicted a devastating defeat on the Ottoman army at Megiddo in September 1918, ending the war in the region.

》 T.E. LAWRENCE

Having joined in expeditions in the Near East, T. E. Lawrence (1888–1935) was a perfect liaison officer to Britain's Arab allies. He stirred up the Arab Revolt of 1916 with a distinctive flamboyance, giving rise to the legend of "Lawrence of Arabia."

✉ **General Allenby** enters Jerusalem after its capture from the Ottomans on December 11, 1917. The damage to Turkish morale from its loss was profound.

Stalemate in the west

W EUROPE   1917

British troops march toward the front line to relieve comrades there. The rotation of units was an attempt to mitigate the hardships of trench life.

1917 was one of the most difficult years for all those involved in World War I. The Allied naval blockade of Germany led to a shortage of wheat there in the winter, while the German U-boat campaign (*see p.294*) led to hardships in Britain. In April, France's Nivelle Offensive gained barely 1,650 ft (500 m) in its first day at a cost of 100,000 casualties, and led to widespread mutinies in the French army. Despite enormous losses, British offensives at Arras (in northeastern France) in April and at Messines (western Belgium) in June failed to gain any significant ground. Both sides tried new weapons, the Germans pioneering poison gas artillery shells at Messines, and the British using tanks on a large scale for the first time at Cambrai (northeastern France) in November. Neither weapon contributed to a decisive breakthrough.

The US enters the war

W EUROPE   1917–1918

In May 1917, the US Congress passed legislation authorizing the drafting of men into the army.

It was German action that finally broke the 1917 stalemate (*see above*). In February, Germany announced it was resuming unrestricted attacks on foreign shipping.

The threat to US interests was clear, and was compounded by a telegram written by the German foreign minister encouraging Mexico to attack the US. President Woodrow Wilson's attempts to maintain neutrality in the conflict, and to act as an honest broker for peace, were over, and in April the US declared war on Germany. However, it was not until June that the first US troops arrived in France, under the command of General John Pershing, and they were posted to the trenches only in October. The initial inexperience of the Americans, and the fact that Pershing at first failed to have his troops operate independently of their allies, meant that for a while their impact was limited.

Yet the German High Command was well aware that each increase in the numbers of US soldiers fighting with the Allies, which reached four complete divisions by 1918, lessened the chance of a German victory.

The end of the war

◻ W EUROPE ⧗ 1918

In March 1918, Germany signed a peace treaty at Brest-Litovsk with the new Bolshevik government of Russia. This freed up some 44 German divisions, which were now shifted to the Western Front. The German Chief of Staff, Erich Ludendorff, argued that these divisions should be used for a massive all-or-nothing assault.

On March 21, the Germans launched Operation Michael, the first element in their "Spring Offensive." They won 45 miles (70 km) of ground, but their largest gains were against the least resistance. As Allied resistance stiffened, Germany's initial momentum stalled. Ludendorff ordered further smaller attacks between April and July, but by then, with the US presence growing at 250,000 men a month, it was clear that his gamble had failed.

The Final Offensive

The Allied counterstroke came with an attack along the Marne River in late July. Another offensive around Amiens led to 27,000 German

❯❯ Armistice Day on November 11 is marked by wearing red poppies, the flowers that bloomed on World War I battlefields.

casualties on August 8 alone, which Ludendorff dubbed "the black day of the German army." In the "Hundred Days Campaign," the Allies then pushed east, finally breaking through Germany's trench lines. In a costly series of actions in September and October, they breached the Hindenburg line, Germany's last fortified defense.

With its main ally, Austria–Hungary, having signed an armistice with Italy after a disastrous defeat by the Italians in late October, Germany was under huge pressure, and a revolution threatened to overthrow the German Kaiser. Finally, the Germans signed an armistice on November 11, bringing World War I to an end.

◻ A German army unit returns home in December 1918. Many soldiers were bitter that the politicians agreed to an armistice while they were still able to fight.

American artist John Singer Sargent's harrowing painting *Gassed* evokes the terrible torment inflicted on soldiers who inhaled poison gas. Gas was first used as a weapon by the Germans near Ypres in April 1915, but eventually all sides employed some form of gas warfare.

The Treaty of Versailles

Although World War I had ended at the armistice of November 11, 1918, a large number of issues remained. The Western Allies wanted arrangements to ensure that Germany never again posed such a threat to peace, including an adjustment to Germany's borders to reflect its reduced status. Other treaties redrew the map of central and eastern Europe in favor of new nations that had emerged there.

The peace conference

On January 18, 1919 in Paris, delegates from more than 20 nations, excluding Germany and Austria–Hungary, gathered to seal peace. The driving forces at the conference were France's prime minister Georges Clemenceau, his British counterpart David Lloyd George, and US president Woodrow Wilson.

The French were intent on reducing Germany's capacity for waging war, extracting reparations, and regaining control of Alsace-Lorraine. The British wanted to avoid the anger that extravagant reparations claims might fuel in Germany, and to protect their imperial interests. President

⊘ **French troops disarm German police** during their 1923–1925 occupation of the Ruhr, western Germany, when Germany refused to pay its reparations.

Wilson, meanwhile, came armed with his Fourteen Points, the most important of which demanded guarantees of self-determination for the national minorities and the establishment of an international body to preserve world peace, the League of Nations.

The settlement

By May the outline of a final settlement stated that Germany was to acknowledge its guilt in the war and Kaiser Wilhelm was to be put on trial. Germany was to reduce its army to fewer than 100,000 men, its navy to a token force, and to have no tanks or aircraft.

The Rhineland was also to be demilitarized. More galling still was the cession of Alsace-Lorraine to France, part of Schleswig to Denmark, large portions of Prussia and Silesia to Poland, and the occupation of the Saarland region for 15 years by an international force. Any future union of Germany with Austria was also forbidden. Huge financial reparations were to be paid. On June 28, 1919, the German delegation signed the

Treaty in its entirety, sowing the seeds of bitterness among the German people that would be a key contributor to the outbreak of World War II just 20 years later. Further treaties imposed conditions on Germany's allies, and contained clauses that also caused considerable political strife in the interwar period.

⌃ **The Hall of Mirrors** at the Palace of Versailles, where the 1919 Treaty was signed.

⌄ **French Prime Minister** Georges Clemenceau signs the Treaty of Versailles on June 28, 1919. His desire to punish Germany harshly caused some debate.

Between the wars

The treaties that ended World War I, such as that signed at Versailles, did little to create a stable political environment in Europe. Resentment at the terms of the peace grew in Germany, and successive governments began to test its limits. In eastern and central Europe, fragile democracies succumbed to dictatorships. More ominously, public unrest in Germany and Italy gave rise to the extremist ideologies of National Socialism and Fascism under Adolf Hitler and Benito Mussolini.

Russia heads for revolution

RUSSIA **1905–1917**

After the Revolution of 1905 (*see p.263*), Tsar Nicholas II had been forced to agree a new constitution for Russia, including the formation of an elected Duma (parliament).

However, the tsar retained the ability to dissolve the Duma, which he did in 1906 and 1907. Two subsequent Dumas met from 1907–1912 and 1912–1917, which were in almost constant conflict with Nicholas. Normal political tensions were suspended in the early stages of World War I, but as the war went progressively worse for Russia, rising prices prompted industrial workers to strike. Violence erupted on the streets of Petrograd (St. Petersburg) and Moscow in the February Revolution, led by the Petrograd Soviet ("council"), and Nicholas abdicated on March 2, 1917.

Power was handed to a Provisional Government under Prince Lvov, but its position was contested by the Petrograd Soviet, which was dominated by Vladimir Lenin's revolutionary Russian Bolshevik Party. In July, riots erupted in Petrograd. Prince Lvov was replaced as leader of the Provisional Government by Alexander Kerensky, but the possibility of restoring stability would soon be ruined by a tide of revolutionary activity.

≫ **Revolutionary officers** drive the tsar's confiscated car around the streets of Petrograd. Ironically, it was later to become Lenin's own personal vehicle.

The 1917 Revolution

⚑ RUSSIA ⌛ OCTOBER 1917

In July 1917 Russia's Provisional Government, under Alexander Kerensky, suppressed an outbreak of revolutionary riots. Vladimir Lenin fled to Finland, but his followers received help from an unlikely source.

Bolshevik power

In August 1917, General Lavr Kornilov, the army commander in chief, ordered troops into Petrograd, ostensibly to protect the Provisional Government from the Bolshevik threat. Suspecting an attempted coup, Kerensky asked the Bolsheviks for help, arming the Bolshevik Red Guard militia.

Kornilov's alleged attempt to seize power was unsuccessful, but Kerensky's regime was fatally weakened. In September Kerensky attempted to organize a "Democratic Conference" to rein in the unruly leftist factions baying for power, but this had no effect apart from bringing into disrepute those parties who cooperated with it. In mid-October, the Central Committee of the Bolshevik Party met to plan the seizure of power, fearful that a left-wing coalition of other parties might take power if the Kerensky government collapsed.

On October 25, Leon Trotsky, the party's chief organizer, launched an almost bloodless coup in Petrograd. Armed squads of pro-Bolshevik revolutionaries occupied key positions such as railroad stations and telephone exchanges. Kerensky surrendered and the Bolsheviks moved quickly to push out the other leftists from positions of influence. Their supremacy ensured, the Bolsheviks moved to implement Lenin's revolutionary program.

⬆ The Bolshevik hammer and sickle symbolized the unity of industrial and agricultural workers.

》 LENIN

After his brother was hanged for his part in a plot to kill Tsar Alexander III, Vladimir Ilyich Lenin (1870–1924) became a revolutionary. In 1895, he was exiled to Siberia. On his release, he spent several years in Europe, where he studied Marxism (see p.267). Lenin came to power in the October Revolution of 1917, but he died less than seven years later, his program for a revolutionary transformation of Russia only partially fulfilled.

 **Leon Trotsky** returned from exile in North America in 1917 to lead the infant Bolshevik Red Army, instigating proper training to turn it into an effective fighting force.

The Russian Civil War

🏳 **RUSSIA** ⚔ **1918–1920**

After seizing the center of power in Petrograd in November 1917, the Bolsheviks fought a multisided civil war. Many high-ranking tsarist officers were determined to fight back against the Revolution, and the left-wing parties whom the Bolsheviks had pushed aside were unwilling to let the matter rest.

In May 1918, the remaining leaders of the leftist Socialist-Revolutionaries (SR) set up their own government at Samara on the Volga River. Anti-Bolshevik ("White") armies began to form, led by General Kornilov (see p.303) in the south, Admiral Kolchak in Siberia, and General Yudenich in the northwest. By late 1918, the situation for the Bolsheviks was critical, with Admiral Kolchak pushing far into the Urals. Trotsky's Red Army defeated Kolchak in April, but Kornilov's army— now under General Denikin's control following Kornilov's death—captured Kiev, Odessa, and Orel in the summer of 1919, almost threatening Moscow. Yet a devastating counterattack pushed Denikin back, and a badly coordinated thrust against Petrograd by Yudenich in October 1919 failed. The last remaining large White force, under General Wrangel, attempted to seize the Crimea, but in late 1920 he evacuated his forces, leaving the Red Army to mop up an assortment of anarchist, nationalist, and Islamic militia, which continued to resist reincorporation by the central government.

Go where you **belong**... into the **dustbin of history**.

Leon Trotsky, dismissing a walkout by the Mensheviks and Socialist-Revolutionaries from the Second All-Russian Congress of Soviets (October 25–26, 1917)

Russia under Lenin and Stalin

⚑ RUSSIA ⚰ 1921–1953

》 STALIN

Born Joseph Djugashvilli in Georgia in
1878, Stalin (1878–1953) joined the Marxist
Social-Democratic Labor Party in 1901,
and when this split in 1904 he joined the
Bolshevik faction. Stalin became a valued
enforcer of Lenin's policies, joining the
Bolsheviks' policy-making Politburo in
1919. By 1922 he was the party's Secretary
General, becoming supreme leader after
Lenin's death. In 1926, he expelled Trotsky
from the party; he went on to rule the USSR
virtually unchallenged for nearly 30 years.

When Vladimir Lenin (*see p.303*) came to
power after the Russian Revolution, he quickly
established a highly centralized system of
government, banning all rival political parties
and empowering the Communist Party's dominant
Central Committee to expel anyone who failed
to follow the party line.

From 1921, Lenin promoted the New Economic
Policy (NEP), in which peasants were given more
control over the levels of agricultural production
than strict Bolsheviks would have liked. A federal
Union of Soviet Socialist Republics (USSR) was
created in 1922.

Stalinism

After Lenin's death in 1922, Joseph Stalin—whom
Lenin had favored—removed, tried, or executed his
rivals in the Central Committee, and pushed for
a tougher line and greater centralized state control.
Between 1928 and 1932, he instituted the first of
the Five Year Plans—huge schemes that aimed to
transform the USSR into an industrialized society.
He also enforced a policy of "collectivization,"
in which land belonging to *kulaks* (prosperous
peasants) was given to cooperative farms.

Enormous hardship ensued, including a famine
in the Ukraine in 1932–1933. A network of prison
camps (the *gulag*) was established, and the
"Great Terror" of 1936–1938
saw the secret police
launching waves of purges
of the party elite and army.
Some 690,000 people were
executed, with many more
consigned to prison camps.
It was only with Stalin's
death in 1953 that the icy
chill of his oppressive
regime began to thaw.

**》 A 1920 propaganda
poster** for the Communist
Party demands:"Are you
a volunteer yet?"

The Great Depression

WORLDWIDE **1929–1932**

During the early 1920s the US economy flourished, but by 1927 the US was overproducing goods for which it did not have a market. European economies, meanwhile, had failed to adjust to the conditions of peacetime following the end of World War I, and in Germany a savage bout of hyperinflation in 1919–1923 had wrecked that country's economy.

The Wall Street Crash

Despite the underlying economic gloom, investors on New York's Wall Street stock exchange continued to push up share prices. In October 1929, however, prices began to decline as investor confidence evaporated. On October 24 ("Black Thursday"), panic set in. It was followed by "Black Monday" and "Black Tuesday," on which stock market prices tumbled by 13 and 12 percent

▲ **A German 1,000 mark note** overprinted with the value 1 billion; by December 1922, printing presses were struggling to keep up with hyperinflation.

respectively, in a collapse known as the "Wall Street Crash." The decline soon infected the US economy, as banks called in loans that could no

⬇ **In London, City workers gather** after the collapse of British investor Clarence Hatry's business empire, which fed into the Wall Street Crash one week later.

longer be repaid, and several banks collapsed as panicked savers withdrew their money. A wave of mortgage foreclosures and business bankruptcies led to a downward spiral of unemployment and homelessness. Many people were forced to take shelter in shantytowns, nicknamed "Hoovervilles" out of resentment against President Herbert Hoover, who declined to extend government aid to the unemployed.

The depression

As a result of the Crash, US investors withdrew many foreign loans. This caused the collapse of the system of international loans set up to handle Germany's war reparations and meant that European countries, including Germany, could not pay for their imports. Trade between Europe and North America was badly hit, and the price of commodities plummeted, by 1932 falling to around 45 percent of their 1929 values.

A wave of economic nationalism erupted as countries sought to protect their domestic industries. President Hoover introduced the Smoot-Hawley Tariff in 1930, which increased taxes on imports by around 20 percent, and European governments responded in kind with similar protectionist measures. This resulted in the crippling of international trade and in further deterioration in the world economy. In Germany, unemployment more than doubled to over 15 percent of the workforce, some 4 million people, by the end of 1930.

The New Deal

Hoover was voted out of office in 1932 when Franklin D. Roosevelt (US president 1933–1945) won a landslide victory on the promise of a "New Deal." This was a series of initiatives designed to kick-start the economy and provide emergency relief, new jobs, and agricultural reforms. A series of successful projects, such as the Tennessee Valley Authority—which constructed a large series of dams—did much to alleviate unemployment while the US economy got back on its feet.

The political response in European countries was less constructive. Mass unemployment and poverty led to civil unrest and the rise of right-wing movements. In the 1920s and '30s, many countries in eastern and central Europe became dictatorships—such as Poland, where Marshal Pilsudski's authoritarian regime came to power in 1926. Even in Britain, where in 1930 unemployment had touched 2.5 million (20 percent of the workforce), Oswald Mosley's Union of British Fascists, founded in 1932, briefly threatened to become a real political force.

 Workers widen curbs, a project of the Works Progress Administration in Roosevelt's "New Deal."

> **I pledge** you, I pledge myself, to a **new deal** for the **American people**.
>
> **Franklin D. Roosevelt, Democratic presidential nomination acceptance speech, 1932**

The rise of Fascism

The economic hardship and political instability that followed World War I contributed to a climate of violence and lawlessness across much of Europe in the 1920s. This atmosphere, and unresolved disputes about national boundaries and Germany's role within Europe, helped to produce new, right-wing nationalist movements, sharing an ideology that became known as fascism.

◽ **In 1922 Benito Mussolini** (fourth from left) led his National Fascist Party in a march on Rome, forcing a handover of power to the Fascists.

Mussolini and Fascism

The new right-wing philosophies were fed by loathing and fear of the Union of Soviet Socialist Republics (USSR) and its open desire to export communism. Ironically, the USSR's totalitarian socialist democracy provided a model of government for extreme right-wing nationalists seeking to reform failing democracies in Europe. Mixed with a militaristic ideology, this style of government turned conservatism into fascism.

First of the fascist leaders to rise to power was Italy's Benito Mussolini (1883–1945), who in 1914 joined one of the revolutionary *fasci* (political groups) agitating for social reform. In 1919 he helped found the Fasci Italiani di Combattimento, a group of extreme nationalists.

The Fascists became seen as the protectors of law, deploying their informal militia—the "Blackshirts"— to terrorize socialists. In October 1922, Mussolini ordered the Blackshirts to march on Rome and seize power. King Victor Emmanuel III refused his prime minister's

Hitler's book *Mein Kampf* (meaning "My Struggle") was a statement of his political ideology.

request for military support and invited Mussolini to form a government. In 1926, Mussolini assumed power, brutally silencing any political opponents. Known as *Il Duce* ("the leader"), he ruled Italy as a dictator until 1943.

Nazism in Germany

In 1918, Germany's new Weimar Republic faced similar problems. Many Germans and Austrians resented the terms of the Treaty of Versailles (*see pp.300–1*).

Among them was Adolf Hitler (1889–1945), an Austrian-born former soldier who in 1919 joined a small Munich-based political group— the German Worker's Party, renamed the following year the NDSAP, or Nazi Party. The Nazis had much in common with Mussolini's Fascists, but also had a hankering for a romanticized German past and a dangerous belief in the superiority of the German *Volk* (or race) and of Aryans (white Caucasians), particularly compared to Slavs and Jews.

The Nazis aimed to unite all German speakers in a greater German Reich. Hitler maneuvered the Nazi Party into power, offering it as the only way to end instability. In 1932, he lost an election for the presidency to Paul von Hindenburg, but the following year Hindenburg offered him the chancellorship, hoping to neutralize the Nazis politically. It was a fatal mistake. In 1933, Hitler pushed through an Enabling Act giving him near-dictatorial powers for a period of four years, and once that time had elapsed the Nazis prevented them from being rescinded.

Hitler in power

Once Führer ("leader") of Germany, Hitler was able to implement his racial and extreme nationalist ideology. This was done with the help of an oppressive state security system bolstered by the Gestapo (political police) and the SS (a paramilitary police force controlled by the Nazis).

Joseph Goebbels was an early follower of Hitler, joining the Nazi Party in 1924. From 1933 to 1945 he was minister in charge of propaganda.

« **The Nazis had held** a party rally in the Bavarian city of Nuremberg as early as 1923, and between 1933 and 1938 it became an annual event. The vast numbers of attendees and the militaristic setting proved the party's power and cemented the cult of Adolf Hitler, the revered Führer.

⏶ A 1937 poster by the UGT—a union aligned with the Republicans—urges its members to fight.

The Spanish Civil War

🏴 **SPAIN** ⚔ **1936–1939**

In February 1936, Spain's newly elected left-wing Popular Front government vowed to uphold liberty, prosperity, and justice, but many feared their policies were too progressive. On July 19, 1936, Francisco Franco took control of Spain's armies in Morocco and led them into Spain; the result was civil war.

The opposing sides

The Republicans (government supporters) were composed of liberal democrats, communists, socialists, and anarchists. They faced roughly equal numbers of Franco's Nationalists, who were backed by monarchists, Catholics, and the Falange—the Spanish fascist party. While the Republicans received support from the USSR, Mexico, and socialist and communist volunteers throughout Europe, the Nationalists received military aid from the fascist regimes in Italy and Germany (including the "Condor" legion, armed with tanks).

The course of the war

By November 1, 1936, 25,000 Nationalist troops had begun a three-year siege of the capital, Madrid. In 1937, a campaign to capture the north's Basque provinces led to the aerial bombing of Guernica and many civilian casualties.

A disastrous attempt to force a way through to Madrid in March 1938 put the Nationalist central front on the defensive. Further east, however, the Nationalists pushed toward the coast near Valencia in April, cutting the Republican territory in two. At the Battle of the Ebro (July 25–November 16, 1938), Republican forces were all but destroyed. On January 26, 1939, Barcelona fell to Franco's forces, and on March 27, 1939, the Nationalists entered Madrid almost unopposed.

» FRANCISCO FRANCO

Born into a military family, Francisco Franco (1892–1975) served in Morocco from 1912 to 1926, becoming the youngest general in Spain. After leading the Nationalist movement to victory in the Spanish Civil War, Franco dominated Spanish politics as head of state for 36 years, though from 1947 he was formally the regent for a restored monarchy in which he chose not to appoint a king. His regime was stifling, militaristic, and conservative—democracy was restored only on his death in 1975.

Women and the vote

UK, USA, EUROPE **1869–1928**

Suffrage (the right to vote) had been considerably extended during the 19th century, particularly in Britain, but it was still denied to women. In 1903, Briton Emmeline Pankhurst formed the Women's Social and Political Union to campaign for the vote. Frustrated by the failure to achieve this through peaceful means, the suffragettes, as they became known, took direct action, including an invasion of the Houses of Parliament.

Many suffragettes went on hunger strike, prompting the British government to pass the "Cat and Mouse" Act in 1913, by which the women could legally be force-fed. The campaign finally achieved success in 1918, when women aged 30 and over obtained the vote, although full voting rights were granted only in 1928.

Suffrage in the USA and elsewhere

A similar but more peaceful campaign began in the USA in the 1840s. The first state to grant female suffrage was Wyoming, in 1869; nationally, women won the vote only in 1920, in

> " **Women** will have, **with us**, the **fullest rights**.
>
> **Stanley Baldwin, prime minister of the UK, 1928**

part as recognition of the role they had played in World War I. Key among the figures campaigning for the vote for American women was Susan B. Anthony, who cofounded the National Woman Suffrage Association in 1869.

In the rest of the world, stories of women's suffrage are mixed. New Zealand was the first to grant women full suffrage, in 1893, while some other countries restrict women's right to vote even today.

The "New Women's Organization" lobbied for French women to be given the vote—a right that they received only in 1944.

World War II

Adolf Hitler's rise to power in Germany seriously destabilized Europe and, after a series of false alarms, war broke out in September 1939. The conflict became global, with the USSR and USA joining the western European powers (the "Allies"), while Japan and Italy joined the German ("Axis") side. By the time the fighting finally ended in 1945, World War II had led to the deaths of some 25 million military personnel, and at least as many civilians.

Germany's path to war

POLAND   SEPTEMBER 1939

Throughout the late 1930s, the chancellor of Germany, Adolf Hitler, had steadily chipped away at the restrictions placed on his country by the Treaty of Versailles (*see pp.300–1*); he had restarted conscription, established an air force and, in March 1936, remilitarized the Rhineland. In March 1938, he went further, sending German troops into Austria and proclaiming its *Anschluss* ("union") with Germany.

The Czech and Polish crises

In September 1938, Hitler demanded concessions for the German speakers of Czechoslovakia's Sudetenland, and the Munich Conference (involving Germany, Britain, France, and Italy) granted him occupation of Sudetenland.

The German foreign minister, von Ribbentrop, brokered a deal with the USSR to divide eastern central Europe into two spheres of influence, leaving western Poland in German hands. On the pretext that Poland refused to allow Germany to occupy the once-German port of Danzig, on September 1, 1939, Hitler ordered German forces to invade Poland, marking the beginning of World War II.

◁ **The Germans used propaganda** to support their annexations, such as this postcard proclaiming that the once-Polish town of Danzig "is German."

Blitzkrieg and the fall of France

⚐ SCANDINAVIA, BELGIUM, THE NETHERLANDS, FRANCE ⌛ SEPTEMBER 1939–JUNE 1940

In 1939 the British and French governments had guaranteed protection for Poland against German aggression, so when German forces invaded Poland on September 1, they responded by declaring war.

Germany's assault had begun with the Luftwaffe (air force) blanket-bombing roads, towns, and villages. Fast-moving mobile units, spearheaded by Panzer (tank) divisions, thrust deep into the Polish heartland. It was a new form of warfare, rapid and devastating, which became known as *Blitzkrieg*.

The fall of Poland and Scandinavia

Within a week, Warsaw was under siege. A Soviet invasion on September 17 dealt the fatal blow, and Polish resistance ended on September 28. There followed months of "Phoney War": the Allies built up weapons stocks, but made no

◀◀ **After French surrender** in June 1940, Philippe Pétain led a regime that governed southern France from Vichy.

move against Germany. Then Hitler invaded Denmark and Norway in April 1940, occupying both nations.

The surrender of France

On May 10, Hitler pushed west toward France, overrunning the Netherlands, Belgium, and Luxembourg. German forces broke through the Ardennes, and reached Abbeville on the northern French coast, trapping the British Expeditionary Force (BEF) sent to aid France. As the German army surged toward Paris, the British prime minister Winston Churchill ordered the BEF, who were hemmed in around the port of Dunkirk, to evacuate. The German army entered Paris on June 14, and a week later the French signed an armistice with Germany.

☑ **The successful removal by sea** of some 338,000 Allied soldiers from Dunkirk in May 1940 preserved the core of an army that could resist Germany.

The Battle of Britain

📖 **BRITAIN** ⌛ **AUGUST–OCTOBER 1940**

Having overcome France in June 1940, Adolf Hitler turned his attention to Britain, the one remaining country of significance that resisted him. He laid plans for the invasion of southern England ("Operation Sealion"), but before they could be put into effect, the Germans needed to achieve dominance of the skies. The aerial conflict that raged between August and October 1940 became known as the Battle of Britain, and it pitted Germany's Luftwaffe, under the command of Herman Göring, against the Fighter Command of the British Royal Air Force (RAF), led by Air Chief Marshal Hugh Dowding.

The first German attacks

Dowding linked the new technology of radar to a system of battle groups and sectors that was able to respond rapidly to German raids. Although the Luftwaffe had superiority in numbers of aircraft, they were often close to their extreme flight range and so could operate for only a short time in British airspace.

On August 12, 1940, concerted German attacks on British airfields began, but an attempt the following day (*Adlertag*, or "Eagle Day") to overwhelm the RAF with a mass attack failed.

>> **WINSTON CHURCHILL**

First Lord of the Admiralty during World War I, Winston Churchill (1874–1965) warned against German rearmament in the 1930s. When he became Britain's prime minister in May 1940, his strong resolve and wooing of US support helped to ensure Britain's final victory in World War II.

The RAF wins out

The Germans assumed that the main force of the RAF was spent, and that they would soon achieve by attrition what they could not with a single blow. The RAF, however, proved resilient, and by early September had some 738 Spitfire and Hurricane fighter aircraft—more than at the start of the campaign. Instead, it was the Luftwaffe that was suffering a steady stream of losses.

At the start of September, Hitler ordered a change of tactics and the bombing of London, which started in earnest on September 7. Although the Battle of Britain carried on until October, in effect the German chances of destroying the RAF had already ended.

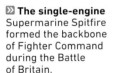

>> **The single-engine** Supermarine Spitfire formed the backbone of Fighter Command during the Battle of Britain.

Air power in World War II

World War II was the first major conflict in which air power played a determining role. During the Polish campaign in 1939, the Luftwaffe deployed some 1,500 aircraft to pulverize Poland and smash its lines of communication. From then on, almost every campaign used air support, with an increasing emphasis on strategic bombing, aiming to destroy the opponent's industries and undermine its morale.

Strategic bombing

The Battle of Britain (*see facing page*) seemed to indicate that there was no decisive strategic advantage in using air power, but both sides continued to deploy massive numbers of aircraft in a tactical role. From 1941, with the arrival of more efficient bombers such as the Vickers Wellington, the British were able to bomb German cities on a large scale, a tactic championed by Arthur Harris, the controversial chief of Bomber Command from February 1942. The bombers were inaccurate, however, and the chances of hitting a specific military or industrial target were remote, so Harris ordered larger raids, containing up to 1,000 bombers. At the attack on Hamburg on July 27–28, the sheer weight of Allied bombing caused a firestorm and 40,000 to 45,000 people died. By 1944, the Luftwaffe's resistance had almost disappeared, and the Allies could bomb at will.

« **German Dornier 217 bombers** attack London during the Battle of Britain in 1940, foreshadowing later, much larger attacks on Germany itself.

" **Bomb the enemy soft** until a comparatively small land force… can **overcome his remaining resistance**.

Air Vice Marshal Arthur ("Bomber") Harris, January 1943

German army helmets were the only part of their gear suitable for the harsh temperatures in the USSR, and the German soldiers suffered terribly from the cold.

The German invasion of the USSR

USSR **JUNE–DECEMBER 1941**

Ever since the 1920s, Hitler had viewed the western USSR as a possible area for German expansion to provide *Lebensraum* ("living space") for a growing population. By 1941, Hitler also feared that the US might join the war on the British side and so, although an uneasy peace had prevailed in eastern Europe since the defeat of Poland in September 1939, he decided on an invasion of Britain's last possible European ally, the USSR.

Operation Barbarossa

The force that Hitler had assembled for the planned invasion, Operation Barbarossa, was truly prodigious, including around four million German troops and their allies, and some 11,000 tanks. At around dawn on June 22, 1941, the German army crossed into the USSR, the invasion having been delayed by several crucial months to deal with a crisis in Yugoslavia. The Soviet Red Army was caught almost completely by surprise and was hampered by a military strategy that insisted on defending every yard of ground, leaving few reserves to contain the intense, rapid attacks of the German *Blitzkrieg* tactic.

The battle for Moscow

The German armored columns sped forward, in the north reaching Leningrad by August 19 and on the central front surrounding Minsk on June 18, where they would capture some 300,000 prisoners—a sign of the large-scale collapse of the Soviet defensive effort. By December 1941, Moscow itself was under threat.

The most advanced German units reached the outer suburbs on December 2. But the offensive ground to a halt in the face of fanatical Soviet resistance and the effects of winter, which froze the lubricant in German tanks. On December 5, the Soviet commander, General Zhukov, ordered a counterattack and within a month, the Germans had been driven back from Moscow.

A Soviet border garrison surrenders in June 1941. Few Red Army units could defend themselves against swift German forces.

The battle of Stalingrad

STALINGRAD, USSR JUNE 1942–FEBRUARY 1943

German troops surrendered at Stalingrad in early February 1943, after holding out for more than two months against besieging Soviet forces.

The industrial city of Stalingrad stood on the west bank of the Volga River in southern Russia, controlling the vital river and rail connections that carried oil supplies to the armament factories of central Russia. Thwarted in his desire to capture Moscow the previous winter (*see facing page*), Hitler ordered a thrust in the spring and summer of 1942 to capture Stalingrad and the oil reserves further south in the Caucasus.

Operations Blue and Uranus

The general German offensive, Operation Blue, began on June 29, 1942, and General Paulus's 6th Army soon moved to secure Stalingrad itself.

Sustained air attacks on August 23 began the main assault, and the same day German troops reached the Volga north of the city. But this was the limit of their success—an astonishingly tenacious Soviet resistance bogged the 6th Army down in house-to-house fighting. On November 19, the Red Army was still somehow clinging onto a small strip along the Volga when Soviet General Zhukov ordered a counterattack, Operation Uranus.

The Soviet forces crashed through the weaker Romanian armies and within four days had the Axis side surrounded. Confounding Zhukov's expectation of an attempt at breakout, Paulus settled down for a siege. But after a German attempt to relieve Paulus failed in December, any hope of victory was gone, and the remnants of the 6th Army finally surrendered on February 2, 1943, at a cost of around 170,000 dead.

Mosin-Nagant M91/30 rifles were used by the Red Army as sniper rifles from 1932, to devastating effect on the streets of Stalingrad.

The God of War
has gone over to the
other side.

Adolf Hitler, February 1943

The war in North Africa

NORTH AFRICA · JUNE 1940–MAY 1943

The vast North African desert provided a theater of war unlike any other in World War II; one in which tanks played a crucial role. Yet the relative strength of the armies deployed there was tiny compared with other fronts. Italy declared war on the Allies on June 10, 1940, and in September, General Graziani—the Italian commander in chief in North Africa—launched an attack toward British-held Egypt.

The Western Desert campaign

After initial successes, by December 1940 Graziani's force was driven back as far as Tripolitania in Libya—the first of the swings in fortune that characterized the desert fighting.

By January 22, 1941, the British had taken the strategic city of Tobruk, but the Germans had started to send reinforcements to bolster their Italian allies and, under the command of General Rommel, the German Afrika Korps commenced a dramatic advance eastward. A British counteroffensive (Operation Crusader) forced the Germans back in December, but in June of the following year, Rommel captured Tobruk, and threatened to push toward the Egyptian capital, Cairo. In a 12-day battle at

△ **At the Battle of El Alamein**, Rommel lost more than 400 tanks, a loss from which the German war effort in North Africa was never really able to recover.

El Alamein in October 1942, the new British commander, General Montgomery (*see p.324*), wore down the Afrika Korps and then struck west.

Operation Torch

Rommel now retreated into Tunisia, but on November 8, 1942, a series of Anglo–American landings (Operation Torch) in Morocco and Algeria tightened the noose on the German and Italian armies in North Africa. Despite stubborn resistance, Rommel's position grew steadily worse. He flew out to Germany in March 1943, and on May 13 the last Axis armies in Tunisia surrendered.

≫ ERWIN ROMMEL

An early proponent of mobile warfare, Erwin Rommel (1891–1944) led a Panzer unit during the Battle of France in 1940. After his failed North Africa campaign of 1941–1943 he was sent to France, where he committed suicide after being implicated in a plot to kill Hitler.

▷ **General Rommel** (far left) was a master of armored warfare, which played a vital part in Germany's efforts in the North African desert.

The war in Italy

⚑ ITALY ⌛ JULY 1943–MAY 1945

At the Casablanca Conference in January 1943, the Allies decided to exploit imminent victory in North Africa (*see facing page*) by launching a new front in Italy. This would enable them to threaten Germany itself from the south, using Sicily as a springboard for the assault.

On July 10, "Operation Husky" began. The Allied advance was sluggish, however, and allowed time for Germany's General Kesselring to evacuate more than 100,000 of his soldiers back to the Italian mainland on August 11–12.

Salerno

The fall of Mussolini's regime on July 25 brought forward Allied plans to invade southern Italy. By the time an armistice with the new Italian government was announced on September 8, British forces had already crossed over into southern Italy. The following day they made a larger amphibious landing at Salerno, south of Naples. However, the Germans had been pouring reinforcements into Italy and resistance was stiffer than the Allies had expected, very nearly pushing their forces back into the sea.

The end of the Italian campaign

The Allied campaign never regained its momentum, and stalled trying to breach a series of strong German defensive lines. A new Allied amphibious landing at Anzio, south of Rome, in December 1943 became bogged down, while it required an enormous effort and almost five months (January to May 1944) to clear the Germans from their positions around Monte Cassino. Even after they finally reached Rome on June 4, 1944, the Allies failed to exploit their victory, and the Germans finally surrendered in Italy only on May 2, 1945, at the very end of the war.

⬈ **In June 1944** US general Mark Clark entered Rome, a German-declared "open city" that escaped bombing.

⬇ **The military cemetery** at Monte Cassino is overlooked by the ruins of the abbey that was destroyed by Allied bombing in February 1944.

Pearl Harbor

⚑ **HAWAII** 🕮 **DECEMBER 1941**

Throughout 1940, US president Roosevelt looked on with alarm as the Japanese steadily encroached on new territory, occupying northern Indochina in July 1940. Meanwhile, the powerful Japanese naval lobby pressed for a preemptive strike against the US to cripple its military capacity before it could react to Japan's advances. Finally, on December 1, 1941, Japanese emperor Hirohito approved the order for an attack on the main US Pacific naval base at Pearl Harbor in Hawaii.

The Japanese attack

Although intercepted intelligence had given indications that an attack of some sort might occur, the Americans were totally unprepared when the large Japanese task force, including six aircraft carriers, began its attack on December 7.

The Japanese commander, Admiral Nagumo, launched two waves of bombers and fighters against the US base, an hour apart. Some 18 US naval vessels were sunk, including eight battleships, and nearly 400 aircraft were destroyed (with the loss of just 29 Japanese planes). The only consolation for America was that its two aircraft carriers were—by chance—absent from Pearl Harbor that day. The following day in Congress, President Roosevelt described the Japanese attack as a "date which will live in infamy" and declared war on Japan. Germany and Italy declared war on the US three days later.

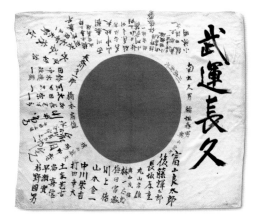

⚓ **This Japanese military flag** inscribed with prayers is an example of the potent mix of nationalism and religious sentiments that inspired Japanese soldiers.

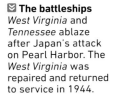

⚓ **The battleships** *West Virginia* and *Tennessee* ablaze after Japan's attack on Pearl Harbor. The *West Virginia* was repaired and returned to service in 1944.

◀ **British troops surrender** to the Japanese at Singapore. Large numbers would be used by the Japanese on labor projects in Southeast Asia.

The Japanese advance

SE ASIA, PACIFIC ISLANDS ⚊ **DECEMBER 1941–MARCH 1942**

The Japanese bombing of Pearl Harbor (*see facing page*) was followed by an attack on the British-held territories of Malaya and Singapore. Japan's armies rapidly swept aside British defenses in Malaya, using surprise and mobility to compensate for a lack of heavy equipment.

By February 12, 1942, Japanese forces had landed in Singapore, a fortress-city that was supposedly the British bastion in Southeast Asia. Three days later its commander, Lieutenant-General Percival, surrendered his 100,000-man command, the largest surrender in British military history.

The Philippines and Burma

At the same time, the Japanese moved against the Philippines—American-held since 1898—from bases on Taiwan. By late December, Japanese air superiority had forced the US general Douglas MacArthur to order a retreat to the island of Corregidor. The US/Filipino defense,

though spirited, proved hopeless, and on May 6 the last defenders surrendered. To complete their defensive perimeter, the Japanese moved to secure Burma in the west and a string of Pacific islands to the east. They captured the Burmese capital Rangoon on March 8, 1942, and the British evacuated their remaining positions in Burma in late April, but the Allies' fighting retreat prevented any large-scale Japanese move into India.

In the early part of 1942, the Japanese made a series of amphibious attacks on Allied colonies in the Pacific, occupying the Dutch East Indies and the British-held portion of Borneo, and on March 8 landing in New Guinea.

It now seemed conceivable that they might even invade Australia from the north, and the catastrophic Japanese defeat of a joint Allied fleet at the Battle of the Java Sea on February 27 made the situation seem even more irrecoverable. In the event, however, this would prove to be the high tide of the Japanese advance.

> **" The worst disaster and largest capitulation in British history.**
>
> **Winston Churchill on the surrender of Singapore to the Japanese, 1942** "

D-Day and the war in the west

⚑ FRANCE **⚔ JUNE–AUGUST 1944**

⌃ US army field telephones enabled rapid communications from the front line to headquarters units.

After almost four years of planning, a combined American, British, Canadian, and Free French force launched Operation Overlord to wrest control of Europe from Germany. It began on "D-Day," June 6, 1944, on the coast of northern France. The Germans believed that any Allied landings would occur near Calais, on the eastern north coast, so were underprepared when the attack came in Normandy.

More than 7,000 Allied naval vessels were involved in the preliminary bombardment of German positions and the subsequent landings. The largest of the five assault areas was at Colleville-sur-Mer, codenamed Omaha Beach. Heavy Allied air and naval bombardment, effective at the four other landing points (Utah, Gold, Juno, and Sword), had made little impact on the well-prepared German positions at Omaha, and the US 1st and 29th Infantry Divisions suffered enormous casualties. By early afternoon, the US had secured a small strip of beach, 6 miles (9.7 km) wide and about 2 miles (3.2 km) deep, but at the cost of 3,000 casualties.

The beachhead expands

Meeting with less resistance at the other beaches, the Allies landed 130,000 troops by nightfall. Six days later, they had linked together the five beachheads into a continuous front and could land armored vehicles, heavy artillery, and a stream of troops. Despite these reinforcements,

the campaign in Normandy went slowly. Allied forces under the British general Bernard Montgomery stalled in front of Caen, which had been a D-Day objective, and it took a major offensive to secure the city's fall on July 18.

The Germans had defended well, but their losses, including 2,000 tanks, made victory impossible. Hitler refused to sanction tactical withdrawals, demanding that every inch of ground be defended. The Allies, in turn, were hampered by the difficult Normandy terrain and by bad weather, which prevented them from effectively employing their more than ten-to-one superiority in aircraft.

> **》 BERNARD MONTGOMERY**
>
> A veteran of World War I (who was severely wounded in France in 1914), Montgomery (1887–1976) took command of the British 8th Army in North Africa during World War II. His meticulous planning led to the defeat of the German field marshal Rommel at El Alamein in October 1942. Montgomery could be overcautious, which hampered his operation to take Caen after D-Day. Confident of his own importance, he quarreled with General Eisenhower, the US commander in chief in western Europe, which almost led to his dismissal in 1945.

The Falaise pocket

On July 25 the US 7th Army advanced south through St. Lô, clearing the way for an advance toward Paris. A German counteroffensive ended with almost all the German troops in Normandy penned into a pocket around Falaise. When Hitler did allow a retreat, on August 16, it was too late for the 25,000 German soldiers who were taken prisoner.

On August 19, the first Allied units crossed the Seine, threatening German control of Paris. A second Allied landing in France, on the southern Riviera, captured Toulon and Marseilles by the end of August. By pushing north toward Lyons, this advance threatened to trap German forces between its forces and the advance from Normandy.

◁ **The French city of Caen** in Normandy was largely destroyed by Allied bombing and the fighting that took place in its streets.

▽ **US troops disembark** in Normandy in June 1944. By June 30, some 850,000 men, 148,000 vehicles, and 570,000 tons of supplies had been put ashore.

The defeat of Germany

 FRANCE, GERMANY, RUSSIA, UKRAINE, BELARUS ☒ **JANUARY 1943–MAY 1945**

The Allies won a morale-boosting victory in France with the recapture of Paris on August 24, 1944, spearheaded by a Free French unit. Yet any hope that the war might soon be over in western Europe was dashed by a German recovery. German units in Normandy began to regroup and a series of strategic miscalculations hampered the Allies' progress.

The Allies captured the Belgian port of Antwerp on September 4, but then stalled. British general Montgomery suggested an operation called Market Garden to push across the lower Rhine and into the vital German industrial heartland of the Ruhr. During the operation, elements of a British airborne division became trapped at Arnhem and 6,000 men surrendered on September 21. In December, Hitler made his last throw of the dice in the west, with a massive assault on Western Allies in the "Battle of the Bulge." More than 500,000 men took part in the advance, which began on December 16. Though initially caught off-balance by the sheer weight of German numbers, the Americans held out at Bastogne, Belgium, counterattacking to narrow the neck of the "bulge" of German troops, and on January 8, 1945 the Germans finally retreated. They had suffered 100,000 casualties and lost 1,000 aircraft.

The Allies finally crossed the Rhine in force on March 24, and against only patchy resistance reached the Elbe, where on April 25 they met up with the Red Army, which had been advancing westward.

☒ **On August 24, 1944,** a small force of the 2nd French Armored Division under Captain Raymond Dronne liberated Paris.

We will fight on to the last.

General Krebs, German army Chief of Staff on May 1, 1945, the day before the final surrender of Berlin

The Soviet hammer and sickle flag was raised on the Reichstag building in central Berlin during the final German surrender.

The triumph of the Red Army

After its sensational victory at Stalingrad (*see p.319*), the Red Army had endured mixed fortunes. They were driven back at Kharkov following a rapid advance westward, but at Kursk on July 12–13, they won the largest tank battle in history (more than 6,000 tanks were engaged). By November 6, 1943, the Red Army had taken Kiev.

After a lull in the fighting necessitated by a harsh winter, Stalin ordered a new offensive, Operation Bagration, to clear the German Army Group Center from Belorussia. On June 24, 1944, the Red Army launched a vast assault around Minsk, with some 2.4 million men facing half that number of German defenders. The German positions collapsed, and by July the Red Army was in Poland. Pausing on the Vistula in fall 1944, while Polish insurgents perished in a failed anti-German uprising in Warsaw, Soviet forces finally took Warsaw on January 17, 1945, and then began the race for Berlin.

In mid-April the final assault began, with two million Soviet troops spearheaded by General Zhukov's 1st Belorussian Army. The one million German defenders, many of them untrained units and some soldiers little more than boys, showed a fanatical determination to resist, but by April 30 even Hitler despaired and committed suicide. Two days later the Berlin garrison surrendered. On May 7, Hitler's successor government at Flensburg in northwest Germany signed a document of surrender. The Allies designated the following day—May 8—as Victory in Europe (VE) Day.

The Red Army's advance into Germany caused a mass exodus of civilians, such as these refugees seeking desperately to escape from Berlin.

The Holocaust

Among the most pernicious aspects of German National Socialist ideology was its view that Aryans (white Caucasians) were racially superior and that other groups, most especially the Jews, were inferior. The practical consequence of this belief was the Holocaust—the deliberate attempt to annihilate the Jewish population of Europe, which resulted in the murder of some six million Jews by 1945.

Early anti-Jewish measures

When Hitler took power in Germany in January 1933, he began a slow process of reducing the civil rights and economic position of the country's half-million Jews. They were excluded from state office and from many professions in 1933–1934.

In September 1935, the Nuremberg Laws stripped Jews of their German citizenship and prohibited marriage or sexual relations between German Jews and Aryans. In November 1938, widespread violence broke out in a pogrom (anti-Jewish riot) known as *Kristallnacht* that destroyed some 7,500 Jewish businesses and killed 91 Jews.

The German invasion of Poland in September 1939 and of the USSR in June 1941 tragically transformed Germany's anti-Semitic policies. With 3.1 million Jews in Poland and 2.7 million

⌃ **Half-starved survivors** of the camp at Ebensee—liberated by the US on May 7, 1945—to which many former inmates of Auschwitz had been sent.

in the western USSR—as well as more than a million in occupied France, the Low Countries, Scandinavia, and the Balkans—Nazi authorities took drastic measures to "clear" Jewish populations. In Poland, the *Einsatzgruppen* (action groups made up from the SS—the elite paramilitary units of the Nazi Party) herded Jews into restricted areas of towns known as ghettoes. Thousands more went to labor camps to work for the German war effort. As German troops swept into the USSR, the SS shot or gassed (in mobile vans) as many Jews as they could find. In Kiev, 33,771 Jews were marched out to the Babi Yar ravine and shot on September 29–30, 1941.

The "Final Solution"

On January 20, 1942, Reinhard Heydrich, head of the Gestapo, summoned senior bureaucrats to a villa at Lake Wannsee in Berlin to ensure their support for a "Final Solution" to the Jewish question. Jews would be transported to camps in eastern Europe, to be worked to death or killed on the spot by mass gassing in sealed chambers.

The bodies were to be burned in huge crematoria staffed by Jews themselves. Trainloads of Jews arrived at the death camps—Auschwitz, Belzec, Chelmno, Majdanek, Sobibór, and Treblinka—from occupied and Axis Europe (except Bulgaria, whose king refused to cooperate).

Only when the Soviet Red Army advanced westward in 1944–1945 did the camps cease work. Even then the suffering was not over. Many thousands died in "Death Marches," during which they were herded, starving and freezing, deeper west into Germany.

After the war the Allies tried 22 leading Nazis at Nuremberg in 1945–1946 for the atrocities. Twelve were sentenced to death and six to long periods of imprisonment. Of the European Jews who had suffered the Holocaust, only around 300,000 survived, and many of these would not return to their homeland, choosing instead to emigrate to the new Jewish State of Israel (*see p.362*).

⊠ **The Star of David**, once a symbol of hope for a Jewish homeland, was used by Nazi Germany as a badge to single out Jews.

⬘ **Top Nazi leaders** faced trial at the Allied Military Tribunal in Nuremberg in January 1946 for atrocities against the Jews.

⊠ **Railroad tracks** lead to the main gates of the Auschwitz concentration camp, in which around a million Jews were murdered.

The principal means used to transport Jewish prisoners to concentration camps was by train. Crowded into cattle cars, with little or no food and water, many perished before they even reached their destination. Once disembarked, the old, sick, and the children were selected for immediate death in the gas chambers.

The defeat of Japan

SE ASIA, PACIFIC ISLANDS **MARCH 1942–AUGUST 1945**

In early 1942, the Japanese sought to complete their outer perimeter in the southern Pacific by seizing the remainder of southern New Guinea. A large Japanese naval force set out in May 1942, but at the Battle of the Coral Sea the Americans turned them back with large losses. A far more significant setback came at the Battle of Midway in early June.

The Japanese admiral Yamamoto intended to surprise the US fleet at the American-held Midway Islands. However, US intelligence had cracked the Japanese message codes, and the US Navy was well prepared for their arrival. Yamamoto, moreover, had wrongly calculated that the two US aircraft carriers would not be present at Midway. In the ensuing battle, Japan lost four aircraft carriers and hundreds of pilots (some 70 percent of its total). At the end of 1942, Japanese success on land also petered out as US naval superiority pushed Japan out of Guadalcanal in the Solomon Islands by February 1943. Later in 1943 the tide of war in the Pacific turned even more in favor of the Allied powers,

The Burma Star was a medal awarded to Commonwealth military personnel who served in Burma between 1941 and 1945.

largely because Japan struggled to match the extraordinary military and industrial resources of the US. In June 1943, General MacArthur ordered Operation Cartwheel, designed to neutralize Japan's bases on New Guinea and the nearby island of New Britain. Although Japanese troops held out until the end of the war, they were confined to the mountains and posed no real further threat to the Allies.

Island-hopping

In November 1943, the Americans continued their "island-hopping" strategy with the conquest of the Gilbert Islands, although the fierce resistance of even very small garrisons there showed the difficulties the US might face in pressing its campaign to a successful conclusion. They then continued on to seize the Marshall and Marianas islands, from where they could launch direct air attacks against Japan.

During 1944 and 1945, US power at sea and in the air began to have a decisive effect. A sea blockade of Japan cut off all imports, strangling the Japanese war economy. Another pivotal US naval victory at the Battle of Leyte Gulf in October 1944 opened the way for the US to regain the Philippines. Landings at Leyte on October 20 met only light resistance, and by March 1945, the US had liberated the Philippine capital of Manila. Meanwhile, in January 1945, the British advanced back into Burma and by early May had secured the entire central area of the country.

A US-supplied M5 tank manned by a Chinese crew in northern Burma in 1944. Longtime adversaries of the Japanese, the Chinese fought for the Allies in Burma.

Iwo Jima to surrender

In February 1945, the US invaded Iwo Jima. It secured the island in several hard-fought weeks, and at the cost of 23,000 Marine casualties, to provide a base for fighters to support US bombing raids on mainland Japan. The US now launched a series of devastating strikes on Tokyo, which on March 9–10 caused a firestorm that killed around 100,000 Japanese citizens.

Japan's island garrisons were isolated and picked off one by one by the US, but although it could clearly no longer win the war, Japan was refusing to accept defeat. The fanatical resistance on the small island of Okinawa, where 120,000 Japanese troops—of whom just 7,500 survived—fought back from March 26 to June 30, demonstrated how bloody the invasion of the Japanese home islands might be. It was this resistance that led President Truman to sanction the dropping of atomic bombs on the Japanese

cities of Hiroshima and Nagasaki on August 6 and 9, 1945 (*see pp.334–5*). As a direct result of these bombings, the Japanese signed an unconditional surrender on September 2 aboard the USS *Missouri* in Tokyo Bay.

≫ GENERAL DOUGLAS MACARTHUR

The Supreme Allied Commander in the Pacific, US general Douglas MacArthur (1880–1964) was born into a military family and began his military career in World War I. He rose to the rank of Army Chief of Staff in the interwar years. At the end of World War II, he became Supreme Allied Commander in Japan, overseeing its reconstruction and the drafting of a new Japanese constitution. In 1950–1951, he led United Nations forces in Korea, but after a disagreement with President Truman was relieved of his command in April 1951.

⊠ **US Marines** raise their national flag on top of Mount Suribachi after the US capture of the island of Iwo Jima in February 1945.

The atom bomb

Scientists discovered the awesome power of nuclear fission
just before World War II, and warring countries raced to develop
the first atomic bomb. The world became aware of America's
scientific victory when it dropped bombs on two Japanese cities—
Hiroshima and Nagasaki—destroying them within seconds.
The development of these weapons was to play a large part
in the ensuing Cold War (*see pp.338–9*).

The nuclear race

In 1938, German scientists Otto Hahn and Fritz
Strassmann had split uranium atoms by bombarding
them with neutrons. Known as "nuclear fission," this
process had obvious military uses, and scientists in
the UK and US grew concerned that Germany
might use it to make bombs.

In August 1939, Albert Einstein wrote to
President Roosevelt urging him to take action.
The president set up the Uranium Committee
to pursue research, and after the US entered
the war in December 1941, he established the
Manhattan Project to accelerate US development
of an explosive nuclear device.

The first bombs

The decision to use nuclear force in World War II
was made by US president Harry S. Truman,
who was frustrated at Japan's resistance to final
surrender and conscious of the huge casualties,
on both sides, that would result from an invasion
of Japan. He chose Hiroshima for its industrial
and military significance.

On August 6, 1945, a US B-29 bomber named
Enola Gay dropped "Little Boy" over the city of
Hiroshima. The bomb exploded 1,950 ft (600 m)
above the city with a blast equivalent to 13 kilotons
of TNT. An estimated 90,000 people were killed
instantly; another 50,000 died later from wounds
or radiation. Around 90 percent of Hiroshima's
buildings were damaged or destroyed in the blast.

≪ **The first nuclear** artillery shell—designed for
firing from ground-based guns—was tested in the
Nevada desert on May 25, 1953.

The ruins of Hiroshima's Museum of Science and Technology in the aftermath of the atomic bomb, which totally destroyed 48,000 buildings.

The second bomb was destined for the town of Kokura, but this was shrouded in clouds on the morning of August 9, 1945, so the US bomber headed for the city of Nagasaki instead. At 11:02am its "Fat Man" bomb delivered 22 kilotons of explosive force over Nagasaki, leading to 70,000 deaths by the end of the year.

Worldwide development

The US quickly lost its nuclear monopoly after the war, as the USSR, Britain, France, and China developed nuclear weaponry. The stockpiling of large nuclear arsenals in the USSR and US created a balance of terror between the two powers that was to play a large part in the Cold War, which dominated world politics from the late 1940s to the early 1990s. Israel, India, Pakistan, and North Korea went on to develop nuclear bombs and arsenals by the early 21st century.

The "Fat Man" plutonium bomb dropped by the B-29 bomber *Bockscar* on Nagasaki was just 5 ft (1.5 m) in diameter, but killed tens of thousands.

I am become **death,** the **destroyer of worlds**.

Robert Oppenheimer, physicist and director of the Manhattan Project, quoting from the *Bhagavad Gita* on the first testing of the atomic bomb, 1945

Europe after World War II

For much of the 20th century after World War II, Europe seemed irrevocably divided into two parts: a democratic, capitalist West, and a communist Eastern bloc. The problems of national self-determination and democratic aspirations were smothered rather than solved by this new order. When communist regimes collapsed from the late 1980s, Europe erupted in a series of savage civil wars.

The Marshall Plan

⚐ **W EUROPE** ⌛ **1948–1952**

In 1945 the Allied powers met at Yalta in the Crimea and Potsdam in Germany to shape post-war Europe. Stalin's insistence that the Soviet sphere be extended to cover eastern Poland and the Baltic states raised anxieties about his expansionist ambitions.

⚏ **George C. Marshall** was awarded the Nobel Peace Prize in 1953 for his development of the Marshall Plan.

Hard times

Concern over Stalin's intentions had led the British government to support Greek anti-Communist rebels in the Greek Civil War that erupted in December 1944. Yet economic hardship in the devastated Western economies threatened to secure communist influence just as much as Stalin's more direct diplomatic thuggery. Shortages were dire in 1947, partly due to the shattered state of European postwar industry, and France and Italy suffered strikes.

The Paris Conference

Allied plans to revive western Germany were opposed by the USSR, which wanted to leech reparations from Germany's economy, not to repair it. US Secretary of State George C. Marshall announced a new European Recovery Program (the "Marshall Plan") in June 1947, offering economic aid to speed Europe's recovery.

Stalin forbade Eastern European countries from participating, so only western European nations assembled in Paris in July to discuss the plan. The US was ultimately to disburse some $12 billion of aid to the 16 participating countries by 1952.

The European Community

After World War II, it was clear to many politicians that Europe needed a mechanism to coordinate its economies, and, among idealists and pragmatists alike, a desire emerged to build a political structure to ensure that no further war between the major European powers would ever again devastate the continent. In 1950, Jean Monnet devised the "Schuman Plan," which led to the founding of the European Coal and Steel Community (ECSC) in 1950. This pooled the coal and steel resources of France, Germany, Italy, Belgium, Luxembourg, and the Netherlands.

In 1957, the Treaty of Rome established the European Economic Community (EEC), with these countries as founder members. The EEC allowed free movement of goods, services, and labor between member states and promoted greater economic integration. Initially Britain stood aside, suspicious of ceding control over its own economic affairs, but it finally joined in 1973, and by 1986 the EEC had 12 members.

The Eastern bloc in Europe

◀ **Czech demonstrators** mount a Soviet tank following the Warsaw Pact invasion in August 1968.

Although Communist parties had actively resisted German occupation in some countries of Eastern Europe, their preeminent role from the late 1940s onward owed as much to Stalin's brutal suppression of other political groups as to their real level of popular support.

The imposition of Communism

In January 1947 the Peasants' Party of Poland was robbed of probable election victory by falsified results. Stubborn anti-Soviet resistance in Czechoslovakia was subdued by the mysterious death of two leading anti-Communist ministers early in 1948. For almost 40 years, most central and Eastern European countries lived under brutal Communist regimes. Following Stalin's death in 1953, some countries made bids for greater independence.

In 1956, the Hungarian leader Imre Nagy announced the end of one-party rule by the Communists, the expulsion of Soviet troops, and Hungary's withdrawal from the Warsaw Pact (see p.339)—but Hungarian hardliners and Soviet forces soon snuffed out his revolution. Similarly, in 1968, Alexander Dubček tried to implement economic and political reforms in Czechoslovakia. His "Prague Spring" was suppressed in August; Warsaw Pact troops invaded Czechoslovakia and imposed a more amenable regime.

The Cold War

Tensions over the post-World War II settlement between Britain and the US on one hand, and the USSR on the other, led one Soviet official to state in 1947 that the world was now split between Western imperialists and socialist anti-imperialists. Countries around the world aligned themselves with one of the two groupings, beginning a Cold War—a state of political hostility that stopped short of actual warfare.

Early confrontations

The first real crisis of the Cold War almost brought the two sides to open warfare. Early in 1948, the Western Allies proposed to unite their sectors of Berlin (which was isolated deep inside the Soviet zone of occupation in Germany) into a single unit.

The Soviets retaliated by cutting off land routes into those sectors. Far from capitulating, however, Britain, France, and the US decided to launch an airlift, and for 11 months they delivered enough supplies to feed West Berlin's two million people.

The Cold War grows

In April 1949, 12 Western countries formed the North Atlantic Treaty Organization (NATO), a mutual self-defense pact clearly aimed at the USSR, and a month later the Western Allies announced the formation of the Federal

⏶ **During the Berlin airlift**, the Western Allies delivered some 2.3 million tons of food to the city on more than 277,000 flights.

Republic of Germany. The Cold War rift between the US and USSR now seemed irresolvable; furthermore, it was given a new edge by the USSR's first atomic weapons test in August 1949.

As each side's sphere of influence in Europe solidified, the Cold War spread globally to areas where the two "superpowers"—the USSR and the US—could operate through proxies. The victory of Mao Zedong's Communists in the Chinese Civil War in 1949 opened up yet another front—one that was

≪ **Cold War allies** Fidel Castro (*left*) and Nikita Khrushchev show fraternal solidarity during the Cuban leader's visit to Moscow in 1963.

> From **Stettin** in the Baltic to **Trieste** in the Adriatic, an **iron curtain** has **descended across the continent**.
>
> Winston Churchill, in a speech at Fulton, Missouri, March 5, 1946

to lead to enormous problems for the US side. Mao began to enact his own foreign policy initiatives, into which the US would become entangled during the Korean War (*see p.372*) and the Vietnam War (*see p.373*).

The Cuban missile crisis

Although Nikita Khrushchev, Soviet leader from 1953, sought to promote a policy of "peaceful coexistence" with the West, it did not prevent him from founding the Warsaw Pact in 1955 as a military organization to confront NATO.

In 1962 a serious crisis developed when Khrushchev dispatched nuclear missiles to bases in Cuba, then controlled by Fidel Castro's communist regime. This posed a very real threat to the US, which considered invading Cuba or launching air strikes in response. Two weeks of knife-edge negotiations finally convinced the Soviets to back down and withdraw their weapons.

The end of the Cold War

The superpowers continued to stockpile nuclear missiles throughout the 1970s and '80s. A period of easing tension in the 1970s, when the two sides ceased to posture quite so openly, was not matched by any reduction in the destructive power of their arsenals.

A series of Strategic Arms Limitations Talks (SALT) had begun in the late 1960s, but agreement on real reductions was reached only in the early 1990s, when the USSR was finally on the verge of collapse and the Cold War was at last coming to an end.

» **The US Navy Trident missile** gave reality to the idea of Mutual Assured Destruction, in which warring sides would both be destroyed by a nuclear conflict.

Ireland and the troubles

⚑ NORTHERN IRELAND ⌛ 1968–1997

In April 1916, the Easter Rising in Dublin helped spark war between the nationalist Irish Republican Army (IRA) and the British authorities. In 1922 Britain sanctioned an independent Irish Free State (later the Irish Republic), which excluded the areas in the north of Ireland that had a Protestant (and pro-British) "Unionist" majority; these were retained within the UK.

The years of violence

In 1968–1969, rising tensions between Catholic and Protestant communities led to renewed violence. A new nationalist group, the Provisional IRA, emerged in 1969 to push for the violent expulsion of the British authorities from Northern Ireland. It was matched by Protestant paramilitary groups, such as the Ulster Volunteer Force (UVF), established in 1966. Two decades of violence followed, including "Bloody Sunday" on January 30, 1972, when British security forces shot dead 13 Catholic protestors, and the IRA bombing of a Birmingham pub on November 21, 1974, killing 21 people.

Normal political life did not return to the province until the late 1990s. The Provisional IRA declared a final ceasefire in 1997 and began negotiations that would finally lead to a power-sharing government with Protestant Unionists. The "Troubles," though, had left in their wake more than 3,000 dead and a legacy of sectarian mistrust.

◰ **A mural in a Protestant district** of Belfast, Northern Ireland's capital, shows the "loyalist" groups that fought nationalist paramilitaries.

> **Bloody sunday**... was sheer **unadulterated murder**.
>
> Coroner Major Hubert O'Neill, August 21, 1973

UFF MEMBER

UDU MEMBER

UDA MEMBER

ULSTER DEFENCE UNION
EST. 1893

ULSTER DEFENCE ASSOCIATION
EST. 1972

ETA

⚑ SPAIN ⚔ 1959–PRESENT

Nationalists in Basque Spain had claimed independence in the 19th century, but the region suffered under Franco's repressive regime (*see p.312*).

Extremists formed the armed group ETA (*Euskadi ta Askatasuna*, or "Homeland and Liberty") in 1959 to fight for independence. At first attacking the local infrastructure, in 1968 ETA moved on to violent terrorist attacks, killing a police chief in August that year. In 1973, the group assassinated Admiral Luis Carrero Blanco, Franco's designated successor. After Franco's death, some autonomy was granted to the Spanish provinces, with particularly wide powers ceded to the government of the Basque region.

ETA, though, did not cease its violent campaign, continuing to demand full independence. A series of abortive ceasefires from 1998 was followed by a new ceasefire in 2010, and the announcement of a permanent cessation of hostilities in 2011.

Perestroika

⚑ USSR, E EUROPE ⚔ 1985–1991

In 1964, Leonid Brezhnev became Soviet leader, succeeding Nikita Khrushchev. Under his governance, the Soviet economy stagnated, and there were often shortages of manufactured goods.

Senior party officials had access to privileges unattainable to many people, and although the Soviet security forces, notably the KGB, relentlessly persecuted dissidents, by the late 1980s the system seemed on the point of collapsing beneath the weight of its own inefficiency and corruption.

The failure of reform

Mikhail Gorbachev became Soviet leader in 1985, and at once publicly acknowledged the faults in the system.

While never questioning Lenin's view of the prime importance to Russia of the Communist Party, he argued that *perestroika* ("restructuring") was needed to streamline it and that a new openness (*glasnost*) was needed to allow a debate on how best to repair the Communist regime.

Cautious reforms included limited rights for private enterprise (introduced in 1987–1988), but talk of change provoked demands for more, and Gorbachev was overtaken by events. In 1988, the Eastern

⬈ British prime minister Margaret Thatcher met Mikhail Gorbachev in Moscow in 1987. He was, she once remarked, a man "we can do business with."

bloc countries threw off communism and in 1991 Gorbachev, who had made himself president with executive powers the previous year, was overthrown.

The collapse of Communism

E EUROPE, THE USSR ⌛ **1989–1991**

Lech Walesa, leader of Solidarity, is carried in triumph through the streets of Krakow, shortly after the August 1980 accord that legalized the trade union.

In 1980 striking shipyard workers in Gdansk, Poland, forced the Communist government to allow workers to form an independent trade union—Solidarity—led by Lech Walesa.

The state struck back in December by declaring martial law, and suppressed Solidarity. The USSR could have intervened but chose not to, and by 1988, with the economic situation deteriorating badly, Poland's government opened talks with the trade unionists and agreed to hold elections in June 1989. These were meant to yield a coalition rule, but ended in Solidarity's victory.

A non-communist, Tadeusz Mazowiecki, became prime minister, dismantling the pillars of communist power. In May 1989, streams of East Germans, disenchanted at being denied even the gradual change occurring elsewhere in the Eastern bloc, began to take refuge in gently reformist Hungary—the only country they could go to without a visa.

Hardline East German leader Erich Honecker demanded Soviet action, but Soviet leader Mikhail Gorbachev had enough on his hands keeping the USSR together, and refused to give Honecker any assistance. Mass demonstrations broke out, and the East German government panicked. First it tried to purge its own hardliners, and then on November 9 it announced that the Berlin Wall,

BORIS YELTSIN

A member of the Communist Central Committee in Sverdlovsk from 1976, Boris Nikolayevich Yeltsin (1931–2007) became the party's chief in Moscow in 1985–1987, but was sacked amid allegations of alcoholism. Yeltsin bounced back and by 1990 was chairman of the Russian component of the USSR. After the USSR dissolved, he became President of Russia, but constitutional crises, Russian losses in two invasions of Chechnya, economic problems, and corruption all tarnished his reputation and he resigned in 1999.

> ❝ The **Soviet Union** could not exist without the **image of the empire**! ❞
>
> Boris Yeltsin, *The Struggle for Russia*, 1994

which had divided the Eastern and Western sectors of the city since 1961, would be opened. East Germany collapsed, and became reunited with West Germany the following August.

The spread of anti-communism was uncontrollable. In early December, a "Velvet Revolution" overthrew the communists in Czechoslovakia, while toward the end of the month the communist dictator of Romania, Nicolae Ceaucescu, was toppled in a much bloodier coup.

The collapse of the USSR

Waves of dissent now began to lap at the USSR itself. Throughout 1990 Gorbachev struggled to stop the Union from dissolving.

He still believed he could "de-Leninize" the Communist Party, and held a referendum in March 1991 in which 78 percent of voters said the USSR (in a modified form) should stay.

However, on August 18, 1991, a committee of communist hardliners staged a coup, arresting Gorbachev and his advisers, and declaring a return to old-style Soviet rule. Boris Yeltsin, president of the Russian Republic (part of the USSR), rallied opinion against the coup and it collapsed. Yet nothing was ever the same again.

On December 1, Ukraine declared its independence, and Gorbachev resigned. At midnight on December 31, 1991, the USSR ceased to exist. The Communist Party, at the heart of public life since 1917, had been banned eight weeks earlier.

» **A colossal statue** of Vladimir Lenin was removed from the Romanian capital of Bucharest in March 1990, at the end of Communist rule.

On November 9, 1989, after weeks of civil unrest, the East German Communist government announced that it would permit travel into West Berlin. Within hours 50,000 East Germans climbed and crossed the Wall, and even started to destroy it; by 1991 it had been demolished.

The war in Yugoslavia

⚑ FORMER YUGOSLAVIA ⌚ 1991–1995

Josip Tito, the communist dictator of Yugoslavia from 1945 to his death in 1980, reorganized the state in 1946 into six socialist republics—Serbia, Croatia, Slovenia, Bosnia-Herzegovina, Montenegro, and Macedonia—in an effort to balance Yugoslavia's potentially explosive mixture of religions and ethnic groups.

After the collapse of communism in 1990, free elections led to nationalist governments in Slovenia and Croatia, which demanded independence. The president of the Serbian republic, Slobodan Milosevic, stridently opposed this notion and whipped up pro-Yugoslav (fundamentally Serb) sentiment. When Slovenia declared its independence from Serbia in June 1991, the Serb-dominated army intervened, but after a short campaign were forced to withdraw.

Smarting from this rebuff, the Serbian army moved in greater force into Croatia, which had also declared its independence. A bloody campaign ensued in eastern Slavonia, where the cities of Vukovar and Vinkovci were destroyed and many Croat civilians massacred. Only in 1992 did a UN-brokered ceasefire bring peace. By then Bosnia, an even more ethnically mixed republic—around 43 percent Muslim, 31 percent Serb, and 17 percent Croat—was sliding into civil war. The vicious conflict saw Europe's worst fighting since World War II, including a brutal siege of Sarajevo conducted by the Bosnian government,

⌃ **General Ratko Mladic**, commander of the Bosnian Serb forces during the civil war there in 1992–1995.

and the massacre of thousands of refugees at a UN "safe haven" in Srebrenica. The violence only ended in August 1995, when a NATO bombing campaign induced Slobodan Milosevic to withdraw support for the Bosnian Serbs and to sign the Dayton peace accord in December.

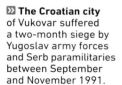

» **The Croatian city** of Vukovar suffered a two-month siege by Yugoslav army forces and Serb paramilitaries between September and November 1991.

New challenges for Europe

⚑ EUROPE ⌛ 1992–PRESENT

Europe had spent nearly all of the 20th century divided by war, but as the Cold War ended, most European leaders looked forward to a new period of peace and prosperity. Events, however, did not unfold quite as they expected. The rapid collapse of communism in Eastern Europe and the USSR (*see pp.342–3*) opened up the prospect of a Europe without fear, but the equally rapid descent of Yugoslavia into civil strife (*see facing page*) suggested that lasting peace was illusory.

European Union

The European Community (*see p.337*) reformed itself in 1992 by means of the Maastricht Treaty, in which it gave itself greater powers, and a new name—the European Union (EU).

A process of enlargement then began, first with the admission of Sweden, Finland, and Austria into the Union in 1995, and then with the strategically more significant additions of ten further countries in 2005, including many former Eastern bloc nations (such as Poland and Hungary) and the former Soviet republics of Estonia, Latvia, and Lithuania. By 2007, when Bulgaria and Romania joined the EU, the organization had 27 member states, making it a large and fractious family in which agreeing on any further changes seemed an almost impossible challenge.

Further hurdles

An ethnic civil war had erupted in Kosovo in 1997–1999, leaving the region in a legal limbo—neither independent nor a part of Serbia—and the EU uncertain as to whether or not to recognize the territory. Similarly, Ukraine had overthrown its old-guard communist regime in late 2004; encouraging the new state to join the EU might provide political stability, but it would alienate the Russian government. Europe still faced many challenges.

> ❝ We **never want** to **wage war** against each other… That is the most important **reason** for a **United Europe**. ❞
>
> **Former German chancellor Helmut Kohl, May 1, 2004**

⬈ Crowds filled the streets of Kiev in support of the Ukrainian opposition leader Viktor Yuschenko during the "Orange Revolution" of December 2004.

The Americas

In the second half of the 20th century, the Americas were marked by extremes of wealth and poverty. The US was the richest and most powerful nation on Earth, but it also struggled with social divisions and prejudices, such as the exclusion of black citizens from the political process. In South America, political and economic crises—combined with occasional direct interventions by the US—created an environment in which stability was hard to achieve.

US economic growth

 USA ⚲ 1945–1960

The US experienced an economic boom during World War II, as its industries expanded to deal with wartime production. This growth continued in peacetime, and the country's buoyant economy created a new middle class that spent its money on consumer goods—some 83 percent of homes in the US had a television by 1958. As a result of an improved diet, American children were on average 2–3 in (5–8 cm) taller in 1950 than their grandparents had been in 1900, and life expectancy for women rose from 51 to 71 years old. There was a large-scale migration to the suburbs, accompanied by a building program to erect a massive 13 million new houses in the ten years between 1948 and 1958. There was consumer choice as never before, and the US developed a "youth culture" for the first time, which fed into a cultural renaissance in the 1960s.

However, the country's growing prosperity had done nothing to halt racial segregation. Many cities became "doughnut-shaped," with a rich business center surrounded by poorer African-American neighborhoods, and then a more prosperous, and largely white-inhabited, outer zone.

« **Increasing affluence** fueled the technological innovation of consumer "must-haves," such as this 1955 TV.

McCarthyism

⚐ USA ⌛ 1950–1954

The growing tensions of the Cold War between the US and the USSR (*see pp.338–9*) soon fed back into US politics, as fears arose that the Soviets would encourage communist subversion or even outright revolution in America. On February 9, 1950, Republican senator Joseph McCarthy gave a speech in which he claimed to have the names of 205 communists working in the US State Department. A political furor erupted in which, to defend himself, McCarthy issued further accusations of communist infiltration.

Bodies such as the House Committee on Un-American Activities investigated alleged communist activity, while McCarthy himself, as Chair of the Senate Permanent Subcommittee on Investigations in 1953–1955, sought to root out communists in all walks of life, particularly in the movie industry and among labor activists. Yet when he turned to attacks on the army, he overplayed his hand: public sympathy for him waned, and in December 1954 his activities were condemned by a vote in the Senate.

⌃ **Senator Joseph McCarthy** testifies to the Senate Foreign Relations Subcommittee in March 1950.

The assassination of JFK

⚐ DALLAS, TEXAS, USA ⌛ NOVEMBER 22, 1963

On Friday November 22, 1963, President John F. Kennedy visited Dallas, Texas, to drum up support for his reelection in the 1964 US presidential race. As the motorcade drove through Dealey Plaza, at least three gunshots rang out, killing the president instantly.

The investigation

The assassination became the subject of a huge controversy. A lone gunman, Lee Harvey Oswald, was arrested shortly after the shooting and charged with murder.

However, two days later he was shot dead while in police custody by Jack Ruby, a gangster who later gave contradictory motives for the killing. Kennedy's successor, vice president Lyndon Johnson, rapidly established the Warren Commission to investigate the assassination. It concluded there was no wider conspiracy to kill Kennedy.

⌄ **President Kennedy** and his wife Jacqueline smile at the Dallas crowds, minutes before his assassination on November 22, 1963.

Civil rights

By the 1950s, discrimination against African-Americans had become entrenched in many southern US states. From the 1870s onward, discriminatory laws had been passed depriving African-Americans of the right to vote, and legalizing a system of segregation in which black people were denied access to whites-only schools and universities, and even from choosing where they might sit on public transportation.

⬆ **Rosa Parks** in the front of a bus, after the abolition of segregation on the Montgomery buses.

The Montgomery Bus Boycott

In the mid-1950s, years of anger and frustration triggered a reaction against discrimination. In December 1955, Rosa Parks refused to give up her seat to a white man on a segregated bus in Montgomery, Alabama. Her arrest ignited a movement for civil rights.

Local activists, including members of the NAACP (the National Association for the Advancement of Colored People), which had long lobbied for African-American rights, organized a boycott of the city's public transportation system, which ended in November 1956 with a Supreme Court ruling that the buses must be desegregated.

Martin Luther King

A boycott organizer and the first African-American to climb aboard a bus when it ended, Martin Luther King, Jr. (1929–1968) was a young Baptist minister who soon became the public face and inspiration of the civil rights movement. Unswerving in his pledge of nonviolence, he followed the lead of Mahatma Gandhi (see p.359) in encouraging civil disobedience to highlight unjust laws.

In 1954, the Supreme Court had ruled that education must be desegregated. This remained largely untested until nine African-American students attempted to attend a high school in Little Rock, Arkansas, in September 1957. The National Guard had to protect them, but they were able to attend class.

Sit-ins and Freedom Rides

In February 1960, black students from Greensboro, North Carolina, staged the first "sit-in" by refusing to move from seats at lunch counters reserved for whites, demonstrating how basic rights were still denied to black Americans. In 1961 groups of black and white people set out to ride buses together— these "Freedom Rides" tested the ruling on desegregated travel.

All the while a campaign grew to promote the voter registration of southern African-American citizens. Martin Luther King organized a mass rally in Birmingham, Alabama, in April 1963 and a "March on Washington" in August, in which he made his iconic speech, "I have a dream...," from the Lincoln Memorial to 250,000 people. Under intense pressure, the government buckled and in 1964 passed the Civil Rights Act, making many forms of discrimination illegal. The achievements of the civil rights movement were crowned 45 years later with the election of Barack Obama, the first African-American president of the US.

◀ **The raised fist** of the "Black Power" movement, popularized by radical activists in the 1960s.

Martin Luther King delivers his "I have a dream" speech. In 1964, he received the Nobel Peace Prize; four years later, he was assassinated in Tennessee.

⌃ Soviet cosmonaut Yuri Gagarin on his mission to become the first human in space in April 1961.

The Space Race

⌕ EARTH'S ORBIT, THE MOON ⛢ 1957–1969

At the end of World War II, both the US and the USSR scrambled to secure the expertise of German scientists who had created the first ballistic missile, the V2. This knowledge could be used to develop rockets capable of reaching space and satellites that would orbit the Earth. A "Space Race" grew out of the Cold War (*see pp.338–9*), with both sides wishing to exploit the propaganda and military benefits of making the first forays beyond the Earth's surface and atmosphere.

The USSR won the early victories in this race, putting the first artificial satellite, *Sputnik 1*, into Earth orbit on October 4, 1957. This was followed by the US *Explorer* in January 1958. Then a Soviet cosmonaut, Yuri Gagarin, became the first human in space, on April 12, 1961. The US got their first astronaut (Alan Shepard) aloft 23 days later.

Piqued by the failure of the US to match its apparently technologically inferior rival, President John F. Kennedy announced in May 1961 that, within a decade, an American would land on the moon and come safely home. So began the Apollo program that culminated in *Apollo 11*. At 10:56pm on July 20, 1969, Neil Armstrong became the first man to stand on the moon. All the astronauts made it back to Earth, and the US declared the Space Race won.

» US astronaut Buzz Aldrin, the second man to stand on the moon, makes his historic walk during the *Apollo 11* mission on July 20, 1969.

The Cuban Revolution

CUBA ⏳ **1953–1959**

The military regime of Fulgencio Batista, which had ruled Cuba since 1933, came under increasing pressure in the 1950s. In 1955, it released a group of political dissidents who had attacked a military barracks in 1953. This turned out to be a disastrous miscalculation: among them was Fidel Castro, a young revolutionary activist.

On December 2, 1956, Castro—who had left Cuba—returned with a group of around 80 fellow revolutionaries aboard the *Granma*. Three days later, Batista's soldiers attacked and most of the revolutionaries were killed, but Castro and a few others, including Ernesto "Ché" Guevara, escaped into the hills. Kept together by Castro's determination, the band grew larger. In 1958, the orthodox Communist Party of Cuba gave its backing to Castro's revolutionaries and, as Batista's forces continually failed to dislodge

him, in August 1958 Castro decided on an offensive of his own. Encountering surprisingly light resistance, by December 31 he had taken the strategic central city of Santa Clara.

Batista panicked and fled Cuba, leaving Castro to enter the capital, Havana, on January 8, 1959. With his idiosyncratic brand of communism, he dominated the country's political life until his death in 2016.

> **Each** and **every one** of us will **pay on demand** his part of **sacrifice**.
>
> **Ernesto "Ché" Guevara (1928–1967), Cuban revolutionary leader**

⌂ Fidel Castro and some of his revolutionaries in 1957, at a time when they were still in hiding in Cuba's Sierra Maestra hills, under pressure from Batista's army.

Allende and Pinochet

CHILE **1970–1988**

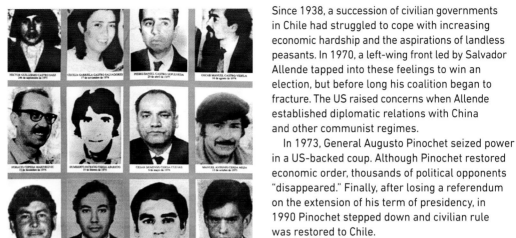

A photo-montage of the *desaparecidos*, more than 3,000 political opponents of Pinochet who were killed or "disappeared" during his dictatorship.

Since 1938, a succession of civilian governments in Chile had struggled to cope with increasing economic hardship and the aspirations of landless peasants. In 1970, a left-wing front led by Salvador Allende tapped into these feelings to win an election, but before long his coalition began to fracture. The US raised concerns when Allende established diplomatic relations with China and other communist regimes.

In 1973, General Augusto Pinochet seized power in a US-backed coup. Although Pinochet restored economic order, thousands of political opponents "disappeared." Finally, after losing a referendum on the extension of his term of presidency, in 1990 Pinochet stepped down and civilian rule was restored to Chile.

Perón and Argentina

ARGENTINA **1946–1974**

Popular with trade-union leaders and the poor, Juan Domingo Perón became president of Argentina in 1946. He immediately embarked on economic reform, nationalizing banks and expanding education. His following, and that of his first wife Eva, was enormous—but there were negative aspects to his rule: he vigorously suppressed all opposition, and sheltered Nazi war criminals fleeing from justice. He also offended the Catholic Church by legalizing divorce.

Perón's populist "Third Way" foreign policy aimed to avoid alienating either side in the Cold War (*see pp.338–9*). But it was too radical for some in the armed forces, and in 1955, the last in a series of military coups unseated him. However, his supporters remained numerous and their effective exclusion from political participation in the 1960s destabilized a series of military-led governments. In 1972 Perón returned from exile to Argentina and in 1973 was elected president, aged 78. His austerity measures calmed inflation, but he died in 1974, leaving his third wife Isabel to complete the last two years of his term.

Former actress Eva Maria Duarte married Juan Perón in 1945, and later became his vice-president.

The US in Latin America

LATIN AMERICA **1952–PRESENT**

Ever since 1823, when President James Monroe sought to exclude the European powers from expanding their hold in the Americas, the US had actively desired to keep the sphere of influence in Latin America purely American. At times this meant intervention: in 1898, war with Spain resulted in temporary occupation of Cuba. As the Cold War flared up, the US sought to exclude communism from its sphere, signing a series of bilateral defense pacts with Latin American countries from 1952.

The Sandinistas

The Cuban Revolution of 1959 marked both the failure of US exclusion policy and the sharpening of US attempts to contain the spread of communism. In 1979, the Marxist Sandinista movement overthrew the Nicaraguan dictatorship

of Anastasio Somoza. The new regime, led by Daniel Ortega, had strong ties to Cuba, and the US tried for years to destabilize it. Ultimately, though, it was a peace plan brokered by other Latin American countries which laid down free elections that finally brought down the Sandinistas in 1990.

Noriega and Panama

Fears of a different kind emerged over Panama, which contained the strategic Canal Zone. Manuel Noriega, commander of Panama's armed forces, had become increasingly involved in the illegal drug trade, which was channeled through Central America.

In 1989, the US finally lost patience and launched an invasion of Panama. Noriega's forces put up little resistance, and the commander was seized, flown to the USA, and put on trial. He was sentenced to 40 years' imprisonment for drug trafficking.

⌃ **Panama's Manuel Noriega** waves to crowds in October 1989 after the suppression of a coup against him.

⌄ **Sandinista fighters advance** along a road during the Nicaraguan Civil War (1972–1979), which ended in the overthrow of Somoza's dictatorship.

Democracy returns to Latin America

◉ LATIN AMERICA ⌛ 1982–PRESENT

The 1980s saw the end of many dictatorships in Latin America, beginning in 1982 with the fall of the Argentinian military government (*junta*) and the restoration of civilian rule to Chile in 1988 (*see p.354*). Democracy provided no easy answers, but produced some strong-minded populists. In 1990, Peru elected as its president Alberto Fujimori, whose "Fujishock" policies tamed hyperinflation and won plaudits from the International Monetary Fund (IMF).

Yet his violations of the constitution and suspicions of corruption led to his overthrow in 2000. Hugo Chávez, a former army chief, served as president of Venezuela from 1999 to 2013. He initiated laws to empower the poverty-stricken majority, but ruthlessly stamped down any opposition. His attempts to forge alliances with other radical Latin American presidents, such as Fidel Castro (Cuba) and Evo Morales (Bolivia), were met with suspicion in the US.

⬆ President Hugo Chávez initiated a "Bolivarian Revolution" of democratic socialism in Venezuela.

The Falklands War

◉ FALKLAND ISLANDS ⌛ APRIL–JUNE 1982

Argentina and the UK had long disputed the ownership of the Falkland Islands in the western Atlantic. Talks between the two countries on the islands' future broke down in early 1982, and on April 2 the Argentines launched an invasion of the Falklands. They overwhelmed the small British garrison, but the Argentine military government under General Leopoldo Galtieri underestimated the British resolve to recover the islands.

Prime Minister Margaret Thatcher ordered the dispatch of a large task force that landed British soldiers on the Falklands on May 21. The British units fought their way east to the Falklands' capital, Port Stanley, by June 14, where they took 11,000 Argentine prisoners, reclaiming the islands and ending the war.

◀ The Argentine cruiser *General Belgrano* was sunk after an attack by a British nuclear-powered submarine on May 2, 1982, with the loss of 321 lives.

NAFTA

NORTH AMERICA **1992–PRESENT**

In December 1992, the leaders of the US, Canada, and Mexico established the North American Free Trade Agreement (NAFTA). This promoted the freedom of movement of goods and services—and labor, but only to a very limited extent—across the borders of their respective countries.

NAFTA became active on January 1, 1994. Central American countries (and others, such as Chile) hoped that they might also be included, but they met strong opposition from US politicians, who were already concerned that products from a lower-wage economy such as Mexico would now be freely available in the US.

Mexico and Canada

Despite the economic benefits Mexico received from NAFTA, it remained vulnerable to economic shocks, as demonstrated by a devaluation of its currency in 1994. Panic set in and the country needed $50 billion in loans, secured against its oil reserves. This situation in turn contributed to the loss of political dominance by the Institutional Revolutionary Party, which had ruled Mexico unchallenged since 1929.

The US's other NAFTA partner, Canada, was generally a model of economic stability, but it suffered persistent political crises over the aspirations for autonomy of its mainly French-speaking province, Québec. First winning elections in the province in 1976, the separatist Parti Québecois was never, however, quite strong enough to force a referendum on the issue. The election of Donald Trump as US president in 2016, committed to protectionist economic policies, raised questions over the future of NAFTA.

△ **US president Bill Clinton** speaks at a public meeting in November 1992 to promote NAFTA.

▽ **The border between** the US and Mexico. Concerns about immigrants and migrant workers entering the US from Mexico contributed to the election of Donald Trump as US president in 2016.

Asia and the Middle East

Asia faced a series of political upheavals after World War II. First the aftermath of British withdrawal from Israel and India turned bloody, then the long-term effects of the communist victory in China's Civil War led to violent struggles in Korea and Southeast Asia. Nevertheless, in the latter half of the 20th century, economic growth in East and Southeast Asia helped improve upon this troubled legacy.

The Indian National Congress

⚑ INDIA ⏳ 1885–1945

In 1885, Western-educated Indians campaigning for greater rights founded the Indian National Congress (INC). Although in principle the congress represented all Indians, its members were mainly Hindu, and in 1906 some Muslims broke away from the INC to form the Muslim League.

Gandhi's protest movements

The 1909 Government of India Act allowed a greater number of Indians to sit on legislative councils alongside the British. However, the changes were deemed to be insufficient, and in March 1919 Mahatma Gandhi launched his *satyagraha* protests—a mass nonviolent movement to force British concessions. At one meeting in Amritsar, the British authorities opened fire on protestors, killing nearly 400 of them. Gandhi did not answer violence with violence, although sporadic riots erupted in the 1920s. In 1930, he symbolically declared Indian independence and conducted a "salt *satyagraha*," marching to the sea near Gujarat to make salt, which was illegal because manufacture of salt was a government monopoly.

Another Act in 1935 allowed more Indians to vote, but still this did not satisfy Gandhi and the INC. World War II suspended the main independence drive, but by its end calls for Indian independence swelled again, with a force almost impossible for Britain to resist.

≪ A line of workers lie down to block strikebreakers from entering a workshop gate in 1930, as part of Gandhi's *satyagraha* protest movement.

The partition of India

INDIA, PAKISTAN, BANGLADESH AUGUST 14–15, 1947

In 1945, the British government sent a delegation of Cabinet ministers to India to try to secure agreement between the Hindu-dominated Indian National Congress (INC; *see facing page*) and the Muslim League on terms for the country's independence. They failed, and communal tensions between Muslims and Hindus festered: on August 16, 1946, the Muslim League leader, Muhammad Ali Jinnah, organized

» MAHATMA GANDHI

Born in Gujarat, India, Mohandas K. Gandhi (1869–1948) studied law in London. He moved to South Africa in 1893, where he helped found the Natal Indian Congress to lobby for greater civil rights for Indians. Returning to India in 1915, he became involved in the INC. His insistence on nonviolence and a united India sometimes put him at odds with other independence leaders, but he earned the name Mahatma ("great soul") for his calm devotion to the cause. He was assassinated in 1948 by a Hindu extremist.

 Three policemen lie injured following riots in the Punjabi city of Lahore over the decision to incorporate it within the borders of the new state of Pakistan.

a "Direct Action Day" in a bid to secure a separate state for Muslims. The ensuing riots led to the deaths of thousands.

The British will to remain in control of the country had by now ebbed away, and they realized that the only way they were going to be able to withdraw from India was to partition the country and transfer power to two separate governments. In July 1947, the British government passed the Indian Independence Act, ordering the demarcation of India and Pakistan.

Post-independence massacres

On August 14–15, 1947, the two new states gained their independence, sparking an exodus of millions of Hindus, Muslims, and Sikhs who found themselves on what they saw as the wrong side of the border. Fighting erupted between India and Pakistan over the disputed region of Kashmir. As many as two million died in the appalling carnage of inter-community violence that tarnished the first days of the infant countries.

Decolonialization

At the end of World War II, European powers, in particular the British, French, Portuguese, and Dutch, still controlled large colonial empires, and there was mostly no timetable for granting the colonies their independence. Yet within ten years, most of Asia—and in a further 20 years, almost all of Africa—had achieved freedom, leaving only small islands or other isolated territories under European colonial rule.

⚌ **King Muhammad V** of Morocco returned home from French-imposed exile late in 1955.

Asian independence

In Asia, it was mostly weakening colonial control as a result of World War II that sparked independence movements, especially in India (*see p.359*). In Indochina the French struggled to beat back the rise of nationalists such as Ho Chi Minh, whose Vietminh fighters had occupied much of Vietnam. In the French Indochina War (1946–1954), the French army failed to dislodge the Vietminh from the north of Vietnam, and had to accept a division of the country into communist northern and capitalist southern states (*see p.373*).

Independence for Africa

In 1956, the US forced the French and British to back down from occupying the Suez Canal area in Egypt, and their will to hold onto their African possessions seemed to evaporate. Britain had already granted independence to Ghana in 1957, after which many former British colonies in Africa became sovereign nations: Tanganyika (now Tanzania) in 1961, Uganda in 1962, Kenya in 1963, and Zambia in 1964. Eventually only Rhodesia remained, to become Zimbabwe in 1980 (*see p.375*).

" The **wind of change** is blowing through this **continent**.

British prime minister Harold Macmillan to the South African parliament, February 3, 1960

⏫ **Political prisoners** were freed onto the streets of Ghana's capital, Accra, in 1966.

French colonies in Africa followed a similar path to independence, though France initially sought to impose a conditional form of freedom in which it continued to control the currency, defense, and foreign affairs of former colonies.

However, full independence was granted to most colonies in 1960. Only in Algeria, with its large minority of French settlers (the *pieds noirs*), did there seem any prospect of Paris retaining control. In 1958, the French colonial authorities staged a coup to prevent a perceived "weak" French government from granting concessions to the Algerian separatist group, FLN. Although the coup was put down by General Charles de Gaulle, fighting raged on until, in 1962, Algeria achieved independence.

The last outposts

Britain handed Hong Kong back to China in 1997, and the Chinese took Macao from the Portuguese in 1999. By 2000 only a handful of colonial territories worldwide were still deemed unable to govern themselves. The colonial era was at an end.

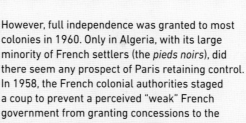

⏬ **A breathtaking fireworks display** marked the transition from British to Chinese rule in Hong Kong on the night of June 30–July 1, 1997.

The birth of Israel

ꖫ **ISRAEL** ⏳ **1917–1949**

⌃ **An ancient symbol of Judaism**, the Star of David was adopted in 1948 as the emblem on the flag of the new State of Israel.

From the 1880s, many Jews emigrated to Ottoman-controlled Palestine with the aim of creating a Jewish state there. This goal was given focus when the First World Zionist Congress convened in Switzerland in 1897. In 1917, the British government drew up a new policy, the Balfour Declaration, that recognized the Zionist aim of a Jewish homeland.

The British mandate

The League of Nations granted Britain formal control of Palestine following the collapse of the Ottoman Empire after World War I. However, the British struggled to reconcile the very different political agendas of Arab and Jewish groups.

Jewish–Arab violence also troubled Britain's authorities, who in 1939 called the St. James Conference to reconcile the two sides. This failed, and the British subsequently conceded to Arab demands for restrictions on Jewish immigration.

However, Jewish fortunes were reversed when the question of allowing Jews to migrate to Israel became a moral rather than political issue following the Holocaust of World War II (*see pp.328–9*). In 1946 US president Harry S. Truman endorsed a proposal to issue 100,000 entry permits to Jews from Europe, and the British determination to hold onto their mandate cracked. A concerted campaign of violence to evict the British from Palestine was also having its

⏵ **A Jewish family** at a *kibbutz* (agricultural commune) near Haifa in 1948. The formation of the State of Israel fulfilled dreams of a Jewish homeland.

effect, in part spearheaded by the Haganah—the official Jewish paramilitary force—as well as more extremist groups such as Irgun Zvai Leumi and the Stern Gang.

The UNSCOP plan

By February 1947 the British despaired of working out a plan for Palestine, and handed matters over to the United Nations (UN), whose Special Committee on Palestine (UNSCOP) produced a report in August that proposed partitioning the territory into an Arab zone of some 44 percent of the land, with a Jewish state receiving around 56 percent. Jerusalem and Bethlehem were to remain UN-controlled in this complex, and in truth unworkable, mosaic.

Civil war

The British announced they would withdraw on May 15, 1948, and fighting erupted as the Jewish and Arab sides sought to gain control of the areas assigned to them in the plan. On May 14, Zionist leader David Ben-Gurion declared the formation of the State of Israel, but already there was full-scale civil war. The fledgling Israeli state also beat back an invasion by six Arab countries that had intervened to support the Palestinian Arabs.

By November Jewish forces had secured not only the sector assigned to them, but large additional areas. This sent a stream of at least 500,000 Arab refugees into neighboring Arab states, where many of them and their descendants remain.

⌃ **The bombing** by Jewish extremists of Jerusalem's King David Hotel on July 22, 1946, crushed the morale of the British in Palestine.

》 **DAVID BEN-GURION**

Born David Grün in Russian-controlled Poland, David Ben-Gurion (1886–1973) was involved in Zionist activities by his mid-teens. In 1906, he arrived in Palestine, establishing the first workers' agricultural commune. Deported by the Ottoman authorities in 1915, Ben-Gurion spent World War I in New York, before returning to help establish a Zionist trade union movement in Palestine. He held the office of prime minister of Israel twice (from 1948 to 1953 and from 1955 to 1963) before finally retiring from political life in 1970.

The Arab–Israeli conflict

⊞ **MIDDLE EAST** ⌛ **1948 TO PRESENT**

≫ **Israeli soldiers** fire shells at Syrian positions on the Golan Heights during the Yom Kippur War in October 1973.

By July 1949, Israel had signed armistice agreements with the Arab countries that had invaded in 1948 (*see p.363*), but as a result the Palestinians, who had fled their homes during the fighting, were deprived of any prospect of immediate return.

In their refugee camps, mostly in Lebanon and the area on the West Bank of the Jordan, they became the responsibility of the United Nations Relief and Works Agency (UNRWA), which operated programs to relieve their plight.

Continued fighting

Bitterness between Israel and Arab countries broke out into open warfare on a number of further occasions. In 1956, the Israelis joined in the Anglo–French operation to occupy the Suez Canal after its nationalization by Egyptian president Nasser, and they briefly occupied much of the strategic Sinai Desert.

In May 1967, a mutual defense pact between Egypt, Lebanon, and Syria looked likely to turn into an invasion of Israel, which provoked the Israelis to a preemptive strike. In the ensuing Six Days' War, the Israelis destroyed much of the Egyptian Air Force on the ground and made large territorial gains in the Sinai from Egypt, took much of the West Bank (including East Jerusalem) from Jordan, and seized parts of the Golan Heights from Syria. These areas became known as the Occupied Territories. In 1973, Egypt and Syria launched an attack

❝ I come **bearing** an **olive branch** in one hand, and the **freedom fighter's gun** in the other. ❞

Yasser Arafat, PLO chairman, November 1974

on Israel on Yom Kippur—the Jewish Day of Atonement—when they knew much of the Israeli military would be at religious observances. The Arab forces made significant early advances, but the Israeli Defense Force (IDF) struck back, pushing their opponents back beyond the 1967 lines. After the conflict, Israel was left with small territorial gains in the Golan Heights; the Arabs with nothing.

The PLO

Resorting to terrorist and guerrilla tactics, in 1964 the Palestinians founded the Palestine Liberation Organization (PLO), which for the next 40 years aimed to help Palestinians realize their hopes of restoring some of their 1948 losses.

Under the leadership of Yasser Arafat from 1969, the PLO sponsored guerrilla raids on Israeli and military targets. It also hijacked international aircraft and murdered members of the Israeli Olympic team at the 1972 Munich games. Setbacks occurred when Jordan expelled militant Palestinians in 1970, and when PLO fighters were pushed out of Lebanon in 1985–1988.

Moves for peace

Israel evacuated the Sinai in 1979 following the Camp David Accords, signed by presidents Sadat of Egypt and Begin of Israel, but hopes for a more permanent settlement proved illusory. In 1987, a low-level insurrection broke out among the Palestinians in Gaza and in the other Occupied Territories, eventually leading the Israeli government to soften its reluctance to negotiate with the Palestinian leadership. This led to the Oslo Accords of September 1993, which allowed the creation of a Palestinian Authority—led by Yasser Arafat—and the Palestinians' gradual assumption of power over much of the Occupied Territories.

However, opposition from extremists on both sides frittered away the chance for lasting peace. Suicide bombers from the radical Islamist Hamas movement struck several times in Israel in 1993–1995, and on November 4, 1995, a Jewish extremist killed the Israeli prime minister Yitzhak Rabin. A new Palestinian *intifada*, or uprising, erupted in the fall of 2000, and since then, peace processes have offered the Palestinians less and less. The Israeli government has sponsored settlements on formerly Palestinian land and built a security wall isolating those Palestinian enclaves it does not seek to control directly.

Radicalism has flourished on the Palestinian side, with Hamas taking power in Gaza in 2007. In 2014 the Israeli army invaded the Gaza Strip in response to rocket attacks on Israel from there. The 70-year Arab–Israeli conflict looks set to continue for a long time yet.

▲ **Yasser Arafat** led the Palestine Liberation Organization from 1969 until his death in 2004.

◀ **Palestinian youths confront** the Israeli army, angered by a Jewish settler's massacre of 29 Arabs in the main mosque in Hebron, the West Bank, in February 1994.

Oil and politics

The awareness among oil-producing nations that they could use the threat of cutting off oil exports as an economic weapon became much stronger after the foundation of the State of Israel in 1948, with one major oil embargo being put into place since then. Outside powers have also sought to exert political or direct military influence over oil-producing nations in a bid to ensure vital fuel supplies.

The 1973 oil crisis

An oil embargo formed part of the Arab response to the Six Days' War with Israel in 1967 (*see p.364*), but was largely ineffective due to a lack of solidarity between the oil-producing countries. This led to the foundation, in 1968, of the Organization of Arab Petroleum Exporting Countries (OAPEC), a body whose purpose was to coordinate and control the use of oil as a political weapon.

The Yom Kippur War of 1973 saw OAPEC flex its political muscles for the first time, as Saudi Arabia and Egypt put an embargo on shipments of crude oil to Western nations that were providing aid to Israel; this tripled world oil prices and

⬆ **President Jimmy Carter** greets Sheikh Ahmed Yamani, Saudi Arabia's Minister of Oil and an architect of the OAPEC oil embargo of 1973.

sent the world into recession. But the oil weapon has never again been used to such conspicuous effect: some members have always been tempted—by the higher profits that could be made—into sidestepping any restrictions or embargo.

In the early 21st century, control of energy reserves and the means of their transmission remains an area of supreme concern for industrialized powers. Russia (which has massive natural gas fields) has become increasingly ready to threaten to cut off supplies or raise prices to countries whose foreign policies are not to its taste.

◀ **A large line** for fuel in Nigeria, which exports most of its crude oil, leaving little for domestic use.

The Iranian Revolution

IRAN ☒ 1979

In the 1960s, Mohammed Reza Pahlavi, Shah (monarch) of Iran since 1941, embarked on a program of economic and social modernization, bolstered by Iran's vast oil reserves. In Iran's mosques, the teachings of the cleric Ayatollah Ruhollah Khomeini—in exile since 1964—were gaining ground.

He preached an end to the Iranian monarchy, with its perceived insensitivity to traditional Shia Islam, and the installation of a theocracy guided by clerics. By 1978, demonstrations against the monarchy had erupted, but were brutally suppressed by martial law.

From monarchy to theocracy

Fearing imminent revolution, the Shah fled Iran on January 16, 1979. Khomeini returned on February 1, and a popular referendum voted for an Islamic Republic.

A new constitution named Khomeini as Iran's supreme leader. Relations between the new regime and the US deteriorated when the US government permitted the Shah to enter the US for cancer treatment in October 1979.

Demanding the Shah's return to Iran to face trial, student radicals invaded the US embassy in Tehran, taking 52 hostages and holding them for over a year. Despite a 2015 agreement on regulating Iran's nuclear industry, relations with the US remain troubled four decades after the hostage crisis.

◀ Iranian women demonstrators carry a placard bearing Ayatollah Khomeini's portrait just after his return to Tehran.

The Soviet invasion of Afghanistan

AFGHANISTAN **1973–1988**

Muhammad Zahir Shah was deposed as king of Afghanistan in a Marxist-led coup in 1973. The People's Democratic Party of Afghanistan (PDPA) government of Nur Muhammad Taraki and Hafizullah Amin then began a program of secularization that offended conservative Muslims and brutally suppressed dissent.

When 50 Russian advisors were murdered in the Afghan city of Herat, the USSR invaded to restore order on December 24, 1978. An Islamic resistance group then declared a *jihad* (holy war) against the USSR and the PDPA. These Islamist *mujahideen* guerrillas fought off the Soviet troops, and even began to threaten Soviet aircraft.

The war was vastly expensive for the USSR, and, in February 1988, under firm international pressure, President Mikhail Gorbachev announced the withdrawal of Soviet troops, leaving the *mujahideen* and PDPA in a stalemate.

A Soviet-made AK-47 Kalashnikov assault rifle used by both Soviet soldiers and Afghan *mujahideen* fighters during the 1978–1988 conflict in Afghanistan.

Indo–Pakistan wars

INDIA–PAKISTAN BORDER **1947–1999**

When the British withdrew from India in 1947 (see p.359), the partition of the Indian subcontinent between India and Pakistan left a question over the future of the princely state of Jammu and Kashmir. Faced with a Pakistani invasion of Poonch, part of his territory, the maharaja appealed to India for help and Indian forces secured the capital Srinagar and eastern Kashmir. The ensuing war continued until a ceasefire was agreed to in January 1949.

The front lines solidified into a "Line of Control" across which the two sides occasionally skirmished, fighting two low-level wars there (in 1965 and 1999). A major Indo–Pakistan war erupted in 1971 when the breakaway regime of East Pakistan (now Bangladesh) successfully bid for independence from the Pakistani government, with significant military assistance from India.

Child refugees fleeing for safety from fighting in East Pakistan during the 1971 Indo–Pakistan war, which led to the region's independence as Bangladesh.

The Iran–Iraq war

IRAN–IRAQ BORDER **1980–1988**

In 1979, Saddam Hussein (*see p.393*) became president of Iraq, following an internal coup in the ruling Ba'ath party. A man of unbridled ambition, he sought to reassert Iraq's position as a strategic power in the Gulf region.

The Iraqi regime was concerned about the possibility of Iran exporting its religious revolution (*see p.367*) to Iraq's large Shia minority, while a festering dispute over territorial rights in the Shatt al-Arab waterway threatened to erupt anew. Sensing a moment of weakness in Iran, Saddam ordered his forces across the border on September 22, 1980. The war, however, was not the walkover that he had expected.

The Iranians defended fanatically, and by March 1981 the Iraqi offensive had stalled. By June 1982, the Iranians had recovered almost all the lost ground.

Thereafter, however, neither side was able to deliver a knockout blow and the war degenerated into a series of offensives that gained little ground at huge cost, as well as sparking the "War of the Cities"— missile attacks on major cities. Finally, both sides accepted that neither could force a victory and agreed to a ceasefire in August 1988, with little to show for the war's 1 million casualties.

The first Gulf War

KUWAIT, IRAQ **AUGUST 1990–FEBRUARY 1991**

In August 1990, the Iraqi president Saddam Hussein invaded the small Gulf sheikhdom of Kuwait. He claimed it as a province of Iraq, with more than half an eye on the country's vast oil reserves, which might help him cover the $100 billion cost of the war with Iran in 1980–1988 (*see above*). The Iraqi army faced precious little resistance to its invasion and the Kuwaiti emir fled.

Operation Desert Storm

The international community was not prepared to acquiesce, and a series of United Nations Resolutions demanded Iraqi withdrawal.

US President George H.W. Bush (president 1989–1993) built an international coalition, including many Arab countries. On January 15–16, 1991, the coalition forces launched Operation Desert Storm, an air offensive that destroyed military and strategic targets.

This was followed by a massive land assault on February 24 known as Operation Desert Sabre. Within less than a week the Iraqi army had retreated from Kuwait and coalition forces had penetrated southern Iraq; then they pulled out, leaving Hussein still in power.

As the Iraqi forces retreated from Kuwait they set off a series of fires in the oilfields, which took weeks to extinguish and caused severe environmental damage.

Communist China

CHINA   1949–PRESENT

In October 1934, Chinese Communists, largely confined by their rivals in the nationalist KMT party to rural areas, abandoned their Jianxi base, broke through a nationalist blockade, and began the "Long March" to find a safer refuge. A trek of around 6,200 miles (10,000 km) ensued, and by the time the Communists established a new headquarters at Yan'an in October 1935, only around a tenth of the 80,000 marchers survived.

The Communists, now led by Mao Zedong, regrouped and in July 1946 launched a civil war to wrest control of China from the nationalists. Despite serious initial setbacks, Mao's forces were able to recruit reinforcements and in the winter of 1947 made gains in Manchuria. The nationalists' best armies perished there and throughout 1948 were in retreat. Finally, in January 1949, Mao

Actors during the Cultural Revolution (1966–1976) perform a play criticizing Confucius, who was seen as symbolic of traditional conservative thinking.

» MAO ZEDONG

Born into a peasant family in Hunan, Mao Zedong (1893–1976) moved to Beijing in 1919 and encountered communism for the first time. He joined the Chinese Communist Party at its inception in 1921 and, in 1927, led the abortive "Autumn Harvest" communist uprising. He took control of the party in 1935. His long tenure as leader of China from 1949 to 1976 left an indelible stamp on the country.

 **President Nixon's** visit to China in 1972 was the start of an improved relationship between the US and the communist Chinese government.

entered Beijing in triumph, while the remaining nationalists fled to the island of Taiwan to establish a Republic of China, with the aim of rivaling the Communist People's Republic of China (PRC). Initially the PRC aligned itself politically with the USSR, agreeing to a Treaty of Alliance and Mutual Assistance in 1950. But in the 1960s Chinese resentment at the cost of the Korean War (*see p.372*), in which Stalin had encouraged Chinese involvement—and a territorial dispute that erupted into military clashes in March 1969 with the USSR itself—strained the relationship.

Domestically, Mao encouraged a radical program of industrialization, in 1958 beginning the "Great Leap Forward," in which industrial and agricultural cooperatives were amalgamated into communes and industrial targets raised. At first it seemed as if China had achieved spectacular increases in output, but later evidence showed that these policies had caused disastrous famines. In 1966, the Cultural Revolution was launched, with the aim of cleansing the country of "bourgeois" influences. Children were recruited as Red Guards, and were encouraged to inform on schoolteachers and relatives who showed any signs of dissent against the regime.

After Mao's death in 1976, his wife Jiang Qing and a party faction known as the "Gang of Four" tried to seize power, but were arrested and jailed. Instead, for the following 15 years China was led by Deng Xiaoping, who introduced a series of measures aimed at turning the Chinese economy away from centralized planning, increasing the volume of foreign trade, and encouraging foreign investment into China.

These new policies reaped spectacular rewards, with the Chinese economy growing at a rate often around 10 percent each year. When other communist regimes collapsed one by one in 1988, China experienced its own pro-democracy movement, which for a time in June 1989 seemed as if it might even dent the party's political monopoly. But Premier Li Peng ordered the army to act, and on June 4, 1989, troops opened fire on the protestors in Beijing's Tiananmen Square, killing some 400 to 800 of them. No opposition movement on a similar scale emerged again. The implicit bargain with the Chinese people became that in exchange for economic well-being, there would be no modification of the Communist Party's central role and that all dissent would be suppressed.

 **The People's Liberation Army** (PLA) is the largest army in the world, with more than 2.25 million service personnel in its army, navy, and air forces.

The Korean War

⊠ KOREA ⊠ 1950–1953

Korea, annexed by Japan in 1910, was partitioned following Japan's surrender in World War II. The division line, at latitude 38°N, was known as the "38th parallel." Soviet forces occupied land north of this line, while the US held the south. In 1949,

both Soviet and US forces withdrew, and tensions between North and South Korea began to rise. Finally, on June 25, 1950, the communist leader of North Korea, Kim Il Sung, ordered an invasion of the south. A United Nations Command (UNC) made up mostly of US forces was sent to assist the south, but they and the South Korean troops were soon penned into a small area in the southernmost tip of the peninsula.

In September, General Douglas MacArthur, commander of the UNC forces, landed troops 150 miles (240 km) farther north at Incheon, catching the North Koreans off guard. By October, UNC forces had crossed the 38th parallel and moved north to the Chinese border. The Chinese government quickly launched a counteroffensive, and pushed the UNC forces back south of the 38th parallel.

The end of the war

The war dragged on for a further two years. Finally, in July 1953, the two sides signed an armistice, leaving the dividing line between the two Koreas close to the 38th parallel, more or less exactly where it had been before the war had started.

◀ US Marines prepare to disembark at Incheon, Korea, in September 1950. The offensive drove pro-communist forces back to the Chinese border.

The first Indochina War

⊠ INDOCHINA ⊠ 1947–1954

At the end of World War II, northern Vietnam came under the control of Ho Chi Minh's communist Vietminh movement, while the French reestablished their administration over what they had named "Indochina" only in the south. Attempts to reach political accord failed; there was fierce fighting throughout 1947–1948, which flared up again in 1950. The able Vietminh general Vo Nguyen Giap thwarted all French offensives and then delivered a final

blow at the Battle of Dien Bien Phu, where a heavily fortified French position was overrun in May 1954.

The Geneva conference

The French will to resist was shattered. On July 21, 1954, a peace conference held in Geneva agreed to a formal partition of Vietnam along the 17th parallel, dividing the country between a communist north and a Western-aligned south.

The Vietnam War

VIETNAM 1963–1973

The division of Vietnam in 1954 did not bring peace. Fearing the spread of communism in the region during 1955, US President Dwight Eisenhower (1890–1969) helped the anti-communist Ngo Dinh Diem to take power in the south via dubious elections, and sent the government hundreds of military advisers. The North Vietnamese reacted by encouraging those in the South who opposed Diem—the Vietcong—to take up arms against the South.

The US military campaign

The US became drawn ever deeper into the conflict, dispatching more than $500 million of US aid to South Vietnam by the end of 1963.

In August 1964, US president Lyndon B. Johnson used an attack by North Vietnamese boats on a US military vessel in the Gulf of Tonkin as a pretext to authorize retaliatory raids on North Vietnam. The first US Marines arrived in South Vietnam in March 1965, and by July they exceeded 50,000. At the peak of the US deployment, in April 1969, there were 543,000 US troops in Vietnam (as well as 47,000 Australians and a New Zealand contingent). A formidable US bombing campaign, Operation Rolling Thunder, failed to dent the Vietcong resistance, and growing US casualties sapped support at home for continued involvement.

A bold series of attacks by the Vietcong on South Vietnamese cities in January 1968 (the "Tet Offensive") also unnerved the Americans, and in August 1969 they began to "Vietnamize" the conflict by withdrawing their forces. On January 27, 1973, the US signed the Paris Peace Accord by which US forces would leave Vietnam within 60 days. Deprived of US backing, the South Vietnamese regime survived until April 1975, when the southern capital Saigon fell to the Vietminh.

⬢ **Dog tags** were used by the US armed forces in Vietnam as an easy means to identify soldiers who had been killed in battle.

⬇ **The Vietnam War** was the first conflict in which helicopters played an important role. Here, a US Chinook resupplies US forces.

Japan, China, and the tiger economies

▣ **EAST ASIA** ⌛ **1945–PRESENT**

After World War II, Allied forces led by US General MacArthur occupied Japan for six years. MacArthur worked with Prime Minister Shigeru Yoshida to draft a new democratic constitution for Japan and reconstruct the Japanese economy.

An economic miracle

From the mid-1950s, the Japanese economy entered a period of rapid growth. Having established heavy industries, such as coal, iron, and steel, the emphasis in Japanese industry shifted in the 1960s to specialist high-tech production, including a lucrative role in the new computing industry.

The 1973 oil crisis (*see p.366*) caused a temporary setback, but by the 1990s Japan's economy was second in size only to that of the US. The long economic boom came to an end in the late 1990s, as an overvalued currency and excessive lending by banks finally resulted in a dramatic slowdown that lasted more than a decade.

The Asian tigers

From the mid-1960s, Japan's economic record had been matched by South Korea, Taiwan, Singapore, and Hong Kong—a group that was nicknamed "the tigers." In the 1990s a second wave of tigers included Thailand, Malaysia, and also China, whose rapid growth in the 1990s placed it in the first rank of world economic powers.

⬓ **In the 21st century**, Asian manufacturing continues to lead the way in consumer goods, electronics (such as this flat-screen television), and technology.

However, Thailand was to overstretch itself, and in 1997, foreign investors began rapidly withdrawing funds, leading to the collapse of the Thai currency. Panic in the financial sector spread to other parts of the Asian economies, as investors offloaded their Asian assets. It took some years for the tigers to recover, but they did so, confounding expectations. Of this group, China emerged the most economically powerful—even after the global economic crisis of 2008—and by 2017 it was challenging the US for the title of the world's largest economy.

◳ **The skyline of Pudong** in Shanghai, China, with its modern, high-tech buildings, is a dramatic contrast to Asian cities of even a few decades earlier.

Africa

The modern history of most African states has been troubled. Decolonialization created nations that cut across ethnic divides, in many cases leading to civil war. Despite Africa's rich reserves of oil, diamonds, and some metals (including gold), inadequate infrastructures hampered attempts to develop modern economies, while many African leaders chose dictatorship over democracy, doing little to enable their countries to compete on the global market.

Rhodesia and UDI

⚑ **RHODESIA (NOW ZIMBABWE)** ⌛ **1962–PRESENT**

In 1962 elections in Southern Rhodesia put the pro-white Rhodesian Front back in power. In 1964, its leader Ian Smith made a show of negotiating with Britain over independence for Rhodesia, on terms that would reflect the will of its black majority. Smith had no intention of allowing black Rhodesians any real political power, and on November 11, 1965, confronted the British with a unilateral declaration of independence (UDI).

The UDI regime

The British government instantly isolated the rebel colony, and the UN condemned the UDI as the act of "a racist minority." But despite the imposition of sanctions, Ian Smith continued to rule. African nationalist groups, notably ZANU, under Ndabaningi Sithole, came to realize that merely lobbying for black majority rule was futile, and were prepared to fight. Smith faced a growing guerrilla insurgency, which placed enormous strain on Rhodesia's resources.

Modern Zimbabwe

Isolated by the collapse of Portuguese rule in Mozambique and Angola in 1973, and with the insurgency reaching the heart of the country by 1976, the Rhodesian government finally agreed to a new constitution in 1978. A moderate black nationalist faction under Bishop Abel Muzorewa took power in 1979, but elections in February 1980

⌃ **Ian Smith** gives a press conference in London shortly before the end of talks that hoped to avert UDI.

returned the hard-line Robert Mugabe, by then leader of ZANU, who remained Zimbabwe's leader for the following four decades.

☐ **Robert Mugabe**, who rose to prominence in the 1960s, became president of Zimbabwe in 1987.

Post-colonial Africa

☐ **AFRICA** ⌛ **1960–PRESENT**

The end of European rule in Africa left more than 50 independent countries facing myriad challenges, often exacerbated by years of colonialism or created by the legacy of the borders that colonial powers had imposed.

The advent of the Cold War (*see pp.338–9*) in the 1940s had aggravated Africa's problems, as the continent became a proxy battlefield between the superpowers. In the Horn of Africa, Cold War tensions exploded into open warfare, as Ethiopia saw the overthrow in 1974 of Emperor Haile Selassie by a Marxist group, the Derg, led by Colonel Mengistu Haile Mariam. With Soviet and Cuban backing, Mengistu secured most of Ethiopia. He also became involved in a war in the Ogaden Desert with Somalia in 1977, a country that then became a US ally until it dissolved into total chaos after 1991.

Famine and civil war

A growing insurgency against the Derg and the regime's policies of agricultural centralization contributed to severe famines in Ethiopia in 1984–1985, in which as many as a million may have died. Climate change (*see pp.386–7*) and continued instability in the region have meant that government policy continues to be dominated by crisis responses to famine rather than long-term solutions.

Marxist groups also seized power in Angola and Mozambique after the Portuguese government abruptly decided to withdraw its colonial control in 1973. In both cases, long-running civil war broke out. In Angola, conflict between the Marxist MPLA and the anti-communist UNITA movement of Jonas Savimbi finally ended only with Savimbi's death in 2002.

The dubious worth of Europe's legacy to Africa was demonstrated in the Belgian Congo, which achieved independence in 1960 under Patrice Lumumba, but almost instantly suffered the secession of the copper-rich province of Katanga. The Belgians sent back troops to Congo, intervening on the side of the Katangan leader Moise Tshombe, before a United Nations force displaced them. Out of this appalling mess the real winner was Joseph Mobutu, the army Chief of Staff, who obtained the presidency in 1965, a post he held until 1997. In common with many African dictators, he viewed the country's treasury as his personal cash cow, sequestering huge sums that impoverished his nation through both the direct losses and the corruption that it encouraged.

Rwanda and Zimbabwe

Rwanda had been French-administered from the end of World War I to its independence in 1964, and the colonial regime had done nothing to ease tensions between the two main ethnic groups:

Hutu and Tutsi. A Hutu massacre of Tutsis in 1964 foreshadowed the genocide of 1994, when Hutu Interahamwe militias slaughtered some 500,000 Tutsis as the Tutsi-led RPF fought its way to the capital of Kigali. The RPF, led by Paul Kagame, took power, but many Hutus fled to Zaire, where they became involved in a multi-sided civil war.

Zimbabwe had entered independence as one of the stronger African economies, but it suffered a dramatic deterioration in fortunes under Robert Mugabe, whose regime became increasingly autocratic. From 2000, "veterans" of the struggle for

« **A sign warns** of land mines in Mozambique, a hazard that persisted years after the end of the civil war there in 1992.

independence seized many white-owned farms, crippling the agricultural economy. By 2008, the economy was in tatters, basic services had seized up, and inflation reached almost unmeasurably high levels. Despite a power-sharing agreement signed between Mugabe and Morgan Tsvangirai in September 2008, Mugabe refused to cede power, and the political and economic prospects for the country look grim.

⊠ **Refugees of the inter-ethnic fighting** in Rwanda in 1994, in which thousands of Tutsis were slaughtered. Large numbers of Hutus also died in its aftermath.

The end of apartheid

SOUTH AFRICA **1958–1999**

Dr. Hendrik Verwoerd, South Africa's prime minister between 1958 and 1966, drew up the system of apartheid—an Afrikaans word meaning "separateness"—in which legalized segregation discriminated against the country's nonwhite population.

Apartheid controlled where nonwhites could live and work, as well as their movements, and denied them political rights. Initially, European powers, still the masters of colonial holdings in Africa, did nothing to oppose the inequalities this created.

In 1960 police turned their guns on a nonviolent demonstration held by the anti-apartheid group the Pan Africanist Congress (PAC) in Sharpeville, killing 69 people and injuring 180 more. The massacre triggered a shift to more militant tactics among activists.

In 1961, Nelson Mandela became leader of the military wing of the African National Congress (ANC) Party, beginning a campaign of sabotage against government installations. He and other ANC members were arrested and sentenced to life imprisonment.

Apartheid persists

As the 1970s and 1980s progressed, violence escalated and resentment grew at a system of Bantustans—impoverished enclaves to which Blacks were relocated as a substitute for any

> " **Never, never**, and **never** again shall it be that this **beautiful land** will again **experience** the **oppression** of one by another. "
>
> **Nelson Mandela, May 9, 1994**

》 NELSON MANDELA

Born in the Eastern Cape, South Africa, Nelson Rolhlahla Mandela (1918–2013) was an early anti-apartheid activist, and after the Sharpeville Massacre in 1960 joined in the ANC's move to a more violent struggle. He was arrested in August 1962 and served 27 years in prison. Mandela emerged in 1990 to become a powerful voice arguing for peaceful reconciliation between South Africa's communities, and served as the country's first nonwhite president from 1994 to 1999.

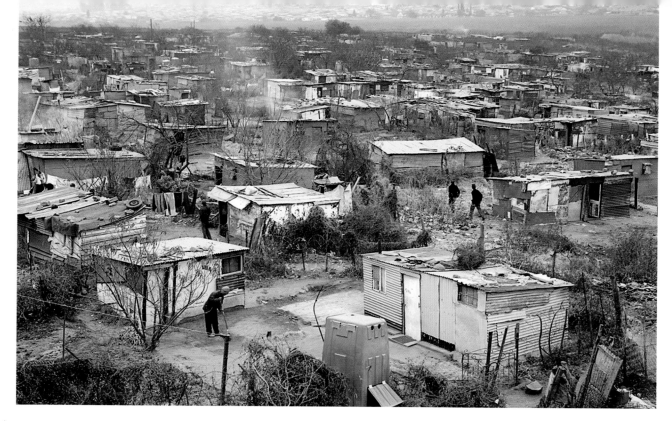

real rights. The police and military clamped down on dissent, violating human rights. A series of anti-government riots, which began in Soweto in June 1976, ended 16 months later after between 600 and 700 people had been killed.

Two events weakened South Africa's position. First, its Rhodesian allies lost power in 1979 (*see p.375*) and second, in 1986, the international community imposed economic sanctions on the country. Yet still the government shied away from real reform.

The end of apartheid

It took a new government administration to open the way for change. In 1989, the country elected F.W. de Klerk as president, and he soon lifted bans on the ANC and other opposition groups. On February 11, 1990, Nelson Mandela was released from the Robben Island prison where he had been held since 1963 and, setting aside any bitterness from nearly 30 years of incarceration, he began

talks with the de Klerk government on ways to achieve a transition to Black majority rule. There were grave obstacles, including the question of how to reconcile different views from political and tribal factions among the Black community, and strong opposition to change from many Whites.

A Convention for a Democratic South Africa met on December 20, 1991, to thrash out the issues, and a referendum among Whites in March 1992—which delivered a 68-percent vote for change—bolstered de Klerk. Negotiations resumed in March 1993 and finally, on April 26–28, 1994, South Africa held its first elections open to universal suffrage. On May 10, 1994, Nelson Mandela became President of South Africa, a post he held until 1999, as the last vestiges of the apartheid system were swept away.

⌃ **Corrugated iron shacks** in the Soweto township are characteristic of the living conditions of many black South Africans during apartheid, and beyond.

❰❰ **South Africa's ANC flag** displays a spear—a symbol of resistance to colonial and apartheid rule.

Of South Africa's 22.7 million registered voters, some 19.7 million voted in the national elections on April 26–28, 1994; a turnout of 86 percent, which caused massive lines in many areas. The ANC, as expected, was the overwhelming winner, receiving 62.6 percent of the vote.

New challenges

In the early 1990s, following the collapse of communism and the end of the Cold War, it seemed for some that "history had ended" and the world had overcome the challenges it once faced. Yet soon the advent of dangerous new diseases, an awareness of man-made damage to the environment, the rise of radical Islamic terror networks, increasing flows of refugees, and a resurgence of populism and nationalism in Europe and the US created a challenging environment for 21st-century governments.

Biotechnology

◻ GLOBAL ⚐ 1945–PRESENT

The founding of the United Nations Food and Agriculture Organization (FAO) in 1945 signaled an international desire to enhance crops and eradicate hunger. In 1960, the International Rice Research Institute was established in the Philippines to improve rice production. Its work has helped rice farmers to increase output by an average of 2.5 percent each year since 1965. Known as the Green Revolution, this transformation has gone a long way to support the burgeoning population of less developed countries.

▽ **Scientists tend to a greenhouse** of GM crops. The problem of cross-contamination of non-GM crops by pollen from GM crops has caused great controversy.

GM Foods and cloning

In the 1990s, scientists developed the technique of Genetic Modification (GM) to alter plants' genetic material and so create crops with better disease and pest resistance. In late 1996 and early 1997, it emerged that the US company Monsanto had been shipping soybeans containing GM material to European ports, resulting in a storm of controversy and strong public fears in Europe about the long-term effects of consuming GM foods.

In July 1996, a sheep ("Dolly") that had been grown from an adult sheep cell (or cloned) was born, giving rise to concerns that the science of biotechnology had far outrun any consideration of the ethical aspects of such manipulations.

Medical advances and new diseases

GLOBAL **1967–PRESENT**

The past century has produced astonishing advances in medicine, most notably the discovery of penicillin—the first antibiotic—by Alexander Fleming in 1928. By the 1950s, antibiotics were being used to provide treatments for many killer diseases, such as syphilis and tuberculosis.

Advances and challenges

Scientists pushed forward other medical boundaries, too. In 1967, surgeons carried out the first successful human heart transplant.

However, while some infectious diseases were eradicated (the last recorded case of naturally occurring smallpox was in Somalia in 1977), many old killers, such as cholera and typhoid, have persisted in underdeveloped countries. As many as 40,000 people a day die from diseases caught by drinking water contaminated by sewage.

⌂ **In 2013, an outbreak** of the Ebola virus in Guinea, West Africa, spread to cause more than 11,000 deaths. Here, Red Cross volunteers disinfect a Guinean hospital in 2014.

The rise of "new" diseases

The sexually transmitted disease AIDS, caused by the HIV virus, was first identified among homosexual men in the US in 1981.

HIV spread globally, and by 2015, AIDS had caused 35 million deaths worldwide, with a further 33 million people infected with HIV. Outbreaks of the acute respiratory disease SARS in 2002–2003, and Mexican "swine 'flu," a strain of the influenza virus that crossed over from pigs to humans in 2009, have provoked fears that it is only a matter of time before a pandemic occurs on the scale of the "Spanish Flu" that killed up to 20 million people just after World War I.

⌂ **Since the early 1990s,** the red ribbon has become a symbol for HIV/AIDS awareness.

Globalization

The increasing interconnectedness of the world economy, with multinational companies cutting across many different jurisdictions, has been termed "globalization." Global consumption of uniform products has led to concerns about the erosion of different cultures and the fear that individual governments have become almost powerless in comparison to the enormous power wielded by global corporations.

⌃ **Barcodes first appeared** on products in the US in 1974, and are now a powerful tool for tracking goods as they make their way around the world.

The growth of global trade

The process of globalization has, in one sense, been going on ever since agricultural villages began trading with more distant neighbors in the Neolithic age. The events of the mid- to late 20th century, however, were of an entirely different order.

In 1944, representatives of 44 nations met at Bretton Woods in the US to establish the International Monetary Fund (IMF) to increase world trade through cooperation between nations. It was a first sign that the world needed an international approach to tackle the globalization of the world economy. From the 1980s onward, many governments began to liberalize their economies, privatizing state assets and encouraging "open" competitive markets. The volume of goods traded worldwide each year in the early 21st century was approximately 22 times larger than that in 1950. Global bodies such as the World Trade Organization—established in

1995, and with 164 member countries by 2016—set ground rules for international trade and solved disputes between governments. The idea behind these organizations was that easier international trade would result in greater growth in the world economy and greater prosperity for its people. The advent of the Internet and digital communications from the 1990s added new dimensions to the world's economic infrastructure, making international trade quicker and more efficient and the exchange of information almost instantaneous.

Anti-globalization

However, globalization has potentially negative effects, too. Multinational companies can shift production to countries where labor costs are lower or health-and-safety legislation is less stringent, cutting their costs and increasing profits. By the 21st century many service jobs—such as those in customer service call centers—had been transferred

《 A McDonald's restaurant in Kuwait City. The "golden arches" are a potent symbol of globalization.

from high-cost Western countries to lower-wage developing countries. Moves such as this have led to an anti-globalization movement, protesting at international agreements that appear to ignore the interests of people in both industrialized and developing nations.

Feelings that globalization and free trade may have damaged domestic industries contributed to the election of Donald Trump as US president in 2016. His message that American economic priorities should come before a commitment to economic openness was attractive to many. Governments in many other countries, especially in Europe, faced similar challenges among elements in their electorates who felt left behind economically. By 2017, globalization was, for the first time, facing serious political challenges.

☑ A car lot outside a Toyota factory near Derby, UK. The Japanese car company began assembling vehicles overseas in 1964.

Climate change and the green movement

GLOBAL ⚬ **1988–PRESENT**

⚑ **A recycling symbol**, a sign of increasing efforts worldwide to reduce the burden of waste.

Since the Industrial Revolution (*see pp.264–5*), average global temperatures have risen by about 1.44°F (0.8°C). This warming has accelerated in the last four decades, so that between 2000 and 2015 the world experienced 15 of the warmest years on record. Many experts believe human activity is to blame for this change in the Earth's climate, and are calling for urgent action to prevent a global crisis and protect the planet for future generations.

The Greenhouse Effect

The Intergovernmental Panel on Climate Change (IPCC) was set up in 1988 to investigate climate change. In 2014, the IPCC produced a report that projected rises in temperature of between 4.7 and 8.6°F (2.6 and 4.8°C) by the end of the 21st century.

The report concluded that a raised atmospheric concentration of the gas carbon dioxide (CO_2) has intensified a natural phenomenon known as the "Greenhouse Effect." This is a process by which the surface and atmosphere of the Earth are warmed as heat radiation from the sun is absorbed by "greenhouse" gases, including methane and CO_2. This effect is magnified as the climate of the Earth

changes, because the warming oceans are less able to remove CO_2 from the atmosphere. Increasing industrialization has caused a rapid acceleration in the production of CO_2 emissions. Coal-burning power stations generate CO_2, as do air, sea, and road traffic; for example, each of the 260 million cars in the US produces more than five tons of the gas each year.

There are several signs that global warming is starting to severely impact our environment, such as a dramatic retreat of glaciers in nonpolar regions, a diminution in sea ice around the Arctic, and a breakup of many ice shelves in the Antarctic. Changes in rainfall patterns in many regions of the world—tens of millions suffered from drought in Africa in the 1980s—and an increase in the number of severe weather events, such as hurricanes, floods, and droughts, are believed to be a result of climate change.

Extinctions and deforestation

Many animal species are now in danger of extinction. In its 2016 report, the International Union for the Conservation of Nature (IUCN) found that in the Democratic Republic of the Congo alone,

there were 235 animal species under threat—30 of them critically endangered. This situation has been aggravated by habitat loss, caused not only by the expansion of human populations into new areas—a process promoted by overpopulation—but also by environmental degradation caused at least in part by climate change. The world's tropical forests play an important part in holding back global warming too, as they "inhale" CO_2. Yet many of these forests are in retreat, having become the victims of overlogging or simply clearance for agricultural expansion.

◀ **Wind turbines** can generate electricity with comparatively little impact on the environment.

The green movement

Many fear that climate change is becoming irreversible, though there is much lobbying for social change to help slow the trend, and perhaps even reverse it. Investment is increasing in renewable sources of energy, such as tidal, wind, and solar power; and in many developed economies, there is a push for consumers to recycle goods. Many policy makers continued to dispute the findings of global-warming experts, and they found a champion in US President Donald Trump, elected in 2016. Yet without urgent action, an increasing consensus believes that climate change will produce an environmental catastrophe.

> **Future generations** may well have occasion to ask themselves, '**What were our parents thinking**?'
>
> **Al Gore,** *An Inconvenient Truth*, 2006

✉ **As rainfall levels** have fallen in many areas, desertification—encroachment by deserts—has become an increasing problem.

>> **A large section** of glacier sheers off into the sea. By the early 21st century, there were fears that rising global temperatures would cause large glacial sheets to melt, raising the level of sea globally and threatening low-lying coasts and islands with flooding.

The communications revolution

⌖ GLOBAL 🕮 1958–PRESENT

Since World War I, advances in technology have transformed global communications and transportation systems. A journey that once took weeks by land or sea can now be made by air in hours, while huge amounts of data can be transmitted almost instantaneously across the world, at the click of a computer mouse.

Road and air travel

The 20th-century boom in travel was largely a result of advances in engine technology that permitted ever more powerful automobiles. Global statistics predict that by 2030 there will be 1.2 billion motor vehicles in use worldwide, operating on a network of roads that cross the land throughout the globe. More dramatic still has been the explosive growth in air travel since World War II, reaching almost 3.6 billion passengers in 2016.

In the Classical era, traveling from Rome to London would have taken weeks and enormous expense, but in the 21st century the journey can be made by air in fewer than three hours and for less than a day's average wage in either country.

The rebirth of communication

By the early 20th century, technological advances were making it possible to exchange messages instantly across the world by radio and telephone (*see pp.268–9*). Then, in 1958, the development of the microchip dramatically transformed the world of communications. Microchips provide the "brains" for computers, personal communications, and cell phones, allowing the storage and transmission of vast amounts of data, often merely at the touch of a button.

A precursor to the Internet became operational in 1969, and the World Wide Web was made available to the public in 1991; while the first cellular telephone network went live in Chicago in 1978. The social media site Facebook was launched in 2004. These innovations are now ubiquitous, and citizens have information and communications tools with a power and scope unimaginable even 30 years ago.

⌃ **The Apple iPhone**, released in 2007, put computer-processing power into a mobile handset.

⌄ **Cell phone technology** provides communication to remote villages, where the cost of installing fixed telephone cables is prohibitive.

9/11

USA ■ 2001

On September 11, 2001, Islamic extremists launched successful attacks on the World Trade Center in New York City and the Pentagon in Washington DC.

The US under attack

At 8:46am American Airlines Flight 11 crashed into the World Trade Center's north tower, followed by an attack on the south tower just 16 minutes later by a hijacked United Airlines Flight 175. In all, around 2,750 people died. Then, at 9:37am, American Airlines Flight 77 crashed into the Pentagon, killing a further 184 people, and at 10:03am another 40 died when United Airlines Flight 93, probably bound for the Capitol Building or the White House in Washington DC, plowed into a field near Shanksville, Pennsylvania.

There had never been such a damaging terrorist attack on US soil. The attackers had used simple methods—knives and the threat of bombs—to take over the aircraft, but the logistics of the operation were well thought out and clearly required months of planning. It took very little time for the prime suspect to emerge as al-Qaeda, an extremist Islamic terrorist network with bases in Afghanistan, led by Osama bin Laden.

》 OSAMA BIN LADEN

From a wealthy Saudi Arabian family, Osama bin Laden (1957–2011) joined the *mujahideen* fight in Afghanistan in the 1980s (*see p.368*). Around 1988 he founded al-Qaeda ("the base"), using extreme terror to oppose US policy toward Muslims.

> " Today, our fellow citizens, our **way of life**, our very **freedom**, came **under attack**.
>
> **President George W. Bush,**
> **September 11, 2001**

⌂ **Smoke billows out** from the World Trade Center, New York City, after the al-Qaeda terrorist attack on September 11, 2001.

The Afghan War

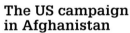
AFGHANISTAN **OCTOBER 2001–PRESENT**

The withdrawal of Soviet troops from Afghanistan in 1988 (*see p.368*) was followed by a bitter civil war, as the *mujahideen* commanders fought for control of the country. In reaction to this chaos, a new political faction arose, the Taliban (meaning "students"), who originated in the *madrassas* (religious schools) of the conservative southern province of Kandahar. From August 1994, the Taliban militia won victory after victory, finally capturing the Afghan capital Kabul in September 1996.

The Taliban, under their leader Mullah Omar, instituted a regime of harsh Islamic rigor, gravely curtailing the rights of women and banning activities such as the playing of music or kite-flying, with severe (including capital) punishment for offenders. Only in the north of the country did a Northern Alliance resist, but they controlled only 10 percent of Afghanistan by 2000. From 1997, the Taliban regime played host to the al-Qaeda movement of Osama bin Laden (*see p.391*), which used its Afghan safe haven as a base to plan terrorist attacks against US interests.

The US campaign in Afghanistan

Once it became clear that al-Qaeda had carried out the 9/11 attacks against the US (*see p.391*), the US government demanded that the Taliban hand over Osama bin Laden. Mullah Omar refused and on October 7 the Americans began to bomb Afghan cities. The Americans also started to provide military aid to the Northern Alliance, who began an offensive southward. The Taliban, faced with US carpet-bombing, largely melted away. Kabul fell on November 13 and the Taliban stronghold of Kandahar at the end of the month. However, Osama bin Laden and much of the al-Qaeda leadership managed to slip away.

The Taliban return

Despite the subsequent dispatch of a multinational armed force to stabilize the country, the Taliban regrouped. The new Afghan government of Hamid Karzai wavered between supporting international offensives against the resurgent Taliban and seeking compromise with more moderate elements. Despite a US troop surge in 2010, the Taliban insurgency grew, particularly after the US army ended combat operations in 2014. By 2017, the Taliban controlled large rural areas of Afghanistan and threatened Kabul and other cities.

Taliban fighters near Kabul in February 1995, after their rapid advance northward from Kandahar.

The war in Iraq

⚑ IRAQ   ⌖ MARCH 2003–PRESENT

From 1993, the Iraqi president Saddam Hussein had been forced to allow the United Nations (UN) to inspect his armaments industries to ensure he did not acquire "weapons of mass destruction" (WMD), such as nuclear, chemical, or biological weaponry. US President George W. Bush (president 2001–2009) exploited Saddam's often patchy compliance with this directive, encouraging the international community throughout late 2002 to pressure the Iraqi government to come clean about its weapons stocks. Saddam blustered, realizing too late that Bush had boxed him into a corner.

The Americans were unable to secure a definitive UN resolution authorizing force, but maintained that previous resolutions contained implicit approval for military action. On March 20, 2003, US airstrikes against Baghdad began. In contrast to the first Gulf War (*see p.369*), a land attack began almost immediately, with US-led coalition forces landing near the southern port of Basra on March 22. As the invasion force pushed northward, many Iraqi units failed to resist or melted away, and the US took Baghdad on April 9, with the last major city, Tikrit, falling four days later.

Iraq after the war

Postwar Iraq descended into chaos, with the breakout of an insurgency against US occupation, mostly by Sunni Muslims, that killed hundreds of US soldiers. The previously supportive Shia population

≫ SADDAM HUSSEIN

A member of the Iraqi Ba'ath party from 1957, Saddam Hussein (1937–2006) played a key role in the coup that brought the party to power in 1968. He ruled Iraq from 1979 with brutal force at home and abroad. The Americans toppled him in 2003.

turned against the coalition, too, and a vicious set of civil wars erupted between the two communities, with the loss of thousands of lives. The insurgency continued to grow, and after the US withdrew its troops in 2011, the extremist Sunni group ISIS (*see p. 397*) seized large parts of the country, including Mosul, in 2014. It took hard fighting, and renewed US aid, including military advisers, to partially roll back these gains by early 2017.

⌄ Flames light up Baghdad on the second night of the US bombing of the Iraqi capital on March 23, 2003, an attack described as "shock and awe."

Beyond the nation state

As early as the 1920s, there was an awareness that the world's nations needed a more international approach to policymaking to avoid the kind of tensions that had led to World War I. Despite this knowledge, the League of Nations, which first met in 1920, failed the challenge of keeping the peace, while its successor, the United Nations, was hampered by the outbreak of the Cold War in the late 1940s.

⌂ **The Taj Mahal hotel** in Mumbai, India, was targeted during the terrorist attacks on the city in November 2008.

Failed states and terrorism

When the Cold War (*see pp.338–9*) ended in the 1990s, many saw it as heralding the "End of History" or a "New World Order," both notions that proved hugely overoptimistic. Nation states with widely varying political traditions could not—or refused to—impose Western democratic systems; while others simply fell apart either as a result of years of misrule or because funding to their governments was removed when they were

no longer required as Cold War allies. The phenomenon of "failed states" (such as Somalia) arose; in such nations, no effective government exists, leading to civil war and warlordism. Enforcing world norms (such as the repression of piracy) is simply impossible on a failed state's national territory.

The world has faced the growth of a new sort of international terrorism, exemplified by al-Qaeda and ISIS (Islamic State of Iraq and

Syria), whose agenda is not a nationalistic one (such as that of the IRA for a united, independent Ireland, or ETA for Basque independence in northern Spain), but aims instead to establish its own new (Islamic) world order. Incidents such as the 9/11 attack on the US (*see p.391*), the 2015 attacks in Central Paris, and the continued rise of ISIS in the Middle East demonstrated a threat that—because it undermines the safety of many countries—cannot be dealt with by one nation acting alone.

World problems with global solutions

The leaders of the 21st century face challenging problems. Large-scale population shifts—such as the vast numbers of migrants seeking to enter the European Union illegally from African countries—as well as climate change, threaten the livelihoods of millions. Globalization is increasing the interdependence of the world economy, so that a fiscal crisis in one country can soon translate into factory closures or banking chaos in another, as happened in 2008–2009.

Controversial US presidential candidate Donald Trump campaigns in 2016. After winning the election, he took office in January 2017.

In the early 21st century, worries about globalization helped the rise of populist movements such as France's *Front National* and contributed to the election of Donald Trump as US president. Although urgent international cooperation is needed to address problems such as global warming, refugee crises, and international terrorism, in 2017 the world seems to be entering a phase where nationalist and regional concern makes such concerted action increasingly difficult.

Syrian refugees fleeing conflict caused by Islamic extremists wait at the Turkish-Syrian border, 2014. In 2016, there were an estimated 65.3 million refugees worldwide.

Crowds gather in al-Tahrir Square, Cairo, which became the main venue for demonstrations against Egyptian president Hosni Mubarak.

The Arab Spring

⚑ **MIDDLE EAST, N AFRICA** ⏳ **2010–PRESENT**

By the early 21st century, discontent was growing in many countries of the Middle East and North Africa. Longstanding dictatorships in Libya, Egypt, Yemen, and Syria stifled dissent, while political corruption went unchecked and poverty increased.

In December 2010, a Tunisian fruit vendor set himself alight in protest of police corruption. A wave of demonstrations broke out in Tunisia after his death, uniting political liberals, radical Islamic factions, and disenchanted youth, all of whom felt marginalized by the country's regime. Unable to contain the protests, President Ben Ali fled Tunisia a month later.

The Arab Spring spreads

The protest movement spread to other Arab countries and became known as the "Arab Spring." Demonstrations grew in size, aided by the opposition's use of new technology: videos of protests shot on mobile phones were rapidly uploaded to websites.

Hosni Mubarak, Egypt's president, tried to suppress protesters, and to offer last-minute concessions to placate them, before stepping down in February 2011. In March 2011, Libyan dictator Muammar Qaddafi's threat to send tanks in to quash protests in Benghazi provoked NATO to begin airstrikes against his forces. After six further months of bitter fighting, Qaddafi was overthrown

and killed. In Syria, the regime of Bashar al-Assad responded violently to protests, sparking a civil war, which was still raging six years later, and caused millions of Syrians to flee their homes.

The effects of the Arab Spring were mixed. The hopes of the original protesters were rarely realized as regimes clung to power, or other military, political, and radical religious factions seized the initiative. Tunisia succeeded in holding democratic elections, but in Egypt a new military regime was established. Libya, Yemen, and Syria all descended into violent factional struggles in which radical Islamic groups such as ISIS flourished (*see opposite*).

Muammar Qaddafi's pro-Russian stance and alleged sponsorship of terrorist attacks alienated NATO countries and helped bring about his downfall.

The Syrian town of Azaz saw bitter fighting in the civil war, as its position on the Turkish border made it a key base for resupplying opposition fighters.

ISIS and global terror

MIDDLE EAST ⌛ 2011–PRESENT

The instability that followed the US invasion of Iraq in 2003, and the outbreak of civil war in Syria, allowed Islamist extremist groups to reestablish themselves, reversing an apparent decline since the expulsion of al-Qaeda from Afghanistan in 2001. Iraqi government policies after 2003 favored the Shia majority and marginalized the minority Sunni community, among whom Saddam Hussein had found his key support. The resulting disaffection helped the growth of al-Qaeda in Iraq (AQI), which joined the insurgency against Iraq's US-backed government until its near destruction in 2007 following a surge in American troop numbers.

AQI remnants regrouped in eastern Syria after the outbreak of the Syrian Civil War in 2011. Now led by Abu Bakr al-Baghdadi, the group renamed itself Islamic State in Iraq and Syria (ISIS) and captured the Syrian regional capital of Raqqa. ISIS proved effective propagandists, using the Internet and social media to spread their message and attract foreign fighters to their cause: by early 2016 an estimated 36,000 had traveled to Syria, nearly 7,000 of them from Western countries. Taking advantage of the weakness of the Iraqi army, ISIS expanded in Iraq and seized the

northern city of Mosul in June 2014. The group now felt strong enough to declare a caliphate, modeled on the political structure of the early Islamic empire, with al-Baghdadi as its caliph, and renamed itself Islamic State (IS).

As ISIS steadily gained territory, outside powers, including the US, Russia, and Iran became alarmed. The US began airstrikes in Iraq in August 2014. American military aid to the Iraqi government and to Kurdish groups in Syria, as well as Russian and Iranian assistance to the Assad regime, helped push back ISIS, until by March 2017 it was threatened in its Mosul stronghold.

ISIS responded to Western assaults by launching a series of attacks in Europe, including one in Paris in November 2015, which left 130 dead. Even as its military position in the Middle East weakened, intelligence services feared that many of those who had traveled to Iraq and Syria to support ISIS might now return and become the nucleus of terrorist cells in their home countries.

⏶ **Mourners in** the Place de la Bourse, Brussels, in March 2016 honor the victims of an ISIS bombing that killed 31 people.

⟫ ABU BAKR AL-BAGHDADI

Born Ibrahim al-Badri, al-Baghdadi founded a small militant group in Iraq in 2003, before joining forces with ISI (the predecessor of ISIS) and becoming its leader in 2010. He was instrumental in the group's expansion, but was rarely seen in public before his declaration of the Islamic State caliphate in 2014.

⏶ **ISIS adopted** an early Islamic black flag as its symbol. Bearing a Muslim declaration of faith, this flag flew over ISIS-controlled towns and villages.

The European Union and the crisis of populism

EUROPE PRESENT

The admittance of Croatia to the European Union (EU) in July 2013 brought the EU's membership to 28 countries. There had been political strains in some member countries for a long time, particularly in the UK, which opposed further integration in the EU. The dislocation that followed the global financial crisis of 2008 heightened a sense that the organization was ignoring the concerns of more deprived socioeconomic groups in favor of those of a trans-national elite.

Refugees in Europe

Rising political instability in the Middle East and North Africa after 2011 led to a corresponding increase in refugees from those areas. Many headed toward the EU, either by land or by boat across the Mediterranean. This influx of asylum seekers fueled an increase in support for far-right and populist parties, which made political capital out of the perceived threat to national identity posed by the largely Muslim newcomers.

In France, the right-wing National Front (FN) won seats in the national legislature for the first time in 2012, and in 2017 its leader, Marine Le Pen, secured a good percentage in the popularity polls and a place in the presidential elections. In the UK, longstanding antipathy to closer integration with

Rescuers from a Maltese organization save some of the tens of thousands of refugees who tried to make the hazardous crossing by boat from Libya to Italy.

Europe crystallized with the rise of the staunchly anti-European UK Independence Party (UKIP), which was a key player in the coalition that secured a 51 percent referendum vote in June 2016 for the UK to leave the EU.

This vote, for what was popularly known as "Brexit," marked a moment of crisis. The challenge of balancing the need for deeper cooperation with the populist groundswell promised a profoundly difficult period for the EU.

British Prime Minister David Cameron faces UKIP leader Nigel Farage in this poster from the June 2016 referendum campaign.

Russia and Ukraine

RUSSIA, E EUROPE PRESENT

≪ A pro-Russian insurgent stands guard over wreckage from Flight MH-17. Subsequent investigations strongly indicated the BUK missile that shot down the Malaysian airlines plane had been fired by a separatist unit.

After the breakup of the Soviet Union in 1991, traditionalists in Russia sought close ties with the other ex-Soviet republics, particularly Ukraine, which was seen as a strategic bulwark against NATO's expansion into eastern Europe.

Russian president Vladimir Putin was enraged when his Ukrainian counterpart Viktor Yanukovych, previously seen as a loyal ally, agreed to sign an Association Agreement with the EU in November 2013. It took strong pressure from Moscow to induce Yanukovych to reverse his decision.

The Donbas crisis

Protests against this move broke out in Kiev, the Ukrainian capital, and Yanukovych fled after a heavy-handed reaction by the security forces backfired, including the shooting of 28 people by snipers on February 20, 2014. Russia sent irregular forces to seize key buildings on the Crimean peninsula, an area that had been part of Russia until 1954, and still housed the bases of the Russian Black Sea fleet.

A Russian-sponsored referendum voted overwhelmingly for Crimea to become part of Russia. Soon afterward pro-Russian insurgents seized territory in the predominantly Russian-speaking Donbas region of southeastern Ukraine. As fighting flared with Ukrainian security forces, there was a strong suspicion that Russia was sending military aid to the insurgents. Commercial passenger jet Malaysian Airlines Flight MH-17 was shot down over Donbas on July 17, with the loss of 298 lives. This, combined with Western anxiety over a possible total collapse of Ukraine, led to the imposition of sanctions on Russia, which reined in Russian enthusiasm for the separatists. However, despite attempts at peace talks, the fighting continued in 2017, albeit at a lower level, and southeastern Ukraine seemed set to become a permanent pro-Russian enclave.

≫ VLADIMIR PUTIN

Putin's early career was as an intelligence officer in the KGB. He entered politics in 1991, and replaced Boris Yeltsin as Russian president in 1999. Putin served in the office until 2008 and then again from 2012, acquiring a reputation as a proponent of an increasingly assertive foreign policy in the Middle East, Ukraine, and elsewhere.

INDEX

Page numbers in **bold** refer to main references to subject.
Page numbers in *italics* refer to illustrations and captions.

C

ACKNOWLEDGMENTS

The publisher would like to thank Neha Samuel for editorial assistance and Heena Sharma for design assistance.

Picture credits
The publisher would like to thank the following for their kind permission to reproduce their photographs:

(Key: a-above; b-below/bottom; c-center; f-far; l-left; r-right; t-top)

1 Getty Images: Travelpix Ltd. (c). **2–3 Alamy Stock Photo**: Deco. **4–5 Getty images**: Jeremy Woodhouse (t). **6 Dreamstime.com:** Gunter Hofer (tl). **Getty Images:** Fine Art Images/Heritage Images (tr). **7 Time Life Pictures/US Coast Guard/The LIFE Picture Collection** (tl); **Getty Images:** NASA (tr). **8–9 Getty Images:** Tom Bonaventure. **11 Getty Images:** Hisham Ibrahim. **12–13 Getty Images:** Fred Mayer. **14** (Panel image) **Getty Images:** DEA / G. Cozzi (t). **14 Corbis:** Anthony Bannister; Gallo Images (ca). **15 Corbis:** Yann Arthus-Bertrand (b). **16 Corbis:** Gianni Dagli Orti (b). **17 Alamy Images:** Mary Evans Picture Library (br). **Getty Images:** Time & Life Pictures (t). **18 Corbis:** The Gallery Collection (bl). **19 Alamy Images:** Keith Heron (b). **Ancient Art & Architecture Collection:** Uniphoto Press Japan (tl). **20 The Art Archive:** Bibliothèque Mazarine Paris (b). **21 akg-images:** akg-images (t). **Corbis:** Angelo Hornak (b). **22 Corbis:** Leonard de Selva (tl). **22–3 Corbis:** William Manning (b). **23 Corbis:** Hulton-Deutsch Collection (tr). **24 Corbis:** Enzo & Paolo Ragazzini (cb). **25 Alamy Stock Photo:** Pictorial Press Ltd. (t); Reuters (b). **26–7 Getty Images:** Joe Cornish. **28–9** Travel Ink (t). **30 Corbis:** Wolfgang Kaehler (b). **DK Images:** Natural History Museum (t). **31 DK Images:** Natural History Museum (br). **The Natural History Museum, London:** The Natural History Museum, London (cla). **32 Getty Images:** The Bridgeman Art Library (b). **33 DK Images:** Natural History Museum (tr). **Science Photo Library:** Javier Trueba/MSF/Science Photo Library (b). **34 Corbis:** Jacques Langevin (b); John Van Hasselt (t). **35 DK Images:** Natural History Museum (cra). **36 Corbis:** The Gallery Collection (tr); Michael Amendolia (bl). **36–7 Getty Images:** Photolibrary (b). **37 DK Images:** American Museum of Natural History (cb). **38 Corbis:** Barry Lewis (crb). **DK Images:** Natural History Museum (clb). **39 Corbis:** Ali Meyer (cb); Pierre Colombel (tr). **40–1 Corbis:** Pierre Vauthey. **42 Corbis:** Alfredo Dagli Orti (t). **43 Alamy Images:** Ozimages (b). **Getty Images:** Japanese School (tr). **44 Corbis:** Adam Woolfitt (tl); **SuperStock:** Reynold Mainse (b). **45 Corbis:** Cordaiy Photo Library Ltd. (b). **Getty Images:** The Bridgeman Art Library (tr). **46 Getty Images:** The Bridgeman Art Library (b). **47 Corbis:** Gianni Dagli Orti (br). **Getty Images:** Nico Tondini (t). **48 Alamy Images:** INTERFOTO (b). **Corbis:** Charles & Josette Lenars (tl). **49 Corbis:** Alfredo Dagli Orti (bl). **Getty Images:** The Bridgeman Art Library (tr). **50–1 Corbis:** Bob Krist. **52–3 Corbis:** Kevin Schafer (t). **54 Corbis:** Bruno Morandi (t); Nik Wheeler (b). **55 Corbis:** Gianni Dagli Orti (br). **Getty Images:** Middle Eastern (cla). **56 Corbis:** Gianni Dagli Orti (bl). **57 Corbis:** Burstein Collection (tr); The Art Archive (b). **58 Corbis:** Gianni Dagli Orti (cra) (bl). **59 Getty Images:** Jane Sweeney (b). **60 Getty Images:** Middle Eastern (tl). **60–1 Corbis:** Brooklyn Museum (b). **61 Getty Images:** Egyptian (tl). **62 Corbis:** Brooklyn Museum (cl); Werner Forman (t). **63 Corbis:** The Gallery Collection (tr). **iStockphoto.com:** Jan Rihak (b). **64–5 Getty Images:** Ary Diesendruck. **66 Corbis:** Atlantide Phototravel (tr). **67 Corbis:** Gianni Dagli Orti (cr). **Getty Images:** Patrick Landmann (b). **68 Corbis:** Neil Beer (cl). **69 Corbis:** Fridmar Damm (t); Sandro Vannini (br). **70 Corbis:** Gail Mooney (b). **Getty Images:** Guy Vanderelst (t). **71 Corbis:** Jean-Pierre Lescourret (bl); Wolfgang Kaehler (tr). **72–3 Getty Images:** Kevin Schafer/Corbis **74 Corbis:** Ladislav Janicek (t); **Getty Images:** Robert Harding (bl). **75 Corbis:** Luca Tettoni (bl); Paul Almasy (tr). **76 Alamy Images:** Liu Xiaoyang (t). **Corbis:** Christie's Images (cl). **77 Alamy Images:** Liu Xiaoyang (b). **Corbis:** Asian Art & Archaeology, Inc. (tr). **78 Corbis:** Charles & Josette Lenars (b); Gianni Dagli Orti (t). **79 Corbis:** Danny Lehman (bl); Gianni Dagli Orti (tr). **80–1 Photolibrary:** CM Dixon. **82–3 Corbis:** Werner Forman (t). **84 Corbis:** Gianni Dagli Orti (t); Paul Almasy (cb). **85 Alamy Images:** Visual Arts Library (London) (tr). **Getty Images:** DEA / W. BUSS (b). **86 Corbis:** Gianni Dagli Orti (b) (bc). **87 Corbis:** Paul Almasy (b). **88 Corbis:** John Heseltine (t). **Getty Images:** Marco Simoni (b). **89 Alamy Images:** Rolf Richardson (r). **90 Corbis:** Wolfgang Kaehler (br). **91 Corbis:** Hoberman Collection (ca); José Fuste Raga (b). **92–3 Alamy Images:** nagelestock.com. **94 DK Images:** Hellenic Maritime Museum (bl). **Getty Images:** Greek (tl). **95 Corbis:** Araldo de Luca (bl). **DK Images:** British Museum (cr). **96 Corbis:** Araldo de Luca (b). **97 Corbis:** Michele Falzone (ca). **98 Corbis:** Sandro Vannini (c). **iStockphoto. com:** David H. Seymour (b). **99 Corbis:** Christophe Boisvieux (crb). **100 Corbis:** Fred de Noyelle (bl). **Getty Images:** Glenn Beanland (t). **101 DK Images:** British Museum (tr). **Getty Images:** Panoramic Images (b). **102–3 Getty Images:** School of Giulio Romano (b). **103 Corbis:** Roger Wood (tr). **104 The Bridgeman Art Library:** (b). **Corbis:** Hoberman Collection (cr). **105 Corbis:** Bob Sacha (br). **106 Corbis:** Sandro Vannini (bl). **107 Corbis:** Barney Burstein (tr); Karl-Heinz Haenel (b). **108 Getty Images:** Roman (cr). **108–9 Getty Images:** Lee Frost (b). **109 Corbis:** image100 (cr). **110–11 Corbis:** Araldo de Luca (b). **111 Corbis:** Hoberman Collection (tr). **112 akg-images:** Tristan Lafranchis (b). **113 Corbis:** The Gallery Collection (crb). **DK Images:** The Board of Trustees of the Armories (ca). **114 Corbis:** Werner Forman (b); **iStockphoto.com:** Trudy Karl (t). **115 Getty Images:** Ary Scheffer (b); Time & Life Pictures (ca). **116 Corbis:** Bettmann (t). **Getty Images:** AXEL SCHMIDT (cb). **117 Alamy Images:** Danita Delimont (b). **Getty Images:** Hulton Archive (cr). **118 Corbis:** Adam Woolfitt (t); Lindsay Hebberd (b). **119 Alamy Images:** (br); Sherab (tr). **120–1 akg-images:** Roland and Sabrina Michaud. **122 Corbis:** Philadelphia Museum of Art (ca). **122–3 Getty Images:** Panoramic Images (b). **123 Getty Images:** Paleo-Christian